THE CLASH OF CAPITALISMS?

Chinese Companies in the United States

Chinese foreign direct investment in the United States has generated intense debates. Some welcome it for the immediate benefits such as job creation; others view Chinese investments, especially those controlled by the Chinese government, as a critical threat. The debates have so far missed an important question: how do Chinese companies investing in the United States react to the host country's law? Ji Li formulates a novel analytical framework to examine the adaptation of Chinese companies to general U.S. institutions and their compliance with U.S. laws governing tax, employment equality, and national security review of foreign investments. The level of compliance varies, and this variation is examined in relation to company ownership, including state ownership. Li's analysis is based on interviews and a unique and comprehensive dataset about Chinese companies in the United States that has never been systematically explored.

Ji Li is Professor of Law and a member of the Associate Faculty of the Division of Global Affairs at Rutgers University.

The Clash of Capitalisms?

CHINESE COMPANIES IN THE UNITED STATES

JI LI
Rutgers University School of Law

CAMBRIDGE
UNIVERSITY PRESS

CAMBRIDGE
UNIVERSITY PRESS

University Printing House, Cambridge CB2 8BS, United Kingdom

One Liberty Plaza, 20th Floor, New York, NY 10006, USA

477 Williamstown Road, Port Melbourne, VIC 3207, Australia

314–321, 3rd Floor, Plot 3, Splendor Forum, Jasola District Centre,
New Delhi – 110025, India

79 Anson Road, #06–04/06, Singapore 079906

Cambridge University Press is part of the University of Cambridge.

It furthers the University's mission by disseminating knowledge in the pursuit of education, learning, and research at the highest international levels of excellence.

www.cambridge.org
Information on this title: www.cambridge.org/9781107157156
DOI: 10.1017/9781316661802

First published 2018

Printed in the United Kingdom by Clays, St Ives plc

A catalogue record for this publication is available from the British Library.

Library of Congress Cataloging-in-Publication Data
NAMES: Li, Ji, 1976– author.
TITLE: The clash of capitalisms : Chinese investors in the United States / Ji Li, Rutgers University School of Law.
DESCRIPTION: Cambridge, United Kingdom ; New York, NY, USA : Cambridge University Press, 2018. | Includes index.
IDENTIFIERS: LCCN 2017051371 | ISBN 9781107157156
SUBJECTS: LCSH: Business enterprises, Foreign – Law and legislation – United States. | Investments, Chinese – Law and legislation – United States. | Business enterprises, Foreign – Social aspects – United States. | Investments, Chinese – Social aspects – United States.
CLASSIFICATION: LCC KF1419 .L55 2018 | DDC 346.7307–dc23
LC record available at https://lccn.loc.gov/2017051371

ISBN 978-1-107-15715-6 Hardback

to my family

Contents

Tables and Figures

Tables

Figures

Acknowledgments

In the course of writing this book, I was fortunate to receive the support of many friends and colleagues. I owe special thanks to Karen Alter, Susan Rose-Ackerman, Curtis Milhaupt, Benjamin van Rooij, Weiyi Shi, Simone Tsigounis, Wei Zhang, and Wentong Zheng, who read the entire manuscript of this book and offered me valuable suggestions and comments. I also benefited enormously from the comments of a large group of specialists who read parts of the manuscript. Weitseng Chen, Jerome Cohen, Douglas Eakeley, Gary Francione, Hualing Fu, Christopher Gane, Yunsong Ge, Jie Gong, Li Guo, Taja-Nia Y. Henderson, Virginia Ho, Robin Huang, Alan Hyde, Jing Leng, John Leubsdorf, Benjamin Liebman, Haitian Lu, Shaowei Mao, Curtis Milhaupt, Kwai Ng, Shitong Qiao, Sabrina Safrin, Victor Shih, and Yingmao Tang read and commented on earlier versions of Chapters 3 and 4, which set forth the analytical framework of the research.

In addition, I would like to thank Cynthia Blum, Thomas Brennan, Dhammika Dharmapala, Alan Hyde, Stuart Deutsch, John Leubsdorf, Omri Marian, David Noll, Mark Ramseyer, Fadi Shaheen, Stephen Shay, and Yan Xu for their comments on parts of Chapter 5, which explores Chinese companies in the U.S. tax system. The chapter also incorporated feedback from several other participants at the 27th Annual Meeting for the American Law and Economics Association at Harvard Law School.

Moreover, for valuable comments on parts of Chapter 6, which examines Chinese companies and U.S. employment law, I would like to thank Stuart Benjamin, Cynthia Estlund, Katie Eyer, Mary Gallagher, Aaron Halegua, Virginia Ho, Alan Hyde, Jedidiah Kroncke, Mingwei Liu, Yan Tian, and a few participants in the conference on the Global Transformation of Work held at Rutgers School of Management and Labor Relations and the 12th Annual Conference on Empirical Legal Studies at Cornell Law School.

Furthermore, for helpful comments on parts of Chapter 7, which investigates the interactions between Chinese companies and the U.S. national security review system, I am grateful to Stuart Benjamin, Adam Chilton, Jim Cox, Stuart

Deutsch, Douglas Eakeley, Taja-Nia Henderson, David Noll, John Leubsdorf, Sabrina Safrin, Reid Weisbord, Huyue Zhang, and other participants of the 11th Annual Conference on Empirical Legal Studies at Duke Law School.

In revising earlier versions of the manuscript, I incorporated comments and suggestions from participants in workshops, seminars, and conferences hosted by Cheung Kong Graduate School of Business, Chinese University of Hong Kong Faculty of Law, Columbia Law School, National University of Singapore Faculty of Law, Northwestern University, Peking University Law School, Peking University School of Transnational Law, Rutgers Business School, Rutgers School of Management and Labor Relations, University of California–Irvine Law School, University of California–San Diego, University of Hong Kong Faculty of Law, and Yale School of Management.

Through the course of this book project, Rutgers Law School has served as a nurturing intellectual home. I have had the honor of learning from a wonderful group of colleagues who at various points reviewed and commented on parts of the book.

A special note of appreciation to Candice Niu, Junchen Pan, Sherry Qu, Evelyn Shi, and other staff members of the China General Chamber of Commerce—USA, whose hard work made possible the annual survey of Chinese companies in the United States and the compilation of the unique data set. I also want to express my appreciation to the group of anonymous business practitioners for generously sharing their views and experience with me, and to the Philip Shuchman Fund for Empirical Research for generous support.

At Cambridge University Press, I am grateful to senior editor John Berger for his guidance, patience and professionalism, and to Sharon McCann and her colleagues whose meticulous work sped the manuscript through the publications process, and to John Gaunt for excellent copyediting. I also thank the two anonymous reviewers for their interest in the project, valuable comments, and support.

Several paragraphs of Chapter 2 and Chapter 3 were published in the *Northwestern Journal of International Law and Business*, Volume 36, Issue 1 (2016); portions of Chapter 5 were published in the *Hastings Law Journal*, Volume 68, Issue 3 (2017); portions of Chapter 7 were originally published in the *Berkeley Business Law Journal*, Volume 14, Issue 1 (2017). I am grateful for the excellent editing assistance by the editors of those journals, in particular Kara Cooper, William Carpenter, and their colleagues at the *Northwestern Journal of International Law and Business*; Amy Holtz, Eric Young, and Jonathan Goldstein at the *Hastings Law Journal*; and Gavin Moler and Eugene Choi at the *Berkeley Business Law Journal*.

My deepest thanks, of course, go to my family.

Abbreviations

ACFTU	All-China Federation of Trade Unions
CCP	Chinese Communist Party
CDIC	Central Discipline Inspection Committee (of the Chinese Communist Party)
CEO	chief executive officer
CFIUS	Committee on Foreign Investment in the United States
CGCC	China General Chamber of Commerce—USA
COD	Central Organization Department (of the Chinese Communist Party)
DPA	Defense Production Act (1950)
FCPA	Foreign Corrupt Practices Act (1977) (United States)
FDI	foreign direct investment
FINSA	Foreign Investment and National Security Act (2007) (United States)
GAO	Government Accountability Office (United States)
GDP	gross domestic product
HBV	hepatitis B virus
HRM	human resource management
IRS	Internal Revenue Service (United States)
LTB	Local Tax Bureau (China)
M & A	mergers and acquisitions
MNE	multinational enterprise
NGO	non-governmental organization
ODI	outbound foreign direct investment
PC	personal computer
SASAC	State-Owned Assets Supervision and Administration Commission
SAT	State Administration of Taxation (China)
SME	small and medium-sized enterprise
SOE	state-owned enterprise
STB	State Tax Bureau (China)
TVE	township and village enterprise
TWEA	Trading with the Enemy Act (United States)
VAT	value added tax

1

Introduction

We came to invest [in the U.S.] for the rule of law; yet our biggest challenge here is also the rule of law.[1]

CEO of a Chinese real estate company in the United States

Merely two decades ago, very few Chinese companies contemplated making investment overseas, and those that did focused mainly on resource-rich developing countries.[2] Today, thousands of Chinese firms have set up or acquired businesses around the globe. By some measure, outbound direct investment (ODI) from China reached about $200 billion in 2016.[3] The surge of Chinese ODI has triggered many controversies and intense debates, most of which revolve around two novel, albeit important, questions. First, how will soaring investment from the world's largest developing country impact host countries' institutions? For the skeptics, Chinese companies that have thrived in a poor legal and regulatory environment at home would "export China's domestic problems" and trample on the laws of their host countries.[4] By comparison, those holding a more sanguine view foresee that Chinese companies venturing abroad, much like multinationals based in developed countries, will react rationally to host-country environments.[5] The optimists also applaud investments from China for the immediate economic and social benefits, such as

[1] Public statement made by the executive at Roads to USA – Greenfield Investment versus Cross-border M & A Forum in Washington, D.C. (June 20, 2017).

[2] Ivar Kolstad and Arne Wiig, "What Determines Chinese Outward FDI?", 47 *Journal of World Business* 26 (2012).

[3] Thilo Hanemann and Mikko Huotari, Record Flows and Growing Imbalances: Chinese Investment in Europe in 2016, Rhodium Group (Jan. 2017), at http://rhg.com/wp-content/uploads/2017/01/RHG_Merics_COFDI_EU_2016.pdf.

[4] See Chapter 2 for more discussion of the critical views.

[5] Ji Li, "I Came, I Saw, I . . . Adapted an Empirical Study of Chinese Business Expansion in the U.S. and Its Legal and Policy Implications," 36 *Northwestern Journal of International Law and Business* 143 (2016).

additional employment. For instance, Joe Biden once remarked that "President Obama and I, we welcome, encourage and see nothing but positive benefits flowing from direct investment in the United States from Chinese businesses and Chinese entities. It means jobs. *It means American jobs*."[6]

Despite growing attention to Chinese ODI and rising temperature of the debate, very few researchers have systematically examined how Chinese investors interact with their host countries' legal and regulatory institutions. The topic is timely and important as Chinese companies have begun to direct more of their foreign investment to countries featuring robust legal systems. Notably, of all the destination countries for Chinese ODI, the United States has emerged as the largest recipient.[7] Will Chinese investors, having long conducted business in an environment where law is often secondary to power and social connections, [8] fully comply with the laws of a developed host state, take an opportunistic approach towards compliance, or defy the host state's laws and regulations? Put differently, will Chinese companies retain most of their home-state characteristics in coping with host-state laws and regulations? If Chinese investors readily adapt and behave like their local counterparts, ODI from China will not give rise to a disproportionately large number of frictions with host-country legal institutions. But if Chinese companies are in recalcitrant disobedience of the laws and regulations, their increasing presence will undoubtedly spawn a great deal of conflicts that may jeopardize existing host-country institutions.[9]

The second key question underlying many of the debates about Chinese ODI pertains to the Chinese state's visible hand in promoting development and steering foreign investments. The Chinese government exerts an intricate control over the economy through, among other things, managing state-owned enterprises and implementing industrial policies. Critics have expressed grave concerns that Chinese ODI, heavily influenced or even controlled by the state, will threaten host countries' national security and wreak havoc on the institutions that have enabled free-market capitalism.[10] State-owned companies (SOEs), featured prominently in Chinese ODI,

6 "Remarks by Vice President Biden and Chinese Vice President Xi at a U.S.-China Business Roundtable," the White House, Office of the Vice President, at www.whitehouse.gov/the-press-office/2011/08/19/remarks-vice-president-biden-and-chinese-vice-president-xi-us-china-busi, last accessed April 19, 2017, added emphasis.

7 Thilo Hanemann and Cassie Gao, "Record Deal Making in 2016 Pushes Cumulative Chinese FDI in the US above $100 billion," Rhodium Group (Dec. 30, 2016), at http://rhg.com/notes/record-deal-making-in-2016-pushes-cumulative-chinese-fdi-in-the-us-above-100-billion. The calculation excludes Hong Kong and the EU.

8 Ji Li, "The Power Logic of Justice in China," 68 *American Journal of Comparative Law* 503 (2017); Wei Zhang and Ji Li, "Weak Law v. Strong Ties: An Empirical Study of Business Investment, Law and Political Connections in China," 13 *Review of Law and Economics* (2016); Yuen Yuen Ang and Nan Jia, "Perverse Complementarity: Political Connections and the use of Courts among Private Firms in China," 76 *Journal of Politics* 318 (2014).

9 Li, "I Came, I Saw, I . . . Adapted," 143, 146.

10 See, e.g., Ian Bremmer, "State Capitalism Comes of Age: The End of the Free Market?", 8 *Foreign Affairs* 40 (2009); Joshua Kurlantzick, *State Capitalism: How the Return of Statism is Transforming the World* (2016); the view is shared by some practitioners; see, e.g., Robert D. Atkinson, "Testimony

have drawn particular suspicion. Some fear that China will use the SOEs "as weapons in conflicts with other countries, as vehicles to control certain types of natural resources, as vehicles for obtaining and stealing sensitive technology from other nations, or as tools for undermining environmental and labor norms in countries where [they] invest."[11]

China's evolving state–business relations have spurred an emerging literature and scholars have attempted to fit the system into one of several familiar theoretical models. For instance, analogies have been made to other East Asian developmental states.[12] True, China resembles them in the way government designs and implements industrial policies to facilitate growth; but equally evident are multiple structural differences, an obvious one being the crucial role SOEs have played and continue to play in China's economy. Other commentators classify the Chinese system more broadly as state capitalism, variably defined as "a system in which the state functions as the leading economic actor,"[13] a regime featuring "widespread influence of the government in the economy, either by owning majority or minority equity positions in companies or by providing subsidized credit and/or other privileges to private companies,"[14] or a political economy characterized by the subordination of private capital to the state and the control of national plans over market operations.[15] However, upon close examination, China distinguishes itself from other countries in this broad category by the high concentration of SOEs' equity interest, the permeation of the ruling party in both state-owned and private enterprises, and the government's superior administrative capacity.[16] Moreover, China is by far the largest of all of state capitalist economies and arguably the most successful.[17] And in contrast to the widely held post-Cold War belief that China would eventually convert to free-market capitalism,[18] recent signs indicate that the Chinese model will likely endure. While the party-state

before the U.S.–China Economic and Security Review Commission, Hearing on Chinese Investment in the United States: Impacts and Issues for Policymakers" (Jan. 26, 2017), at www.uscc.gov/sites/default/files/Atkinson_USCC%20Hearing%20Testimony012617.pdf, last accessed April 15, 2017.

11 Kurlantzick, *State Capitalism*, 239.

12 John B. Knight, "China as a Developmental State," 37 *World Economy* 1335 (2014); Seung-Wook Baek, "Does China Follow 'the East Asian Development Model'?", 35 *Journal of Contemporary Asia* 485 (2005).

13 Bremmer, "State Capitalism Comes of Age," 40.

14 Aldo Musacchio and Sergio Lazzarini, *Reinventing State Capitalism: Leviathan in Business, Brazil and Beyond* (2014), 2.

15 Alex Dupuy and Barry Truchil, "Problems in the Theory of State Capitalism," 8 *Theory and Society* 1 (1979).

16 Mark Wu, "The 'China, Inc.' Challenge to Global Trade Governance," 57 *Harvard International Law Journal* 261 (2016).

17 Benjamin L. Liebman and Curtis J. Milhaupt, eds., *Regulating the Visible Hand? The Institutional Implications of Chinese State Capitalism* (2015).

18 Garry D. Bruton, Mike W. Peng, David Ahlstrom, Ciprian Stan, and Kehan Xu, "State-Owned Enterprises around the World as Hybrid Organizations," 29 *Academy of Management Perspectives* 92 (2015), 95.

lately renewed its pledge to press on with the market reform,[19] it has at the same time advocated the use of both the "visible hand" and the "invisible hand."[20] A radical transformation being unlikely, how, then, do China's rather unique, yet enduring, state–business relations influence the adaptation of Chinese companies to host-country institutions? Do state-owned Chinese investors exhibit different compliance behavior in liberal market economies such as the United States?

In short, surging Chinese ODI raises two sets of important yet underexplored questions: how Chinese investors react to host-country legal institutions; and whether and how the rather unique state–business relations matter. This book attempts to answer these questions by investigating how Chinese companies in the United States react to U.S. legal and regulatory institutions, and whether state ownership in Chinese investors makes a difference in their reactions. Drawing on insights from selected theories of compliance and international business, I construct an analytical framework that combines comparative institutional analysis with firm-level research. To be concrete, the framework organizes the analysis of foreign investors' responses to a host country's institutions into three parts: (1) the institutional distances between the investors' home and host states; (2) the investors' desire to conform to the host-country institutions; and (3) the investors' ability to make the requisite adaptation. Put in plain English, the framework guides the analysis through three inquiries about the *need* for, and the *desire* and the *ability* of, foreign investors to adapt and conform to a host country's legal and regulatory environment.

Let me briefly expand on the first inquiry, *the need* for foreign investors to adapt to host-country legal institutions. In areas of significant cross-country learning and institutional transplant, there will be no pressing need for foreign investors to make material behavioral adjustments. For instance, few Canadian companies investing in the United States would have to markedly alter the way they conduct business (e.g., how they set prices and collaborate with other firms), in order to comply with U.S. antitrust law. In areas where substantial institutional gaps exist across different countries, foreign investors' adaptation and compliance with host-country rules will then hinge on their *desire* and *ability* to make the necessary adjustments. If the investors show adequate inclination as well as capacity, they will cross the institutional gaps and their business expansion in the host state will not entail surging frictions. On the other hand, if they possess neither the desire nor the ability to adapt, numerous conflicts will follow. Applying this analytical framework, this book examines how Chinese companies doing business in the United States react to the general U.S. institutional environment as well as how they cope with U.S. legal and regulatory institutions in three subject matter areas (i.e., tax, employment discrimination, and national security review of foreign investments). For

[19] Cary Huang, "Party's Third Plenum Pledges 'Decisive Role' for Markets in China's Economy," *South China Morning Post* (Nov. 12, 2013), at www.scmp.com/news/china/article/1354411/chinas-leadership-approves-key-reform-package-close-third-plenum.

[20] James Stent, *China's Banking Transformation: The Untold Story* (2016), 6.

instance, do Chinese firms cautiously comply with U.S. tax law, aggressively exploit the loopholes in the system, or willfully disregard the law? In addition, this book explores the association, if any, between state ownership in Chinese investors and their adaptation. Are state-owned Chinese investors, for instance, less likely than their privately owned counterparts to engage in opportunistic compliance with U.S. law prohibiting employment discrimination?

To address these questions, the book employs both qualitative and quantitative methods. A unique dataset was compiled from three comprehensive annual surveys (2014, 2015, and 2016) targeting executives of sizable Chinese companies in the United States. The survey was conducted in collaboration with China General Chamber of Commerce—USA (CGCC), by far the largest business association of Chinese companies in the United States. This book presents both descriptive and statistical analysis of the data in a reader-friendly way. Moreover, I personally reached out to dozens of individuals with firsthand knowledge about Chinese investments in the United States, such as managers of the Chinese businesses and the U.S. lawyers who have advised them. From the Rashomonian observations and comments, I extracted insights to formulate the hypotheses for the statistical tests and to supplement or substantiate the institutional and quantitative analyses. Furthermore, information about Chinese ODI was gleaned from secondary materials such as media reports and studies by NGOs, professional service providers, and government agencies.

The remainder of this book proceeds as follows. To provide readers with necessary background knowledge, Chapter 2 begins by reviewing the incremental changes in China's foreign direct investment (FDI) policies and the long-term growth trajectory of Chinese ODI. It then shifts the focus to Chinese investments in the United States. Besides a synopsis of the topic, the chapter recounts the experiences of three major Chinese companies (Lenovo, Bank of China, and Huawei) that have made or attempted to make substantial investments in the United States. As will be shown, their experiences vary dramatically. Last, the chapter describes the comprehensive surveys of Chinese companies in the United States and presents an overview of the results.

Chapter 3 is divided into two parts. The first part formulates the general analytical framework for researching foreign investors' reactions to a host country's legal institutions. As just noted, to explore this broad topic, one should begin by examining relevant institutional gaps between the investors' home and host countries, and, in cases of large institutional gaps, by further analyzing the investors' desire and ability to conform to the host country's institutions. Applying this framework, the second part of the chapter empirically examines Chinese companies in the United States. It finds that the Chinese investors generally encounter substantial institutional gaps, yet many of them demonstrate both the desire and the ability to cross the gaps. To be more concrete, long-term commercial interests instead of home-state policies drove most of the Chinese investments in the United States, and the managers held in high regard various U.S. social, legal, and business institutions.

Meanwhile, many of the Chinese companies have to a great extent localized decision-making concerning U.S. legal and compliance matters and relied heavily on U.S. professionals to cope with the host country's institutional setting. Consequently, the Chinese companies in general should adapt and comply reasonably well with U.S law. That being said, significant variations across the Chinese firms are evident.

The variations are empirically explored in Chapter 4. The tests of the chapter concentrate on whether and how state ownership in Chinese investors is associated with the varying institutional distances and the firm-level factors. The connections between state ownership and the institutional distances are complex and context-sensitive. Everything else held constant, Chinese SOEs that bear relatively low noncompliance costs in the domestic setting usually have to traverse longer institutional distances when investing in the United States, because most U.S. laws pertinent to foreign investments either disregard state ownership or discriminate against state-owned or state-controlled investors. However, due to the multilayered agency problem inherent in Chinese SOEs, the managers' interests are not well aligned with those of the firms and their nominal owners.[21] In addition, senior managers of Chinese SOEs typically multitask, and profit maximization is but one metric for their performance evaluation.[22] Hence, despite low noncompliance costs in the home state, managers of Chinese SOEs may still avoid taking the risk. When Chinese SOEs invest in the United States, the same logic applies and it complicates their reactions to U.S. legal institutions. Second, on the desire of Chinese investors to adapt, the chapter finds preliminary evidence that state-owned Chinese investors are more responsive to the home government's policies and less likely than private investors to reinvest their U.S. profits. Yet, on the other hand, managers of state-owned Chinese firms do not differ from private-company managers in holding generally positive views of U.S. institutions. Third, regarding the ability to adapt to U.S. legal institutions, the chapter uncovers evidence that ties Chinese investors' state ownership to more centralized management. At the same time, however, state-owned Chinese investors are indistinguishable from private investors in terms of reliance on local professionals. The mixed empirical findings suggest that,

21 See, e.g., Zhou Mi and Xiaoming Wang, "Agency Cost and the Crisis of China's SOE," 11 *China Economic Review* 297 (2001); Bruton et al., "State Owned Enterprises Around the World as Hybrid Organizations," 92; Yingyu Zhang, Hui Luan, Wei Shao, and Yingjun Xu, "Managerial Risk Preference and Its Influencing Factors: Analysis of Large State-Owned Enterprises Management Personnel in China," 18 *Risk Management* 135 (2016); Alvaro Cuervo-Cazurra, Andrew Inkpen, Aldo Musacchio, and Kannan Ramaswamy, "Governments as Owners: State-Owned Multinational Companies," 45 *Journal of International Business Studies* 919 (2014).

22 See, e.g., Ji Li, "State-Owned Enterprises in the Current Regime of Investor–State Arbitration," in Shaheea Lalani and Rodrigo Polanco, eds., *The Role of the State in Investor–State Arbitration* (2014); Lin Cui, Klaus E. Meyer, and Helen Wei Hu, "What Drives Firms' Intent to Seek Strategic Assets by Foreign Direct Investment? A Study of Emerging Economy Firms," 49 *Journal of World Business* 488 (2014), 491–2; Jiangyu Wang, "The Political Logic of Corporate Governance in China's State-Owned Enterprises," 47 *Cornell International Law Journal* 631 (2014).

everything else held constant, Chinese state-owned firms may be less efficient in coping with major U.S. legal and regulatory issues than privately owned Chinese investors.

The institutional distances between China and the United States, though large in general, vary across different subject matter areas, and so should the reactions of Chinese companies. Chapters 5 to 7 of this book examine how Chinese companies deal with the U.S. legal institutions governing taxation, employment discrimination, and national security review of foreign investment. I choose these three areas of U.S. law because they implicate, actually or potentially, almost all Chinese companies in the United States, and they relate to some of the core issues in the ongoing debates about Chinese ODI as well as emerging-market FDI.

Chapter 5 examines Chinese companies in the U.S. tax system. Thanks to learning and institutional transplant from the United States to China in the past four decades, the two countries' tax systems share quite a few core concepts and principles. But beyond that, the two differ strikingly. How do Chinese firms respond to the impenetrable U.S. tax system? The chapter finds, quite surprisingly, that Chinese investors on average prefer the complex yet law-based U.S. tax system to the one back home. They also rely extensively on local professionals to handle U.S. tax matters. Moreover, the chapter finds that Chinese companies have in general adopted a conservative approach towards U.S. tax planning and have not experienced extraordinary audits or disputes with the IRS. Furthermore, state ownership in Chinese investors does not correlate significantly with their opinions about U.S. tax institutions, nor is it linked to how the firms handle technical or routine tax matters such as tax planning. However, preliminary test results indicate that Chinese investors with majority state ownership are more likely to experience audits and disputes with the IRS, which serves as initial evidence confirming the finding in Chapter 4, namely that state-owned Chinese investors may be less efficient in dealing with major U.S. legal and regulatory matters.

Chapter 6 explores how Chinese companies respond to the U.S. law prohibiting employment discrimination. Again, thanks to transnational learning and legal transplants, the formal Chinese law against employment discrimination has incorporated the basic principles of the U.S. law, though the latter is undoubtedly more comprehensive and operative. In contrast, the compliance and enforcement gaps remain wide open. How do Chinese companies fair under the elaborate U.S. rules for employment equality? According to the findings of this chapter, Chinese managers hold on average a positive view about U.S. employment laws and rely to a certain extent on local professionals to handle personnel matters. The majority, therefore, have adopted local practices for managing human resources and taken measures to prevent workplace discrimination; and contrary to popular belief, discrimination has not been a major issue for doing business in the United States. At the same time, however, the evidence indicates inadequate compliance efforts and therefore the potential for more workplace friction as Chinese companies further expand and diversify their U.S. workforces. The chapter also investigates the potential effects of state ownership of Chinese investors on how they view and react to the U.S. rules, and discovers no significant effects.

Chapter 7 explores the reactions of Chinese investors to national security review of foreign investments (also known as CFIUS review). Chinese investors, having no experience with national security review of investment at home, encounter an enormous institutional gap in this subject matter area. Consequently, many of the Chinese managers lack any knowledge about this peculiar U.S. institution. Moreover, the U.S. law governing CFIUS is ambiguous and the interagency body enforcing the law enjoys broad discretion. Hence most of the Chinese managers with knowledge about the system consider it politicized and non-transparent. That is in sharp contrast to their views on U.S. tax and employment institutions. Given the enormous institutional gaps and the negative view, it is no surprise that most of the Chinese investors have either neglected CFIUS review or taken a more opportunistic approach towards the CFIUS risk. Such reactions have led to conflicts with the enforcement agency that culminated in the first and only lawsuit challenging its actions (*Ralls* v. *CFIUS*), which eventually altered the legal contour of the CFIUS review process. The chapter further examines the effects of state ownership in Chinese investors. Contrary to U.S. tax law and employment law, the CFIUS rules subject foreign government-controlled investments to enhanced agency scrutiny. Unsurprisingly, statistical analysis finds state ownership in Chinese investors to be significant. That is, those working for Chinese companies with significant state ownership think negatively of the regime. In addition, state-owned Chinese investors are more likely to consider notifying CFIUS about their acquisitions of U.S. assets.

Chapters 5 to 7 highlight varying institutional distances across different subject matter areas. Among the three studied herein, the institutional gaps between China and the United States are wide in their respective employment laws, wider in tax, and much wider in national security review of foreign investment. Moreover, while U.S. tax law and employment law generally disregard ownership types (e.g., state-owned or private), CFIUS rules single out foreign investors with state ownership for heightened scrutiny. Consequently, most of the Chinese managers see U.S. laws in the areas of tax and employment neutrally or positively; yet the same managers either lack any knowledge or are critical about the CFIUS process. Meanwhile, and to a certain extent related to the varying institutional gaps, Chinese companies have relied heavily on local professionals for handling complex tax matters and CFIUS review, less so in managing human resources in the United States. Overall, the findings of the book suggest that Chinese companies investing in the United States are generally adaptive to host-country legal institutions that are neither discriminatory nor highly discretionary. Yet notable variations exist, and state ownership in Chinese investors makes a difference in areas with large institutional gaps that vary according to ownership types and when major legal and compliance matters are implicated. On the other hand, in dealing with routine and technical legal and compliance issues, state-owned Chinese investors tend to adopt similar or even more cautious approaches than private Chinese investors in the United States.

This book makes several contributions. First, drawing on insights from various literatures, the book presents a unified analytical framework to investigate how foreign investors comply with host-country laws and regulations. The existing scholarship that has tangentially touched on the topic has either disregarded subnational institutional disparities and cross-national institutional homogeneity, or assumed away certain key firm-level variations in the adaptation to host-state contexts. The analytical frame articulated herein fills the holes. It is also broadly applicable. For instance, one may use it to guide the analysis of how Chinese firms investing in Germany respond to various German laws, or how Brazilian investors in Japan cope with different Japanese laws.

Second, the book contributes to the theoretical debate about Chinese ODI and its impacts on host countries, especially developed countries such as the United States. Ample empirical evidence herein suggests that Chinese business elites have internalized the basic concepts of free-market capitalism and embraced its enabling institutions. Decades of market reform in China may be incomplete, but it has been market-oriented nonetheless. The shared faith in market efficacy among the Chinese business elites, regardless of their employers' ownership type, paves the way for Chinese companies to conform to market-enabling institutions in the United States. Somewhat ironically, in a time when more politicians from the developed world begin to endorse isolationism and protectionism, Chinese companies may take actions, intentionally or not, to sustain the host-country institutions that are crucial to free-market capitalism. The *Ralls* v. *CFIUS* lawsuit, which will be discussed in Chapter 7, illustrates the point. A Chinese investor's suit against the federal agency and President Obama fortified, at least in theory, the legal protection of property rights for foreign owners of U.S. assets.

Third, the book adds to the discussion of state capitalism. Its findings should ease the fear that Chinese companies, either SOEs or privately owned national champions, will conquer global business. At least in the United States, Chinese companies have not been a formidable force. On average they suffer a loss, and those that survived the fierce competition of the U.S. market and overcame the various liabilities of foreignness have localized and shed nearly all defining Chinese characteristics. In addition, host-state governments have ample regulatory tools (e.g., CFIUS review) to regulate SOEs and other investors subject to their home state's influence.

Fourth, the book contributes to the debate about SOEs. Are they strategic and policy tools of the state owners, as alleged by their detractors, or fully commercialized business organizations identical to private companies in every aspect except for ownership? Also, do SOEs significantly differ from private companies in the way they operate in host countries where many of their home state advantages no longer exist? Moreover, to what extent do they vary from private companies when doing business in a mature market with relatively less, but more institutionalized, government intervention? This book offers some preliminary answers. Differences certainly exist between Chinese investors with significant state ownership and private Chinese investors, but they are not reflected in the dealings with technical and routine matters in the United States. Overall, Chinese SOEs, especially those subject to multiple capital market regulations, have been commercialized to a great extent and largely adaptive to host-country institutional contexts. Hence soaring Chinese investment in the United States by itself will unlikely trigger a clash of capitalisms.

2

Chinese Foreign Direct Investment in the United States

We are a Fortune 500 company. It would be embarrassing if we did not have any investment in the United States.[1]

CEO of the U.S. affiliate of a large Chinese company

The decade-long Cultural Revolution that came to an end in the late 1970s left China a hermit state in dire poverty. Few Chinese traveled abroad, and outbound foreign direct investment (ODI) was unheard of. Economically and diplomatically isolated, China had marginal impact on the outside world beyond the ramifications of the Cold War power play. Fast forward four decades, China is now the world's second-largest economy (or the largest if measured in purchasing-power parity[2]) and has been fully integrated in the global market. Domestically, an incremental, albeit massive, institutional creative destruction is unfolding, which manifested as the Chinese state capitalism. Though state-owned enterprises (SOEs), a legacy of the morbid planned economy, have survived the reforms and continue to play a vital role, private and foreign-invested businesses in China employ more workers, pay more taxes, and patent more inventions. Outside China, the country's influence reaches the remotest corners of the world; each year millions of Chinese travel abroad and thousands of Chinese companies invest in foreign countries.[3] At a time

[1] Interview with the CEO of the affiliate of a large Chinese company in real estate and investment (June 14, 2017).

[2] 2015 GDP ranking, PPP based, World Bank (Oct. 11, 2016), at http://databank.worldbank.org/data/download/GDP_PPP.pdf, last checked on Nov. 14, 2016.

[3] In 2015, 120 million Chinese traveled abroad. Ma Chi, "Chinese Travelers Lead 2015 Global Outbound Tourism," *China Daily* (Jan. 28, 2016), at www.chinadaily.com.cn/china/2016–01/28/content_23288004.htm, last checked on Nov. 14, 2016. In 2015, Chinese investors invested in 6,532 overseas companies, an increase of 14.7% from 2014. Summary Statistics of Chinese Outbound Direct Investment (Non-banking) 2015, Ministry of Commerce of the PRC, at http://hzs.mofcom.gov.cn/article/date/201601/20160101239873.shtml, last checked on Oct. 11, 2016.

when many politicians in the United States and Europe trumpet protectionism, China champions free trade and globalization.

Of this great transformation, this chapter concentrates on the changes in Chinese government policies regarding foreign investment and the long-term growth of Chinese ODI. After a chronological recap, this chapter introduces the ongoing debate about the impacts of Chinese ODI on host countries. On one side of the debate, scholars and policymakers welcome Chinese investment. In their view, Chinese firms, being either uncompetitive or highly adaptive, do not threaten host-country institutions. On the opposite side of the debate, however, critics and skeptics stress the incompatibility of China's state capitalism with free-market capitalism and express concerns that Chinese investors would "export China's domestic problems"; China's surging ODI, if not properly managed and regulated, will wreak havoc on the extant global economic order.

The debate, having for years revolved around Chinese ODI in resource-rich developing countries, has followed the recent geographic shift of Chinese ODI towards the United States. Scholars and policymakers have raised the same set of questions. For instance, will Chinese outbound investors transplant their home practices to their U.S. businesses? In other words, will Chinese companies doing business in the United States violate U.S. labor and employment laws, evade U.S. tax, or impair U.S. national security? This book addresses these questions by exploring how Chinese investors react to various U.S. legal and regulatory institutions. As a necessary background, this chapter offers an overview of Chinese ODI and growing China-sourced investments in the United States. The chapter also describes the research methodology and presents some key descriptive data about, among other things, why Chinese firms invest in the United States, how they fare in the complex and unfamiliar institutional context, and what they plan to do with U.S. profits.

I FOUR DECADES OF CHINESE ODI

A review of Chinese ODI necessarily begins with the launching of the "reform and opening" policy in 1978–9, because prior to that "China had no ODI to speak of."[4] Due to its diplomatic and economic isolation, the Chinese government had minimal foreign-exchange reserves at its disposal in the early 1980s (see Figure 2.1 below), so the initial policies regarding foreign investment were designed mainly to attract inbound FDI.[5] From 1979 to 1982, due to the severe shortage of foreign exchange, all ODI projects had to be reviewed and approved by the State Council or the National Planning Commission on a case-by-case basis.[6] As the number of proposed projects rose

4 David Shambaugh, *China Goes Global: The Partial Power* (2013), 177.

5 Yadong Luo, Qiuzhi Xue, and Binjie Han, "How Emerging Market Governments Promote Outward FDI: Experience from China," 45 *Journal of World Business* 68 (2010), 72.

6 Ibid., 73.

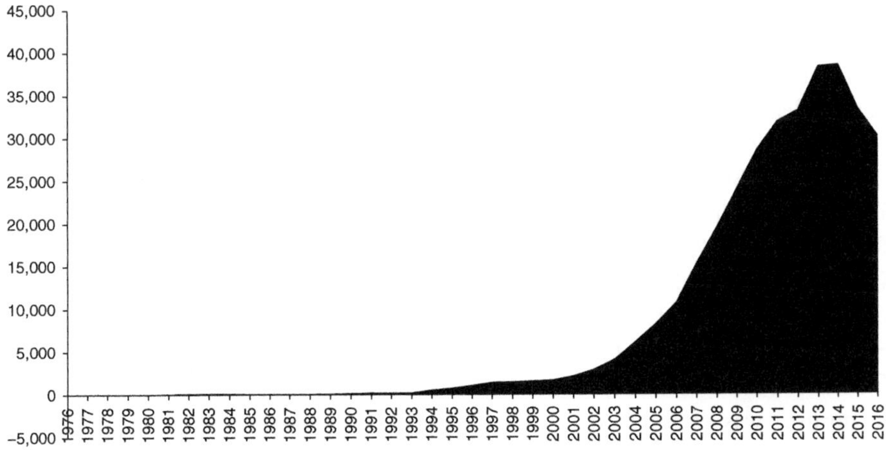

FIGURE 2.1 Chinese foreign exchange reserve (1976–2016; unit = US$100 million)
Source: State Administration of Foreign Exchange

over time, the State Council delegated review authority to the former Ministry of Commerce, which promulgated the first formal ODI guideline in 1984.[7] Various restraints capped the total amount of ODI during this early period at about $200 million.[8]

Like Chinese government policies in other areas, those regarding foreign investment "ebbed and flowed with shifts in the factional balance of power."[9] From 1986 to 1991, the balance tilted towards the reformers and the central government experimented with a range of economic liberalization policies.[10] Within that context, Chinese ODI surged, reaching a total of $1.2 billion.[11] However, when the power balance made a conservative turn after 1989, the government tightened its ODI policies. In 1991, the State Council endorsed the opinion of the National Planning Commission that China was "unprepared for large-scale foreign investment."[12] Review authority was reassigned to the National Planning Commission and the State Council, which imposed more onerous restrictions.[13] Consequently, the number of ODI projects declined from 1992 to 1996 at an annual rate of 20%.

7 Ibid. 8 Shambaugh, *China Goes Global*, 177.

9 Hongbin Cai and Daniel Treisman, "Did Government Decentralization Cause China's Economic Miracle?", 58 *World Politics* 505 (2006), 507.

10 Shambaugh, *China Goes Global*, 177. 11 Ibid., 177.

12 Paragraph 1, Guowuyuan Pizhuan Guojia Jiwei Guanyu Haiwai Touzi Xiangmu Guanliyijian de Tongzhi (State Council Notice about Circulating the Opinion of National Planning Commission about Strengthening the Administration over Foreign Investment Projects), Guofa [1991] No. 13.

13 "Woguo 'Zouchuqu' Zhanlue de Xingcheng ji Tuidong Zhengce Tixi Fenxi" (Analysis of the Formation and Promotion of the "Go Global" Policy), Economic Information Department of China Council for the Promotion of International Trade (2007).

Meanwhile, two decades of economic growth, fueled partially by inbound FDI and international trade, boosted the foreign-exchange reserve and enabled Chinese investors to acquire more foreign assets. Against this backdrop, some central leaders began to advocate less restrictive policies for ODI. In February 1998, Jiang Zemin propounded that the government should organize and support competitive SOEs to "go abroad" and invest in Africa, Central Asia, Central Europe, and South America.[14] At a Politburo meeting in January 2000, Jiang formulated the "go global" strategy, which was subsequently endorsed at the Fifth Plenary Session of the Chinese Communist Party (CCP) 15th National Congress as one of the strategic national policies to foster development.[15] Subsequently, the State Council put in place a variety of rules and institutions to facilitate ODI. For example, the China Export & Credit Insurance Corporation (Sinosure) was established to extend credit and provide insurance to Chinese outbound investors. The government also started to negotiate bilateral investment agreements that were more protective of investors.[16]

In addition, the central government streamlined and clarified the approval procedure for Chinese ODI. The Ministry of Commerce and the Ministry of Foreign Affairs jointly issued the *Guidelines for Investments in Overseas Countries' Industries and the Overseas Investment Guidance Catalogue*, directing Chinese firms to invest in selected industrial sectors and "priority recipient nations."[17] Moreover, the central government delegated considerable authority to local governments to review and approve ODI projects.[18] Once the floodgates opened, Chinese investments rushed out. In contrast to the policy fluctuations of the 1980s and early 1990s, state support for an open economy has not waivered ever since.[19] All the subsequent Five-Year Plans have emphasized "go global" as a government policy of strategic importance.[20] Having switched its role from a regulator to a proponent of ODI, the Chinese government offered various incentives for Chinese firms to invest abroad. For instance, state-owned banks were instructed to facilitate Chinese enterprises' outbound investments;[21] the State Administration of Foreign Exchange simplified the procedures for acquiring foreign currency for ODI;[22] and the Ministry of Commerce

[14] Shambaugh, *China Goes Global*, 175.

[15] Luo, Xue, and Han, "How Emerging Market Governments Promote Outward FDI," 68, 54.

[16] Karl P. Sauvant and Michael D. Nolan, "China's Outward Foreign Direct Investment and International Investment Law," 18 *Journal of International Economic Law* 893 (2015), 933.

[17] Shambaugh, *China Goes Global*, 176.

[18] Luo, Xue, and Han, "How Emerging Market Governments Promote Outward FDI," 68, 72.

[19] Cai and Treisman, "Did Government Decentralization Cause China's Economic Miracle?", 505.

[20] Shambaugh, *China Goes Global*, 176.

[21] Yuan et al, "Zhongguo Yinhangye 'Zhou Chu Qu' Yinlai Kuaisu Fazhanqi" (Chinese Banking Industry "Going Global" Entering a Period of Fast Growth), *People's Daily* 3 (Aug. 4, 2016), at http://finance.people.com.cn/n1/2016/0804/c1004-28609135.html, last checked on Sept. 20. 2016.

[22] Guo Song, "'Zouchuqu' Waihui Zhengce Zhichi Tixi" (Facilitating Foreign Exchange Policiies for "Go Global"), *Zhongguo Jirong* (China Finance) 31 (2015).

and the Ministry of Foreign Affairs provided free services such as investment information to Chinese investors.[23]

As China's extraordinarily large foreign-exchange reserve turned into a fiscal liability and the Chinese economy began to suffer over-capacity on the supply side, the central government, clearly intending the global expansion of Chinese firms to kill both birds,[24] further loosened the restrictions by replacing the approval system with a reporting system. Unless an outbound investment concerns sensitive regions or countries, or sensitive industries, investors need only file a notice with the Ministry of Commerce or provincial departments of commerce.[25]

The volume and composition of Chinese ODI well reflect the shifts in the governmental policies. Because of the initial restrictions and the state's extensive intervention, large state-owned conglomerates historically dominated China's ODI. Up until 2010, SOEs, benefiting from all sorts of government support,[26] accounted for 75% of the total Chinese ODI.[27] Moreover, the ODI in this period was concentrated in a few sectors crucial to China's economic development, e.g., energy and transportation.[28] Recently, however, private Chinese companies in diverse sectors have ratcheted up their ODI; the latest data suggest that they have already overtaken non-banking SOEs.[29]

In summary, the meteoric rise of the Chinese economy and the loosening of government control led to a recent surge in investment outflows (see Figure 2.2), catapulting China to the position of the world's second-largest source of ODI.[30] Also, Chinese ODI recently exceeded the investment inflows, rendering the developing country a net capital exporter.[31] Though concerns with capital flight and an abrupt depletion of foreign-exchange reserves led the central government to claw back some authority to review outbound investment deals, it is unlikely to reverse the long-term upward trend.[32] By some estimates, Chinese ODI could reach $367.3 billion by 2022;

23 The Ministry of Commerce website, for instance, offers free information about the investment environment of almost every foreign country.

24 "China Stresses Finance for Companies 'Going Global'," (Dec. 24, 2014), at http://news.xinhuanet.com/english/china/2014–12/24/c_133876895.htm.

25 Section 6, Chapter 2, Jinwai Touzi Guanli Banfa (Measures for the Administration of Overseas Investment), Shangwubuling (MOFCOM Directive) No. 3 (2014).

26 Shambaugh, *China Goes Global*, 177. 27 Ibid., 178.

28 Shannon Tiezzi, "China Urges Companies to 'Go Global'," *The Diplomat* (Dec. 25, 2014), at http://thediplomat.com/2014/12/china-urges-companies-to-go-global.

29 Lyu Chang, "Private Firms Taking the Lead in ODI," *China Daily* (Sept. 30, 2016), at http://europe.chinadaily.com.cn/epaper/2016-09/30/content_26943752.htm.

30 Courtney Fingar, "China Becomes Number One in Outbound Greenfield FDI," *Financial Times* (June 14, 2016), at https://next.ft.com/content/8d55adf0-321e-11e6-bda0-04585c31b153.

31 Wang Youling and Liu Hui, "2015 Woguo Shixian Ziben Jingshuchu, Duiwai Zhijie Touzi Shouci Yueju Quanqiu Di'er" (China Realized Net Capital Outflow, ODI Ranked Second in World), Xinhua News Agency (Sept. 22, 2016), at http://news.xinhuanet.com/fortune/2016–09/22/c_1119608646.htm, last accessed on Nov. 14, 2016.

32 Gabriel Wildau, Don Weinland, and Tom Mitchell, "China to Clamp Down on Outbound M & A in War on Capital Flight," *Financial Times* (Nov. 29, 2016), at www.ft.com/content/2511fa56-b5f8-11e6-ba85-95d1533d9a62, last checked on Dec. 6, 2016.

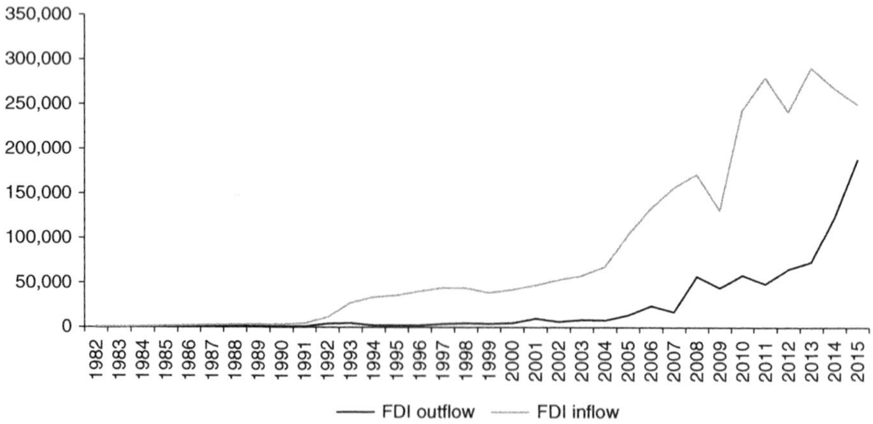

FIGURE 2.2 FDI inflows and outflows (China 1982–2015, current US$ million)
Source: World Bank: World Development Indicators, downloadable at http://data.worldbank.org/country/china?view=chart

the developing country will then surpass the United States as the world's largest source of FDI.[33] The surge of Chinese ODI, just like the phenomenal growth of the Chinese economy, poses numerous novel and important questions. This book explores one such question – how Chinese investors interact with host-country legal and regulatory institutions.

II DEBATES ABOUT THE IMPACTS OF CHINESE ODI

Chinese ODI, given its sheer scale and growth rate, has attracted great attention from scholars and policymakers worldwide. The subsequent debates can be categorized into two diverging views: one welcoming the expansion as broadly beneficial and the other considering it a critical threat. Those holding the former view observe an ascending China opting to play by the existing rules.[34] Enabled partially by embracing global capitalism,[35] the Chinese ODI will fortify the current international system in the long run.[36] Also, the existing global order is sufficiently open and inclusive to accommodate a rising superpower without major disruptions; in other words, China is distinguishable from previous emerging powers in the large stake it holds in preserving the status quo.[37] Of course,

33 Zhong Nan, "China to be Largest Source of FDI, Surpassing the US," *China Daily* (Nov. 11, 2015), at www.chinadaily.com.cn/bizchina/2015–11/11/content_22424743.htm.

34 Edward S. Steinfeld, *Playing Our Game: Why China's Rise Doesn't Threaten the West* (2010), 265.

35 Ibid.

36 Aaron L. Friedberg, "The Future of U.S.–China Relations: Is Conflict Inevitable?", 1 *International Security* 12–14 (2005).

37 G. John Ikenberry, "The Rise of China and the Future of the West," 87 *Foreign Affairs* 23 (2008).

Chinese ODI also brings immediate benefits to host countries, such as new jobs, cheap capital, and additional R & D.[38]

Somewhat ironically, a few scholars have reached the same optimistic conclusion by trivializing the ability of Chinese multinational enterprises (MNEs), especially the gigantic multinational SOEs, to pose any existential threat to competitive private companies from the West,[39] as "profitable" Chinese firms mostly depend on various government subsidies and/or their politically secured oligopolistic positions in the Chinese market.[40] Some contend that the gap between China and the United States has barely narrowed in the past three decades in terms of technological capacity. If anything, the United States appears to have further consolidated its absolute lead.[41] So to this group of scholars and commentators the concern with Chinese business expansion is merely déjà vu.[42] Despite the fear in the 1980s of Japan replacing the United States as the world's economic hegemon,[43] the U.S. system eventually proved more resilient and competitive.[44]

Another group holding the non-threat view, consisting mostly of business scholars, sees Chinese investors as rational and their global expansion as tracking conventional patterns of cross-border investment. The investment's net effect on the host country is a function of multiple factors, such as investment motives and the development gap between the host and the home states.[45] Companies from developed countries, for instance, tend to transplant their corporate governance and management style to their overseas operations. By comparison, investors from developing countries, unable to rely on home-developed efficiency measures or techniques, are more inclined to adapt to the host-state environment. The theory suggests that a greater institutional distance raises the liability of foreignness, which "arises from a broad unfamiliarity with the local market, local practices, and local regulations."[46] In response, foreign investors tend to adopt local

38 See, generally, Theodore Moran and Lindsay Oldenski, *Foreign Direct Investment in the United States: Benefits, Suspicions, and Risks with Special Attention to FDI from China* (2013).

39 See, e.g., George J. Gilboy, "The Myth Behind China's Miracle," 83 *Foreign Affairs* 33 (2004); Peter Nolan, *China and the Global Economy National Champions, Industrial Policy and the Big Business Revolution* (2001), 193.

40 Unirule Institute of Economics, "The Nature, Performance, and Reform of the State-Owned Enterprises" (April 12, 2011), at www.unirule.org.cn/xiazai/2011/20110412.pdf, 34.

41 Michael Beckley, "China's Century? Why America's Edge Will Endure," 36 *International Security* 41 (2011), 70–2.

42 Curtis J. Milhapt, "Chinese Investment: A Case of Déjà Vu for the United States," 4 *East Asian Forum Quarterly* 1 (2012), 34.

43 The most famous work is probably by Paul M. Kennedy, *The Rise and Fall of the Great Powers: Economic Change and Military Conflict from 1500 to 2000* (1989).

44 Sean Starrs, "American Economic Power Hasn't Declined? It Globalized! Summoning the Data and Taking Globalization Seriously," 57 *International Studies Quarterly* 817 (2013).

45 Randall Morck, Bernard Yeung, and Minyuan Zhao, "Perspectives on China's Outward Foreign Direct Investment," *Journal of International Business Studies* 337 (2008).

46 Robert Salomon and Zheying Wu, "Institutional Distance and Local Isomorphism Strategy," 43 *Journal of International Business Studies* 343 (2012), 343.

isomorphism strategies.[47] In other words, Chinese firms investing in countries that are vastly different from China in terms of the cultural, regulatory, and economic institutions will adopt the practices of their local counterparts "to acquire legitimacy and to mitigate the liability of foreignness."[48] Because Chinese investors will behave like local firms, there should be minimal detrimental effects on host-country institutions.

On the opposite side of the grand debate are those who perceive Chinese economic expansion as a critical threat.[49] Some in this camp are concerned with the practical risks of Chinese outbound investment, especially investment in developing countries, because "Chinese companies and their management display an inability to escape their own national corporate culture and business practices."[50] Chinese companies investing in Africa, for instance, have allegedly spawned corruption, disrespect for the law, and human rights violations, and have on occasion supported ruthless dictators.[51] Even Chinese officials lamented that outbound investors might be "exporting China's domestic problems."[52] The threat may persist as Chinese companies show a tendency to invest in resource-rich countries with weak institutions[53] and a tolerance for high political risk due to government subsidies.[54] Studies of foreign individuals and corporations in the United States also offer evidence suggestive of home-state effects. In their seminal work, Fisman and Miguel find that, everything else being equal, U.N. diplomats from corrupt countries were more likely to violate New York City traffic rules.[55] Similarly, corporations with foreign owners from corrupt countries are more prone to tax evasion in the United States.[56] Moreover, scholars of international business have shown that parent

47 Ibid., 344. 48 Ibid., 343.

49 For a summary of the pessimistic views, see Friedberg, "The Future of U.S.–China Relations," 17–22.

50 Shambaugh, *China Goes Global*, 187; Chih-shian Liou, "Rent-Seeking at Home, Capturing Market Share Abroad: The Domestic Determinants of the Transnationalization of China State Construction Engineering Corporation," 54 *World Development* 220 (2014), 228.

51 For examples of the "China bashing," see Barry Sautman and Yan Hairong, "Bashing 'the Chinese': Contextualizing Zambia's Collum Coal Mine Shooting," 23 *Journal of Contemporary China* 1073 (2014).

52 "Zhongguo Qiye 'Zouchuqu' Yao Tupo 'Xingxiang Kunju'" (Chinese Companies Going Abroad Should Change their Negative Image), *Liaowang* (Oct. 2, 2012), at http://finance.chinanews.com/cj/2012/10–22/4265426.shtml.

53 E.g., Bala Ramasamy, Matthew Yeung, and Sylvie Laforet, "China's Outward Foreign Direct Investment: Location Choice and Firm Ownership," 47 *Journal of World Business* 17 (2012); Peter J Buckley, L. Jeremy Clegg, Adam R. Cross, Xin Liu, Hinrich Voss, and Ping Zheng, "The Determinants of Chinese Outward Foreign Direct Investment," 38 *Journal of International Business Studies* 499 (2007).

54 Diego Quer, Enrique Claver, and Laura Rienda, "Political Risk, Cultural Distance, and Outward Foreign Direct Investment: Empirical Evidence from Large Chinese Firms," 29 *Asia Pacific Journal of Management* 1092 (2012).

55 Raymond Fisman and Edward Miguel, "Corruption, Norms, and Legal Enforcement: Evidence from Diplomatic Parking Tickets," 115 *Journal of Political Economy* 1020 (2007).

56 Jason DeBacker, Bradley T. Heim, and Anh Tran, "Importing Corruption Culture from Overseas: Evidence from Corporate Tax Evasion in the United States," 117 *Journal of Financial Economics* 122 (2015).

companies' ownership structure and the home-state institutions have measurable impacts on the firms' investment strategies and reactions to host-state institutional pressure.[57]

To other naysayers, the threat of Chinese ODI originates from China's practice of state capitalism.[58] Supported by a highly interventionist government with vast resources, Chinese SOEs pose a formidable challenge to free-market capitalism.[59] And such challenge may not come only from the SOEs because private Chinese companies, once recognized as national champions, will be co-opted and receive the state's largesse.[60] Given the vast resources controlled by the Chinese government, its "corporate agents" stand a good chance of prevailing over Western firms in the global market.[61]

Still others take note of the Chinese government's discontent with the extant international system shaped and guarded by the United States and its allies. To have more voice in global political and economic affairs, China has begun to build alternative multilateral institutions. It recently co-ordinated and sponsored the establishment of the BRICS New Development Bank, widely viewed as the developing-country alternative of the Bretton Woods institutions for financing global development.[62] China has also created the Asian Infrastructure Investment Bank,[63] a regional multilateral institution mostly funded by the Chinese government to substitute the Asian Development Bank dominated by the United States and Japan.[64] And soon after the global financial crisis, China put forward a plan to replace the U.S. dollar as the world reserve currency with special drawing rights based on a bundle of currencies.[65] In sum, the ascent of China, if not properly

57 Lin Cui and Fuming Jiang, "State Ownership Effect on Firms' FDI Ownership Decisions under Institutional Pressure: A Study of Chinese Outward-Investing Firms," 43 *Journal of International Business Studies* 264 (2012); Yadong Luo and Stephanie Lu Wang, "Foreign Direct Investment Strategies by Developing Country Multinationals: A Diagnostic Model for Home Country Effects," 2 *Global Strategy Journal* 244 (2012).

58 "The Rise of State Capitalism," *The Economist* (Jan 21, 2012), at www.economist.com/node/21543160.

59 Ian Bremmer, "State Capitalism Comes of Age: The End of the Free Market?", 8 *Foreign Affairs* 40 (2009).

60 Curtis J. Milhaupt and Wentong Zheng, "Beyond Ownership: State Capitalism and the Chinese Firm," 103 *Georgetown Law Journal* 665 (2015).

61 "The Rise of State Capitalism."

62 Raj M. Desai and James Raymond Vreeland, "What the New Bank of BRICS Is All About," *Washington Post* (July 17, 2014), at www.washingtonpost.com/blogs/monkey-cage/wp/2014/07/17/what-the-new-bank-of-brics-is-all-about, last accessed on Sept. 22, 2014.

63 Jane Perlez, "U.S. Opposing China's Answer to World Bank," *New York Times* (Oct. 9, 2014), at www.nytimes.com/2014/10/10/world/asia/chinas-plan-for-regional-development-bank-runs-into-us-opposition.html?hpw&rref=business&action=click&pgtype=Homepage&version=HpHedThumbWell&module=well-region&region=bottom-well&WT.nav=bottom-well&_r=0, last accessed on Oct. 10, 2014.

64 "What China Wants?", *The Economist* (Aug. 23, 2014), at www.economist.com/news/essays/21609649-china-becomes-again-worlds-largest-economy-it-wants-respect-it-enjoyed-centuries-past-it-does-not.

65 Jamil Anderlini, "China Calls for New Reserve Currency," *Financial Times* (March 24, 2009), at www.ft.com/intl/cms/s/0/7851925a-17a2-11de-8c9d-0000779fd2ac.html#axzz3DcTbEkqs.

managed by the West, heralds "a dark era of ideological contention and geopolitical rivalry."[66] And Chinese investors, acting as agents of the regime, may undermine the U.S.-led international system.

To summarize, within a short span of four decades, China has transformed from a poverty-struck hermit state to the world's second-largest economy boasting a relatively dynamic and open market. The subsequent surge of Chinese ODI has spurred intense debates that culminated in two diverging views: one critical about the global expansion of Chinese companies for the threat they pose to host-country institutions and the global order, the other embracing Chinese ODI for its contribution to host-country economies and fortification of the extant international institutions. Though the debates have produced valuable insights about China's global expansion, they offer inadequate answers to the most pressing questions about how the expansion may impact U.S. legal and regulatory institutions. First, the literature review has clearly evidenced the lack of consensus. Some studies found adaptation and isomorphism, whereas others demonstrated enduring home-country effects. Which of the two holds more predictive power when it comes to Chinese investment in the United States? The truth may lie somewhere in between, i.e., Chinese investors in the United States exhibit some signs of isomorphism while retaining certain home-state practices. That hypothesis then raises the question: to what extent do Chinese investors adapt to the U.S. institutional setting? On that the existing literature has been silent.

Second, the extant literature has largely neglected Chinese investment in developed countries, especially the United States. Because Chinese investors only recently ventured into competitive markets in the West, quality empirical data are in short supply. Therefore, with a few exceptions,[67] most of the studies about Chinese ODI focus on investments in developing countries. Findings of those studies and the theories deduced therefrom may not apply to Chinese investment in the United States, since its robust formal institutions are absent in most Third World countries.

Third, the scholarship on Chinese ODI has overlooked the host-country legal and regulatory institutions. Most of the research on Chinese outward investment, having been conducted by business scholars and social scientists, rarely touches on the dynamic interactions between the investors and host-country law. Some simply

66 Charles Kupchan, *No One's World: The West, the Rising Rest, and the Coming Global Turn* (2012), 205.

67 See, e.g., Brian Burgoon and Damian Raess, "Chinese Investment and European Labor: Should and Do Workers Fear Chinese FDI?", 12 *Asia Europe Journal* 179 (2014); A. Szamosszegi, "An Analysis of Chinese Investments in the U.S. Economy," report prepared for the U.S.–China Economic and Security Review Commission (2012); L. Liu and Y. Tian, "The Internationalisation of Chinese Enterprises: The Analysis of the UK Case," 4 *International Journal of Technology and Globalisation* 87 (2008); Theodore H. Moran, "Toward a Multilateral Framework for Identifying National Security Threats Posed by Foreign Acquisitions: With Special Reference to Chinese Acquisitions in the United States, Canada, and Australia," 7 *China Economic Journal* 39 (2014).

dismissed the question with an unsubstantiated claim that Chinese companies have "difficulties adapting to foreign legal, regulatory, tax and political environments."[68] Yet in contrast to most developing countries, formal rules in the United States should play a key role in shaping the behavior of Chinese investors. Having neglected the legal dimension, the literature has huge gaps to fill.[69]

Lastly, many of the extant studies have relied on the analyses of a small number of Chinese companies.[70] While ethnographic research can certainly present valuable details and context about Chinese investment in host countries, the induced theories tend to be limited in application. While the more recent research began to use quantitative methods,[71] much has relied on government-provided macro-level firm or industrial data.[72] Such data fail to adequately account for frequent use of tax havens and offshore holding companies by Chinese outbound investors, resulting in "large geographical, industrial composition and volume biases."[73] Moreover, such data do not aid research involving subjective aspects of foreign investment. As a result, and given that soaring ODI from China is a relatively new phenomenon,[74] we

68 Shambaugh, *China Goes Global*, 189.

69 For example, the differences between Chinese FDI and Japanese FDI in terms of local hiring are attributed mostly to the different stages of development of the two home countries. Xiaohua Yang, Yi Jiang, Rongping Kang, and Yinbin Ke, "A Comparative Analysis of the Internationalization of Chinese and Japanese Firms," 26 *Asia Pacific Journal of Management* 141 (2009), at 156. The author did not greatly discuss any possible impact of the Japan–US FCN Treaty that allowed Japanese companies to appoint managers of their choice and the absence of such favorable treaty benefits for Chinese investors in the U.S. Though a few legal scholars have begun to pay attention to Chinese investment in the U.S., lacking empirical data, their research remains descriptive and speculative. See, e.g., Curtis J. Milhaupt, "Is the U.S. Ready for FDI from China? Lessons from Japan's Experience in the 1980s," in Karl Sauvant, ed., *Is the U.S. Ready for FDI from China?* (2009).

70 See, e.g., Steinfeld, *Playing Our Game*, 265; Yang et al., "A Comparative Analysis of the Internationalization of Chinese and Japanese Firms," at 141; Ping Deng, "Why do Chinese Firms Tend to Acquire Strategic Assets in International Expansion?", 44 *Journal of World Business* 74 (2009); Huaichuan Rui and George S. Yip, "Foreign Acquisitions by Chinese Firms: A Strategic Intent Perspective," 43 *Journal of World Business* 213 (2008).

71 For instance, a critical literature review of all articles on the internationalization of Chinese firms published in major scholarly journals found thirteen studies that used the survey method. Ping Deng, "The Internationalization of Chinese Firms: A Critical Review and Future Research," 14 *International Journal of Management Reviews* 411 (2012).

72 See, e.g., Ramasamy, Yeung, and Laforet, "China's Outward Foreign Direct Investment," at 17; I. Kolstad and A. Wiig, "What Determines Chinese Outward FDI?", 47 *Journal of World Business* 26 (2012); P. J. Buckley, S. Elia, and M. Kafouros, "Acquisitions from Emerging Countries: What Factors Influence the Performance of Target Firms in Advanced Countries?", 4 *European Journal of International Management* 30 (2010); P. E. Tolentino, "Home Country Macroeconomic Factors and Outward FDI of China and India," 16 *Journal of International Management* 102 (2010); Lin Cui and Fuming Jiang, "FDI Entry Mode Choice of Chinese Firms: A Strategic Behavior Perspective," 44 *Journal of World Business* 434 (2009); Peter J. Buckley et al., "Historic and Emergent Trends in Chinese Outward Direct Investment," 48 *Management International Review* 715 (2008).

73 Dylan Sutherland and John Anderson, "The Pitfalls of Using Foreign Direct Investment Data to Measure Chinese Multinational Enterprise Activity," 221 *China Quarterly* 21 (2015), 45.

74 Szamosszegi, "An Analysis of Chinese Investments in the U.S. Economy," at 30.

remain in the dark as to why Chinese firms invest in the United States and how they react to U.S. institutions.

In sum, fast ascending the international pecking order economically and politically, China and its global business expansion have caught a great deal of scholarly and public interest. Yet previous studies about the impacts of Chinese ODI have left important questions unexplored. Taking an interdisciplinary approach, this book begins to fill the void by empirically investigating the reactions of Chinese investors to U.S. legal and regulatory institutions, and the effect, if any, of state ownership.

III CHINESE FDI IN THE UNITED STATES

As discussed at the beginning of this chapter, four decades of continuous growth have transformed China from an isolated country in dire poverty to the world's second-largest economy,[75] and from a capital-importing country to one of the largest sources of global ODI.[76] While the investments initially flowed to resource-rich developing countries, an increasing number of Chinese firms have invested in mature and competitive markets. Some estimate that in 2015 alone Chinese investors made direct investments of US$40 billion in Europe and North America,[77] and the vast majority of the investments were in four sectors unrelated to natural resources, i.e., real estate, automotive industries, corporate services, and information technology.[78] This section presents an overview of Chinese investments in the United States and a more detailed account of the experiences of three Chinese companies.

A *An Overview of Chinese Investment in the United States*

Chinese investments in the United States, largely following the general trajectory of Chinese ODI (see Figure 2.3), have been undergoing explosive growth.[79] The United States recently emerged as the largest national recipient of China's ODI.[80] Meanwhile, the composition of Chinese investors has changed. While for many years SOEs dominated Chinese investments in the United States, private investors now play an increasingly important role. A recent study estimates that privately

75 Ji Li, "I Came, I Saw, I . . . Adapted."

76 Jamil Anderlini, *China to Become One of World's Biggest Overseas Investors by 2020, Financial Times* (June 25, 2015), available at www.ft.com/cms/s/0/5136953a-1b3d-11e5-8201-cbdb03d71480.html#axzz4ERYKV4Sa.

77 "Bird's Eye View: Comparing Chinese Investment into North America and Europe," June 2016, *Baker & McKenzie*, at www.bakermckenzie.com/en/insight/publications/2016/06/birds-eye-view.

78 Ibid.

79 China Going Global Investment Index, Economist Intelligence Unit (2013), at http://china.ucsd.edu/_files/odi-2013/09232013_Paper_Liu_ChinaGoingGlobal.pdf.

80 Thilo Hanemann and Cassie Gao, "Chinese FDI in the US: Tripling Down on America," July 22, 2016, at http://rhg.com/notes/chinese-fdi-in-the-us-tripling-down-on-america.

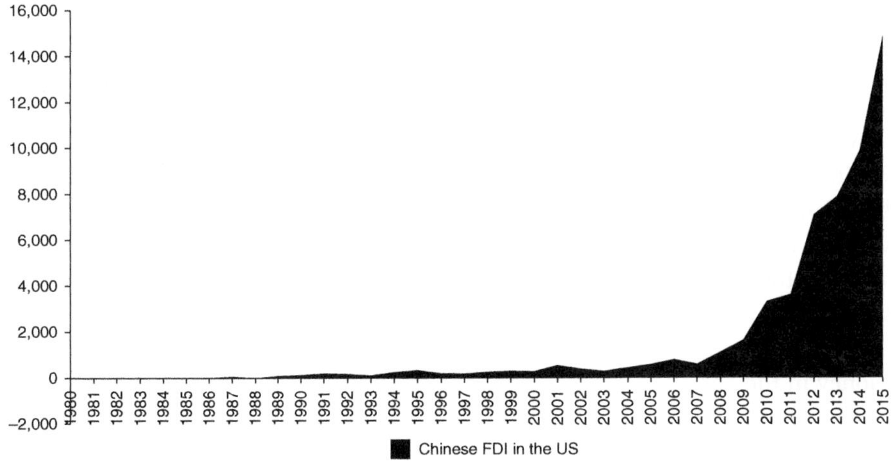

FIGURE 2.3 Chinese FDI in the United States 1980–2015 (direct investment position on a historical-cost basis; US$ million)
Source: Bureau of Economic Analysis, U.S. Department of Commerce, available at www.bea.gov/international/di1fdibal.htm

owned companies accounted for up to 84% of total Chinese investment in the United States, a 65% increase from merely five years ago.[81]

Most Chinese investments in the United States have involved mergers and acquisitions,[82] which is not surprising given the vast differences between the two countries. Foreign investors without advantageous firm-level or institutional resources inevitably face daunting challenges when operating in well-developed markets. SOEs, with financial backing of their governmental owners, may take on such a task, as exemplified by the risky investments they made in some of the least developed countries.[83] For private Chinese companies less able to afford long-term risks, acquiring established businesses affords a quick entry into the competitive U.S. market. A recent survey counted more than a hundred mergers and acquisitions by Chinese investors of U.S. firms in 2015 alone, with an aggregated book value of US$13.5 billion.[84] In stark contrast to Chinese investments in developing countries, those in the United States span diverse sectors, from real estate to entertainment.[85] In sectors tied closely to national security, however, Chinese investors are largely absent. Chapter 7 of the book will elaborate on

81 Thilo Hanemann and Cassie Gao, "Chinese FDI in the US: 2015 Recap," Jan. 19, 2016, at http://rhg.com/notes/chinese-fdi-in-the-us-2015-recap.

82 "New Neighbors: 2016 Update," report by the National Committee on US–China Relations and Rhodium Group, April 2016, at http://rhg.com/wp-content/uploads/2016/04/RHG_New-Neighbors_2016-Update_Full-Report.pdf, 2.

83 Jing-Lin Duanmu, "Firm Heterogeneity and Location Choice of Chinese Multinational Enterprises (MNEs)," 47 *Journal of World Business* 64 (2012).

84 "New Neighbors: 2016 Update," 2.

85 Hanemann and Gao, "Chinese FDI in the US: 2015 Recap."

how they cope with the U.S. regime for national security review of foreign investments (also known as CFIUS review). Chinese investors also avoid those U.S. sectors where foreign investments are either heavily regulated or restricted, such as nuclear energy.[86]

Moreover, Chinese investments in the United States spread across many states. California and New York lead the others in attracting the investments. The former has drawn Chinese investors in sectors such as semiconductors and entertainment; whereas the latter has lured Chinese capital in real estate and financial services;[87] states in the Midwest (e.g., Michigan and Illinois) have also attracted substantial Chinese investments in the manufacturing sector (e.g., the production of auto parts);[88] and states in the South such as Texas have become a magnet for Chinese money in the energy sector.[89] Chinese investments have generated many employment opportunities for American workers; by the most recent account, U.S. affiliates of Chinese companies employ approximately 90,000 Americans. Some have estimated that the number could reach as high as 400,000 by 2020.[90]

To summarize, Chinese investments in the United States have been growing exponentially.[91] In contrast to their investments in developing countries, Chinese firms invest in myriad sectors and diverse locations in the United States, and employ a rising number of American workers.

B *Three Chinese Companies in the United States*

The preceding subsection presented a bird's-eye view of Chinese ODI and Chinese investments in the United States. To supplement abstract numbers with more concrete examples, this subsection sketches the investments of three Chinese companies in the United States: Lenovo, Bank of China, and Huawei. The three are well-known Chinese firms with different ownership structures and in different sectors. Lenovo, listed on the Hong Kong stock exchange, is one of the largest manufacturers of personal computers (PCs), mobile phones and other consumer

86 For a summary of the restrictions on foreign investment in the US nuclear energy sector, see Sachin Desai and Kathleen Schroeder, "US Nuclear Foreign Ownership Policy Ready for a Refreshed Interpretation," 37 *Energy Law Journal* 85 (2016), 92–3.

87 "New Neighbors: 2016 Update," 3.

88 Ellen Sheng, "Michigan Prioritizes China with New Investment Center," *Forbes* (July 14, 2016), at www.forbes.com/sites/ellensheng/2016/07/14/michigan-prioritizes-china-with-new-investment-center/2/#175a2dee1220.

89 Chris Tomlinson, "Chinese Companies Invest Big in Texas and Houston, Oil and Services Companies Have Invested $7.4 billion in the Last 15 Years," *Houston Chronicle* (April 20, 2016), at www.houstonchronicle.com/business/outside-the-boardroom/article/Chinese-companies-invest-big-in-Texas-and-Houston-7258436.php.

90 Thilo Hanemann and Adam Lysenko, "The Employment Impacts of Chinese Investment in the United States," Rhodium Group (Sept. 27, 2012), at http://rhg.com/articles/the-employment-impacts-of-chinese-investment-in-the-united-states, last accessed on Nov. 10, 2016.

91 Chinese FDI in the United States increased by 200% in 2016. Hanemann and Gao, "Record Deal Making in 2016."

electronics. Bank of China is one of the five major state-owned Chinese banks and the world's fourth-largest bank by capitalization;[92] its stock is publicly traded in China and Hong Kong. Huawei, an employee-owned company headquartered in Shenzhen, is the largest Chinese maker and seller of telecommunications equipment and services. I select these three companies as examples because they pioneered Chinese investments in the United States, yet their experiences vary dramatically. The following comparative description underlines the urgent need for an analytical framework and systematic empirical study of how Chinese companies interact with U.S. institutions.

1 Lenovo

Lenovo, having been a dominant PC seller in China, was little known globally before it acquired IBM's PC business in 2005.[93] The acquisition, partially in response to the Chinese government's then nascent "go global" policy[94] and widely anticipated to fail,[95] proved to be Lenovo's first successful move towards building a globalized business. The Chinese government played a critical role in the acquisition as both the majority stake-holder of the acquirer and its financial underwriter.[96] Lenovo managed to retain most of the former IBM employees and delegated to them broad management authority. Soon after the acquisition, Lenovo established a global headquarters in North Carolina and by 2013 had expanded its U.S. workforce to more than 2,700 employees.[97] A senior executive of Lenovo commented that out of the several thousand employees in the United States, only a handful were expatriated from China. Because of the extent of Lenovo's overseas expansion, he would label it "a global company with a Chinese heritage."[98]

Riding on the momentum of the early success, Lenovo further increased its U.S. investment. In 2014, it acquired Motorola Mobility for $2.91 billion from Google and became the world's number-three smartphone manufacturer. When

92 Liyan Chen, "2015 Global 2000: The World's Largest Banks," *Forbes* (May 6, 2015), at www.forbes.com/sites/liyanchen/2015/05/06/2015-global-2000-the-worlds-largest-banks/#41747a4824f1, last accessed on Dec. 6, 2016.

93 Neil Gough and David Gelles, "Lenovo Agrees to Buy IBM Server Business for $2.3 Billion," *New York Times* (Jan. 23, 2014), at http://dealbook.nytimes.com/2014/01/23/lenovo-buys-ibm-server-business-for-2-3-billion.

94 Chuan Zhi Liu, "Lenovo: An Example of Globalization of Chinese Enterprises," 38 *Journal of International Business Studies* 573 (2007), 573.

95 Sumner Lemon, "Concerns Mount over Lenovo's IBM Deal," *PCWorld* (Jan. 27, 2005), at www.pcworld.com/article/119476/article.html.

96 Ping Deng, "Why do Chinese Firms Tend to Acquire Strategic Assets in International Expansion?", 44 *Journal of World Business* 74 (2009), 80.

97 "Lenovo in the United States," available at www.lenovo.com/transactions/pdf/Lenovo-USA-Fact-Sheet.pdf.

98 Presentation by Lawrence Yu, director of Lenovo Global Marketing, at Rutgers Business School (March 16, 2016).

the deal closed, another 2,800 U.S. workers joined the Chinese company.[99] In the same year, Lenovo bought IBM's lower-end server business for $2.3 billion and retained thousands of the seller's former employees.[100] The acquisitions led to a further shift in the composition of Lenovo's global businesses. Today, only 28% of the company's annual revenue originated from China, compared to 30% from the Americas.[101] During the aggressive expansion in the United States, Lenovo did not encounter significant legal or regulatory hurdles, except for some national security concerns that were promptly addressed without affecting the company's core U.S. business.[102]

The experiences gained from the earlier U.S. investments, however, cannot guarantee long-term success. After the acquisition of Motorola Mobility, the sale of Motorola phones dropped by more than 30% in 2015,[103] due to which Lenovo reported in March 2016 its first quarterly loss in over seven years. Lenovo's executives acknowledged that they underestimated the difficulties of integrating Motorola operations. To improve its financials, the company announced a global layoff of 3,200 employees, 500 of which worked for Motorola.[104]

To summarize, as one of the first Chinese companies to invest in the United States, Lenovo made history by acquiring IBM's PC business. Despite the widely shared skepticism, the acquisition transformed Lenovo into a competitive China-based MNE, or, in its executive's words, a "global company with a Chinese heritage." Riding on the initial success, Lenovo multiplied its investments in the United States. The recent acquisitions, however, posed serious challenges that have pressed Lenovo to reduce its global workforce and trim down its U.S. operations.[105]

2 Bank of China

Bank of China, one of the five major state-owned banks in China, was among the first Chinese companies to set up operations in the United States. It opened a U.S. branch in New York Chinatown in 1981, much earlier than other Chinese

99 "Becomes World's #3 Smartphone Maker; Prepares for Even More Growth," *Lenovo Newsroom* (Oct. 30, 2014), available at http://news.lenovo.com/news-releases/lenovo-completes-acquisition-motorola-mobility-from-google.htm.

100 Gough and Gelles, "Lenovo Agrees to Buy IBM Server Business."

101 Annual Report of Lenovo for Fiscal Year of 2015, at www.lenovo.com/ww/lenovo/pdf/report/[illegible]20160603a.pdf, 20.

102 In 2014, CFIUS approved the acquisition by Lenovo of the IBM server business. Alex Barinka and David McLaughlin, "IMB Obtains US Approval for Sale of Server Business to Lenovo," *Bloomberg Technology* (Aug. 15, 2014), at www.bloomberg.com/news/articles/2014–08-15/ibm-gets-u-s-approval-for-sale-of-server-business-to-lenovo, last accessed on Oct. 12, 2016. In 2005, CFIUS reviewed but raised no objections to the acquisition of the IBM PC business. Mike Musgrove, "US Panel Clears IBM Deal with Chinese Firm," *Washington Post* (March 10, 2005), 5.

103 Ji Jiapeng, "Shouji Bumen Jukui 18yi Lianxiang Quanqiu Caiyuan 3200ren Ying Handong" (Cell Phone Department Suffered 1.8 Billion Loss, Lianxiang Laid Off 3,200), 21st *Century Business Herald* (Aug. 15, 2015), at http://m.21jingji.com/article/20150815/622463c02988d9ee15c24e822721dc31.html.

104 Ibid. 105 "New Neighbors: 2016 Update," 3.

companies.[106] For many years the bank's U.S. operations were profitable, yet the management bore typical attributes of a state-owned Chinese bank prior to the radical reforms of the SOEs and the Chinese banking system. In the hierarchical decision-making structure, governance and internal control were perfunctory, and personal relationships with clients exerted a heavy influence on loan decisions. Such traits carried a high risk of fraud and violating banking regulatory rules in the United States.

From 1991 to 1999, some former employees of the bank's New York branch colluded with certain borrowers to defraud the bank, causing losses of more than $30 million.[107] Of course, few banks, Chinese or not, can be fully immune to fraud. What set Bank of China apart was the structural vulnerability of the bank's traditional governance. In 2002, Office of the Comptroller under the U.S. Treasury Department issued a fine of US$10 million to Bank of China for misconduct committed by its U.S. branches. It found that

> numerous unsafe and unsound banking practices occurred in the period 1991 through 1999 by senior executive management and other former personnel of the branches, including the facilitation of a fraudulent letter of credit scheme, the facilitation of a loan fraud scheme, the unauthorized release of collateral and the concealment of such action, and other suspicious activity and potential fraud.[108]

Pursuant to the consent order issued by the U.S. Treasury Department, Bank of China agreed to systematically reform the management of its U.S. branches. It expanded the duties and authority of the risk-management department and hired a chief risk officer whose qualifications included "education and training focused on bank operations in the U.S.," "expertise in the banking laws and regulations of the U.S.," and "significant experience in fraud control."[109] And the chief risk officer reported directly to Bank of China and the general manager of all the U.S. branches.[110] When asked to comment on the lessons learned from the fraud

[106] Amy He, "Bank of China New York Opens Queens Branch," *China Daily USA* (June 27, 2014), at http://usa.chinadaily.com.cn/2014–06/27/content_17620960.htm, last accessed on Oct. 11, 2016.

[107] For more details about the fraud, see *Bank of China* v. *NBM LLC*, 2005 U.S. Dist. LEXIS 14783 (S.D.N.Y., July 21, 2005).

[108] Consent Order #2002–1, US Department of the Treasury Office of the Comptroller of the Currency, at www.occ.gov/static/news-issuances/news-releases/2002/nr-occ-2002–7-consent-order-1.pdf, 35.

[109] Section 2, Article I, Consent Order #2002–1, US Department of the Treasury Office of the Comptroller of the Currency, at www.occ.gov/static/news-issuances/news-releases/2002/nr-occ-2002–7-consent-order-1.pdf.

[110] Section 4, Article I, Consent Order #2002–1, US Department of the Treasury Office of the Comptroller of the Currency, at www.occ.gov/static/news-issuances/news-releases/2002/nr-occ-2002–7-consent-order-1.pdf.

cases, senior officers of the bank suggested that employees should keep some distance from clients,[111] and the role of compliance should be elevated.[112]

After Bank of China implemented the consent order and strengthened its compliance, its U.S. businesses continued to grow. The growth accelerated even after the 2008 financial crisis, when the U.S. government tightened the regulation of the banking sector. In 2012 Bank of China opened a fourth branch, in Chicago, and expanded its U.S. workforce to more than 500 employees. Like Lenovo, the bank's U.S. operations have been highly localized. For instance, more than 90% of the bank's New York workforce was recruited locally, including some of the top executives.[113] Riding on the wave of Chinese ODI, the bank has participated in financing some of the largest investments in the United States.[114] In 2014 the bank's U.S. assets surpassed $50 billion, a threshold over which banks are subject to more rigorous regulatory oversight.[115] Nonetheless, the bank continued its expansion, and is planning to open yet another branch in Houston and hire 100 more employees.[116]

In summary, Bank of China pioneered the entry by Chinese companies into the U.S. market. In the 1990s, as its U.S. operations grew, the bank's traditional practices resulted in fraud and in violations of U.S. banking rules. Pursuant to the consent order of the U.S. banking regulator, the U.S. branches of Bank of China implemented structural reorganization that elevated the role of compliance and risk control, and relied heavily on U.S. professionals. The bank has since played an active role in facilitating trade and investments by Chinese firms and its U.S. businesses have undergone explosive growth, though it faces more regulations and sometimes still falls short of full compliance.[117]

3 Huawei

In stark contrast to Lenovo and Bank of China, Huawei has encountered mounting challenges when investing in the United States. This telecommunications equipment manufacturer, founded by a former army engineer, set up its U.S. headquarters

[111] "Zhongguo Yinhang Pilu Niuyue Fenhang Susong Zhouqiang Anjian Shimo" (Bank of China Reveals Lawsuit against Zhou Qiang), *China Business News* (Sept. 30, 2002), at www.cctv.com/financial/zhongguocjbd/caijingtt/20020930/51.html.

[112] Hu Shuli and Gu Wei, "Zhongguo Yinhang Niuyue Fenhang Fashengle Shenmo" (What Happened at Bank of China New York Branch), *Caijing* (Feb. 10, 2002), at http://finance.sina.com.cn/g/20020210/172143.html.

[113] Carolyn Cui and Daniel Huang, "The Bank of China Takes Manhattan," *Wall Street Journal* (May 2, 2016), at www.wsj.com/articles/coming-to-midtown-bank-of-china-1462008602.

[114] For instance, the bank extended a loan to Anbang Insurance to acquire a stake in New York real property. "The Bank of China Takes Manhattan."

[115] "Zhongguo Yinhang Buju Yanke Jianguan Jiji Zaimei Tuozhan Yewu," *Wall Street Journal* (May 3, 2016), at http://cn.wsj.com/gb/20160503/biz085222.asp.

[116] Cui and Huang, "The Bank of China Takes Manhattan."

[117] Jesse Hamilton, "Bank of China Targeted by U.S. for Money-Laundering Controls," *Bloomberg* (Jan 20, 2016), at www.bloomberg.com/news/articles/2016–01-20/bank-of-china-targeted-by-u-s-over-money-laundering-controls.

as early as 2001.[118] Like Lenovo, Huawei made a few attempts to acquire U.S. businesses; however, the deals were repeatedly blocked by the U.S. government. In 2008, the U.S. government prohibited Huawei from purchasing 3Com on grounds of national security.[119] In 2011, after Huawei bought some assets from a bankrupt U.S. firm, 3Leaf, CFIUS opened an investigation of the acquisition and forced a divestiture.[120] The U.S. government also intervened to restrain Huawei's sale of telecommunication equipment. In 2010, under pressure from the U.S. government, Sprint excluded Huawei from a bid to modernize its cellular network, a contract worth billions of dollars.[121]

No one can fault Huawei for not working hard enough to dispel the national security concerns. Like Lenovo, Huawei relied heavily on U.S. talent in managing its U.S. business. Almost all of the senior executives in the United States are Americans recruited from the firm's U.S. competitors or partners.[122] Also, the company spared no efforts in lobbying the U.S. government. To get the Sprint contract, for instance,

> Huawei enacted an all-out lobbying effort in Washington. It helped set up a company with the reassuring name Amerilink Telecom to resell Huawei gear to Sprint. Amerilink had big-name board members such as former congressman Richard A. Gephardt and World Bank ex-President James D. Wolfensohn, who gave the enterprise a political class seal of approval. It didn't work.[123]

In 2011, Huawei even invited the U.S. government to investigate its operations to clear any national security concerns, to no avail. In 2012, the House Intelligence Committee produced a report that urged the U.S. government to block Huawei from acquiring U.S. assets and to exclude its equipment from the market.[124] That was the last straw that broke the camel's back. Ren Zhengfei, founder of Huawei,

[118] Cecilia Kang, "Huawei's US Competitors among Those Pushing for Scrutiny of Chinese Tech Firm," *Washington Post* (Oct. 10, 2012), at www.washingtonpost.com/business/technology/huaweis-us-competitors-among-those-pushing-for-scrutiny-of-chinese-tech-firm/2012/10/10/b84d8d16-1256-11e2-a16b-2c110031514a_story.html.

[119] Steven R. Weisman, "Sale of 3Com to Huawei Is Derailed by U.S. Security Concern," *New York Times* (Feb. 21, 2008), at www.nytimes.com/2008/02/21/business/worldbusiness/21iht-3com.1.10258216.html, last accessed on Nov. 22, 2016.

[120] Sinead Carew and Jessica Wohl, "Huawei Backs Away from 3Leaf Acquisition," *Reuters* (Feb. 19, 2011), at www.reuters.com/article/us-huawei-3leaf-idUSTRE71I38920110219.

[121] Joann S. Lublin and Shayndi Raice, "Security Fears Kill Chinese Bid in U.S.," *Wall Street Journal* (Nov. 5, 2010), at www.wsj.com/articles/SB10001424052748704353504575596611547810220.

[122] Ashlee Vance and Bruce Einhorn, "At Huawei, Matt Bross Tries to Ease U.S. Security Fears," *BloombergBusinessweek* (Sept. 15, 2011), at www.bloomberg.com/news/articles/2011-09-15/at-huawei-matt-bross-tries-to-ease-u-dot-s-dot-security-fears.

[123] Ibid.

[124] David E. Sanger and Nicole Perlroth, "N.S.A. Breached Chinese Servers Seen as Security Threat," *New York Times* (March 22, 2014), at www.nytimes.com/2014/03/23/world/asia/nsa-breached-chinese-servers-seen-as-spy-peril.html?_r=0.

announced its exit from the U.S. market, citing concerns that the company's U.S. business would impact U.S.–China relations.[125]

Soon after the announcement, however, Huawei's defensive position reversed thanks to Snowden's revelations in 2013 that the NSA had hacked all major telecommunication systems. The agency had been spying on Huawei ever since 2007. According to Huawei's spokesperson, the revelations "leveled the playing field between Huawei and the U.S. government and U.S.-based competitors. It has caused a reset of the trust issues on both sides."[126] Moreover, citing concerns about the national security threat, the Chinese government imposed restrictions on the access of Cisco (Huawei's major competitor based in the United States) to the Chinese market.[127] It appears that large telecommunications equipment providers, whether China- or U.S.-based, simply cannot insulate their foreign investments from complex bilateral relations.

Like Lenovo, Huawei is a China-headquartered company that has globalized. Its founder insisted that the company was a global MNE with 17,000 employees worldwide.[128] Huawei reported 2015 revenue of US$60.8 billion, of which only 42% came from the Chinese market.[129] But the U.S. market plays a small part in Huawei's overseas business, accounting for less than 5% of its revenue.[130] Nonetheless, Huawei is still expanding in the United States, focusing primarily on R & D and areas with no national security implications.[131]

To summarize, this subsection has sketched the diverging experiences of three Chinese companies that made early investments in the United States. Lenovo took advantage of the Chinese government's "go global" policy and acquired IBM's PC business, which jump-started its ascent as a competitive global company. Its U.S. business expanded until recently, when its acquisition of Motorola's mobile phone business generated substantial losses. Subsequent downsizing has rendered Lenovo one of only a very few sizable Chinese companies in the United States to cut back its U.S. operations.[132] In comparison, Bank of China was initially slow in adapting to

[125] Kathrin Hille, "Huawei 'Not Interested in the US Any More'," *Financial Times* (April 23, 2013), at www.ft.com/content/7b212314-ac28-11e2-a063-00144feabdc0, last accessed on Dec. 20, 2016.

[126] Joseph Kovar, "Huawei and U.S. Spying: 'Snowden Revelations Level Playing Field On Both Sides'," *CRN* (May 2, 2014), at www.crn.com/print/news/channel-programs/300072702/huawei-and-u-s-spying-snowden-revelations-level-playing-field-on-both-sides.htm?itc=refresh&page=0%2C1.

[127] Eva Dou, "For Cisco, Empty China HQ Shows Localization Not Always Quick," *Wall Street Journal* (Sept. 23, 2015), at http://blogs.wsj.com/chinarealtime/2015/09/23/for-cisco-empty-china-hq-shows-localization-not-always-quick.

[128] Zhou Zhanggui, "Ren Zhengfei de Kunan Huihuang" (Bitter Glory of Ren Zhengfei), *Financial Times Chinese* (July 27, 2016), at www.ftchinese.com/story/001068631?full=y.

[129] Annual Report 2015 Huawei, at www.huawei.com/en/about-huawei/annual-report/2015.

[130] Michael Hiltzik, "Suspicions Keep Chinese Telecom Firm Huawei Out of U.S. Market," *Los Angeles Times* (Dec. 5, 2014), at www.latimes.com/business/hiltzik/la-fi-hiltzik-20141207-column.html.

[131] Linda Deng, "Huawei to Open New Office in Seattle, Go on Hiring Spree," *China Daily* (March 4, 2016), at http://usa.chinadaily.com.cn/2016–03/04/content_23740864.htm.

[132] "New Neighbors: 2016 Update."

the U.S. institutional context. As its U.S. operations multiplied, its traditional practices led to fraud and sanctions by the U.S. regulator. The external shock forced the bank to adapt in accordance with U.S. rules. Thereafter, bank branches localized their operations and have played a crucial role in facilitating Chinese investments in the United States. By contrast, Huawei's investments have confronted numerous setbacks. Labeled a national security threat, Huawei's acquisitions or sales in the U.S. market have been repeatedly stalled by the U.S. government. And its efforts to adapt to the U.S. context have failed to improve the situation. As a result, Huawei has targeted only certain markets with no potential national security risk and concentrated its U.S. investment in R & D. Despite the differences, the U.S. investments of the three Chinese companies share a few common features. First, except for the recent workforce reduction at Lenovo, all three experienced continuous growth in their U.S. businesses. Second, all three companies localized their U.S. operations, though state-owned Bank of China appears to have lagged behind the private companies in this regard. Third, all three companies adjusted their corporate behavior in accordance with U.S. institutional settings; again, it appears to have taken Bank of China longer to make the adjustments.

However, to what extent can these three represent Chinese companies in the United States in terms of how they react to the host country's institutions? The rest of this book attempts to answer this and several related questions using both qualitative and quantitative methods. I interviewed several dozen individuals with firsthand knowledge about the topic, such as current or former managers of Chinese companies in the United States and lawyers who have assisted these clients.[133] The interview subjects were selected in three ways. First, I reached out to qualified individuals in my personal network and then let the sample snowball. I conducted semi-structured formal interviews with this group of subjects, which lasted from twenty minutes to about three hours. Second, I spoke to panelists or participants at public events about Chinese investments. These informal interviews were typically short and focused on specific questions. Third, the China General Chamber of Commerce (CGCC) connected me with some its members and I followed up with a number of interviews. I used the information gleaned from all these interviews to formulate the hypotheses, substantiate findings from the empirical analysis, and contextualize the abstract data on Chinese investments in the United States. Besides interviews, I also analyzed secondary materials pertaining to Chinese FDI published or distributed by consulting firms, NGOs, and service providers, as well as government agencies. However, the primary source of empirical evidence for this book is the data derived from three comprehensive surveys of Chinese businesses in the United States. More details of the surveys follow below.

133 To keep the anonymity of the interviewees, the description of the interviews throughout this book will include only time and general identifiers such as the interviewees' position and the firms' sector.

IV THE SURVEY OF CHINESE INVESTMENTS IN THE UNITED STATES

As noted earlier, most of the existing research about Chinese ODI relies on anecdotal reports, case studies, or tests using official data of dubious quality.[134] In addition, much of the scholarship has concentrated on Chinese ODI in developing countries, as Chinese companies only recently began to invest in advanced economies. In particular, systematic studies of Chinese ODI in the United States are numbered. Topic-wise, very few scholars have examined how Chinese investors respond to host-country legal and regulatory institutions. Filling the gaps, this book investigates the interactions between Chinese companies in the United States and various U.S. legal institutions. The analysis draws on primary empirical data extracted from three annual surveys of Chinese businesses in the United States. This section describes the surveys and presents some summary descriptive data as a background for in-depth analyses in the following chapters.

A *Surveys of Chinese Companies in the United States*

The surveys were conducted in 2014, 2015, and 2016 in collaboration with the China General Chamber of Commerce (CGCC), the most prominent association of Chinese companies in the United States.[135] The questionnaires, prepared in simplified Chinese, cover a wide array of topics ranging from the investors' business performance to their compliance with several major U.S. laws and regulations. Some questions appeared repeatedly in all three surveys, others in just one or two due to shifting thematic focuses.[136] For example, the 2014 survey included a set of questions about the Chinese respondents' dispute resolution in the United States, which were left out in the other two surveys; the 2015 survey contained more questions about human resource management at the responding firms than the other two annual surveys; and the 2016 survey incorporated a section of questions about intellectual property that were not included in the prior questionnaires.[137]

In summer 2014, when CGCC first began to survey its members, it distributed the survey instrument in two ways. One, the survey was circulated to all CGCC members with valid contact information; in the end most of CGCC board members completed the questionnaires, which ensured a diverse sample of Chinese companies in the United States. Two, a senior staff member of CGCC interviewed about a dozen Chinese executives, many of whom returned completed questionnaires in a

[134] See, in general, Dylan Sutherland and John Anderson, "The Pitfalls of Using Foreign Direct Investment Data to Measure Chinese Multinational Enterprise Activity," 221 *China Quarterly* 21 (2015).

[135] The author participated in the survey project as a non-paid academic advisor, and provided comments on its administration and the analysis of the survey results.

[136] Some of the questions in 2015 were slightly modified in response to feedback from the 2014 survey respondents and comments from the 2015 survey design team.

[137] The use of three surveys and the change of some survey questions ameliorate common method biases typical of research that relies on only one survey instrument.

timely manner.[138] By the end of the summer CGCC had collected completed and partially completed questionnaires from 101 firms. In summer 2015, the CGCC staff relied solely on the survey questionnaires and collected 122 responses. The 2016 survey was distributed early in the year, and the CGCC managed to collect a total of 141 responses.

Because of high response rates among the board directors (e.g., 74.2% for the 2015 survey), the survey sample is stratified. Pursuant to its organizational policy and by-laws, CGCC elects Chinese companies representing different sectors, locations, corporate structure, and ownership type to be members of its boards. The diversity of the board composition and the members' prominence in Chinese FDI is evident upon a casual look at the list of CGCC board leaders, which includes all of the largest Chinese companies in banking (e.g., ICBC, Bank of China, and China Construction Bank), in energy and natural resources (e.g., PetroChina, Sinopec, State Grid, and Sinochem), in telecommunication (e.g., China Unicom, China Telecom, China Mobile, ZTE, and Huawei), in transportation and construction (e.g., Air China, HNA, China Construction, COSCO Shipping), in manufacturing (e.g., Haier, Sany, Broad, Fuyao Glass, BYD Motors, SAIC, Wanxiang, Angang, and Baosteel), and in real estate and insurance (e.g., Wanke, Greenland, People's Insurance, and Fosun). The list goes on (see Table 2.2 in the chapter appendix for a complete list of 2016 CGCC board directors). As illustrated below, the diversity is well reflected in the sample on multiple dimensions.

First, as shown in Figure 2.4, the respondents vary in terms of their sectoral background. According to the 2015 and 2016 survey results, the top two sectors most popular with Chinese investors are manufacturing and finance and insurance. The 2014 survey used different sectoral classifications, but the diversity is no less obvious.

In line with the general trend of Chinese ODI, most of the Chinese companies made their U.S. investments in the past decade. According to the 2016 survey, the median duration of investment in the United States is approximately eight years, and the mean is slightly more than eleven years. Moreover, the survey respondents are diverse in terms of ownership character (see Figure 2.5). In the 2014 survey, 43% of the respondents reported their Chinese investors to have less than 10% state ownership (i.e., they are either wholly privately owned investors or investors with insignificant Chinese government ownership). The 2015 survey includes about the same percentage of respondents (41%) with predominantly private Chinese investors. Reflecting the rise of private Chinese investors in Chinese ODI, the 2016 survey had 56% of the responding firms with either no state ownership or less than 10% state owernship.[139] Meanwhile, state-owned

138 A CGCC staff member other than the interviewing director compiled the survey results to avoid possible feedback bias.

139 The shift also reflects changing sample compositions.

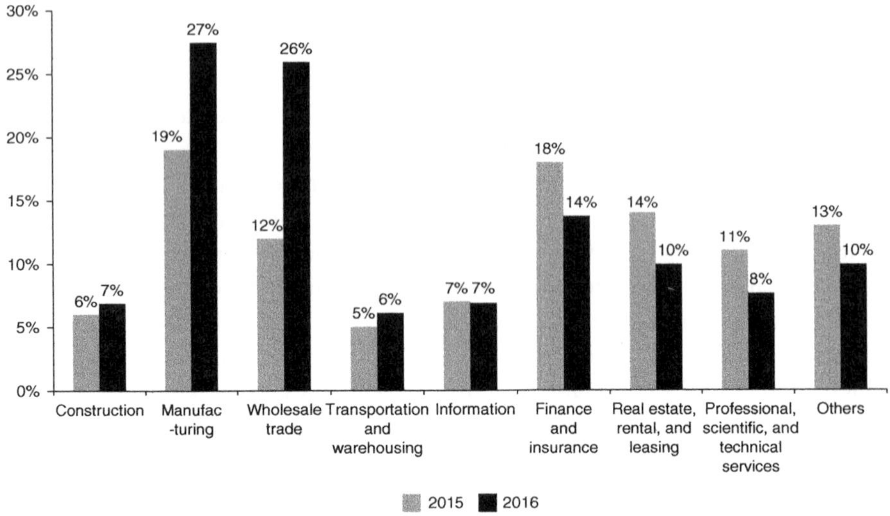

FIGURE 2.4 Sectoral distribution of survey respondents (showing top eight out of nineteen sectors from the 2016 CGCC survey)
Source: 2015 and 2016 CGCC survey; note: multiple choices, nineteen altogether, were allowed for this question (131 responded to this question in 2016; 108 responded to this question in 2015)

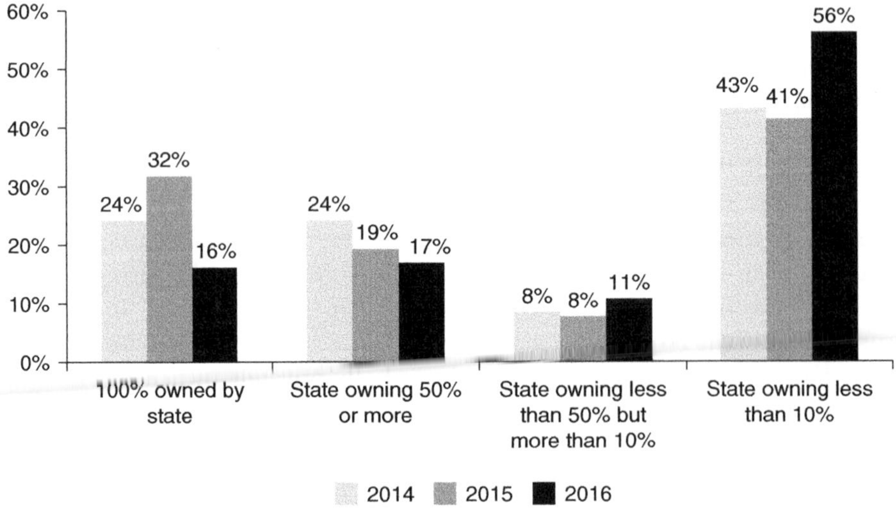

FIGURE 2.5 Ownership structure of the Chinese investors
Source: 2014 to 2016 CGCC surveys (95 counts in 2014 for this survey qustion, 104 in 2015, 130 for 2016)

Chinese investors are well represented in the three surveys. For instance, 48%, 51%, and 33% of the 2014, 2015, and 2016 survey respondents respectively reported at least majority Chinese government ownership in their investors. The distribution of ownership evidences SOEs' dominance of Chinese ODI in the United States.[140] The relatively high percentage of SOEs in the sample serves well the purposes of this study, as they have occupied the central stage of the debates about Chinese ODI and state capitalism.[141]

To what extent do the Chinese investors own their U.S. businesses? Put differently, do they own 100% of their U.S. businesses, substantial parts of them (e.g., as investors in joint ventures), or just a small share? According to the surveys, the vast majority of the Chinese investors owned at least a majority interest of their U.S. business (98% for the 2014 survey and 97% for the 2015 survey). Note that the sample does not include Chinese companies with only portfolio U.S. investments.[142]

Moreover, the survey respondents hold investments in diverse locations (see Figure 2.6). Consistent with other studies of Chinese ODI in the United States, New York and California stand out as the most popular states for the surveyed Chinese firms.[143] According to the 2015 survey, forty of the respondents invested in the former and thirty-five in the latter. Illinois, Texas, New Jersey, and Michigan, in decreasing order of popularity, also attracted fair amounts of the Chinese investment. Moreover, at least twenty-seven other states each had at least one Chinese company responding to the survey (for the number of survey respondents for each state, see Table 2.1 in the appendix).

To summarize, the analysis presented in this book is based on data extracted from three comprehensive annual surveys targeting a diverse sample of sizable Chinese investors doing business in the United States. The surveys cover a broad range of topics and open a valuable window into the Chinese FDI in the United States, especially firm-level data and Chinese investors' perceptions, considerations, and motives that are unobservable using archival data. That said, the dataset has several limitations. For instance, Chinese ODI in industrialized countries being a nascent phenomenon, the pool of sizable Chinese firms in the United States remains relatively small.[144] More will be said about the limitations of the research later.

140 Szamosszegi, "An Analysis of Chinese Investments in the U.S. Economy," at 22.

141 Note that the sample is not a random representation of all Chinese companies in the United States. Small Chinese-invested businesses such as take-out restaurants are not the target of the ongoing debates about Chinese ODI. Rather, the population of interest for this study is the prominent Chinese firms doing business in a variety of sectors in the United States. This sample approximates that population. More will be said about the limitations of the surveys at the end of Chapter 4.

142 Portfolio investment refers to the holding of interest or share of less than 10% of the invested entity. Their nonrepresentation in the sample is not an issue for the purposes of this study because *passive* holders of U.S. interests tend to be loosely regulated and they usually do not to have any substantial impacts on host-country legal institutions.

143 "New Neighbors: 2016 Update," 3.

144 China does not rank highly on the list of countries investing in the United States. See, e.g., Foreign Direct Investment in the United States 2014 Report, Organization for International Investment, at www.ofii.org/sites/default/files/FDIUS2014.pdf, 4.

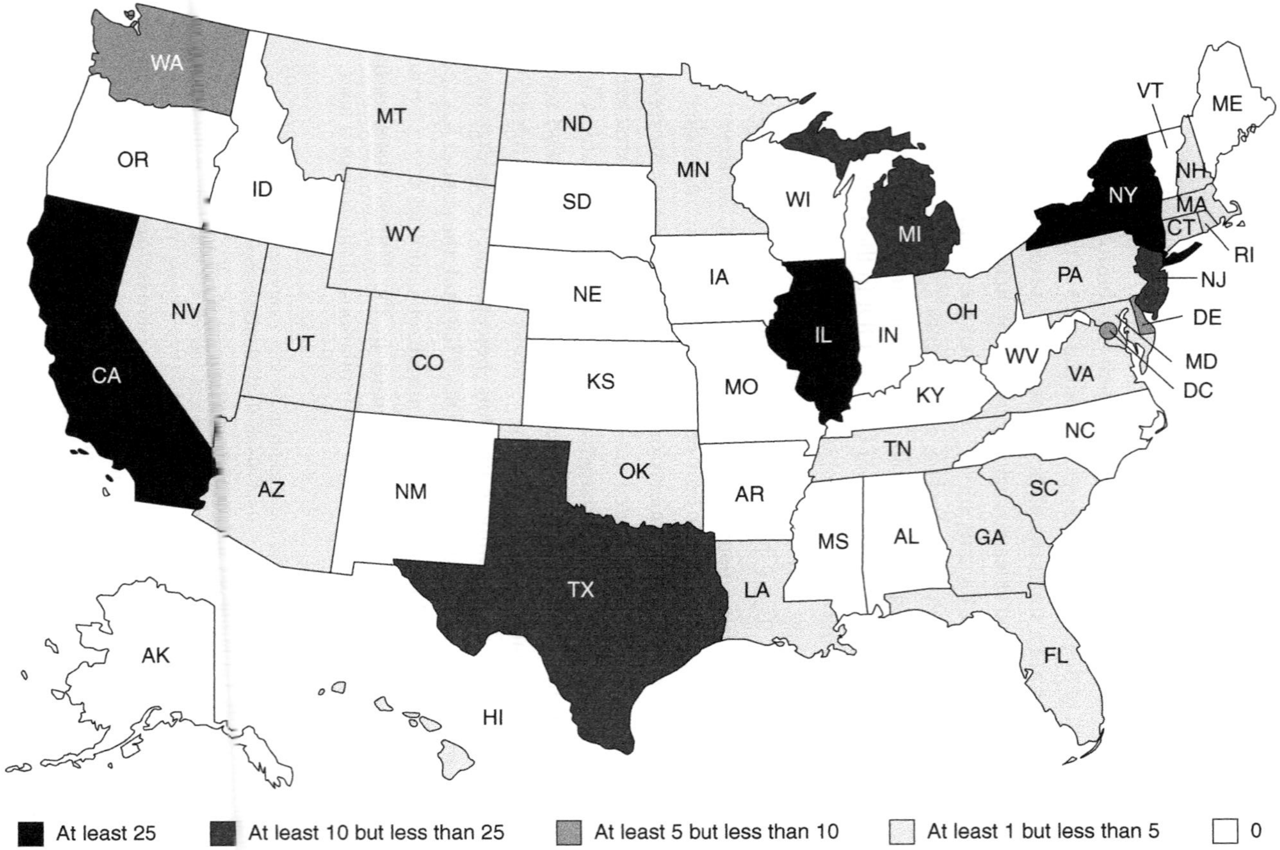

FIGURE 2.6 Investment location choice of survey respondents
Source: 2015 CGCC survey

B Descriptive Survey Data about Chinese Investments in the United States

Chinese companies only recently made substantial investments in advanced economies, so systematic studies of the phenomenon are spotty, to say the least. In particular, little is known about Chinese investments in the United States besides a few recently published policy briefs and case studies.[145] One of this book's objectives is to narrow the gap. But before proceeding to in-depth data analysis, section B here summarizes some descriptive data derived from the surveys that will shed light on several key aspects of Chinese investments in the United States (e.g., their motives and investment performance). The summary also serves as a helpful background for the following chapters.

1 Investment Motives

Firms may engage in FDI for a variety of reasons, and traditionally scholars categorized them into four groups: resource seeking, market seeking, efficiency seeking, and/or strategic asset seeking.[146] Because China's political economy bears many unique features, the motives of soaring Chinese outbound FDI have stimulated new research. Yet so far scholars have been at odds. Some portray the Chinese government as a puppeteer pulling the strings of the ODI projects.[147] Under this account, investment decisions are driven primarily by state policies, not by business concerns that neatly fit in the four categories;[148] and SOEs act as zealous agents of their government owners. Others, while acknowledging possible incentive distortion due to the distinct state–business relations in China, contend that years of reforms have by and large commercialized Chinese SOEs.[149] Moreover, the lack of effective central state control also contributes to the corporate autonomy of the SOEs' foreign subsidiaries.[150] Thus one may infer that, in spite of the delicate balancing between state policy interests and corporate commercial interests, most Chinese SOEs are mostly profit-driven most of the time.

145 See, e.g., Szamosszegi, "An Analysis of Chinese Investments in the U.S. Economy"; Steven Globerman and Daniel Shapiro, "Economic and strategic considerations surrounding Chinese FDI in the United States," 26 *Asia Pacific Journal of Management* 163 (2009).

146 John H. Dunning and Sarianna M. Lundan, *Multinational Enterprises and the Global Economy* (2008).

147 For a summary of this camp of scholars, see J. -M F. Blanchard, "Chinese MNCs as China's New Long March: A Review and Critique of the Western Literature," 16 *Journal of Chinese Political Science* 95 (2011).

148 E.g., Mark Yaolin Wang, "The Motivations behind China's Government-Initiated Industrial Investments Overseas," 75 *Pacific Affairs* 189 (2002); Szamosszegi, "An Analysis of Chinese Investments in the U.S. Economy," 29.

149 E.g., Steinfeld, *Playing Our Game*; Erica Downs, *Inside China, Inc: China Development Bank's Cross-border Energy Deals* (2011).

150 Antoine Kernen and Katy N. Lam, "Workforce Localization among Chinese State-Owned Enterprises (SOEs) in Ghana," 23 *Journal of Contemporary China* 1053 (2014).

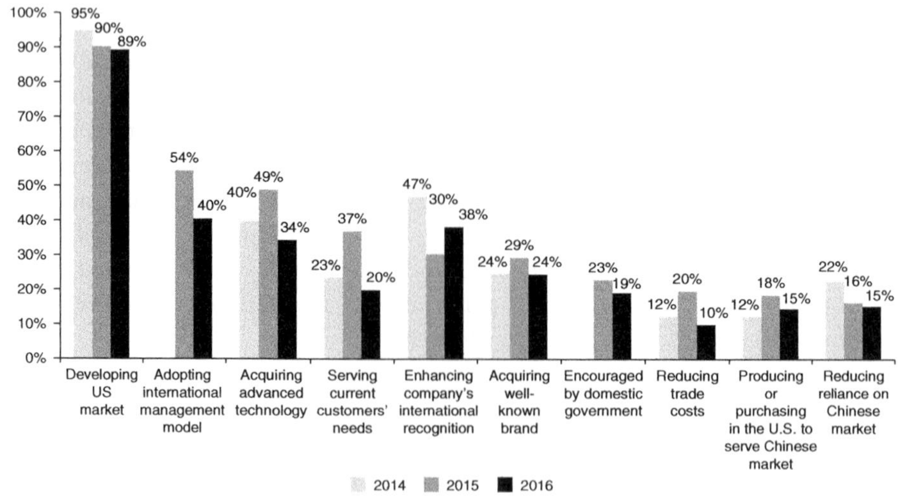

FIGURE 2.7 Top ten motives for Chinese MNEs to invest in the United States
Source: 2014–16 CGCC surveys; note: multiple choices allowed for this question (98 responded to the question in 2014; 92 in 2015; 131 in 2016)

The survey results indicate that commercial motives play a dominant role in Chinese investments in the United States. To explore the U.S. market is by far the most important driver (see Figure 2.7). A large number of Chinese companies also invest in the United States to learn "advanced" management practices. As will be discussed in the following chapter, this finding confirms the generally positive perceptions of Chinese MNE managers about U.S. institutions.[151] The survey results also indicate that Chinese investors eagerly seek advanced technologies in the United States. Moreover, for many of the respondents, investing in the United States is tied closely to their intent to climb the business food chain (e.g., enhancing brand recognition or acquiring globally recognized brands).[152] Gaining control over natural resources – the incentive that has drawn extensive international media coverage – plays a negligible role in the firms' decisions to invest in the United States. As a result, prior research about Chinese ODI in resource-rich developing countries may not be very helpful for analyzing Chinese investments in the United States.

Moreover, the survey results reveal the clustering of Chinese investors in the United States.[153] A significant minority marked "meeting the needs of current Chinese customers to expand in the United States" as an investment incentive.

[151] The 2015 CGCC survey added a few new choices for the question about investment motives.

[152] This is consistent with the findings from the studies of overall Chinese FDI. See, e.g., Agyenim Boateng, Wang Qian, and Yang Tianle, "Cross-Border M&As by Chinese Firms: An Analysis of Strategic Motives and Performance," 50 *Thunderbird International Business Review* 259 (2008).

[153] Yang notes that Chinese SOEs are unlike Japanese *keiretsu* in exhibiting the clustering effect in FDI. Yang et al., "A Comparative Analysis of the Internationalization of Chinese and Japanese Firms."

How about the "go global" policies of the Chinese government? As discussed earlier, the government has adopted a variety of measures to encourage outbound investment, and several studies highlight the influence of such state intervention.[154] The survey results indicate that the government incentives do play a role in some Chinese companies' decisions to invest in the United States.

Furthermore, some Chinese investors invest in the United States to hedge business risk and reduce their reliance on the domestic market. Given the slowdown of the Chinese economy and the risks associated with its restructuring, a growing number of Chinese investors are diversifying their businesses by investing in more stable economies. In summary, according to the survey data, Chinese companies invest in the United States primarily for commercial considerations such as developing the U.S. market, acquiring advanced technology, and enhancing brand recognition, which fall squarely into the established categories of FDI motives.

2 Investment Overview

Chinese FDI in the United States, generally motivated by commercial factors, has undergone an explosive growth. How well have the Chinese companies done in the competitive and sophisticated U.S. market? Some critics of Chinese ODI have argued that many Chinese firms suffered losses from their overseas investments since they lacked the requisite capacity to thrive in foreign markets.[155] The survey results, however, portray a mixed image. The majority of the surveyed firms have reported a revenue increase (60% reported revenue increase in 2015 and 51% in 2016). With regard to profit level, however, the data are highly variable. In the 2015 survey, about a quarter of the respondents reported their U.S. profits to match their global profit level. 38% reported U.S. profits higher than global profits, and the same percentage recorded lower U.S. profits. In 2016, more than 30% of the surveyed firms reported that their U.S. profits were on par with the global profit level. For about a quarter of the firms, the U.S. investments were more profitable than their global business. Some 41% reported U.S. profits lower than the global level. In addition, the survey data indicate that Chinese companies in the United States on average suffer a slight loss, which is not uncommon for companies that recently invested in a mature and fiercely competitive foreign market.

154 Buckley et al., "The Determinants of Chinese Outward Foreign Direct Investment"; Quer, Claver, and Rienda, "Political Risk, Cultural Distance, and Outward Foreign Direct Investment," at 1089; Alessia A. Amighini, Roberta Rabellotti, and Marco Sanfilippo, "Do Chinese State-Owned and Private Enterprises Differ in Their Internationalization Strategies?", 27 *China Economic Review* 312 (2013).

155 According to a 2015 study by UNDP of sustainable Chinese ODI, 24% of the respondents reported losses from foreign investments. See "Zhongguo Qiye Haiwai Kechixu Fazhan Baogao" (Report on Sustainable Overseas Development of Chinese Enterprises 2015), at www.undp.org/content/dam/china/docs/Publications/UNDP-CH-2015%20report%20on%20the%20sustainable%20development%20of%20chinese%20enterprises%20overseas%20CN.pdf, last accessed on Dec. 11, 2016.

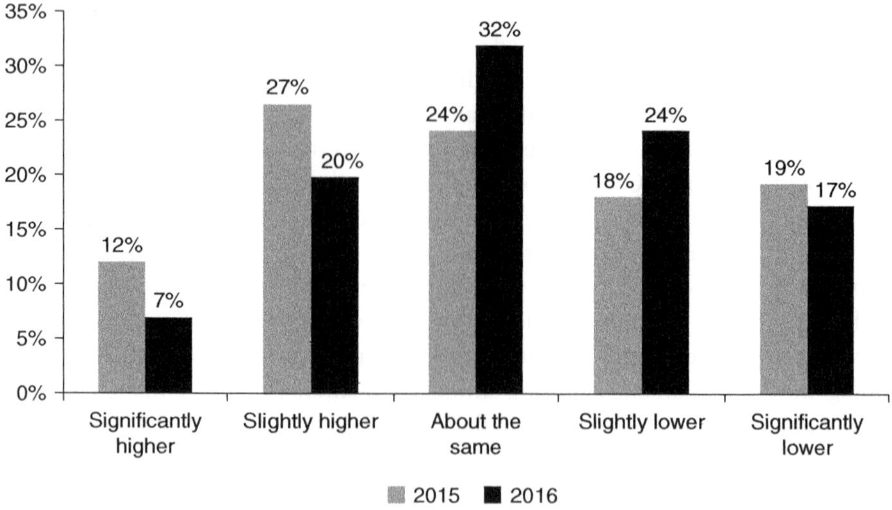

FIGURE 2.8 U.S. profits compared to global profits
Source: 2015 and 2016 CGCC survey

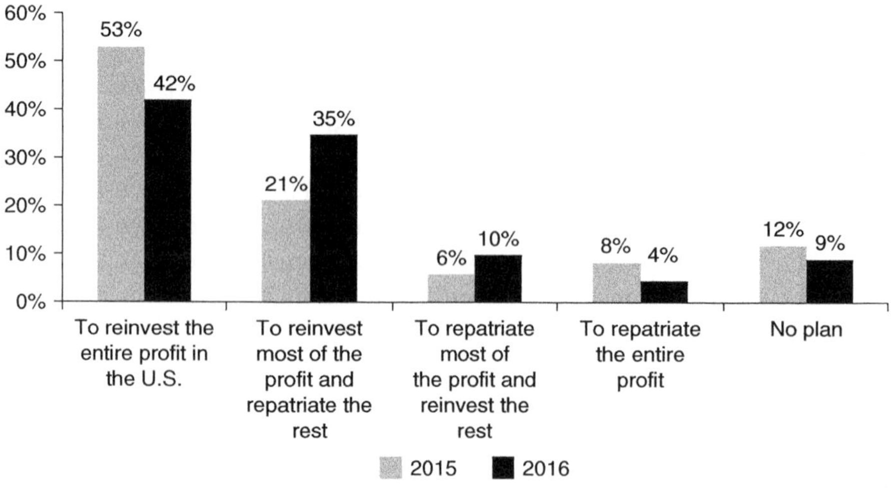

FIGURE 2.9 Plans for U.S. profits
Source: 2015 and 2016 CGCC survey

Most of the survey respondents invest in the United States for the long term. According to the survey data, the vast majority would reinvest all or most of their U.S. profits in the United States. Only less than 10% intend to repatriate all their U.S. profits back to China (see Figure 2.9). The distribution remains very stable over time, and the differences between the two surveys are marginal. As will be elaborated in the following

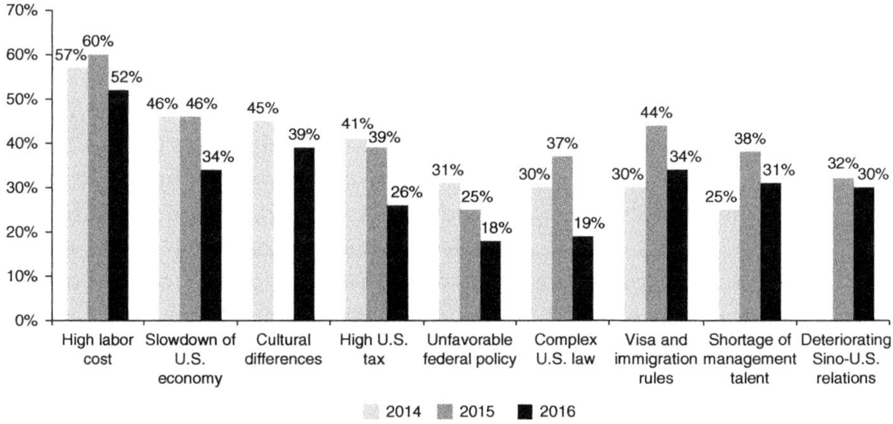

FIGURE 2.10 Major challenges and risks of doing business in the United States
Source: 2014–16 CGCC surveys (in the 2016 survey, "cultural differences" refers specifically to the difference in management culture between China and the United States; 99 responded to this question in 2014, 95 in 2015, 121 in 2016)

chapter, the long-term investment prospects, which portend repeated interactions between Chinese investors and U.S. institutions, play a crucial part in the former's legal compliance.

Chinese investments face numerous risks and challenges of doing business in the U.S. market. According to the survey data, high U.S. labor costs concern the most Chinese firms. Chinese ODI occurs at a relatively precocious stage compared to the ODI from other countries such as Korea and Japan, which experienced fast investment outflow only after domestic labor costs had reached a high level.[156] Though wages have been escalating in China, they still lag far behind the market rates in the United States. According a Chinese businessman, labor costs in China for blue-collar jobs is about one-eighth of that in the United States, and about one-half for white-collar jobs.[157]

Many of the survey respondents also expressed concern with a potential slowdown of the U.S. economy. The vast majority of the Chinese investors are committed to long-term investment in the United States and have been rapidly expanding their U.S. businesses (see Figure 2.9). Additionally, some have intended the U.S. market as a hedge against the deceleration of the Chinese economy. Hence, an abrupt slowdown of the U.S. economy would derail the investment plans. Many of the investors also consider cultural differences between the two countries to be a major challenge to doing business in the United States. Moreover, a high percentage of respondents

[156] Chris Smith and Yu Zheng, "The Management of Labour in Chinese MNCs Operating Outside of China: A Critical Review," in Mingwei Liu and Chris Smith, eds., *China at Work: A Labour Process Perspective on the Transformation of Work and Employment in China* (2016), 361, 375.

[157] Lin Lishuang, "Cao Dewang Huiying Paolu Chuanwen" (Cao Dewan Responds to Rumors about Fleeing Chinese Market), *Beijing Qingnian Bao* (Dec. 21, 2016), at http://epaper.ynet.com/html/2016-12/21/content_232571.htm?div=0, last accessed on Jan. 16, 2017.

reported deteriorating China–U.S. relations as a major business risk. The managers of these prominent Chinese firms fully recognize that FDI is intertwined with bilateral relations, as vividly illustrated by the experiences of Huawei in the United States and the sales loss of Cisco in the Chinese market after the Snowden fiasco.

Given all these challenges and risks, managers competent enough to run Chinese-invested businesses in the United States must be in short supply. Indeed, it was so perceived by many of the survey respondents. In addition, central to this book, a significant minority of the survey respondents considered complex U.S. laws to be a major challenge. Moreover, quite a few considered heavy U.S. tax to be a major concern. More detailed analysis of how Chinese firms react to the U.S. tax system will be postponed until Chapter 5.

To summarize, the survey results portray average Chinese firms in the United States as driven primarily by business motives, incurring a slight loss, confronting a wide range of challenges and risks such as high labor costs, complex U.S. law, and heavy tax. Nonetheless, the vast majority are committed to long-term investment in the United States.

V CONCLUSION

This chapter began with an overview of Chinese ODI of the past four decades. At the beginning of the "reform and opening-up" period, the Chinese government lacked foreign reserves and therefore designed its FDI policies to attract investment. Meanwhile, most of the Chinese SOEs operating in the planned economy had neither commercial incentives nor the requisite capacity to expand overseas. Thus, few Chinese firms ventured abroad. Subsequent restructuring of the Chinese economy boosted the foreign reserves, and some of the largest companies grew to be competitive conglomerates. Correspondingly, the government adjusted its policies to encourage Chinese firms to "go global," and put in place a variety of policy and institutional tools to facilitate the process. As a result, Chinese ODI surged in the past decade, and a great deal of the investments recently flew into developed markets.

The phenomenon has drawn enormous attention worldwide, and interested scholars, policymakers, and commentators hold two opposing views. On one side, many consider Chinese ODI as posing a grave threat to the existing national and international order. Chinese investors, "exporting China's domestic problems," will have detrimental effects on host countries' institutions. On the contrary, the other side views Chinese companies as commercial actors pursuing business goals no different from MNEs based in developed countries. They will play by the extant rules governing the global economy and will promptly adapt to host countries' institutional settings.

While the debate continues, the United States has emerged as the most attractive destination for Chinese investment. Though the cumulative FDI from China remains at a relatively low level,[158] it has been growing at an exponential rate. By some estimates, China will become the largest source of FDI in the United States within a decade. However, few have so far examined how Chinese companies in the United States react to stringent and sophisticated U.S. legal and regulatory institutions. Will the Chinese firms, having thrived in a poor and state-centered legal environment, export their domestic problems to the United States, or will they react to U.S. laws and regulations in ways analogous to their local counterparts?

To answer these questions, this book sets out to empirically investigate how Chinese companies in the United States react to various U.S. legal and regulatory institutions. I rely on a unique set of survey data, interviews with individuals having firsthand knowledge about Chinese ODI, and multiple sources of secondary materials. The survey data were collected in collaboration with CGCC, the most prominent business association comprising almost all sizable Chinese investors in diverse sectors. According to the survey data, Chinese firms invest in the United States primarily for commercial reasons, such as developing the U.S. market, learning management practices, acquiring advanced technology, and enhancing brand recognition. Most of the Chinese businesses in the United States are expanding. However, given substantial differences between the two countries, the Chinese firms face numerous challenges and risks, including high labor costs, complex laws, and deteriorating China–U.S. relations. The U.S. investments have not returned significant profits to most of the surveyed companies. Nonetheless, the vast majority of the Chinese companies are committed to long-term investment in the United States, which further underscores the importance of understanding how they comply with U.S. law.

Appendix

TABLE 2.1 *Investments by state*

Alabama	0	Indiana	0	Nebraska	0	South Carolina	1
Alaska	0	Iowa	0	Nevada	1	South Dakota	0
Arizona	1	Kansas	0	New Hampshire	1	Tennessee	1
Arkansas	0	Kentucky	0	New Jersey	13	Texas	15
California	35	Louisiana	2	New Mexico	0	Utah	1
Colorado	1	Maine	0	New York	40	Vermont	0

(*Continued*)

[158] China did not rank among the top eight countries in terms of cumulative FDI in the U.S. by the end of 2014. See "Foreign Direct Investment in the United States" (2016 Report), Organization for International Investment, at http://ofii.org/sites/default/files/Foreign%20Direct%20Investment%20in%20the%20United%20States%202016%20Report.pdf, 3, last checked on Dec. 20, 2016.

TABLE 2.1 *(Continued)*

Connecticut	1	Maryland	2	North Carolina	0	Virginia	2
Delaware	7	Massachusetts	2	North Dakota	1	Washington	8
Florida	4	Michigan	11	Ohio	1	West Virginia	0
Georgia	1	Minnesota	2	Oklahoma	1	Wisconsin	0
Hawaii	1	Mississippi	0	Oregon	0	Wyoming	1
Idaho	0	Missouri	1	Pennsylvania	1	Washington, D.C.	6
Illinois	27	Montana	1	Rhode Island	1		

Source: 2015 CGCC survey (survey respondents were asked to list the states in which they have made direct investments)

TABLE 2.2 *Companies of board directors of China General Chamber of Commerce—USA (2016)*

Bank of China USA
China Construction America Inc.
COSCO Shipping (North America) Inc.
Hua Hong International Americas Inc.
Sinochem American Holdings, Inc.
China Telecom Americas
SINOPEC America & SINOPEC USA Representative
Wanxiang America Corporation
Bank of Communications New York Branch
AVIC (USA), Inc.
China Center New York
China Unicom Americas
Minmetals, Inc.
HNA Group North America LLC
Waitex Group of Companies
Agricultural Bank of China New York Branch
Baosteel America Inc.
China Construction Bank New York Branch
CICC US Securities, Inc.
US Management Committee, ICBC
PetroChina International America Inc.
China Merchants Bank New York Branch
Chicago Chapter
Wanxiang America Corporation
SAIC USA Inc.
Wanda Group
CAIGA US Co., Ltd.

(Continued)

TABLE 2.2 *(Continued)*

Houston Chapter
PetroChina International America Inc.
SINOPEC America & SINOPEC USA Representative
Sinochem American Holdings, Inc.
China Communications Construction Company USA
Sany America Inc.
OOGC America LLC
ZTE USA
TPCO America Corp.
Los Angeles Chapter
AVIC (USA), Inc.
BYD Motors Inc.
China Mobile International (USA) Inc.
COMAC USA Office
East West Bank
China Interocean Transport Inc.
New York Chapter
Bank of China USA
China Construction America Inc.
COSCO Shipping (North America) Inc.
Bank of Communications New York Branch
China Center New York
Minmetals, Inc.
HNA Group North America LLC
Waitex Group of Companies
Air China New York Office
Baosteel America Inc.
China Construction Bank New York Branch
US Management Committee, ICBC
Agricultural Bank of China New York Branch
CICC US Securities, Inc.
SCG America Group Inc.
China Merchants Bank New York Branch
Fosun International Ltd. c/o Summit Glory LLC
Vanke (USA) Holding
Angang America Inc.
BWI Group
Cathay General Bancorp
China Eastern Airlines New York Representative Office
CITIC Group New York Office
COFCO (USA) Inc.
Haier America Inc.
The People's Insurance Company of China

(Continued)

TABLE 2.2 *(Continued)*

New York Representative Office
SNPTC USA Office
State Grid US Representative Office
China Unionpay (USA) LLC
China Southern Airlines Company Limited New York Office
Greenland USA
International Vitamin Corporation
Broad U.S.A. Inc.
China Re New York Liaison Office
Hongdou New York Inc.
Kang Long Group, Inc.
Tianyuan Overseas (CNMI) Engineering LLC
Crystal Window & Door Systems, Ltd.
FUYAO Glass Group Industries Co., Ltd.
XIN Development Group International, Inc.
Eccom Network (USA) Inc.
China Taiping Starr Holding Company
Representative Office in the USA, China Council for the Promotion of International Trade
CRRC Corporation Limited
San Francisco Chapter
Hua Hong International (Americas) Inc.
Genertec America Inc.
Washington, D.C. Chapter
China Telecom Americas
China Unicom Americas
Huawei Technologies USA

Note: more updated information about the board of directors of China General Chamber of Commerce—USA may be obtained at its website, www.cgccusa.org.

3

Chinese Investments and U.S. Legal and Regulatory Institutions

significant are the perceived, and sometimes real, political backlash and regulatory risks associated with [Chinese] investments in the United States. The struggle to operate within the [U.S.] legal, regulatory, and political systems is a mutual concern for China and the United States.[1]

David M. Marchick, managing director, Carlyle Group

Do Chinese companies really "*struggle* to operate within the U.S. legal and regulatory institutions"? This chapter attempts to find an answer. To briefly recapitulate, the preceding chapter reviewed the evolution of Chinese government policies regarding foreign direct investment (FDI), the proliferation of China-sourced outbound direct investment (ODI), and the recent surge of Chinese investments in the United States. Should the investments continue to grow at the current or even a slightly lower rate, China would soon surpass other countries to be the largest source of FDI in the United States. While Chinese ODI has gripped enormous media attention, few have systemically examined how Chinese companies in the United States react to the U.S. institutional context. Will they readily conform to U.S. legal and regulatory institutions, or defy any U.S. rules contrary to their core interests, or, worse yet, export China's domestic problems, as they have allegedly been doing in some other host countries (e.g., evade tax, violate labor rights, and impair national security)? What will ensue from the burgeoning Chinese FDI in the United States – the Americanization of the Chinese investors or a tectonic clash of capitalisms?

If conflicts are inevitable, what will be their impacts on U.S. institutions? Will Chinese investment spur major changes to U.S. laws and regulations in areas

[1] David M. Marchick, "Fostering Greater Chinese Investment in the United States," Council on Foreign Relations Policy Innovation Memorandum No. 13 (Feb. 2012), at www.cfr.org/china/fostering-greater-chinese-investment-united-states/p27310.

pertinent to it, as heralded by *Ralls* v. *CFIUS*, a recent lawsuit filed by a Chinese-invested company against the U.S. government that has a significant long-term impact on the regulatory regime (details of the case can be found in Chapter 7)? As discussed in the preceding chapter, the existing scholarship on Chinese ODI, having focused primarily on developing countries where robust institutions are lacking, does not quite aid our understanding of Chinese investments in the United States.

This chapter begins to answer these questions; it proceeds in three steps. First, taking an eclectic approach, I formulate a general analytical framework for investigating how foreign investors react to host-country institutions. Second, applying the analytical frame, I examine how Chinese companies react to U.S. legal and regulatory institutions. As will be elaborated, Chinese investors in the United States, though confronting wide institutional gaps, are generally adaptive to the host country's institutional context. Third, I conclude this chapter and raise the question to be explored in the following chapter – the effect, if any, of state ownership of Chinese investors.

I ANALYTICAL FRAMEWORK FOR FOREIGN INVESTORS' ADAPTATION

The reign of multinational enterprises (MNEs) over the global economy has spawned a vast literature.[2] Yet despite the enduring academic attention, few scholars have systematically studied how MNEs react to the legal and regulatory institutions of their host countries. Drawing on insights from scholarship in international business, FDI, and legal compliance, I present a new analytical framework that will guide the research of Chinese investors' reactions to U.S. legal and regulatory institutions and their potential impacts. The framework comprises three components (see Figure 3.1): (1) the legal and regulatory distance between foreign investors' home state and host state, (2) the investors' desire to adapt to host-country institutions, and (3) the investors' ability to adapt. More details follow.

A *Relevant Legal and Regulatory Distances*

The concept of "institutional distance" is not new. Scholars in international business and management have long investigated the link between institutional distance, broadly defined to include political, cultural, social and regulatory distances, and

[2] See, e.g., John H. Dunning, "The Eclectic (OLI) Paradigm of International Production: Past, Present and Future," 8 *International Journal of the Economics of Business* 173 (2001); Peter J. Buckley and Pervez N. Ghauri, *The Internationalization of the Firm: A Reader* (1999); Jay B. Barney, "Firm Resources and Sustained Competitive Advantage," 17 *Advances in Strategic Management* 203 (2000); A. Edward Safarian, "Internalization and the MNE: A Note on the Spread of Ideas," 34 *Journal of International Business Studies* 116 (2003); Jean-François Hennart, "Theories of the Multinational Enterprise," *Oxford Handbook of International Business* 127 (2001).

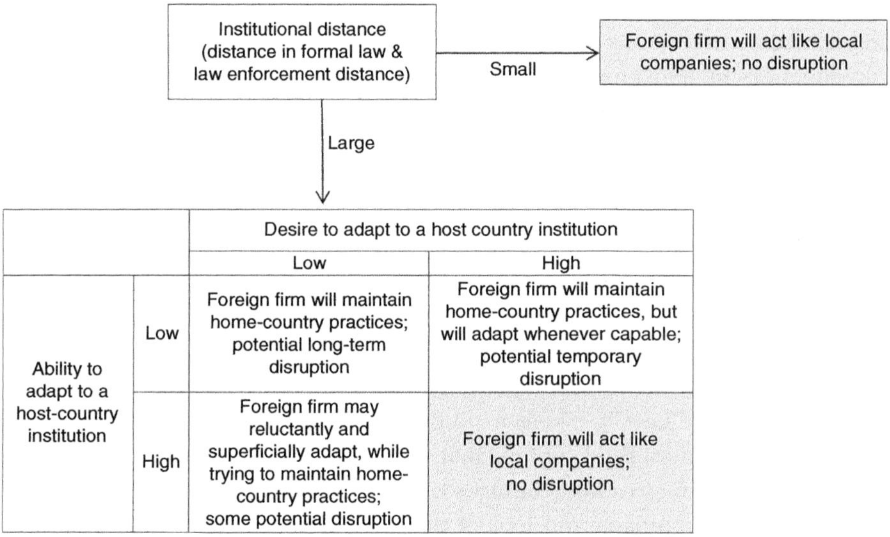

FIGURE 3.1 Analytical framework

foreign firms' isomorphic behavior.[3] When the institutional distance between two countries is large, foreign firms lacking legitimacy or familiarity with host-country institutions typically suffer acute "liability of foreignness."[4] To overcome the liability, so it is argued, foreign investors tend to imitate domestic firms.[5] Insightful as it is, the literature has largely adopted a comparative approach at the national level, i.e., comparing broad normative, cognitive, and regulatory systems of different countries.[6] However, to analyze how foreign investors react to host-country laws and regulations, high-level analysis is inadequate as it neglects both intra-state variations and inter-state homogeneity of laws and regulations in certain subject matter areas.[7]

[3] Salomon and Wu, "Institutional Distance and Local Isomorphism Strategy"; Lorraine Eden and Stewart R. Miller, "Distance Matters: Liability of Foreignness, Institutional Distance and Ownership Strategy," 16 *Advances in International Management* 187 (2004).

[4] Salomon and Wu, "Institutional Distance and Local Isomorphism Strategy," 343.

[5] Ibid.

[6] See, e.g., Tatiana Kostova and Srilata Zaheer, "Organizational Legitimacy Under Conditions of Complexity: The Case of the Multinational Enterprise," 24 *Academy of Management Review* 64 (1999); Agnès Bénassy-Quéré, Maylis Coupet, and Thierry Mayer, "Institutional Determinants of Foreign Direct Investment," 30 *World Economy* 764 (2007); Stav Fainshmidt, George O. White, and Carole Cangioni, "Legal Distance, Cognitive Distance, and Conflict Resolution in International Business Intellectual Property Disputes," 20 *Journal of International Management* 188 (2014); Belay Seyoum, "Formal Institutions and Foreign Direct Investment," 51 *Thunderbird International Business Review* 165 (2009).

[7] Recent scholarship has questioned the explanatory power of institutional distance in international business research. Anne-Wil Harzing and Markus Pudelko, "Do We Need to Distance Ourselves from the Distance Concept? Why Home and Host Country Context Might Matter More than (Cultural) Distance," 56 *Management International Review* 1 (2016); Srilata Zaheer, Margaret Spring Schomaker, and Lilach Nachum, "Distance without Direction: Restoring Credibility to a Much-Loved

Let me elaborate on the inadequacy. First, within the same national context, legal and regulatory institutions can differ significantly in terms of enforceability and the consequences of noncompliance. It is one thing to violate parking rules, quite another to be caught cheating on tax. Yet the concept of institutional distance, or regulatory distance more specifically, has been broadly defined to encompass "rules and laws that exist to ensure the stability and order of a society."[8] When applied, often in research about multinational institutional distances, the broad concept rarely accounts for intra-state variations. Second, transnational learning and institutional transplants can generate comparable regulatory systems in otherwise vastly different countries. For instance, Chinese legislation that enables and facilitates a "socialist market economy" has borrowed heavily from advanced market economies and international conventions (e.g., the Chinese Contract Law[9] and the Chinese Company Law[10]). There is no denying that the broadly defined institutional distance matters. But I contend that, for purposes of analyzing the reactions of foreign-invested firms to a host country's laws and regulations, one will have to take a more nuanced approach and look at the institutional differences between two countries in the same subject matter area, e.g., the differences between U.S. tax law and Chinese tax law, or the differences between U.S. employment law and its equivalent in China.[11] Therefore, the term "institutional distance" for this book refers more narrowly to the differences between the institutions of a foreign investor's home state and host state in the same legal and regulatory area. Though this book concentrates on Chinese companies in the United States, the analytical framework

Construct," 43 *Journal of International Business Studies* 18 (2012); Rosalie L. Tung and Alain Verbeke, "Beyond Hofstede and GLOBE: Improving the Quality of Cross-cultural Research," 41 *Journal of International Business Studies* 1259 (2010) This author agrees with the critiques that more attention should be paid to foreign investors' home- and host-state contexts.

8 Dean Xu, Yigang Pan, and Paul W. Beamish, "The Effect of Regulative and Normative Distances on MNE Ownership and Expatriate Strategies," 44 *Management International Review* 285 (2004), 288.

9 Jing Leng and Wei Shen, "The Evolution of Contract Law in China: Convergence in Law but Divergence in Enforcement?", in Yun-chien Chang, Wei Shen, and Wen-yeu Wang, eds., *Private Law in China and Taiwan: Legal and Economic Analyses* (2017) 63, 67.

10 See, e.g., Wang, "The Political Logic of Corporate Governance."

11 Only a few recent studies have explored sector-specific institutional distances. Stewart R. Miller and Arvind Parkhe, "Is There a Liability of Foreignness in Global Banking? An Empirical Test of Banks' X-efficiency," 23 *Strategic Management Journal* 55 (2002); Bennet A. Zelner, Witold J. Henisz, and Guy LF Holburn, "Contentious Implementation and Retrenchment in Neoliberal Policy Reform: The Global Electric Power Industry, 1989–2001," 54 *Administrative Science Quarterly* 379 (2009); Salomon and Wu, "Institutional Distance and Local Isomorphism Strategy," 343. However, these quantitative studies have neglected variations in regulatory enforcement likely due to the lack of available data and good measurement. Also overlooked by the existing theory is the extent of exposure to nuanced institutional distances. Foreign investors may insulate themselves in bubble communities populated by home-country expatriates or immigrants in host countries. A case in point would be Chinese investors in the United States that do most of their businesses in Chinatowns and primarily serve Chinese-speaking customers. These investors, with only partial exposure to U.S. institutions and institutional differences between the two countries, tend to exhibit compliance behavior typical of home-state firms. This will not be discussed extensively as the sample for the instant study comprises sizable China-based MNEs that do not target Chinese communities in the United States.

applies generally to research about how foreign investors, regardless of their states of origin, react to host-country laws and regulations.

Throughout the book, I use the terms "institutional distance," "institutional gap," and "legal and regulatory distance" interchangeably.[12] Because the terms are rather abstract, I further divide them into *"distance in formal law"* and *"law enforcement distance."* As noted above, cross-national convergence of formal laws may result from legal transplants and globalization of knowledge. Take antimonopoly laws as an example. As one of the early national antimonopoly laws, the Sherman Act was passed by the U.S. Congress more than a century ago.[13] It was subsequently adopted in various revised forms by lawmakers in Europe and Japan.[14] In 2007, the Chinese legislature enacted the Chinese Antimonopoly Law that embodied the key concepts and principles of the U.S. law and those of the other advanced economies. Such legal transplants narrow the gaps in a variety of formal laws across different countries, especially those laws crucial to running a market economy in the global context.

While formal laws in multiple areas may be converging, their enforcement often exhibits significant cross-country variations. Again, consider antimonopoly laws as an example. The effect of the global legal transplant on market competition hinges on the structural institutions of the host states.[15] Though the formal Chinese Antimonopoly Law incorporated the key concepts and principles of the corresponding U.S. and E.U. laws, government agencies in China enforce the law in ways vastly different from the other two jurisdictions.[16] Enforcement is crucial in shaping compliance behavior.[17] Most developed countries feature governments capable of basic law enforcement, which raises the cost of noncompliance. In contrast, many developing countries lack the capacity to enforce rules in a fair and effective manner, and laws are often made to be ignored when they do not further the interest of powerful stakeholders.[18] Thus, even

[12] The model should apply equally to less formal institutions such as social norms and codes of business conduct.

[13] Some U.S. states passed antimonopoly laws well before the Sherman Act was enacted. George J. Stigler, "The Origin of the Sherman Act," 14 *Journal of Legal Studies* 1 (1985), 5.

[14] In the case of Japan, the antimonopoly law was imposed by the U.S. government after World War II. Alex Y. Seita and Jiro Tamura, "The Historical Background of Japan's Antimonopoly Law," *University of Illinois Law Review* 115 (1994).

[15] Tay-Cheng Ma, "Legal Transplant, Legal Origin, and Antitrust Effectiveness," 9 *Journal of Competition Law and Economics* 65 (2013).

[16] Angela Huyue Zhang, "Bureaucratic Politics and China's Anti-monopoly Law," 47 *Cornell International Law Journal* 671 (2014).

[17] According to the mainstream literature on the economics of legal compliance, rational actors will comply with a law if doing so produces net benefit, the calculation of which takes into account the probability of being caught violating a law multiplied by the subsequent penalties. Gary S. Becker, "Crime and Punishment: An Economic Approach," in Nigel G. Fielding, Alan Clarke, and Robert Witt, eds., *The Economic Dimensions of Crime* 13 (1968).

[18] Ji Li, "When Are There More Laws? When Do They Matter? Using Game Theory to Compare Laws, Power Distribution, and Legal Environments in the United States and China," 16 *Pacific Rim Law and Policy Journal* 335 (2007).

in areas with narrow formal-law gaps, companies from developing countries often have to cross a large law enforcement distance when operating in developed countries.

The distance in law enforcement also exhibits intra-state variations. Given limited judicial and administrative resources, a government inevitably enforces some laws and regulations more rigorously than others. Even for the same law, enforcement and noncompliance costs may vary temporally. For instance, the U.S. government stepped up its enforcement of the Foreign Corrupt Practices Act (FCPA) in the last decade, which raised the legal risk of operating in countries with a corrupt business culture.[19] Another type of intra-state variation stems from the power distribution of enforcement agencies and companies. Non-state actors that command abundant resources can often bend the rules in their favor, especially in countries with relatively weak institutions.[20] In sum, for purposes of researching foreign investors' reactions to host-country legal institutions, the concept of "institutional distance" (or "regulatory distance"[21]) as currently defined and used in the international business and management literature is inadequate. I refine the concept to incorporate formal-law distance and distance in law enforcement at the subnational level.

B Desire to Adapt to Host-Country Institutions

What happens if a foreign investor confronts a large legal and regulatory distance in a certain subject matter area in a host country? The existing literature on the isomorphism of foreign firms assumes that, whenever large institutional distances are identified, the foreign investors possess both the intent and the capacity to "imitate the practices of domestic firms."[22] By neglecting firm-level variations in these two aspects, however, the scholarship cannot explicate why foreign firms from the same home country might react differently to a host country's legal institutions. I contend that to fully understand the reactions of foreign investors, the analytical framework has to incorporate a structured firm-level analysis of the investors' desire and ability to conform. In other words, once a significant institutional gap is found between a foreign investor's home state and host state in a particular subject matter area, how the investor reacts to the legal institution of the host state turns on its desire and ability to make the requisite behavioral adjustments (see Figure 3.1). Of these

[19] Issac A. Binkovitz, "Recent Changes in US and UK Overseas Anti-Corruption Enforcement Under the FCPA and the UK Bribery Law: Private Equity Compliance," 3 *Michigan Journal of Private Equity and Venture Capital Law* 75 (2013), 76.

[20] Li, "When Are There More Laws?", 335.

[21] Ajai S. Gaur and Jane W. Lu, "Ownership Strategies and Survival of Foreign Subsidiaries: Impacts of Institutional Distance and Experience," 33 *Journal of Management* 84 (2007), 87.

[22] Salomon and Wu, "Institutional Distance and Local Isomorphism Strategy," 343; Eden and Miller, "Distance Matters," 187; Xu, Pan, and Beamish, "The Effect of Regulative and Normative Distances," 285.

TABLE 3.1 *Relationship between investment motives and foreign investors' desire to adapt*

	Commercial	Home-state policy
Long-term commitment	Strong desire to adapt and act like local companies	Medium desire to adapt
Short-term commitment	Medium desire to adapt	Weak desire to adapt and act like local companies

two factors, I first explore the desire to adapt in two dimensions: (i) investment motives, and (ii) the managers' perceptions of the host-state institution.[23]

1 Investment Motives

Motives are essential in setting behavior; and investment motives are crucial to the desire of foreign investors to conform to host-country institutions. First, to study foreign investment from countries featuring state capitalism, researchers and policymakers invariably ask whether political concerns or commercial interests drive the foreign investors. Companies obeying their home state's fiat to "go global" do not necessarily behave rationally in the business sense (i.e., with maximizing corporate profits as the sole objective);[24] that presumably influences their desire to adapt to the host-country contexts.[25] For one thing, policy-driven investors may be less sensitive to noncompliance costs, since commercial interests form only a part of their calculation.[26] In contrast, foreign investors motivated by commercial considerations should respond to host countries' law enforcement mechanisms in ways analogous to their local peers, especially in countries featuring free-market capitalism. Second, one should inquire whether the foreign investors make a long-term or a short-term commitment to their host-country business. Everything else being equal, long-term commitments naturally induce a stronger desire to conform to the host country's institutions.

Table 3.1 demonstrates how the investment motives relate to the desire of a foreign investor to adapt and conform to its host country's legal institutions. To be concrete, other variables in the analytical framework held constant, foreign investors driven by long-term commercial considerations typically have a stronger desire to adapt and mimic local firms; in contrast, those motivated by short-term policy or political

23 Note that these are not exhaustive of all factors that may affect the desire of foreign investors to adapt and conform to host-country institutions. As will be elaborated at the end of this book, future research should expand the study of other explanatory variables.

24 Luo, Xue, and Han, "How Emerging Market Governments Promote Outward FDI," 71.

25 Ji Li, "I Came, I Saw, I . . . Adapted."

26 In the same vein, they should be less sensitive to compliance cost as well. But in a country with adequate law enforcement capacity like the United States, it is reasonable to assume that noncompliance cost is generally higher than compliance cost.

considerations will be less inclined to conform to host-country institutions; various mixtures of the two factors are associated with different levels of inclination to make behavior adjustments in response to host-country institutions. Because the renaissance of state capitalism has blurred the boundary between commercial and political incentives for FDI from countries such as China,[27] the two may often be interlinked in practice, especially for state-owned investors.

It merits emphasizing that, in applying the analytical model, adaptation does not necessarily imply compliance with formal host-country laws. For instance, research has shown that the commercialization of some Chinese state-owned MNEs might have caused the deterioration of their treatment of local workers in certain developing countries.[28] In those cases, short-term commercial incentives for the Chinese managers induced them to adopt substandard labor practices of the host countries. By contrast, adaptation implies compliance when similarly positioned domestic companies in the host country generally obey the laws and regulations. Because this book focuses on Chinese investments in the United States, I equate adaptation to compliance.

2 Perceptions of Host State Institutions

Since Tom Tyler's seminal work, a rich literature has documented the importance of individuals' perceptions of laws and institutions in their compliance behavior.[29] A person obeys a law not only for fear of noncompliance penalties, but also for the perception that the law, its enforcement, and the authority behind it are fair and legitimate.[30] The logic should apply to the adaptation of foreign investors to host-country legal and regulatory institutions. Everything else being equal, foreign investors holding positive views of their host-country institutions should be more inclined to conform. Though some studies have examined foreigners' subjective assessment of host-country institutions, none have connected the variable with legal and regulatory compliance.[31] In addition, the factor merits scrutiny because foreign investors, in contrast to domestic actors, typically hold a comparative perspective. An institution viewed in a positive light by

27 Xiaoming He, Lorraine Eden, and Michael A. Hitt, "The Renaissance of State-Owned Multinationals," 58 *Thunderbird International Business Review* 117 (2016); Cuervo-Cazurra et al., "Governments as Owners."

28 Dan Haglund, "In It for the Long Term? Governance and Learning among Chinese Investors in Zambia's Copper Sector," 199 *China Quarterly* 627 (2009), 645–6.

29 Tom R. Tyler, *Why People Obey the Law* (2006); Jonathan Jackson, Ben Bradford, Mike Hough, Andy Myhill, Paul Quinton, and Tom R. Tyler, "Why do People Comply with the Law? Legitimacy and the Influence of Legal Institutions," 52 *British Journal of Criminology* 1051 (2012).

30 Kristina Murphy, Tom R. Tyler, and Amy Curtis, "Nurturing Regulatory Compliance: Is Procedural Justice Effective When People Question the Legitimacy of the Law?", 3 *Regulation and Governance* 1 (2009).

31 Jean-Paul Roy and Christine Oliver, "International Joint Venture Partner Selection: The Role of the Host-Country Legal Environment," 40 *Journal of International Business Studies* 779 (2009).

domestic subjects may disappoint investors from a foreign country that has established a more efficient institution or an institution better tailored to the home-state value system.

To summarize, foreign firms' investment motives and the managers' perceptions of host-country institutions are essential to their desire to conform. Everything else being equal, a foreign investor motivated by long-term commercial interests and holding positive views of host-country institutions should be more inclined to conform. In contrast, foreign investors driven by short-term state policy concerns and critical of host-state institutions tend to preserve home-state features.

C *Ability to Adapt to Host-Country Institutions*

Besides the desire to adapt, how foreign companies react to host-country institutions also hinges on their ability to make the necessary behavioral adjustments. Although many factors may affect that ability, I focus on the following two: (i) the allocation of corporate decision-making power, and (ii) access to and use of local knowledge.[32]

1 The Allocation of Decision-Making Power

The topic of management localization in FDI has been extensively explored,[33] and some have demonstrated the link between institutional distances and the dependence of MNEs on local partners and personnel.[34] Hence, I add this dimension to the analytical framework and contend that how decision-making power is allocated between local managers and home-country headquarters plays an important part in the company's ability to adapt. Everything else being equal, localized decision-making should generally facilitate adaptation.[35] Fully embedded in the host-country environment, local managers possess not only better information, but more incentives to conform to the legal and regulatory institutions. In contrast, managers at the headquarters obtain filtered, if not distorted, information about the host-country circumstances. Nor do they bear all direct consequences of the local business's reaction to host-state rules. For instance, U.S. courts can usually assert personal jurisdiction over managers of MNEs stationed in the United States, not so much over managers located in foreign countries. In addition, adding more individuals to a decision-making process not only slows it down but also raises the transaction cost. Thus, everything else being

[32] The amount of material resources a foreign investor commands is essential for the capacity to adapt, but I assume the effect of varying resources is intermediated by and better analyzed via the use of local professional services.

[33] Mezias, "Identifying Liabilities of Foreignness," 232.

[34] Xu, Pan, and Beamish, "The Effect of Regulative and Normative Distances," 285, 298.

[35] Mezias, "Identifying Liabilities of Foreignness," 229, 232.

equal, allocating decision-making power away from local managers tends to impede adaptation to host-state institutions.

2 Reliance on Local Knowledge

To cross wide institutional gaps, knowledge and skills necessary for coping with host-country institutions are critical. The issue is particularly acute for foreign investors operating in countries with sophisticated legal and regulatory systems. Consider, for example, Chinese investors that have to comply with U.S. tax law. Those that do not rely on local professionals will face mounting challenges in navigating the complex system. Even if local managers are granted decision-making power, they will have to consult in-house or external professionals in dealing with specific legal and compliance matters in a country like the United States. However, despite its theoretical and practical importance, few scholars have explored this topic. The existing literature on FDI and service providers focuses primarily on how service companies globalize or engage in foreign investment;[36] to the best of my knowledge, the literature is silent about how developing-country investors rely on host-country service providers to comply with local laws and regulations.

In summary, it is crucial to consider foreign investors' capacity when exploring their adaptation to host-state legal institutions. Everything else being equal, investors that allocate decision-making authority to local managers and rely on local professionals adapt more effectively; by comparison, foreign investors that make such decisions in the home state and refuse local professional services will likely fail to adapt to host-state institutions.

Before proceeding to the next section, it merits emphasizing that the variables of the analytical framework are not necessarily independent or mutually exclusive. Institutional distances, for example, should affect how foreign investors perceive host-country institutions as well as the cost of adaptation. Nor are the factors exhaustive for understanding how foreign investors react to host-country legal and regulatory institutions; personal characteristics of foreign business managers, for instance, may well play some role in explaining companies' coping

[36] Arnold K. Weinstein, "Foreign Investments by Service Firms; The Case of Multinational Advertising Agencies," 8 *Journal of International Business Studies* 83 (1977); M. Krishna Erramilli, "The Experience Factor in Foreign Market Entry Behavior of Service Firms," 22 *Journal of International Business Studies* 479 (1991); Jiatao Li and Stephen Guisinger, "The Globalization of Service Multinationals in the 'triad' Regions: Japan, Western Europe and North America," 23 *Journal of International Business Studies* 675 (1992); Lilach Nachum, "Economic Geography and the Location of TNCs: Financial and Professional Service FDI to the USA," 31 *Journal of International Business Studies* 367 (2000); Glenn Morgan and Sigrid Quack, "Institutional Legacies and Firm Dynamics: The Growth and Internationalization of UK and German Law Firms," 26 *Organization Studies* 1765 (2005); Michael A. Hitt, Leonard Bierman, Klaus Uhlenbruck, and Katsuhiko Shimizu, "The Importance of Resources in the Internationalization of Professional Service Firms: The Good, the Bad, and the Ugly," 49 *Academy of Management Journal* 1137 (2006).

behavior.[37] Obviously, much remains unknown about Chinese firms' adaptation to legal institutions of the developed world, and this framework is more a serious attempt to organize the analysis of this important topic and to stimulate conversation about it than a comprehensive formula that will answer all possible questions. In short, the analytical framework, drawing on insights from diverse fields and combining institutional with firm-level analysis, enables an organized examination of foreign investors' reactions to host-country legal and regulatory institutions, which has to date eluded most scholars.

To apply the analytical frame, one starts with a comparative institutional analysis in the area of interest (e.g., tax law or employment law) to gauge the institutional distance between foreign investors' home state and host state. If the institutional distance is insignificant, both formally and in terms of enforcement, the foreign investors will act like their local counterparts in coping with the local legal institution at issue. Hence, in that area the foreign investors do not have to alter their compliance behavior and their growing presence will not have major impacts on the host state's institutions. If, however, the institutional distance is large, how the investors react to the host state's institutions turns on their desire and ability to make the necessary behavioral adjustments. To be concrete, foreign investors that pursue long-term commercial objectives, perceive host-country institutions positively, delegate decisions to local managers, and rely on local professionals will mimic their counterparts in the host state. Contrarily, foreign firms will be slow to adapt if they are motivated by home-state policies and short-term investment, disrespect host-state institutions, and distrust local managers and professionals. They will clash with and may even unsettle the existing host-state institutions. In the following section, I will apply this analytical framework to assess preliminarily how Chinese companies in the United States generally react to U.S. legal and regulatory institutions.

II HOW CHINESE BUSINESSES REACT TO U.S. INSTITUTIONS

The eclectic analytical framework presented above applies broadly to understanding the adaptation (or lack of it) of foreign investors to the host country's legal and regulatory institutions. Its application is not limited by the investors' home or host states. For instance, the heuristic device may guide the examination of how Japanese investors in China react to Chinese tax law, as well as how Indian investors in the UK comply with UK employment law.[38] Applying the framework,

[37] See, e.g., Wen-Tsung Hsu, Hsiang-Lan Chen, and Chia-Yi Cheng, "Internationalization and Firm Performance of SMEs: The Moderating Effects of CEO Attributes," 48 *Journal of World Business* 1 (2013).

[38] Scholars of international business and management have combined institutional analysis with firm-level analysis to explore cross-border investments and the operations of multinational enterprises. See, e.g., Christine Oliver, "Sustainable Competitive Advantage: Combining Institutional and

the rest of this book analyzes the reactions of Chinese firms in the United States to U.S. legal and regulatory institutions. This section begins with an institutional comparison that underscores the typically large legal and regulatory distance between China and the United States. As noted earlier, in researching foreign investors' adaptation to a particular legal or regulatory institution, one should take into account intra-state variations in legal institutions. That I will do in Chapters 5, 6, and 7, which present in-depth analysis of the way Chinese firms cope with U.S. tax law, U.S. employment law, and the U.S. regime on national security review of foreign investments.

Leading into those area-specific analyses, this chapter presents a broad-stroke sketch of Chinese companies' reactions to general U.S. institutions. Apart from the institutional comparison to follow, I undertake firm-level analysis by empirically exploring the desire and the ability of Chinese companies to adapt to U.S. institutions in general. Using survey data, I demonstrate that the vast majority of Chinese investments in the United States were motivated by long-term commercial interests, and most of the Chinese managers think highly of structural U.S. institutions. Meanwhile, Chinese companies have to a large extent localized the management of their U.S. investments and relied extensively on local knowledge in dealing with U.S. legal and regulatory institutions. In short, Chinese companies in the United States typically face large institutional distances, yet they are generally adaptive to the host country's institutional environment.[39]

A General Institutional Distances between China and the United States

I first examine the general institutional distances between China and the United States. Everything else being equal, noncompliance by foreign investors will more likely occur in case of a wide institutional gap. To underscore the large institutional distances for those unfamiliar with the Chinese political economy, the following paragraphs chronicle how various business actors in China have evolved and interacted with domestic legal and regulatory institutions over the past four decades. As will be shown, both the formal-law distances and the law enforcement distances between China and the United States are significant in general; at the same time, the

Resource-Based Views," *Strategic Management Journal* 697 (1997); Klaus E. Meyer, Saul Estrin, Sumon Kumar Bhaumik, and Mike W. Peng, "Institutions, Resources, and Entry Strategies in Emerging Economies," 30 *Strategic Management Journal* 61 (2009); Dean Xu and Oded Shenkar, "Note: Institutional Distance and the Multinational Enterprise," 27 *Academy of Management Review* 608 (2002); Keith D. Brouthers, Lance Eliot Brouthers, and Steve Werner, "Resource-Based Advantages in an International Context," 34 *Journal of Management* 189 (2008). However, no one has articulated a framework for analyzing how foreign investors react to a host country's legal and regulatory institutions in different subject matter areas.

39 It is worth emphasizing again that the sample is a largely unbiased representation of the interested population for the purposes of this book, i.e., prominent Chinese firms from diverse sectors investing in the United States.

distances also vary across different subject matter areas. Readers who are familiar with the topic should skip these paragraphs.

As described in Chapter 2, the past four decades have witnessed China's transformation from an isolated state with a stagnant planned economy to the world's second-largest economy featuring a relatively open and dynamic market, in which firms of various ownership characteristics participate. During the great transformation, business organizations coevolved with the legal and regulatory institutions governing them. At the dawn of the reform, the Chinese government owned and micro-managed nearly all business enterprises in China,[40] which suffered inefficiency and massive losses. To improve their performance, the government devised and experimented with a variety of new incentive measures. Yet most of them failed.[41] Meanwhile, enterprises of alternative ownership types emerged. Without the organizational weaknesses of state-owned enterprises (SOEs) and under less control of the state, these business enterprises were much more competitive.[42] Their fast ascendance eroded public faith in the SOEs, undermined political support for the state sector, and enabled the reformers among the political elite to make the case for radical restructuring.[43]

In the mid-1990s, the reformers began to massively privatize the SOEs,[44] as part of the campaign to establish a "socialist market economy" with Chinese characteristics.[45] The central government adopted the policy of "grabbing the big and letting go [of] the small," under which the state privatized small and medium-sized SOEs, but continued to own large SOEs in strategic and important sectors.[46] The state sector contracted in the period immediately following the restructuring.[47] Meanwhile, a dynamic market gradually took shape.

Concurrent to building a less restricted market, the central government set out to "modernize" the SOEs that remained under its control.[48] Evidencing the

40 Sujian Guo, "The Ownership Reform in China: What Direction and How Far?", 36 *Journal of Contemporary China* 553 (2003).

41 Ibid.

42 Barry Naughton, "Chinese Institutional Innovation and Privatization from Below," 84 *American Economic Review* 266 (1994).

43 Hongbin Cai and Daniel Treisman, "Did Government Decentralization Cause China's Economic Miracle?", 58 *World Politics* 505 (2006).

44 Ross Garnaut, Ligang Song, and Yang Yao, "Impact and Significance of State-Owned Enterprise Restructuring in China," 55 *China Journal* 35 (2006).

45 Gary Sigley, "Chinese Governmentalities: Government, Governance and the Socialist Market Economy," 35 *Economy and Society* 487 (2006).

46 Yongnian Zheng and Minjia Chen, "China's State-Owned Enterprise Reform and Its Discontents," 56 *Problems of Post-communism* 36 (2009).

47 "Between 1995 and 2001, the number of State-owned and State-controlled enterprises in China fell from 118,000 to 47,000 and total employment in the SOE sector fell by 36 million." Garnaut, Song, and Yao, "Impact and Significance of State-Owned Enterprise Restructuring in China," 52.

48 Chi-Wen Jevons Lee, "Financial Restructuring of State Owned Enterprises in China: The Case of Shanghai Sunve Pharmaceutical Corporation," 26 *Accounting, Organizations and Society* 673 (2001).

reformers' embrace of global capitalism, most of the corporatized SOEs adopted a quasi-holding-company structure,[49] which, while maintaining ultimate state control, allowed minority ownership by non-governmental actors.[50] As part of the reform, the state listed many of the largest Chinese SOEs on stock exchanges in China, Hong Kong, and even the United States,[51] so that they would be subject to rigorous regulations of the securities markets. As a result of the "institutional outsourcing,"[52] the corporate governance and organization of most central-level SOEs bore formal resemblance to public firms in advanced market economies.

The state also altered the control mechanism through which it manages the SOEs. First, new agencies such as the State-Owned Assets Supervision and Administration Commission (SASAC) were set up to supervise some of the largest SOEs in China. Against the background of corporatizing the SOEs, the institutional reform aimed at separating "ownership from control" and "business from politics."[53] Aware of the importance of managerial discretion and the balance of power between the SASAC and the SOEs it oversees, the central government did not task the agency with micro-managing individual SOEs.[54] The SASAC reviews only the most important corporate proposals, participates in the evaluation of senior corporate officers, and makes long-term strategic business plans along with the SOEs.[55] It also takes part in making rules and regulations for managing the SOEs.[56] Below the central level, provincial governments also control some sizable Chinese SOEs, which tend to cluster in heavy industries such as automobile manufacturing, mining, power generation, and steelmaking.[57] Moreover, a fraction of large Chinese SOEs are

49 Scott Waldron, Colin Brown, and John Longworth, "State Sector Reform and Agriculture in China," *China Quarterly* 186 (2006), 290.

50 Jonathan G. S. Koppell, "Political Control for China's State-Owned Enterprises: Lessons from America's Experience with Hybrid Organizations," 20 *Governance* 266 (2007).

51 Laixiang Sun and Damian Tobin, "International Listing as a Mechanism of Commitment to More Credible Corporate Governance Practices: The Case of the Bank of China (Hong Kong)," 13 *Corporate Governance: An International Review* 81 (2005), 82.

52 Steinfeld, *Playing Our Game*, 265. 53 Koppell, "Political Control," 265. 54 Ibid., 265–6.

55 Law of the People's Republic of China on the State-Owned Assets of Enterprises, Oct. 28, 2008, ch. 6, at www.lawinfochina.com/display.aspx?lib=law&id=7195&CGid=.

56 While the SOEs under the nominal management of the SASAC are clearly among the largest in China, there are many sizable centrally controlled SOEs that, for historical reasons, remain outside SASAC's jurisdiction. Currently about 6,000 such SOEs exist and are controlled by approximately eighty central-government agencies. Unirule Institute of Economics, "The Nature, Performance, and Reform of the State-Owned Enterprises" (April 12, 2011), 34, at www.unirule.org.cn/xiazai/2011/20110412.pdf, accessed Feb. 25, 2014. For these SOEs, the Ministry of Finance exercises "ownership rights" on behalf of the central government. Moreover, state agencies traditionally in charge of propaganda still hold control over assets such as most television stations, mass media publishers, and movie producers.

57 The government of Beijing, for instance, supervises SOEs in areas such as real estate, utilities, public transportation, steel making, pharmaceuticals, construction, insurance, and commercial retailing. See official webpage of the SASAC of Beijing Municipal Government, 2014, at www.bjgzw.gov.cn/QtCommonAction.do?method=xxcx&type=0000006010&flag_qt=6, accessed Feb. 25.

subject to dual leadership of central government agencies and regional governments.[58]

The government, having withdrawn from micro-managing most SOEs, continues to exercise its control through a sophisticated *nomenklatura* system.[59] In other words, the corporatization reform, as a result of which large SOEs adopted a "modern" corporate governance structure, did not substantially alter the political status of the SOE managers who remain in the *nomenklatura*. And it is not uncommon for ranking SOE officers to actually assume government positions.[60] Given the size and diversity of the multilayered Chinese bureaucracy, the central government limited its direct personnel control to officials of the vice ministerial or vice provincial level and above.[61] Promotion of managers to this level is managed by the Central Organization Department (COD) of the CCP, but ultimately decided by the Politburo;[62] in the process, however, the opinions of the SASAC are given significant weight.[63] For SOEs not supervised by the SASAC, the appropriate regulatory agencies will opine on a candidate's fitness for promotion.[64] As an integral part of the political apparatus, SOEs are also subject to oversight by the Central Discipline Inspection Committee (CDIC) and its regional and departmental units.[65] But the CDIC tends to concentrate its firepower on serious violations of CCP rules, such as corruption and embezzlement of state assets.

Besides control through the agencies and senior personnel management, the government implements industrial policies and subsidizes selected firms with favorable loans and discounted land use.[66] Although the SOE reform was no doubt transformational,[67] the contraction of the state sector was nonlinear. Subsequent to the global financial crisis, the Chinese government rolled out an enormous stimulus package that significantly

58 For instance, there are thirty-eight SOEs in Beijing that have their corporate CCP organizations administered by Beijing SASAC and the rest controlled by twenty-four national agencies and SOE parents, including the Railway Ministry, the State Post Bureau, the State Bureau of Tobacco Administration, the Ministry of Public Security, and the Ministry of National Security. These Beijing SOEs employ 430,000 employees and 120,000 are CCP members. There are 6,700 basic Party organizations in these SOEs. See the official website of the SASAC, 2014, at www.sasac.gov.cn/n1180/n1583/n10363/n7225820/n8998361/12089895.html, accessed Feb. 25.

59 Liou, "Rent-Seeking at Home," 225.

60 Nan Lin, "Capitalism in China: A Centrally Managed Capitalism (CMC) and Its Future," 7 *Management and Organization Review* 63 (2011), 73.

61 Pierre F. Landry, *Decentralized Authoritarianism in China: The Communist Party's Control of Local Elites in the Post-Mao Era* (2008), 41–51.

62 Chen Li, "Holding 'China Inc.' Together: The CCP and the Rise of China's Yangqi," 228 *China Quarterly* 927 (2016), 937.

63 Ruilong Yang, Yuan Wang, and Huihua Nie, "Zhunguanyuan Jinsheng Jizhi: Laizi Zhongguo Yangqi de Zhengju" (Promotion Mechanism for Quasi-officials: Evidence from Chinese Centrally-Controlled Enterprises), Munich Personal RePEc Archive (MPRA) paper, April 1, 2012, at http://mpra.ub.uni-muenchen.de/50317/1/MPRA_paper_50317.pdf.

64 Katharina Pistor, *The Governance of China's Finance*, in Joseph P. H. Fan and Randall Morck, eds., *Capitalizing China* (2013), 35–62.

65 Li, "Holding 'China Inc.' Together," 939.

66 Li, "State-Owned Enterprises in the Current Regime."

67 Steinfeld, *Playing Our Game*, 265, 51.

empowered the SOEs.[68] Since then the central government has been sending contradicting signals about the future of Chinese SOEs. While some top officials insisted on letting the market play a "decisive role,"[69] others encouraged the SOEs to grow "larger and stronger."[70] Moreover, the CCP has recently strengthened its grip over SOEs, signaling a reversal of the policy to "separate management from politics."[71]

Though SOEs still dominate many parts of the Chinese economy, non-state-owned enterprises have become the driver of growth. Township and village enterprises (TVEs) first emerged in the legal vacuum for the protection of private property ownership.[72] Compared to SOEs, the TVEs had simpler management structures and were able to take advantage of the distortions in the Chinese planned economy.[73] Meanwhile, private businesses also sprouted from the cracks in the regime.[74] Lacking state support and institutional legitimacy, privately owned enterprises initially lagged behind TVEs in profitability.[75] But the central government's market reform improved the macro environment for non-state-owned businesses, and most TVEs, having lost their comparative advantages, privatized.[76] Meanwhile, massive privatization and partial privatization of SOEs in the past two decades further enlarged the private sector. The reforms have reversed the composition of the Chinese economy – the private sector now accounts for a higher percentage of China's GDP and offers more jobs than do SOEs.

To summarize, years of incremental reform gave rise to a unique type of state capitalism featuring, on the one hand, a government that dominates strategic and important industries through control over SOEs and many other industries through variable equity ownership or myriad policy tools,[77] and, on the other, a dynamic and

68 By the end of 2011 there were totally 144,715 Chinese SOEs. See Weibing Qiao, *China's State-Owned Assets Supervision and Administration Yearbook* (2012).

69 Cary Huang, "Party's Third Plenum Pledges 'Decisive Role' for Markets in China's Economy," *South China Morning Post* (Nov. 12, 2013), at www.scmp.com/news/china/article/1354411/chinas-leadership-approves-key-reform-package-close-third-plenum, last accessed Jan. 2, 2017.

70 Xiaoyi Shao and Matthew Miller, "China Aims to Make State-owned Firms 'Stronger, Better, Larger'," *Reuters* (Sept. 13, 2015), at www.reuters.com/article/china-soe-reform-idUSB9N11D01920150914, last accessed Dec. 12, 2016.

71 Emily Feng, "Xi Jinping Reminds China's State Companies of Who's the Boss," *New York Times* (Oct. 13, 2016), at www.nytimes.com/2016/10/14/world/asia/china-soe-state-owned-enterprises.html, last accessed Dec. 22, 2016.

72 Victor Nee, "Organizational Dynamics of Market Transition: Hybrid Forms, Property Rights, and Mixed Economy in China," *Administrative Science Quarterly* 1 (1992).

73 Naughton, "Chinese Institutional Innovation and Privatization," 266, 267; Enrico C. Perotti, Laixiang Sun, and Liang Zou, "State-Owned versus Township and Village Enterprises in China," in Josef C. Brada, Paul Wachtel, and Dennis Yang, eds., *China's Economic Development* (2014), 33.

74 "Productivity Effects of TVE Privatization: The Case Study of Garment and Metal-Casting Enterprises in the Greater Yangtze River Region," Governance, Regulation, and Privatization in the Asia-Pacific Region, NBER East Asia Seminar on Economics, 2004, Volume 12, 231–50.

75 Ibid.

76 Hongbin Li and Scott Rozelle, "Privatizing Rural China: Insider Privatization, Innovative Contracts and the Performance of Township Enterprises," 176 *China Quarterly* 981 (2003).

77 Barry Naughton and Kellee S. Tsai, *State Capitalism, Institutional Adaptation, and the Chinese Miracle* (2015).

relatively open market. To facilitate the market and regulate increasingly complex state–business relations, the government established a comprehensive network of laws and regulations. Though some laws have incorporated special provisions to accommodate the interests of SOEs, most treat Chinese firms of different ownership types alike. In refashioning the legal infrastructure, the government borrowed heavily from existing laws and legal principles of advanced market economies,[78] which has tapered formal institutional gaps between China and the United States, especially in areas where the laws enable or regulate the market (e.g., contract law and company law).

Yet law enforcement distances between the two countries remain large. To understand how laws are implemented and complied with in China requires some basic knowledge about the courts and regulatory agencies. In the past decades, along with the economic transformation, a series of judicial reforms has taken place. From bare existence during the Cultural Revolution, the Chinese judiciary has vastly expanded its size and workload. The number of judges increased from 60,439 in 1981 to 195,000 in 2011,[79] and the number of first-instance cases surged from 906,051 in 1981 to 11,444,950 in 2015.[80] Meanwhile, the quality of Chinese courts has improved. It was historically a common practice to staff the courts with veterans.[81] The Chinese Law on Judges, as amended in 2001, requires all judgeship candidates to have at least a college degree and to pass the competitive national judicial examination. As a result, the percentage of Chinese judges with university degree leapt from 9.6% in 1995 to 51.6% in 2004.[82] However, the remarkable progress has not altered the judiciary's subordination to the CCP,[83] and the power distribution of the stakeholders in a lawsuit, rather than relevant statutory language, often determines how laws apply in China.[84]

Compared to the judiciary, government agencies often play a much more important enforcement role in China.[85] The authority of an agency depends on the

78 Gao Hongjun, "The Globalization of American Law: Typical Examples and Jurisprudential Reflections," 1 *China Legal Science* 3 (2011).

79 Jingwen Zhu, *Report on China Law Development* (2007), 33; He Fan, "Faguan Duoshao Cai Gouyong" (How Many Judges Are Needed), *Renmin Fayuan Bao* 6 (June 7, 2013).

80 Cheng Guowei, "2015 Nian Quanguo Fayuan Shenpan Zhixing Qingkuang" (2015 Report on Adjudication and Enforcement by Chinese Courts), *Renmin Fayuan Bao* (March 18, 2016), at www.court.gov.cn/zixun-xiangqing-18362.html, last accessed Aug. 15, 2016.

81 Benjamin L. Liebman, "China's Courts: Restricted Reform," 191 *China Quarterly* 620 (2007).

82 Zhu, *Report on China Law Development*, 34.

83 Carl Minzner, "China's Turn against Law," 59 *American Journal of Comparative Law* 50 (2011); Stanley B. Lubman, *Bird in a Cage: Legal Reform in China after Mao* (1999); Liebman, "China's Courts," 620.

84 Ji Li, "The Power Logic of Justice in China," 65 *American Journal of Comparative Law* 95 (2017).

85 Gongmeng Chen, Michael Firth, Daniel N. Gao, and Oliver M. Rui, "Ownership Structure, Corporate Governance, and Fraud: Evidence from China," 12 *Journal of Corporate Finance* 424 (2006), 425–6; Nicholas Howson, "Protecting the State from Itself? Regulatory Interventions in Corporate Governance and the Financing of China's 'State Capitalism'," in Liebman and Milhaupt, *Regulating the Visible Hand?*.

resources at its disposal, its ranking position in the political hierarchy, and the stature of its leaders. Similar to the judiciary, Chinese government agencies, especially those at the central level, have improved the quality of their staff over time. In addition, to rationalize administration the state has been promoting "governance in accordance with law."[86] Through a series of legislation, the state has established a comprehensive regime of administration laws, which subject a wide array of agency actions to judicial scrutiny.[87] However, suing the government continues to be an uphill battle in China as the courts usually side with officials.[88]

Little wonder compliance in China should differ from that in the United States. The power hierarchy of Chinese business organizations has significant impacts on their compliance behavior and on how laws and regulations are enforced. Large Chinese SOEs at the pinnacle of the hierarchy can directly influence legislation to safeguard their core interests.[89] Thus, compliance normally does not alter the status quo for the large SOEs.[90] If conflicts with enforcement agencies ever occur, their resolution, which tends to be through informal channels,[91] turns on the power distribution among the stakeholders. Given their political status, large SOEs, especially those centrally controlled, often have the regulators or the courts, if they ever get involved, on their side.[92] Thus, noncompliance costs tend to be lower for SOEs than for private companies in China. At the same time, however, SOEs suffer the triple-agency problem.[93] The interests of the ultimate shareholders (i.e., the people) are nominal and dispersed. Their ownership control is typically delegated through multiple layers to several state agencies; therefore, SOE managers usually share less or none of the benefits from taking the risk of noncompliance despite its relatively low cost.[94] Consequently, the reactions of SOEs to Chinese laws and regulations tend to be more complex and sensitive to contextual factors such as the state's policy priorities.[95]

86 Kevin J. O'Brien and Lianjiang Li, "Suing the Local State: Administrative Litigation in Rural China," 51 *China Journal* 75 (2004).

87 Ji Li, "Suing the Leviathan: An Empirical Analysis of the Changing Rate of Administrative Litigation in China," 10 *Journal of Empirical Legal Studies* 815 (2013); Minxin Pei, "Citizens v. Mandarins: Administrative Litigation in China," *China Quarterly* 832 (1997).

88 O'Brien and Li, "Suing the Local State," 75; Li, "Suing the Leviathan," 815; Xin He and Yang Su, "Do the 'Haves' Come Out Ahead in Shanghai Courts?", 10 *Journal of Empirical Legal Studies* 120 (2013).

89 Ji Li, "The Leviathan's Rule by Law," 12 *Journal of Empirical Legal Studies* 815 (2015).

90 Ibid.

91 Ruoying Chen, "Legal Informality and Human Capital Development in China," in Liebman and Milhaupt, *Regulating the Visible Hand?*.

92 He and Su, "Do the 'Haves' Come Out Ahead in Shanghai Courts?", 120; Margaret M. Pearson, "The Business of Governing Business in China: Institutions and Norms of the Emerging Regulatory State," 57 *World Politics* 296 (2005); Zheng Lei, Benjamin L. Liebman, and Curtis J. Milhaupt, "SOEs and State Governance: How State-Owned Enterprises Influence China's Legal System," in Liebman and Milhaupt, *Regulating the Visible Hand?*, 203.

93 Cuervo-Cazurra et al., "Governments as Owners," 919.

94 Ibid.

95 Alex L. Wang, "Chinese State Capitalism and the Environment," in Liebman and Milhaupt, *Regulating the Visible Hand?*, 251.

By comparison, owners of large private companies keep a delicate relationship with the state, even for those who managed to gain access to formal political power.[96] On the one hand, large companies with nationwide business, even those with good connections, are incentivized to take law and compliance more seriously. Despite the authoritarian nature of the state, power is fragmented.[97] Very few officials are capable of wielding influence in all provinces, over all regulatory agencies, and across all branches of the state. Even if a private firm succeeded in cultivating close ties with such officials, the valuable *guanxi* capital will be reserved "for matters of life and death,"[98] such as criminal prosecution, instead of resolving legal and compliance problems arising from business transactions. In other words, as successful Chinese private firms expand their businesses beyond the original locale, the cost and risk of building reliable political ties multiplies, so they invest in law and compliance as a supplemental measure of risk control. In addition, many of the companies have listed shares on capital markets in China and abroad, which generally raises the cost of manifest disregard of law.[99] On the other hand, however, for private companies to survive and prosper in China, it is still crucial to "remain close to the government."[100] They will face insurmountable challenges in navigating the maze of Chinese rules without good personal relations with regulatory agents, which normally lower noncompliance costs. Moreover, without the triple-agency problem ubiquitous among Chinese SOEs, large private firms are more likely to engage in opportunistic compliance to further the owners' interests.

The vast majority of business entities in China are small and medium-sized private enterprises (SMEs). So far they have not been the focus of the debates about Chinese ODI, simply because most of them lack the capacity to invest overseas.[101] Without formal political status, SMEs in China sit at the bottom of the power hierarchy. The agency problem confronting SOEs and, to a lesser extent, sizable private companies, is insignificant in SMEs. A dollar saved from compliance is a dollar earned for the owner. And Chinese legislation, rarely incorporating the

96 Hongbin Li, Lingsheng Meng, and Junsen Zhang, "Why Do Entrepreneurs Enter Politics? Evidence from China," 44 *Economic Inquiry* 559 (2006).

97 See, e.g., Kenneth Lieberthal and Michel Oksenberg, *Policy Making in China: Leaders, Structures, and Processes* (1988); Andrew Mertha, "'Fragmented Authoritarianism 2.0': Political Pluralization in the Chinese Policy Process," 200 *China Quarterly* 995 (2009); Andrew C. Mertha, "China's 'Soft' Centralization: Shifting Tiao/Kuai Authority Relations," 184 *China Quarterly* 791 (2005).

98 Interview with an anonymous businesswoman whose extended family runs a billion-dollar business in China (Sept. 5, 2015).

99 In this book, "private companies" refers to non-SOEs and includes companies, listed on stock markets, that may be partially owned by state institutions. Note that in the United States listed companies are normally called public companies.

100 Matthew Miller, "Wang Jianlin, China's Property Tycoon, Finds Golden Path to Billions," *Reuters* (Dec. 23, 2014), at www.reuters.com/article/wanda-properties-wang-idUSL3N0U23XF20141222.

101 I discuss them because, with luck and business acumen, a tiny proportion of the SMEs grow into large private companies with global businesses. Those that experienced the fastest growth, however, have not fully shed the habits and features characterizing Chinese SMEs, which will affect their compliance behavior in the United States.

interests of the SMEs, often imposes on them exorbitant compliance costs. More importantly, Chinese laws tend to lag behind the fast-transforming economy and society. As an entrepreneur once commented, "in China what is good for development is often illegal."[102] Indeed, to a certain extent, the Chinese development miracle exemplifies an incremental institutional creative destruction. SMEs pushed the institutional boundaries with unsolicited and often post hoc support from the reformers among the political elite; gradually more market-friendly institutions took shape.[103] Had the Chinese regulators and courts enforced the laws strictly in the 1970s and 1980s, much of the bottom-up economic reforms would not have happened in the first place. However, the flip side of the institutional creative destruction is disrespect for formal rules, and a highly unpredictable legal environment for Chinese SMEs. Therefore, on legal and regulatory compliance, Chinese SMEs act in a highly opportunistic and pragmatic manner.[104] They muddle through the shifting mess of Chinese laws and regulations.

To summarize, compliance in China varies in accordance with the ownership character and size of a Chinese company. An integral part of the formal power structure, large SOEs can influence lawmaking so that the formal rules codify the status quo for the SOEs; hence subsequent compliance usually does not impair their core interests. Moreover, given SOEs' "bureaucratic ties and administrative rank," regulators and courts in China take their interests into consideration.[105] However, while SOEs' political status lowers their noncompliance costs, the managers have less personal incentive to violate a law for the sake of the employers, not to say the nominal owners. Thus, SOEs' reactions to Chinese laws and regulations tend to be sensitive to context. Possessing less political power, large private firms with extensive businesses in China avoid high-stakes government interventions by investing in law and compliance. But at the same time, with less of an agency problem, private companies are more sensitive to compliance costs. Hence, they tend to be more speculative and comply at the level where the expected risk reduction equals the cost. Private SMEs in China generally have poor compliance records as they typically lack compliance capacity and disrespect formal laws, which often conflict with their interests.

Comparatively speaking, formal laws in the United States are an integral part of the business fabric. Courts in the United States, especially those at the federal level, are more independent and powerful than Chinese courts. U.S. laws undergo constant change, but at a more predictable pace. For better or worse, business interests,

[102] Comments from a Chinese entrepreneur participating in the 2008 Chicago Conference on China's Economic Transformation (July 10, 2008).

[103] Naughton, "Chinese Institutional Innovation and Privatization," 266.

[104] For instance, most Chinese SMEs underpay their taxes. Ji Li, "Dare You Sue the Tax Collector? An Empirical Study of Tax-Related Administrative Lawsuits in China," 23 *Pacific Rim Law and Policy Journal* (2014). SMEs also have a poor compliance record for Chinese employment and labor law.

[105] Liou, "Rent-Seeking at Home," 220, 226.

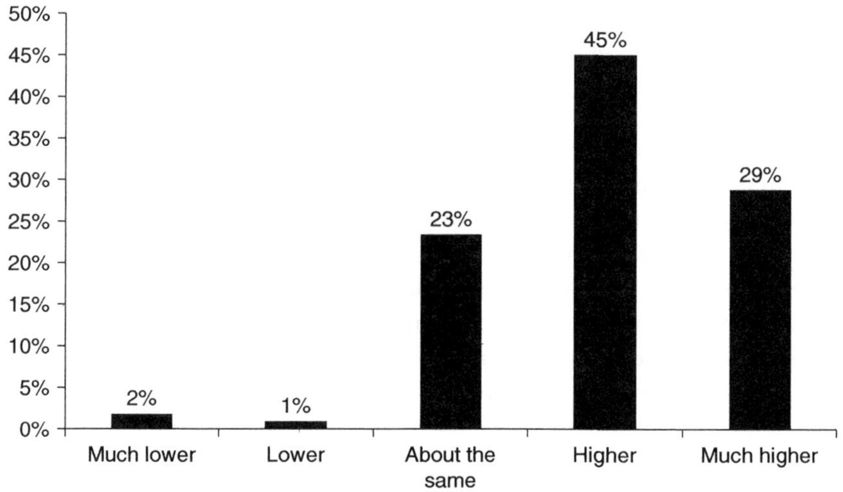

FIGURE 3.2 Legal and compliance costs (U.S. versus China)
Source: 2016 CGCC survey (total 111 responses for this question)

even those of SMEs, shape legislation in the United States. In general, laws and regulations are enforced more strictly in the United States than in China.

Thus, compliance costs in the United States should in general exceed the cost at home for Chinese companies. The CGCC survey in 2016 asked the Chinese managers to share their opinions on this issue. The results show that, consistent with the anecdotal evidence, about 74% of the Chinese managers considered that U.S. legal and compliance costs surpassed costs in China; only about 3% thought the costs to be lower in the United States (see Figure 3.2).

In summary, significant general institutional distances exist between China and the United States. Quite a few formal laws governing business actors have been converging in the two countries, but the gaps in actual compliance and law enforcement are enormous. How do Chinese companies cope with the institutional distances? Following the analytical framework, I now shift the focus to the desire and ability of the investors to adapt to host-country legal institutions.

But before proceeding, I want to point out once again that this section sketches the general legal and regulatory distances between China and the United States. As noted earlier, regarding Chinese firms' reactions to specific U.S. legal institutions (e.g., tax, employment, etc.), one still needs to examine the institutional distance between the two countries in that legal area in order to account for cross-area variations. For example, violating Title VII generally results in a fine on the employer and remedies for disgruntled employees,[106] whereas tax evasion may

[106] Rebecca Hanner White, "Vicarious and Personal Liability for Employment Discrimination," 30 *Georgia Law Review* 509 (1995), 516.

lead to criminal prosecution. Varying noncompliance costs should affect foreign investors' compliance behavior. Moreover, the institutional distances between China and the United States may vary for firms of different ownership types. Though SOEs and private companies possess different political resources in China, U.S. laws and agencies normally treat them equally as long as the SOEs engage in commercial activities. Yet some rules do differentiate SOEs from businesses of other ownership types. For instance, the current U.S. regime of national security review of foreign acquisitions singles out foreign state-owned investors for heightened scrutiny. Because of the discriminatory treatment, Chinese SOEs react in ways different from private Chinese firms. Such institutional variations should be considered when studying compliance of Chinese businesses in the United States. I will address them in Chapters 4 to 7.

B Desire to Adapt to U.S. Institutions

Chinese companies generally face wide institutional gaps when investing in the United States; to traverse the distances takes both the desire and the ability to make the necessary and often costly behavioral adjustments. Should they lack either or both, we stand to witness more friction with U.S. laws and regulations as investment from China continues to grow. But if Chinese investors are both inclined to adapt to the U.S. institutional context and capable of doing so, their investment will not have impacts beyond occasional disputes or conflicts emerging during a brief learning period. Of the two firm-level factors, this subsection examines the desire of Chinese investors to adapt from two angles: (i) investment motives and (ii) Chinese managers' opinions about various U.S. institutions.

1 Investment Motives

As noted in Chapter 2, the motives of Chinese ODI have attracted a great deal of attention worldwide.[107] Skeptics see the investment as driven primarily by policy considerations of the Chinese government; others find that the investors pursue mainly commercial goals. But few have linked the investment motives to Chinese investment in the United States or to Chinese investors' legal compliance. As previously discussed, investment motives form an important part of the investors' desire to adapt and comply with host-country legal institutions. Those motivated by long-term commercial considerations should be more inclined to conform to a host country's legal environment than investors driven by short-term policy concerns of

[107] Jiangyong Lu, Xiaohui Liu, and Hongling Wang, "Motives for Outward FDI of Chinese Private Firms: Firm Resources, Industry Dynamics, and Government Policies," 7 *Management and Organization Review* 223 (2011); Ivar Kolstad and Arne Wiig, "What Determines Chinese Outward FDI?", 47 *Journal of World Business* 26 (2012); Ping Deng, "Outward Investment by Chinese MNCs: Motivations and Implications," 47 *Business Horizon* 8 (2004).

the home government. So, what motivates Chinese companies to invest in the United States?

Anecdotal evidence suggests that Chinese companies, even those state-owned, pursue business objectives in their global expansion.[108] The head of the Chinese sovereign wealth fund, for instance, insisted that his entity would not make any unprofitable investments "just because we're told to."[109] But how representative are these cases? According to the survey data, the vast majority of the Chinese companies have invested in the United States for business reasons, such as to explore the market, to acquire advanced technologies, and to enhance their brand recognition (see Figure 2.7 in Chapter 2). Only a minority factored the Chinese government's "go global" policy into their investment decisions.

In addition, how committed are Chinese investors to the U.S. market? As discussed earlier, the acquisition by Lenovo of IBM's PC business demonstrated a long-term commitment. The company established a global headquarters in North Carolina right after the deal. Similarly, when Chinese Wanda Group purchased AMC, the American movie theater chain, it promised to fully reinvest all the U.S. profits.[110] Consistent with the anecdotal reports, the survey results show that the vast majority have planned to reinvest their U.S. profits and almost all anticipate further expansion of their U.S. businesses (see Figure 2.9). In summary, long-term commercial motives drive most of the Chinese investors in the United States.

2 Perceptions of U.S. Institutions

Besides investment motives, the perceived legitimacy and efficacy of formal institutions are crucial to foreign investors' compliance.[111] Executives that consider their home-state corporate governance and institutional environment to be superior will hesitate to adapt to host-country settings. How do Chinese MNE managers view U.S. institutions? One can make a case that they opine positively of U.S. institutions because the Chinese business elites have embraced global capitalism.[112] The transition of China in the past decades reflected a gradual and selective internalization of established institutions in advanced market economies.[113] Though the process was complicated by diverging political interests, the quest for

[108] Erica Downs, *Inside China, Inc: China Development Bank's Cross-border Energy Deals* (2011).

[109] Allen T. Cheng, "China's CIC Boosts Direct Investments in Search of Returns," *Institutional Investor* (Sept. 5, 2016), at www.institutionalinvestor.com/article/3583237/investors-sovereign-wealth-funds/chinas-cic-boosts-direct-investments-in-search-of-returns.html#.WGvk2FMrLIU, last checked on Dec. 20, 2016.

[110] Wang Jianlin, "Chuli Zhengshang Guanxi Bazijue: Qinjin Zhengfu Yuanli Zhengzhi" (Principles for Managing Government–Business Relations: Stay Close to Government and Away from Politics), *Zhongguo Qiyejiawang* (Sept. 20, 2012), at http://finance.sina.com.cn/china/20120920/083313189125.shtml, last accessed Dec. 22, 2016.

[111] See, e.g., Jackson et al., "Why do People Comply with the Law?"; Tyler, *Why People Obey the Law*.

[112] Steinfeld, *Playing Our Game*, 265.

[113] See, e.g., Nicholas R. Lardy, *Markets Over Mao: The Rise of Private Business in China* (2014).

modernity has led Chinese thought leaders to accept, consciously or not, the superiority of market capitalism.[114] For instance, the campaign to "modernize" large Chinese SOEs centered on imposing Western corporate structure over traditional state enterprises. In their appearance, most sizable Chinese SOEs resemble large U.S. companies after the reform. If one surveys business research and education in China, it is easy to spot a clear dominance by U.S. academia. Take CKGSB, one of the top business schools in China, as an example; almost all the management professors at the school received their doctoral degrees from U.S. universities.[115] Hence, one may contend that a market-oriented system has gained unquestioned legitimacy in the eyes of Chinese business elites.

On the other hand, one may expect Chinese managers to share critical views of U.S. institutions after the 2008 financial crisis. Having spent years learning from the West, Chinese leaders suddenly realized that "the teachers now have some problems."[116] Further inspired by its relevant insulation and quick recovery from the global recession, some in China now zealously advocate development models that depart radically from free-market capitalism.[117] A growing number of scholars have joined the enterprise of finding, constructing, and debating a Beijing Consensus.[118] In other words, some may argue that Chinese managers have forsaken faith in the free market and its enabling institutions.[119]

In short, whether Chinese investors set out to conquer the United States or adapt to the U.S. "rules of the game" hinges in part on their perceptions of the system. If confident about the efficacy of the Chinese ways of doing business, managing companies, interacting with regulators, and resolving disputes, Chinese investors

114 Steinfeld, *Playing Our Game*, 265, 18.

115 Educational background information is available at the school's website, www.ckgsb.edu.cn/faculty, last accessed Sept. 13, 2016.

116 "When Fortune Frowned," *The Economist* (Oct. 9, 2008), at www.economist.com/node/12373696, last accessed Sept. 17, 2014.

117 Barry Naughton, "China's Distinctive System: Can It Be a Model for Others?", 19 *Journal of Contemporary China* 438 (2010).

118 For the debate about Beijing Consensus, see Suisheng Zhao, "The China Model: Can It Replace the Western Model of Modernization?", 19 *Journal of Contemporary China* 419 (2010); Stephan Ortmann, "The 'Beijing Consensus' and the 'Singapore Model': Unmasking the Myth of an Alternative Authoritarian State-Capitalist Model," 10 *Journal of Chinese Economic and Business Studies* 337 (2012); Matt Ferchen, "Whose China Model Is It Anyway? The Contentious Search for Consensus," 20 *Review of International Political Economy* 390 (2013). For those who question the duplicability of the Beijing model, see Naughton, "China's Distinctive System," 437; Scott Kennedy, "The Myth of the Beijing Consensus," 19 *Journal of Contemporary China* 461 (2010). For those who argue against such a Beijing model, see Yang Jiang, "Rethinking the Beijing Consensus: How China Responds to Crises," 24 *Pacific Review* 337 (2011); Yasheng Huang, "Rethinking the Beijing Consensus," 11 *Asia Policy* 1 (2011).

119 Ian Bremmer, "State Capitalism Comes of Age: The End of the Free Market?", 8 *Foreign Affairs* 40 (2009). Yet according to an opinion survey by *The Economist*, the Chinese public was still more in favor of the free-market system than the U.S. See "Public Opinion on Capitalism: Market Troubles," *The Economist* (April 6, 2011), at www.economist.com/blogs/dailychart/2011/04/public_opinion_capitalism, last accessed Dec. 11, 2016.

will probably strive to maintain them, which may generate numerous frictions with the extant U.S. system. Conversely, if Chinese investors view U.S. institutions positively, they should be more inclined to make the necessary adjustments to the host-country environment. To answer the question, this subsection examines the opinions expressed by the survey respondents. As will be demonstrated, the vast majority hold general U.S. institutions in high regard, which bodes well for prompt adaptation. This subsection focuses on a variety of contextual institutions; discussion about Chinese investors' opinions of U.S. law in specific areas will be postponed to Chapters 5 to 7.

A U.S. SOCIAL, POLITICAL, AND ECONOMIC SYSTEMS. As noted, several recent developments may have eroded the reputation of basic U.S. institutions. To some, the global financial crisis revealed the flaws and dire consequences of blind faith in free-market capitalism,[120] and the subsequent government intervention in economic restructuring has vindicated those preaching a more proactive regulatory role of the state. Meanwhile, Chinese official media have not spared U.S. institutions negative publicity. American politics has been portrayed as conservative, chaotic, and U.S.-centered,[121] and as heralding the decay of Western democracy.[122] By comparison, the Chinese model, allegedly characterized by political stability, social harmony, and sustained economic development, has been presented as a desirable alternative to U.S. institutions.[123] Have Chinese managers internalized this rhetoric? If so, they may be hesitant to board a sinking ship.

The survey findings indicate quite the opposite: the Chinese managers share highly positive opinions of U.S. social, political, and economic systems. On the question of social openness and tolerance, merely 6% and 5% expressed a negative view in the 2016 and 2015 surveys respectively. In the 2014 survey, merely 2% considered U.S. society to be unfair (see Figure 3.3 and Figure 3.8 in the Appendix). Moreover, Chinese managers admire the United States for its capacity

120 See, e.g., Richard A. Posner, A *Failure of Capitalism: The Crisis of '08 and the Descent into Depression* (2009).

121 See, e.g., "Meiguo Zhengfu Guanmen: Qiandaishang de Duikang" (American Government Shut Down, A Fight for Money), *Xin Jing Bao* (Oct. 19, 2013), at http://news.xinhuanet.com/world/2013–10/19/c_117783388.htm, accessed Sept. 11, 2014; "Meiguo Lianbang Zhengfu Guanmen Fengbo Shuoming Shenmo?" (What Does the US Government Shutdown Tell Us?), *Guangmingwang* (Oct. 28, 2013), at www.gmw.cn/xueshu/2013–10/28/content_9305492.htm, accessed Sept. 18, 2014.

122 "Touxi Meiguo Zhengfu Guanmen Fengbo" (Analysis of American Government Shutdown), *Qiushililunwang* (Sept. 18, 2013), at www.qstheory.cn/zs/201310/t20131023_281996.htm, accessed Sept. 2, 2014.

123 Sun Tiexiang, Luo Sha, and Wang Youling, "Zhidu Zixin Genzhi Zhongguo" (Confidence in Chinese Institutions), *Xinhuanet* (Sept. 16, 2014), at http://news.xinhuanet.com/2014–09/16/c_1112498276.htm, accessed Sept. 18, 2014; Xie Yahong et al., "Hao Zhidu Rang Zhongguo Anding Youxu Chongman Huoli" (Good Institutions Stabilize and Energize China), *People's Daily* (Sept. 7, 2014), at http://world.people.com.cn/n/2014/0907/c1002-25617441.html, accessed on Sept. 3, 2014.

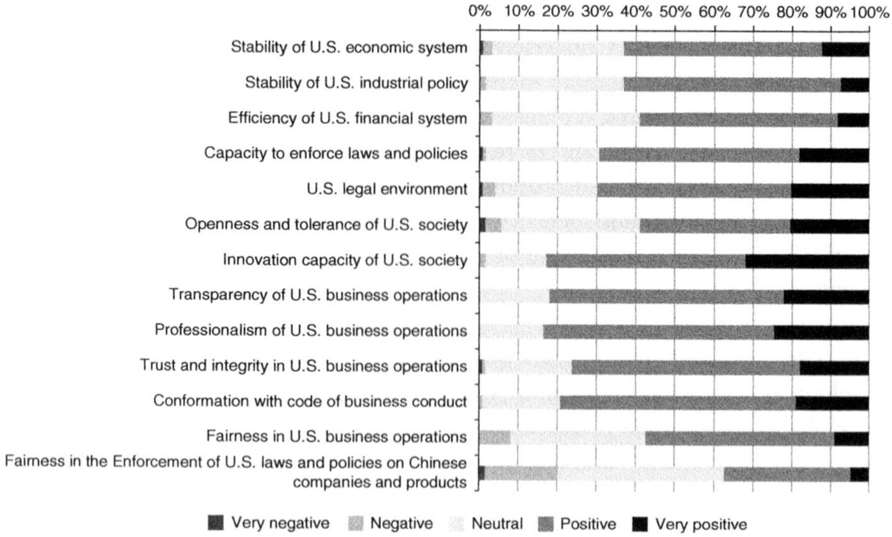

FIGURE 3.3 Chinese managers' views of various U.S. institutions and systems
Source: 2016 CGCC survey

to innovate, with 82%, 90%, and 95% of the respondents considering U.S. society to be innovative or highly innovative in the 2016, 2015, and 2014 surveys respectively. In addition, according to the 2014 survey, 75% of respondents considered the U.S. political system to be stable or very stable, in contrast to only 2% who considered it unstable. Regarding the U.S. economic system, the perceptions are equally positive. Close to 90% of 2015 survey respondents considered it stable. The 2016 survey, however, recorded a drop in the positive view to 62%, and the percentage holding a neutral view rose to 34%. Still, less than 5% opined negatively of U.S. economic stability.

B U.S. BUSINESS ENVIRONMENT. The environment for doing business in China differs considerably from that in the United States.[124] Yet similar to the findings above, Chinese managers opined favorably of the host state's business environment. Some 81%, 85%, and 91% of 2016, 2015, and 2014 survey respondents respectively considered the business transactions and conduct of U.S. firms to be transparent or highly transparent. In addition, more than 83% of 2016 survey respondents held high regard for the professionalism of U.S. firms. Moreover, close to 76% held positive or highly positive views about trust and integrity regarding U.S. businesses. On the question about conformity with the code of business conduct, 79% of survey

[124] For one, transactions and investments depend heavily on informal institutions. Zhang and Li, *Weak Law v. Strong Ties*.

respondents considered U.S. companies to be in good standing. Finally, regarding fairness in the U.S. business environment (i.e., no discriminatory treatment of foreign companies, customers, or investors), only 8% of the 2016 survey respondents felt unfairly treated, in comparison to 57% who saw the U.S. business environment as fair or very fair. The results echo comments from a Chinese manager. "It is hard to gain entry into the U.S. market due to high barriers. But once in, they treat you fairly. Everyone plays by the rule. It's much better than other developing countries where hardly any transaction is certain."[125]

C U.S. LEGAL SYSTEM. Huge institutional gaps exist between China and the United States in judicial independence and authority, and it is plausible that Chinese companies, when expanding abroad, carry attitudes towards the law and courts with them, as illustrated by anecdotal reports of Chinese investors violating labor rights, disregarding environmental protection law, and bribing host-country officials.[126] The issue is crucial for understanding their adaptation, for the reading of U.S. law and courts as corrupt or systemically biased will affect investors' compliance inclination.

As shown in Chapter 2, many survey respondents considered U.S. laws to be complex and confusing. But the perception does not appear to affect the generally positive opinions held by Chinese investors about the U.S. legal system. Some 70% of the 2016 survey respondents thought highly about the U.S. legal system, in comparison to only 4% negative responses. Additionally, 69% of 2016 survey respondents considered the U.S. government to have sufficient capacity to enforce laws and policies. Only 2% thought the opposite. While Chinese firms tend to distrust the courts or take advantage of judicial bias back home,[127] those that have invested in the United States shared a generally positive view of the U.S. judiciary. For instance, 51% of 2014 survey respondents considered U.S. courts to be fair or very fair, while 46% expressed a neutral opinion and merely 3% of respondents saw U.S. courts as unfair.

The general impression of Chinese investors about public administration in the United States is also positive. When asked to compare government review and approval procedures in the United States with those in China, 45% and 60% of the 2015 and 2014 survey respondents respectively found the burden to be less onerous in the United States, and only 17% and 12% thought the opposite.

125 Interview with a manager working for a Chinese SOE's U.S. affiliate in the transportation sector (Jan. 12, 2017).

126 Alfred Atakora, Wilson Kwaku Nimsaah, Benjamin Adjei Danquah, and Julia Agyapong Poku, "Globalization and Emergent Africa–Asia Dialogue: The Good, the Bad and the Ugly," 7 *African Journal of Business Management* 3697 (2013); Angela Dziedzom Akorsu and Fang Lee Cooke, "Labour Standards Application among Chinese and Indian Firms in Ghana: Typical or Atypical?", 22 *International Journal of Human Resource Management* 2730 (2011).

127 Yuen Yuen Ang and Nan Jia, "Perverse Complementarity: Political Connections and the Use of Courts among Private Firms in China," 76 *Journal of Politics* 318 (2014).

Moreover, 63% and 66% of the 2015 and 2014 survey respondents respectively considered the procedures in the United States to be more transparent than in China, on which only 8% and 5% disagreed. In short, Chinese managers think highly of contextual U.S. institutions, which should contribute to their compliance in the host country. One may suspect that the survey responses do not truly reflect the views of Chinese managers, as many of them work for Chinese SOEs and may feel the pressure to toe the party line. Had that been the case, however, the survey data should tilt towards negative perceptions of U.S. institutions given that Chinese official rhetoric about U.S. institutions has been overwhelmingly critical. Moreover, as will be detailed in Chapter 4, state ownership in Chinese investors is not significantly associated with managers' opinions about U.S. institutions.

To summarize, this section has assessed the desire of Chinese investors to adapt to general U.S. institutions. According to the survey data, long-term commercial interests motivated most Chinese investments and Chinese managers generally held positive views of the U.S. institutional environment. Both would catalyze investors' behavioral adjustments to the host country's setting.

C *Ability to Adapt to U.S. Legal and Regulatory Institutions*

Besides the desire to adapt, foreign investors must possess adequate capacity to cross institutional gaps as wide as those currently existing between the United States and China. This section discusses two factors crucial to that capacity: (i) localized decision-making and (ii) reliance on local professionals. First, overcoming the significant liability of foreignness generally necessitates management localization.[128] Lenovo's expansion in the United States is a case in point. Since its acquisition of IBM's PC business, the Chinese company has relied extensively on local employees to run the U.S. business. According to a Lenovo executive, only a few of the several thousands of U.S. employees were expatriated from China.[129] Similarly, Huawei has relied heavily on U.S. employees to explore the U.S. market. When lack of trust hampered its business expansion, the company went as far as hiring former U.S. government officials.[130] However, to what extent do these two cases represent Chinese companies in the United States?

Second, reliance on local professionals is equally important. U.S. legal and regulatory institutions being highly complex, Chinese investors have to engage local service providers in their day-to-day operations. From negotiating a contract to hiring an employee, firms in the United States confront a wide array of actual and potential legal and regulatory issues. Given the intricacy of U.S. laws, even domestic firms routinely rely on professionals such as lawyers and in-house counsel to handle

128 Xu, Pan, and Beamish, "The Effect of Regulative and Normative Distances," 285, 289.

129 Presentation by Lawrence Yu, Director of Lenovo Global Marketing, at Rutgers Business School, March 2016.

130 Ashlee Vance, "At Huawei, Matt Bross Tries to Ease U.S. Security Fears."

such matters. Unlike most developing countries, the United States has a fully grown service sector. Professionals specializing in assisting foreign investors abound. Readers may recall the experience of Bank of China from Chapter 2. When it relied on nonprofessionals to handle compliance matters and internal control, rampant violations led to regulatory sanctions. It then agreed to hire experienced compliance officers and granted them substantial authority. Subsequently, the bank has improved its record and been expanding rapidly in the U.S. market. Yet again, is the anecdotal case representative of Chinese firms in the United States?

This section examines the extent to which Chinese companies in the United States localize and professionalize their U.S. operations. Everything else being equal, Chinese investors that tightly control their U.S. operations and refuse to engage local professionals will encounter more challenges and frictions in coping with U.S. legal institutions. In contrast, a high degree of localization and dependence on U.S. professionals will facilitate prompt adaptation.

1 Allocation of Decision-Making Power

Overwhelmingly, Chinese investors are either majority or sole owners of their U.S. businesses,[131] and therefore should be legally entitled to absolute control over the operations of their U.S. affiliates. Yet it will be costly and inefficient for Chinese investors to dictate their U.S. operations in light of the disparities between the two markets.[132] Thus, certain decisions have to be delegated. For this study, how Chinese investors allocate decision-making power is important because the headquarters' decisions will reflect more of the Chinese political, business, and legal context.[133] Since it is difficult to gauge accurately how decision-making power, a broad and nebulous concept, is allocated between the Chinese headquarters and local managers, I begin with a proxy variable, i.e., the authority to decide on important personnel matters concerning U.S. operations.

Given that the vast majority of Chinese investors wholly own their U.S. businesses, it is unsurprising that most of them retain the authority to recruit or dismiss senior managers in the United States. Even Lenovo expatriated several senior managers to hold key positions in their U.S. affiliates. Some 40% of the 2015 survey respondents reported that such decisions were made solely by the headquarters in China. About 35% reported that the Chinese headquarters made such decisions after consulting with U.S. managers. Still, about 25% delegated

131 This is likely a show of faith in the certainty of property protection in the U.S. Witold J. Henisz, "The Institutional Environment for Multinational Investment," 16 *Journal of Law, Economics, and Organization*, 334 (2000).

132 Xu, Pan, and Beamish, "The Effect of Regulative and Normative Distances," 285, 289.

133 A recent empirical study of Chinese companies investing in Germany found no rigid rules regarding the allocation of decision-making power between Chinese parents and their German subsidiaries. Yun Schüler-Zhou and Margot Schüller, "An Empirical Study of Chinese Subsidiaries' Decision-Making Autonomy in Germany," 12 *Asian Business and Management* 321 (2013).

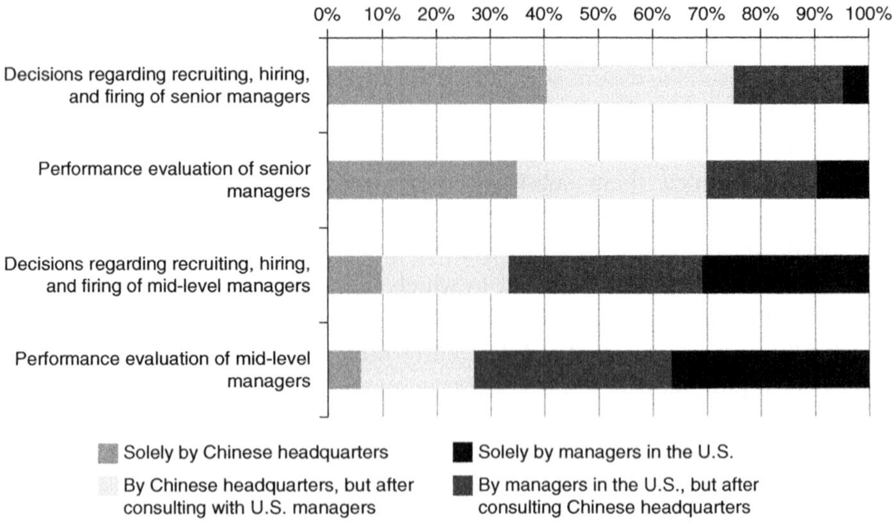

FIGURE 3.4 Allocation of power re major U.S. personnel decisions
Source: 2015 CGCC survey

the decision-making power to managers in the United States. By contrast, U.S. management exercises more control over mid-level personnel decisions, as 66% reported that such decisions were made locally. By comparison, the performance evaluation of the managers at senior and mid-level is even more localized.

The 2016 survey did not break down the personnel decisions by management levels. Instead, the relevant question inquired generally about how different types of U.S. personnel decisions were made. For decisions on recruitment and dismissal of U.S. employees, about 9% of the Chinese respondents reported that the Chinese headquarters had the final say; another 13% reported that the Chinese headquarters made the decisions, but based on consultation with local managers. Among the rest, in 54% of the cases local managers made personnel decisions, after consulting with the Chinese headquarters; and 24% reported U.S. managers to have full authority over personnel decisions regarding U.S. operations. The results from the 2014 survey were similar.

In addition to the data for the proxy variable, the 2016 survey specifically inquired about the allocation of power to decide major U.S. legal and compliance matters. Among the 120 respondents to this question, about 58% reported that the Chinese headquarters made the decision either independently (13%) or based on consultation with managers in the U.S. (45%). Among the 42% that reported localized decision-making, 26% consulted with the Chinese headquarters, and about 17% decided matters without consultation. Evidently, managers in the United States play a varying but important role in deciding major U.S. legal and compliance matters.

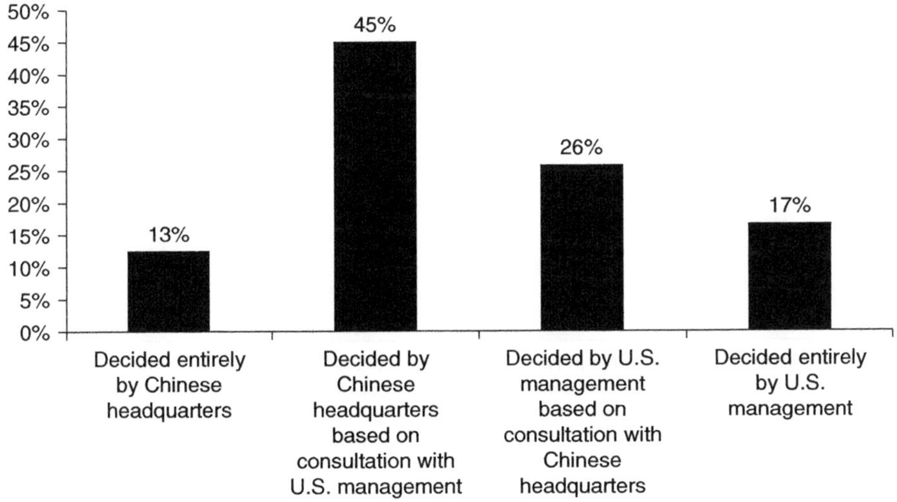

FIGURE 3.5 Decisions re major U.S. legal and compliance issues
Source: 2016 CGCC survey

To summarize, most Chinese investors, as the sole or majority owners of their U.S. businesses, are legally entitled to full control over U.S. operations; and control they have imposed, especially over top managers at U.S. affiliates. Nonetheless, in practice the Chinese headquarters will consult with local managers about such decisions; the latter's input plays a vital role in mid-level U.S. personnel matters. Likewise, for slightly more than half of Chinese investors, major U.S. legal and compliance decisions are rendered by the headquarters in China, but not without consulting U.S. managers in most cases.

2 Reliance on Local Professionals

The U.S. legal and regulatory systems are nothing but complex; it usually takes years of training and practice to develop expertise in any area of U.S. law. To Chinese investors accustomed to lax law enforcement at home, access and use of professional knowledge is critical to their compliance capacity in the United States. In theory, foreign companies facing formidable "liability of foreignness" may overcome it by forming a joint venture with U.S. parties. An earlier study found the method to be highly popular among Chinese firms investing overseas.[134] However, as discussed above, sizable Chinese companies prefer investing in the United States via subsidiaries. The lack of local partners accentuates the need to rely on professionals to cross the knowledge gap.

To assess reliance on local professionals, I first look at the extent to which Chinese investors employ in-house legal and compliance staff. As shown in Figure 3.6, about

134 Yang et al., "A Comparative Analysis of the Internationalization of Chinese and Japanese Firms," 152.

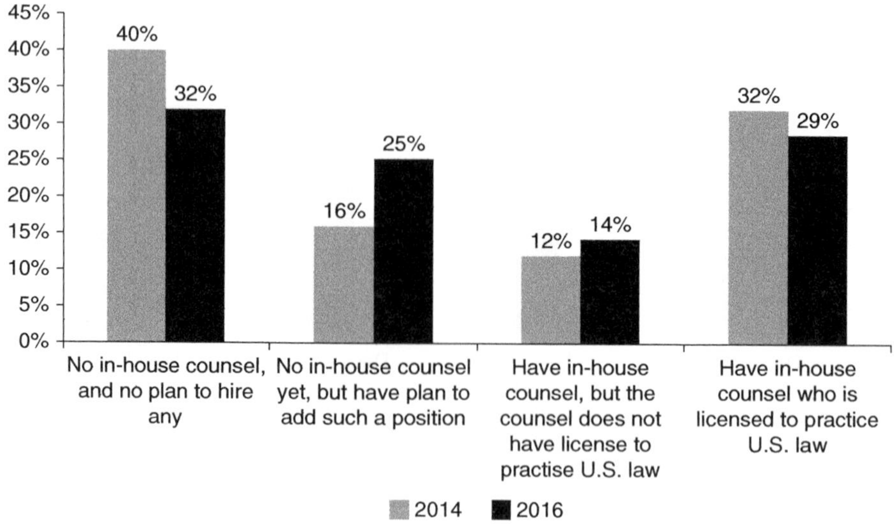

FIGURE 3.6 Full-time in-house legal capacity of Chinese companies in the United States
Source: 2014 and 2016 CGCC survey

30% of Chinese companies reported having in-house counsel licensed to practice U.S. law. Some 60% and 68% of 2014 and 2016 survey respondents respectively employed or planned to employ in-house legal staff. Meanwhile, more than 20% of respondents reported having full-time staff in charge solely of compliance work. Similar percentages of companies had their in-house counsel handle compliance matters. Only about a third of respondents did not have full-time compliance staff or any plan to add such a position (see Figure 3.7).

Given the complexity of U.S. laws, in-house counsel and compliance staff can barely handle all the legal matters that may implicate Chinese investors. Most have to rely on outside advisors. According to the 2014 survey, 65% of respondents frequently engaged U.S. lawyers and 33% had occasionally used their service, which leaves only 2% having never consulted a U.S. lawyer. In selecting U.S. lawyers, Chinese investors assigned the most weight to the lawyers' practice experience in relevant areas, followed by legal fee and the lawyers' or law firms' general reputation. Only a few paid attention to U.S. lawyers' government connections and Chinese background, and even fewer cared about the lawyers' educational credentials. As reflected by the preference ordering, Chinese managers are rather sophisticated consumers of U.S. legal services.

From the supply side, the well-developed U.S. legal market produces enough lawyers and compliance professionals to serve Chinese clients, as evidenced by the overall positive feedback for their services. When requested to rate their level of satisfaction with the work of U.S. lawyers on a one-to-five scale (one being very unsatisfied, five being very satisfied), 55% of Chinese managers chose four and 9%

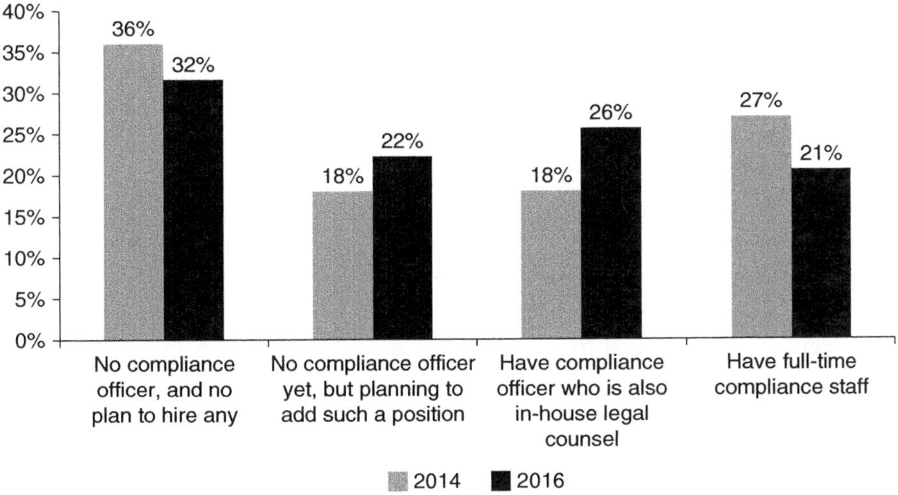

FIGURE 3.7 Compliance capacity of Chinese companies in the United States
Source: 2014 and 2016 CGCC survey

chose five. Only 3% chose two, and no one chose one. In summary, according to the survey, Chinese companies in the United States rely extensively on local professionals to interact with various host-country institutions, and the U.S. service market is able to meet their demand. Access to and use of local knowledge facilitate adaptation by Chinese firms to U.S. legal and regulatory institutions.

To recapitulate, Chinese companies, when investing in the United States, generally encounter wide legal and regulatory gaps. Bridging the gaps necessitates both the desire and the ability to adapt. Motivated largely by long-term commercial interests and viewing U.S. institutions positively, Chinese investors should be inclined to adapt. Meanwhile, Chinese firms in the United States rely extensively on local professionals in coping with the host state's legal and regulatory institutions. Though the majority of investors still retain the power to decide major personnel matters, local managers' input has played a vital role in matters concerning mid-level personnel and major U.S. legal and compliance issues. Therefore, most Chinese companies in the United States should be inclined and able to adapt and comply with U.S. legal and regulatory institutions, especially when compliance involves mainly routine and technical decisions.

III CONCLUSION

Will Chinese investors in the United States, rising fast in number, find themselves entangled in troubles with the complex and stringent U.S. legal and regulatory institutions? In other words, will the surge of Chinese FDI in the United States entail frictions or even "clashes" with the host-country systems? To address these questions, the chapter first formulated a new analytical framework that comprises three inquiries about the institutional distances between foreign investors' home and host states, their desire to adapt to host-state institutions, and their ability to adapt. In plain English, whether and how foreign investors adapt to a set of host-country laws turns on the need, the desire, and the ability to do so.

Applying the framework to the question at issue, I examined the general institutional distances between China and the United States. The formal-law gaps between the two countries, though large in general, vary across different areas. Due to decades of transnational learning and legal transplants, those Chinese laws enabling and regulating the market to a great extent resemble U.S. laws in corresponding areas. However, the gaps in law enforcement and compliance remain large due to the vast political differences between the two countries.

Would Chinese investors, on the edge of this institutional chasm, take the leap forward? According to the survey data, Chinese investors think the grass is greener on the other side. Long-term business considerations motivated most Chinese investment in the United States and Chinese managers viewed various U.S. institutions positively. Hence, they should be inclined to play by the host-country rules. Next, I examined the ability of the Chinese firms to adapt. Despite their ownership control of the U.S. businesses, the Chinese firms delegated considerable decision-making authority to local managers on mid-level personnel matters and U.S. legal and compliance matters. Moreover, they have relied extensively on local professionals in coping with complex U.S. laws. In summary, the empirical analysis demonstrates the need, the desire, and the ability of Chinese investors to adapt to general U.S. legal institutions.

The overall finding, however, cannot disguise significant cross-firm variations on each of the three dimensions. Some Chinese firms pay more attention to home-state policies, hold more critical opinions about U.S. institutions, centralize the power to decide matters concerning their U.S. investments, and distrust local professionals. What explains the variations? Among multiple possible explanatory factors, Chapter 4 below focuses on the one that distinguishes Chinese ODI and has spawned intensive debate – state ownership in Chinese investors. To be concrete, Chapter 4 will empirically investigate possible links between, on the one hand, state ownership in Chinese investors and, on the other, variations in the institutional distances between China and the United States, the investors' desire to adapt to U.S. institutions, and their ability to do so.

Appendix

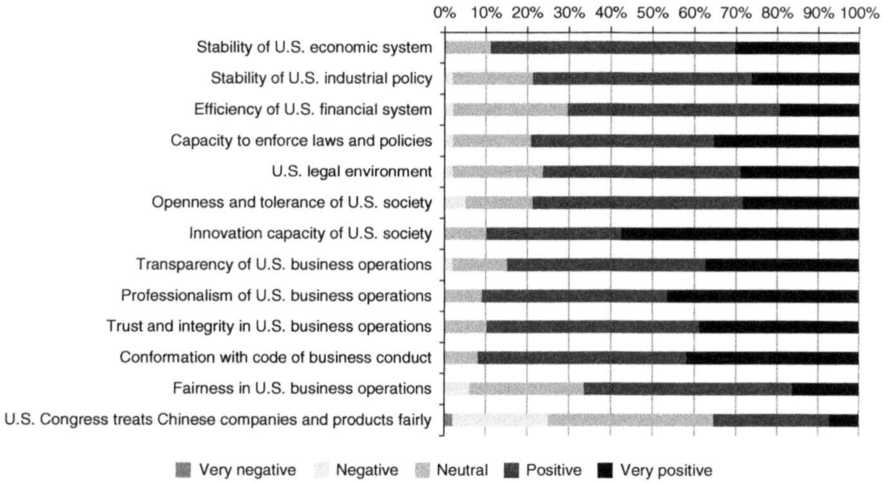

FIGURE 3.8 Perceptions of U.S. institutions
Source: 2015 CGCC survey

4

State Ownership and Chinese Investors' Reactions to U.S. Institutions

What you read in the newspapers about Chinese SOEs is bullshit. They are well organized and efficient . . . they play by the rules.[1]

Wall Street professional who worked as investment manager at a large Chinese state-owned company

The manager's glowing view of Chinese SOEs is probably biased. The state-owned company he worked at is known for its globalized operations and seasoned management. Yet not all Chinese SOEs defy the conventional wisdom. A vast literature has demonstrated the differences that companies' state ownership makes. Due to the renaissance of state capitalism, more scholars have joined the enterprise of exploring SOEs, especially those in China. Yet the existing literature has overlooked the question to be addressed in this chapter, i.e., whether and how state ownership influences Chinese investors when they adapt to U.S. legal and regulatory institutions.

Let me pause and restate this book's twofold goal. First, it examines how Chinese companies react to U.S. legal and regulatory institutions. Applying a novel analytical framework, the preceding chapter examined the comprehensive survey data on Chinese foreign direct investment (FDI) and demonstrated that Chinese companies typically confront large institutional gaps when investing in the United States, yet on average they have both the inclination and the capacity to conform to U.S. institutions. That being said, significant variations across the firms manifest in almost all respects of the general findings. Granted, variations across different firms are inevitable, given the diversity and size of the Chinese economy. Of interest are potential systematic variations. The second goal of this book is to explore the

[1] Interview with a former investment banker who worked for a large Chinese state-owned company in finance (March 29, 2017).

connection, if any, between state ownership in Chinese investors and the various aspects pertinent to their adaptation to U.S. institutions.

Widespread state ownership, a defining feature of China's state capitalism, sets Chinese outbound investments apart from earlier waves of FDI (e.g., FDI from Japan) and poses novel theoretical and policy questions. Scholars have long explored the rationale for state ownership in corporate actors and its effects, yet most of their studies have revolved around the efficiency consequence. To many, principle-agent conflicts at multiple levels undercut the efficiency of SOEs, so they lag behind private firms in terms of performance or innovation.[2] Others highlight the multi-tasking of SOEs. In addition to preserving the value of state assets and generating profits, SOEs also serve a variety of social and political functions, such as maintaining stability, reducing unemployment, lowering inequality, filling institutional gaps, and even promoting diplomatic relations.[3] Some of the tasks spill out positive externalities, which may justify the efficiency loss of state ownership. While the literature has enriched our knowledge about SOEs, it has been silent about how investors with government ownership react to legal institutions at home and abroad. This chapter begins that line of inquiry.

Applying the analytical framework articulated in the preceding chapter, I empirically investigate whether and how state ownership is associated with the following three factors: (1) the institutional distances between China and the United States, (2) the desire of Chinese investors to adapt to U.S. institutions, and (3) their ability to do so. This chapter proceeds in that order. First, it explores the link between state ownership and the institutional gaps confronting Chinese companies in the United States. As will be detailed, the gaps in formal laws do not usually vary for firms of different ownership types, yet Chinese companies with significant state ownership typically confront larger law enforcement distances in the United States. Second, the chapter examines whether and how state ownership in Chinese investors bears on their investment motives and the Chinese managers' perceptions of U.S. institutions, both of which are crucial to the desire to adapt. It uncovers preliminary evidence that state-owned Chinese investors are more likely to take into account investment policies of the Chinese government, whereas the ownership type has no apparent effect on the managers' views of the host country's institutions. Third, the chapter tests possible connections between, on the one hand, state ownership in Chinese investors, and, on the other, their management localization and reliance on local professionals. The test results strongly suggest that

[2] Aldo Musacchio, Sergio G. Lazzarini, and Ruth V. Aguilera, "New Varieties of State Capitalism: Strategic and Governance Implications," 29 *Academy of Management Perspectives* 115 (2015), 118.

[3] Chong-En Bai and Lixin Colin Xu, "Incentives for CEOs with Multitasks: Evidence from Chinese State-Owned Enterprises," 33 *Journal of Comparative Economics* 517 (2005); Dani Rodrik, *One Economics, Many Recipes: Globalization, Institutions, and Economic Growth* (2007); Paul M. Vaaler and Burkhard N. Schrage, "Residual State Ownership, Policy Stability and Financial Performance Following Strategic Decisions by Privatizing Telecoms," 40 *Journal of International Business Studies* 621 (2009); Deborah Brautigam, *The Dragon's Gift: The Real Story of China in Africa* (2009).

Chinese investors with significant state ownership tend to centralize decision-making for their U.S. businesses. Yet at the same time, Chinese investors, regardless of their ownership type, rely extensively on local professionals in the United States. In the end, I conclude the chapter by briefly discussing the contributions and limitations of the empirical findings, followed by an introduction to the following three chapters, which explore in more detail how Chinese companies react to U.S. institutions in three areas most relevant to their investments, i.e., tax, employment, and national security review.

Before proceeding, a few words are in order on the empirical tests in this chapter. I extract the data for the regression analysis from the annual CGCC surveys. As previously noted, except for a set of core questions, CGCC altered the survey contents each year according to its shifting interest. Hence, the data available for some of the tests are limited to one or two years, so some of the test results offer merely suggestive evidence. But taken together, the regression results make a convincing case that state ownership in Chinese investors has a significant effect on how they cope with major legal and compliance matters in the United States.

I STATE OWNERSHIP AND THE LEGAL AND REGULATORY DISTANCES BETWEEN CHINA AND THE UNITED STATES

Chapter 3 demonstrated that Chinese companies investing in the United States generally confront large institutional distances. According to the existing literature, the natural course to follow is to examine how foreign investors adapt. That, however, would miss the complexity of the question due to the unique nature of China's state capitalism. Unlike earlier waves of FDI in the United States, the current one from China has seen investors of diverse ownership types play important roles. That raises the question about the effect of ownership types. In other words, do state-owned firms that enjoy privileged status in China have to overcome higher hurdles in order to comply with U.S. law? To answer the question, this section factors the ownership character into the comparative institutional analysis. Following the framework articulated in Chapter 3, the analysis proceeds in two parts: the distances in formal laws between China and the United States, and law enforcement distances.

Except for a few areas where foreign government ownership of U.S. assets is either restricted or triggers heightened governmental scrutiny,[4] most U.S. laws pertinent to foreign investment treat SOEs pursuing commercial objectives and private investors the same. Given the general non-differentiation, state ownership matters in the analysis of formal institutional distances to the extent that formal Chinese laws

[4] FINSA, for instance, instructs CFIUS to investigate acquisitions of U.S. assets that will result in foreign government control. Moreover, foreign ownership, whether public or private, is restricted in some areas, such as nuclear energy. Sachin Desai and Kathleen Schroader, "US Nuclear Foreign Ownership Policy Ready for a Refreshed Interpretation," 37 *Energy Law Journal* 85 (2016), 92.

treat SOEs more favorably than private Chinese firms. As noted in Chapter 3, though several formal Chinese laws still contain provisions that arguably favor SOEs, e.g., the Chinese Anti-monopoly Law,[5] in most areas state ownership of a business is no longer a distinct legal feature. For example, the Chinese Contract Law generally treats SOEs and privately owned companies alike. The "socialist market reform" of the past decades has transformed Chinese SOEs from a distinct type of organization to legal persons endowed with the same rights and obligations under Chinese laws as privately owned business organizations.[6] Therefore, except for the few subject matter areas where either Chinese law or U.S. law differentiates SOEs from firms of other ownership types, government ownership is generally not associated with varying formal legal distances between China and the United States. In other words, Chinese companies investing in the United States may encounter wide gaps in formal laws and regulations, but in most areas the gaps do not further vary according to the companies' ownership character.

However, regarding law enforcement distances between the two countries, state ownership in Chinese investors often makes a difference. As briefly discussed in Chapter 3, in their home state Chinese SOEs that command enormous political resources interact with regulators in a dynamic and tangled state–SOE relationship.[7] On the one hand, powerful SOEs "good at maneuvering China's fragmented bureaucracy with conflicting departmental interests" can capture regulatory agencies.[8] On the other, supervising government agencies may exert some control over SOEs by influencing the political careers of the top managers.[9] The unique institutional setup of China's state capitalism determines the negotiated nature of SOE regulation and compliance.[10] In the United States, however, the Chinese SOEs can hardly influence the decisions of U.S. judges, state or federal prosecutors, or other federal enforcement agents. Therefore, powerful Chinese SOEs will bear the same cost of noncompliance in the United States as those without much political capital at home. Hence, formal laws held constant, noncompliance costs in the United States should be greater for powerful Chinese investors. Moreover, state ownership in foreign investors often raises suspicion and concerns in host countries (especially those featuring free-market capitalism such as the United States) that may lead to selective law enforcement and higher compliance costs.[11]

Let me add a quantitative layer to the discussion. The 2016 CGCC survey contains a question that enables a preliminary assessment of the relationship between state ownership in Chinese investors and the cost of complying with U.S. laws. The scale question asks the respondents to compare their U.S. compliance costs with those in

5 Article 7, Chinese Anti-monopoly Law.

6 Wang, "The Political Logic of Corporate Governance," 665.

7 Liou, "Rent-Seeking at Home," 226. 8 Ibid., 221. 9 Ibid., 220, 225. 10 Ibid., 226.

11 Klaus Meyer, Yuan Ding, Jing Li, and Hua Zhang, "Overcoming Distrust: How State-Owned Enterprises Adapt Their Foreign Entries to Institutional Pressures Abroad," 45 *Journal of International Business Studies* 1005 (2014).

TABLE 4.1 *Summary statistics*

Variable	Observations	Mean	Std. dev.	Min.	Max.
State ownership (50%)	130	0.33	0.47	0	1
State ownership (10%)	130	0.43	0.497	0	1
Investment duration	129	8.47	9.32	0	36
Net U.S. asset	123	2.02	1.18	1	4
U.S. compliance costs versus compliance costs in China	111	3.98	0.85	1	5

Source: 2016 survey

TABLE 4.2 *State ownership and U.S. compliance costs relative to costs in China*

	1	2	3	4
State ownership (50%)	0.469 (0.424)		0.4795 (0.4325)	
State ownership (10%)		0.735* (0.407)		0.763* (0.419)
Investment duration	0.0107 (0.0226)	0.0044 (0.0227)	0.0102 (0.0238)	0.005 (0.0236)
Net U.S. assets			−0.0069 (0.1694)	−0.0442 (0.1708)
number of observations	106	106	103	103

Source: 2016 survey; significance level: ***p < 1%; **p < 5%; *p < 10%; ordered logistic regressions

China. Unsurprisingly, most of the respondents consider compliance costs in the United States to be higher (3.98 out of 5) (see Table 4.1), but significant variation exists. I ran a series of preliminary statistical tests to investigate whether state ownership in Chinese investors is systematically linked to the variation.[12]

How to measure the variable of interest throughout the book – state ownership in Chinese investors? In each of the three annual CGCC surveys, the respondents reported the ownership character of their Chinese investors as one of the following five types: wholly state-owned, majority-owned by the state, the state owning a significant minority share (less than 50% but more than 10%), the state owning a minority stake (less than 10% but more than 0), and no state ownership. From the collected data, I create a state-ownership dummy that equals 1 if a Chinese state entity owns at least a majority interest of the Chinese investor, 0 otherwise. However, due to the intricate state–business relations in China, government control may not

[12] Because the dependent variable, i.e., data derived from the scaled answers, is ordinal, I use ordered logistic regression to assess the hypothetical connection with state ownership in the Chinese investors.

rest solely on majority ownership.[13] To capture possible effects of extended state influence or control, I construct an alternative dummy that equals 1 if the state owns at least 10% of the Chinese investor, 0 otherwise. I will use these two dummies alternately to represent state ownership throughout the rest of this book.

Given the limited sample size, only two control variables are included in the tests. First, how long a Chinese investor has operated in the United States may correlate with both its relative compliance costs (e.g., declining costs due to established legitimacy) and its ownership character (e.g., SOEs dominated earlier ODI from China). Hence, the tests include investment duration as a control. Second, it is plausible that Chinese SOEs make more large investments in the United States.[14] So I also add U.S. investment size as a control variable.

According to the test results, relative U.S. compliance costs are positively associated with significant state ownership (more than 10%). Everything else being equal, Chinese investors with the state owning at least a significant minority stake are more likely to report high U.S. compliance costs than private Chinese investors. In China's model of state capitalism, the government exerts control and influence over business actors through multiple means beyond majority equity ownership.[15] A substantial state interest is probably sufficient to guarantee privileged treatment in an otherwise adverse institutional environment. Meanwhile, state ownership in a Chinese company, even a minority one, may cause suspicion and raise compliance costs in the United States. Hence the finding of statistical significance for the state-ownership variable. However, readers should take the test results as suggestive evidence. One may come up with alternative interpretations. For instance, state-owned Chinese investors may cluster in certain sectors that are heavily regulated in the United States but weakly controlled in China, which naturally increases relative U.S. compliance costs. Due to the limited sample size, this alternative hypothesis cannot be adequately evaluated.[16]

Majority state ownership is not significant. One possible explanation is that Chinese companies with significant minority ownership are indistinguishable from state-owned investors when it comes to the difference in compliance costs. Alternatively, one may attribute the nonsignificance to the small sample size. Moreover, neither of the control variables is significant. Because the focus of this chapter is on state ownership in Chinese investors, I will not elaborate on the test

13 Milhaupt and Zheng, "Beyond Ownership"; Musacchio, Lazzarini, and Aguilera, "*New Varieties of State Capitalism*," 115.

14 As shown in Table 4.1, U.S. investment size is measured by using net U.S. assets on a scale of 1 to 4 (1 if the responding firm's net U.S. assets are less than US$5 million, 2 if between US$5 million and US$10 million, 3 if between US$10 million and a US$100 million, and 4 if more than US$100 million).

15 Chen Li, "Holding 'China Inc.' Together"; Milhaupt and Zheng, "Beyond Ownership," 665.

16 A proper sectoral variable will comprise many dummies and will greatly reduce the degree of freedom of the regression analysis. Also, ordered logistic tests normally require large samples. A sample with a little more than a hundred observations is testing the limit of the modeling. Thus, the findings are suggestive evidence that call for further empirical analysis.

results for the control variables. Suffice it to say that investment duration and size appear to have no more than marginal effects on Chinese firms' U.S. compliance costs relative to those in China. Yet again, given the limited sample size, one would err to draw definitive inference from the nonsignificant coefficients.

To summarize, Chinese companies in the United States face large legal and regulatory gaps. The gaps further vary according to the ownership type of the Chinese investor. Although formal-law distances between the two countries remain roughly constant except in a few subject matter areas, the law enforcement distance appears larger for state-owned Chinese investors. Thus, all else being equal, Chinese companies with significant state ownership have to make more efforts to comply with various U.S. legal institutions. Such efforts may take many forms, such as briefing or training in U.S. law. For instance, a Chinese state-owned airline company has engaged experts on U.S. legal compliance to train its employees before they are positioned in the U.S. offices. Much to the author's surprise, during an interview for this research project the New York representative of the company could still recall the instructions received almost two years before about avoiding the type of collaboration with competitors that would violate U.S. antitrust law.[17]

II THE DESIRE TO ADAPT TO U.S. INSTITUTIONS

Having examined the ties between state ownership in Chinese investors and the institutional gaps they have to traverse when investing in the United States, I now empirically explore the two company-level factors in the analytical framework: the desire and the ability of Chinese investors to conform to U.S. legal institutions. Applying the previously articulated analytical frame, this section examines the possible effects of state ownership on the desire to adapt from the following two angles: (1) the investment motives of Chinese companies and (2) the Chinese MNE managers' views about general U.S. institutions.

A *Investment Motives*

As discussed in Chapter 3, investment motives are crucial for understanding foreign investors' behavior in host countries; long-term commercial interests are typically more conducive to adaptation than short-term home-state policy concerns. Chapter 3 demonstrated that long-term commercial considerations, such as market expansion and brand enhancement, drove most of the Chinese investment in the United States. Nonetheless, a significant minority of the survey respondents also reported that the Chinese government's encouragement had played a part in their investment decisions. Among Chinese companies in the United States, are those

[17] Interview with the CEO of the U.S. affiliate of a large Chinese company in transportation (June 14, 2017).

with significant state ownership more likely to have considered government stimulation when making the investment decision?

An affirmative answer will not be surprising. The Chinese government controls SOEs through multiple mechanisms, including senior personnel management.[18] "SOE managers are economic actors, but they are political officials even more so."[19] Decision-makers in SOEs, therefore, "are motivated by both political achievement and business achievement, and can be moved back and forth across the political hierarchy and state-controlled business hierarchy under the Party's direction."[20] Hence, Chinese investors with state ownership should enforce state policies regarding FDI more vigorously than privately owned companies.[21] Prior research has documented cases where Chinese SOEs, encouraged by the government, took on risky projects in developing countries that were shunned by private firms.[22] How about Chinese FDI in developed countries such as the United States? Some anecdotal evidence appears to confirm the effect of state ownership on investors' motives. "SOE managers always balance political achievement (*zhengji*) and business achievement (*yeji*)," observed a former manager at a state-owned firm with substantial U.S. investment:

> political achievement often trumps business achievement in their decisions. For instance, the firm expanded its U.S. business to multiple areas even though in some they did not expect to make any profit. They wanted the firm to look like an "all-round" U.S. business [in the sector]. It is good "political achievement" since no other Chinese firms [in the sector] have done it.[23]

Another echoes the observation. "Chinese firms seem to focus on long-term specific investments, not short-term revenue or profits."[24] In short, SOEs participate in various business activities "to mount the political hierarchy."[25]

Yet on the other hand, the government's "go global" policy does not specifically target SOEs. At least in writing, the policy is supposed to benefit all Chinese companies investing abroad, SOEs as well as privately owned firms. Additionally, the line between SOEs and private companies has blurred and private Chinese companies have also become beneficiaries of government subsidies and champions of its policies.[26] Thus, it is possible that Chinese outbound investors, irrespective of ownership type, are equally responsive to government policy incentives.

[18] Li, "State-Owned Enterprises in the Current Regime"; Liou, "Rent-Seeking at Home," 220, 221.
[19] Liou, "Rent-Seeking at Home," 220, 225. [20] Li, "Holding 'China Inc.' Together," 927, 944.
[21] Lin Cui, Klaus E. Meyer, and Helen Wei Hu, "What Drives Firms' Intent to Seek Strategic Assets by Foreign Direct Investment? A Study of Emerging Economy Firms," 49 *Journal of World Business* 488 (2014), 491–2.
[22] Amighini, Rabellotti, and Sanfilippo, "Do Chinese State-Owned and Private Enterprises Differ in Their Internationalization Strategies?".
[23] Interview with a former manager of the U.S. affiliate of a major Chinese company (Jan. 24, 2017).
[24] Interview with a manager of an SOE's U.S. businesses in insurance and finance (July 19, 2017).
[25] Liou, "Rent-Seeking at Home," 220, 225. [26] Milhaupt and Zheng, "Beyond Ownership," 665.

TABLE 4.3 *Summary statistics (variables for testing state ownership and investment motives)*

Variable	Observations	Mean	Std. dev.	Min.	Max.
State ownership (50%)	327	0.422018	0.494638	0	1
State ownership (10%)	327	0.510703	0.500652	0	1
Investment duration	323	11.34056	9.844212	0	40
U.S. revenue	181	2.160221	1.225547	1	4
Government encouragement as a reason for investing in the U.S.	252	0.186508	0.390291	0	1
Net U.S. asset	123	2.02439	1.183655	1	4

Source: 2014–16 surveys

I empirically assess the conflicting hypotheses. As noted earlier, the 2015 survey and the 2016 survey contain multiple-choice questions about the responding firms' main investment motives. From the data I construct a dependent dummy variable that equals 1 if the survey respondent chose "Chinese government encouragement" as one of the main motives, 0 otherwise (see Table 4.3).

The independent variable of interest is state ownership in a Chinese investor. I use the same two dummy variables of state ownership as described above (i.e., at 50% level and 10% level). The goal is to test whether one of the two dummies is significantly associated with the likelihood that a Chinese firm considered government stimulation as a main driver of U.S. investment.

A number of variables are added as controls. First, investment duration. As discussed in Chapter 2, the Chinese government only began to seriously promote ODI in the last decade. Prior to that, its FDI policies were oriented towards boosting inbound FDI.[27] Therefore, it is possible that earlier Chinese investments in the United States, which were mainly spearheaded by the SOEs, were not driven by the "go global" policy.

Second, U.S. investment size is included in the tests to control for its possible association with both the ownership character of the Chinese investors and the policy motivation. Investors that make substantial U.S. investments may rely more heavily on a supportive home-state government than do those that intend to test the waters. In 2014 and 2015 the respondents were asked to report the dollar amount of their U.S. assets. But the majority skipped the question. So in 2016, the survey respondents were asked to select a range of amounts in which their net U.S. assets fell. That greatly raised the response rate for this question.[28] An alternative proxy of U.S. investment size is U.S. revenue for the responding firms. For the same reason, a scale question was used to collect the data in 2016.

27 Luo, Xue, and Han, "How Emerging Market Governments Promote Outward FDI."

28 The question was also clarified to ask for the responding firm's U.S. net assets.

As shown in Table 4.4, state-ownership dummies are positively associated with the likelihood that government policies drive U.S. investment (at varying levels of significance). The preliminary results from most of the specifications suggest that, everything else being equal, Chinese investors with at least a significant minority state ownership are more likely to report "government encouragement" as a main reason for investing in the United States. The results are stronger for the tests using the 2016 survey data, which have less of a missing-data problem, than those using the combined 2015–16 data. Note that the conclusion is tentative, given the limited sample size and the sensitivity of the test results to model specifications.

Neither of the two control variables is significant. U.S. investment duration and U.S. investment size appear to have no more than marginal effects on how likely Chinese firms factor government encouragement into their investment decisions. Again, given the sample size, readers should refrain from drawing conclusions based on the nonsignificant coefficients.

Having shown that Chinese investors with significant state ownership tend to be more policy-driven, I now move on to the second question, i.e., whether they are more likely to make long-term commitment to U.S. business. Conventional wisdom holds that Chinese SOEs are less constrained by shareholder demands for short-term profit maximization and able to make stable and long-term foreign investments.[29] Yet some argue the opposite: certain features of SOE governance such as management rotation actually encourage short-term investment and management strategies.[30] The ongoing debate, however, has centered on Chinese FDI in Africa, where the business environment is volatile and long-term investment incurs high risks. Few have explored the tie between state ownership in Chinese investors and their time horizon for investments in the highly stable United States.

In order to assess the tie, I construct a new dummy variable as a proxy for long-term commitment of Chinese investors to their U.S. businesses. The 2015 and 2016 survey inquired about the actual or planned use of U.S. profits (to reinvest or to repatriate the U.S. profit). From the data I create a dummy variable that equals 1 if a responding firm planned to reinvest all or most of its U.S. profits, 0 otherwise.

The independent variable of interest is ownership type, represented by the same two dummy variables (50% state ownership and 10% state ownership) as used in the prior tests. A number of control variables are included in the tests. First, newly arrived investors, which are more likely to be private companies, may allocate a larger fraction of their profits to expanding their U.S. businesses. Therefore, I include investment duration to account for the possible confounding effects. Second, Chinese companies with substantial U.S. investments may reinvest more profits either out of necessity or as a result of self-selection, so I add the companies' net U.S. assets as a control for some of the tests. Third, firms may not have any plan for their profits if their U.S. operations

29 Ian Taylor, "Unpacking China's Resource Diplomacy in Africa," 35 *China in Africa* (2007); Li, "State-Owned Enterprises in the Current Regime."

30 Haglund, "In It for the Long Term?", 644.

TABLE 4.4 *State ownership and "government encouragement" as a main reason for U.S. investment*

	2016 survey data				2015 and 2016 survey data			
	1	2	3	4	5	6	7	8
State ownership (50%)	0.983*		1.306**		0.5448		0.747*	
	(0.512)		(0.5555)		(0.3655)		(0.4519)	
State ownership (10%)		0.887*		1.058*		0.702*		0.716
		(0.507)		(0.553)		(0.368)		(0.455)
Investment duration	−0.0177	−0.0155	−0.012	−0.0047	0.0039	0.0035	0.0065	0.0089
	(0.0273)	(0.0273)	(0.0291)	(0.0282)	(0.0176)	(0.0174)	(0.0207)	(0.0204)
Net U.S. asset			−0.2597	−0.3036				
			(0.236)	(0.2341)				
U.S. revenue							−0.243	−0.262
							(0.1805)	(0.184)
Number of observations	124	124	116	116	218	218	168	168

Source: 2015–16 surveys; significance level: ***p < 1%; **p < 5%; *p < 10%; logistic regression tests

TABLE 4.5 *Summary statistics (additional variables for testing long-term commitment to U.S. business)*

Variable	Observations	Mean	Std. dev.	Min.	Max.
U.S. profit level	119	2.798319	0.8980188	1	5
U.S. profit level (2015–16)	256	0.3203125	0.4675106	0	1
Reinvest most U.S. profits	205	0.7170732	0.4515238	0	1

Source: 2015–16 surveys

barely produce any; and the profitability of state-owned businesses may differ from that of their privately owned counterparts. Hence, profit level is included as a control in two tests.[31]

As shown in Table 4.6, state ownership is negatively associated with the likelihood of reinvesting U.S. profits in the host state. In other words, everything else held constant, Chinese investors with significant state ownership are less likely than private investors to invest their U.S. profits back to the United States. The finding, sensitive to model specifications, may be interpreted as the former either having no reinvestment plan or having plans to reinvest U.S. profits at levels lower than privately owned Chinese investors. Both may be ascribed to state control over SOEs. Details vary, but profitable SOEs are generally required to submit certain percentages of their post-tax earnings and profits to the state, and, due to fiscal pressure, the central government has been raising the percentages.[32] The government's demand may not directly affect the allocation of SOEs' U.S. investment profits, but its indirect ripple effects or the SOEs' internal governance mechanisms to meet the demand can still diminish the overseas managers' ability to reinvest the profits or even to plan for the reinvestment.

The tests also return some non-robust results that negatively link profit level to actual or planned reinvestment of U.S. profits. Less profitable respondents may be motivated to further expand their U.S. investments, or their headquarters simply discount them as a major source of profits. In addition, according to the tests using the 2016 data, net U.S. assets are positively associated with reinvesting U.S. profits. Not surprisingly, larger investments tend to absorb more locally generated profits.

To summarize, the test results offer preliminary statistical evidence that Chinese investors with significant state ownership (at least 10%) are more likely to have considered government encouragement when investing in the United States.

31 The variable of U.S. profit was measured differently in 2015 and 2016. In 2015, it is a dummy that equals 1 if the Chinese company was profitable, 0 otherwise. In 2016, U.S. profit was measured in a scale from 1 to 5, with 1 being "suffering heavy losses" and 5 being "highly profitable." For tests that use both years' data, I convert the 2016 data into the same dummy as used for the 2015 data.

32 Zhao Jing, "Lou Jiwei: Tigao Guoqi Shangjiao Lirun Minbu Caizheng Quekou" (Lou Jiwei: Raise SOE Profit Submission to Cover Fiscal Deficit), *Jingji Cankao Bao* (Sept. 7, 2015), at http://news.xinhuanet.com/fortune/2015-09/07/c_128202417.htm, last accessed on June 18, 2017.

TABLE 4.6 *State ownership and plan to reinvest most of U.S. profits*

	2016 survey data				2015–16 survey data			
	1	2	3	4	5	6	7	8
State ownership (50%)	−1.085** (0.448)		0.339 (0.5214)		−0.6066* (0.347)		−0.2257 (0.4255)	
State ownership (10%)		−1.256*** (0.4544)		−0.9656* (0.523)		−0.884** (0.3488)		−0.4164 (0.4248)
Investment duration	0.00148 (0.0045)	0.00147 (0.00495)	−0.023 (0.0269)	−0.022 (0.0263)	−0.0269 (0.0166)	−0.0256 (0.0164)	−0.018 (0.0192)	−0.0174 (0.0189)
Net U.S. asset			0.4003* (0.2376)	0.4398* (0.242)				
U.S. revenue							−0.0438 (0.1756)	−0.0098 (0.17998)
U.S. profit			−0.5281 (0.3329)	−0.468 (0.339)				
U.S. profit (2015–16)							−0.793* (0.4365)	−0.7888* (0.429)
Number of observations	112	112	106	106	190	190	151	151

Source: 2015–16 surveys; significance level: ***p < 1%; **p < 5%; *p < 10%; logistic regressions

Meanwhile, they are less likely to commit to reinvesting the U.S. profits. These findings suggest that state-owned Chinese investors differ from private firms in terms of their investment motives.

B Chinese MNE Managers' Perceptions of U.S. Institutions

The CEO of Shanghai CURA, a large Chinese private equity firm, observed that "no country wants to learn from the United States as much as China does."[33] Indeed, the preceding chapter showed that Chinese managers in the United States generally hold U.S. institutions in high esteem. Yet cross-firm variations, though not significant, still exist. Why do some Chinese investors think less positively than others of the various U.S. institutions? Is government ownership of Chinese investors associated with variation in managers' views? It is possible to come up with opposing arguments. On the one hand, managers of SOE-invested businesses, as primary beneficiaries of China's state capitalism, are heavily invested in sustaining the regime. So, out of self-interest, the managers may be inclined to denigrate U.S. institutions. Moreover, as discussed in Chapter 3, the 2008 financial crisis and its aftermath have cast serious doubt on the efficacy of free-market capitalism. Even some of its long-term proponents in the United States began to question its foundations.[34] A number of experts who follow China closely have noted the attitudinal shift among Chinese elites – a more confident China has begun to assert its "rightful" position in the international community.[35] Moreover, the CCP exhorted the Chinese people to "have every confidence in our path, in our theories and in our system."[36] Given that the SOEs remain integrated in the Chinese political hierarchy, one may reasonably expect that managers of SOEs, "confident" in the Chinese model of political economy, would express more critical views about U.S. institutions.[37] Meanwhile, one may observe a negative association between state ownership in Chinese investors and the managers' views if those working for private Chinese firms hold exceedingly favorable views of U.S. institutions. That is certainly possible; for instance, a senior executive of a large private Chinese company thought the U.S. business environment to be vastly superior; "unlike back in China, here we never have to please any government officials."[38]

33 Lin Lu, statement made during a panel discussion at Roads to U.S.–Greenfield Investment vs. Cross-border M & A Forum (June 20, 2017).

34 See, for example, Posner, *A Failure of Capitalism*.

35 Wang Jisi, "China's Search for a Grand Strategy: A Rising Great Power Finds Its Way," 90 *Foreign Affairs* 68 (2011); Thomas J. Christensen, "The Advantages of an Assertive China: Responding to Beijing's Abrasive Diplomacy," 90 *Foreign Affairs* 54 (2011).

36 Shiping Zheng, "Rising Confidence behind the 'Chinese Dream'," 19 *Journal of Chinese Political Science* 35 (2014), 36.

37 Wang, "The Political Logic of Corporate Governance," 631, 654.

38 Interview with a senior executive of a large private Chinese company that manufactures security equipment (Sept. 10, 2012).

TABLE 4.7 *Summary statistics*

Variable	Observations	Mean	Std. dev.	Min.	Max.
U.S. social innovation	313	4.332268	0.7058458	2	5
Congressional attitude towards Chinese companies and products	189	3.031746	0.8926697	1	5
U.S. legal environment	317	3.949527	0.7819005	1	5
U.S. law enforcement capacity	217	3.97235	0.7752959	1	5
U.S. business transparency	317	4.135647	0.6683798	2	5
U.S. business professionalism	221	4.21267	0.6571444	3	5
Trust and integrity in U.S. business	192	4.296875	0.6143064	3	5
Conformity with code of business conduct	316	4.208861	0.6379909	2	5
U.S. business fairness	220	3.663636	0.785453	2	5

Source: 2014–16 surveys

Yet the opposite may also be true. The "assertive" China may reflect ill-coordinated responses to perceived external threats or a power vacuum, not fundamental changes in the perceived efficacy of the Chinese model.[39] The Party's plea for the Chinese people to have confidence in "our path" might also be interpreted as the ruling elite's burgeoning insecurity. Moreover, as discussed in Chapter 3, SOE managers may not differ from those of private firms as they are both immersed in China's embrace of global capitalism.[40] In short, the opinions of the managers may not relate to their employers' ownership type.

To evaluate the conflicting hypotheses, I ran a series of regression tests of the Chinese managers' perceptions about various U.S. institutions. As elaborated in Chapter 3, the CGCC surveys contain multiple questions assessing how the Chinese managers in the United States view the legal, social, political, and business environment of the host country. I use the perception data as dependent variables and assess how ownership in Chinese investors might be associated with them.

For the independent variable of interest, i.e., the ownership character of a Chinese investor, I use the same two state-ownership dummies created earlier. I also control for the following variables that may have some confounding effects. First, the duration of a respondent's U.S. business operation may relate to both the perception of U.S. institutions and state ownership. Chinese companies that have done business in the United States for an extended period, which tend to be state-owned due to previous FDI restrictions, may have been acculturated.[41] Second, the

39 Andrew Scobell and Scott W. Harold, "An 'Assertive' China? Insights from Interviews," 9 *Asian Security* 111 (2013); Andrew J. Nathan and Andrew Scobell, "How China Sees America," 91 *Foreign Affairs* 32 (2012).

40 Steinfeld, *Playing Our Game*, 265.

41 Buckley et al., "Historic and Emergent Trends," 723 (2008).

size of a Chinese investor's U.S. business may also correlate with both its ownership type and the managers' views about the United States. SOEs tend to invest in larger projects. Meanwhile, U.S. investment size, a valid proxy of a Chinese investor's resources available to adapt to the host-country environment, may have an effect on the managers' views.[42] Furthermore, executives running profitable businesses may be more likely to hold positive views about the institutional context, and state ownership may correlate with profitability, so I control for the profit level of a Chinese-invested business in the United States.

As shown in Table 4.8 and Table 4.9, the tests find no significant evidence that state ownership is associated with the Chinese managers' perceptions. In other words, the managers of Chinese companies, regardless of their ownership type, think favorably of U.S. legal, social, and business institutions. Profit level is significant in several model specifications and the coefficients are positive, indicating that managers doing well in the United States are more inclined to justify some of the institutions. Or, alternatively, managers showing faith in U.S. institutions tend to adapt quickly and make their businesses profitable. As noted, research about causality is for a future time. None of the other tested variables is significant. U.S. investment size, for instance, does not affect the overall positive view of Chinese managers about the U.S. business environment. Nor does investment duration seem to matter. The United States charms newcomers and seasoned expatriates alike. Overall, the variations of the opinions are highly idiosyncratic.

In separate tests I add year dummies to assess changes in the perceptions over time. The results for the state-ownership variables remain largely the same. The 2016 year dummy, however, is significant for several of the perceptions; and the coefficients are negative, indicating that the Chinese managers viewed U.S. institutions less favorably than before. If the trend continues, it may eventually have a measurable effect on Chinese investors' desire to adapt. Yet given how positive the current opinions are, a reversal will unlikely materialize in the near future.

In summary, this section empirically tests the associations between state ownership in Chinese investors and their desire to adapt to U.S. institutions. The tests about the investment motives and the Chinese managers' perceptions of U.S. institutions return mixed results. Regarding investment motives, I find some preliminary and non-robust evidence that state ownership is associated with investments driven by short-term policy concerns. To be more concrete, Chinese investors with significant state ownership are more likely to consider government stimulation when investing in the United States and less committed to reinvesting most or all of their U.S. profits. Meanwhile, the Chinese managers, regardless of their employers' ownership character, hold generally positive views about a wide array of U.S. structural institutions. After decades of economic reform, Chinese business elites, including SOE managers, have invariably embraced market capitalism and the institutions that enable it.

42 I use the U.S. revenue variable in the prior tests to approximate investment size.

TABLE 4.8 *State ownership and perceptions of U.S. institutions (state ownership > 50%)*

	Social innovation	Congressional attitude	U.S. legal system	U.S. law enforcement capacity	Business transparency	Business professionalism	Trust and integrity in U.S. business	Code of business conduct	Business fairness
State ownership (50%)	0.[illegible]26	−0.256	0.248	0.088	0.128	0.489	0.165	0.0179	0.406
	(0.[illegible]54)	(0.3596)	(0.352)	(0.353)	(0.359)	(0.366)	(0.374)	(0.362)	(0.355)
Investment duration	0.[illegible]19	−0.0227	0.0216	0.002	0.004	0.013	−0.0102	0.022	−0.0013
	(0.[illegible]167)	(0.0178)	(0.016)	(0.0158)	(0.0166)	(0.017)	(0.019)	(0.0167)	(0.0159)
U.S. revenue	−0.[illegible]22		0.0105	−0.013	−0.023	−0.111		−0.135	−0.146
	(0.[illegible]53)		(0.1436)	(0.145)	(0.145)	(0.147)		(0.15)	(0.152)
U.S. profit	0.[illegible]46*	0.293	−0.079	0.6788*	0.846**	0.5198	0.516	0.992**	−0.069
	(0.[illegible]87)	(0.359)	(0.378)	(0.385)	(0.385)	(0.388)	(0.377)	(0.398)	(0.388)
Number of observations	[illegible]57	121	156	156	157	157	123	156	157

Source: 2014–16 surveys; significance level: ***p < 1%; **p < 5%; *p < 10%; ordered logistic regression

TABLE 4.9 *State ownership and perceptions of U.S. institutions (state ownership > 10%)*

	U.S. social innovation	Congressional attitude	U.S. legal system	U.S. law enforcement capacity	Business transparency	Business professionalism	Trust and integrity in U.S. business	Code of business conduct	Business fairness
State ownership (10%)	.0219	.073	.0727	.0582	.091	.0404	.269	.292	.0997
	(.266)	(.354)	(.347)	(.345)	(.27)	(.343)	(.37)	(.354)	(.326)
Investment duration	.0127	.025	.0241	.0026	.0008	.016	-.0107	.0251	.00066
	(.014)	(.0175)	(.0162)	(.0155)	(.0135)	(.0167)	(.0188)	(.0167)	(.0154)
U.S. revenue			.0345	.0167				.106	
			(.1486)	(.1486)				(.153)	
U.S. profit	.468	.267	.0124	.694*	.635**	.566	.52	1.047***	.0405
	(.288)	(.357)	(.369)	(.376)	(.287)	(.357)	(.376)	(.3919)	(.348)
Number of observations	231	121	156	156	234	158	123	156	158

Source: 2014–16 surveys; significance level: ***p < 1%; **p < 5%; *p < 10%; ordered logistic regression

III ABILITY TO ADAPT TO U.S. INSTITUTIONS

"For Chinese companies, investing in the United States is like an uphill journey without any shortcut," noted the CEO of a large Chinese private equity firm. "We need to rely on the professionals, even though the cost is exorbitant."[43] Echoing the comment, another corporate executive advised Chinese investors to trust local managers if they want to succeed in the United States.[44] The business advice dovetails well with the analytical framework set forth in Chapter 3, which explored foreign investors' ability to conform to local institutions through two lenses: (1) the allocation of decision-making power between the Chinese headquarters and the managers in the United States, and (2) the use of local professionals. According to the findings in Chapter 3, Chinese investors have in general heeded the advice; many of them have localized decision-making and most have relied extensively on U.S. professionals to navigate the complex rule-based business environment. But one can hardly miss the cross-firm variations. Why, then, do some Chinese investors rely more on local managers and professionals than others? This section attempts to answer the question, with a focus on possible connections between the investors' ownership type and their ability to cope with the host country's institutional environment.

A *Allocation of Decision-Making Power*

As noted earlier, personnel management serves as a key mechanism through which the Chinese government controls SOEs.[45] To be specific, SOEs of different levels have their managers appointed by government agencies at corresponding levels. For instance, the CCP Organization Department administers and the Politburo decides the career paths of all the top executives of the largest central SOEs.[46] In addition to personnel control, SASAC, its regional counterparts, and other relevant government agencies oversee the operations of SOEs within their jurisdictions. They review the overall management of state assets, set major targets for the operation of SOEs, and regularly evaluate the performance of managers.[47] Vertical state control naturally extends beyond the Chinese border to SOEs' overseas investments as they constitute a growing portion of total assets. For instance, SASAC has promulgated a series of substantive and procedural rules governing ODI by Chinese SOEs, which in the

43 Lu Lin, CEO of Shanghai CURA, public statement made during a panel discussion at Roads to US–Greenfield Investment vs. Cross-border M & A Forum (June 20, 2017).

44 Fang Peng, president of GCL International, public statement made during a panel discussion at Roads to US–Greenfield Investment vs. Cross-border M & A Forum (June 20, 2017).

45 Zhang et al., "Managerial Risk Preference"; Li, "State-Owned Enterprises in the Current Regime"; Li, "Holding 'China Inc.' Together," 927.

46 Andrew Szamosszegi and Cole Kyle, *An Analysis of State-Owned Enterprises and State Capitalism in China* (2011); Li, "Holding 'China Inc.' Together," 927.

47 Bai and Xu, "Incentives for CEOs with Multitasks," 517.

view of executives have overly restrained outbound investment.[48] The agency also conducts third-party audits of SOEs' overseas assets.[49] In this hierarchical system of state control and supervision, managers at the Chinese headquarters, expecting to be held responsible for the performance of the foreign businesses, naturally want to retain a proportionate amount of decision-making authority.

Moreover, the multilayered agency conflict distinguishes SOEs from private Chinese companies.[50] Because SOE managers' interests and those of the nominal state owners are poorly aligned, the former typically receive highly discounted and distorted returns from corporate performance. Thus SOE managers tend to be highly risk-averse in carrying out their official duties.[51] For the same reason, SOE employees tend to closely follow established procedures. "The outcome from a decision, even if undesirable, is not important as long as we have gone through the set process."[52] In situations where established procedures are lacking, as is often the case when SOEs enter a vastly different foreign market, SOE employees in the foreign market are strongly incentivized to seek instructions from their Chinese superiors in order to limit their own risk exposure. An interviewee who worked closely with numerous state-owned Chinese companies in the United States commented that no large deals can be done because local managers relied too much on instructions from the Chinese headquarters.[53] In sum, for various structural reasons, state-owned Chinese investors may retain more authority to decide matters concerning their U.S. investments.[54]

Yet some scholars have argued the opposite. Chinese SOEs, after the corporatization reform, largely behave like sizable private companies driven by commercial interests.[55] In other words, since the SOEs have adopted a "modern" corporate structure, the incentive structure is such that SOE managers prioritize profit maximization. At least at the middle level, management of large SOEs has "in general become more depoliticized, technically more professional and more market-oriented

48 Li Shaofei, "Yangqi Laozong Lundao 'Zou Chu Qu'" (CEOs of Central SOEs Discuss "Go Global"), 1506 *Liaowang* 22 (2013).

49 Hua Huadi, "Guoziwei Haozi Qianwan Pinqing Disanfang Jiancha Yangqi Jingwai Zichan" (SASAC Spent Millions on Third-Party Audit of Central SOEs' Overseas Assets), *Xinhuawang* (April 15, 2015), at http://news.xinhuanet.com/fortune/2015–04/15/c_1114980695.htm.

50 Cuervo-Cazurra et al., "Governments as Owners."

51 Zhang et al., "Managerial Risk Preference," 1.

52 Interview with a mid-level employee of the U.S. affiliate of a large Chinese state-owned company in information and telecommunication (June 20, 2017).

53 Interview with an executive of a U.S. nonprofit organization that interacts frequently with Chinese companies in the United States (Dec. 7, 2016).

54 Readers should bear in mind that this study does not consider cases where managers use FDI to engage in embezzlement.

55 Erica Downs, *Inside China, Inc.: China Development Bank's Cross-border Energy Deals* (2011); David A. Ralston, Jane Terpstra-Tong, Robert H. Terpstra, Xueli Wang, and Carolyn Egri, "Today's State-Owned Enterprises of China: Are They Dying Dinosaurs or Dynamic Dynamos?", 27 *Strategic Management Journal* 825 (2006); Steinfeld, *Playing Our Game*, 265.

TABLE 4.10 *Summary statistics (additional variables for tests of this subsection)*

Variable	Observations	Mean	Std. dev.	Min.	Max.
U.S. personnel decision (high-level)	170	2.205882	0.966278	1	4
U.S. personnel decision (mid-level)	167	2.688623	0.968816	1	4
U.S. business ownership	191	0.842932	0.364821	0	1

Source: 2014 and 2015 surveys

than the top level."[56] Moreover, building globally competitive SOEs is a strategic goal of the Chinese government.[57] Hence, the management of SOEs' outbound investments should not vary systematically from that of private Chinese firms.

To test the diverging hypotheses, I ran a number of statistical tests. In the first set of tests I used the power to decide major U.S. personnel matters as a proxy for key management decisions concerning U.S. investments. As noted, the survey inquired about the extent to which local managers decide major U.S. personnel matters. The respondents were asked to make a selection that best described their situations: (1) the Chinese headquarters make all the major personnel decisions concerning the U.S. business; (2) the Chinese headquarters make the major personnel decisions after consulting with U.S. managers; (3) the U.S. managers make all the major personnel decisions after consulting with the Chinese headquarters; (4) the U.S. managers make all the major personnel decisions.[58]

Again, the independent variable of interest is state ownership in a Chinese investor. I use the same two dummy variables as previously described. I also include the following control variables. First, U.S. investment size may matter. Chinese investors may be inclined to exert more centralized control over large U.S. investments. Yet the opposite may also be true. Running large U.S. businesses requires immediate attention from employees with local knowledge, whose performance is in turn best assessed by local superiors. For instance, after Wanda Group acquired AMC, the U.S. movie theater chain, for $2.6 billion, it dispatched only one Chinese employee to co-ordinate with local managers.[59] Second, investment duration may matter. Chinese investors who recently entered the U.S. market may continue to exercise tight control over its U.S. businesses. When they have established fully functioning operations, more of the control may be delegated to local managers. For instance, an executive of a Chinese state-owned firm in the United States attributed its high degree of localization

56 Li, "Holding 'China Inc.' Together," 927, 944. 57 Steinfeld, *Playing Our Game*, 265.

58 The 2015 survey broke down the question into decisions about top U.S. managers, mid-level U.S. managers, and nonmanagement employees. In order to combine the two years of data for the statistical tests, I treat the 2014 survey question as equivalent to the question about decisions regarding mid-level U.S. managers in the 2015 survey. Separately, I equate the 2014 question to the 2015 one on high-level U.S. managers. I ran two series of tests using these two alternative variables.

59 Matthew Miller, "Wang Jianlin, China's Property Tycoon, Finds Golden Path to Billions," *Reuters* (Dec. 22, 2014), at www.reuters.com/article/wanda-properties-wang-idUSL3N0U23XF20141222.

TABLE 4.11 *State ownership and management localization (personnel decisions re mid-level U.S. managers)*

	1	2	3	4	5	6
State ownership (50%)	−0.915***		−1.299***		−1.377***	
	(0.314)		(0.405)		(0.426)	
State ownership (10%)		−0.862***		−1.11***		−1.15***
		(0.309)		(0.393)		(0.41)
Investment duration	0.026	0.0218	0.034*	0.027	0.0335	0.025
	(0.016)	(0.0156)	(0.02)	(0.0198)	(0.02)	(0.0203)
Log U.S. asset			−0.072	−0.061	−0.056	−0.0387
			(0.156)	(0.157)	(0.171)	(0.171)
U.S. business ownership					0.5597	0.4998
					(0.538)	(0.54)
number of observations	160	160	102	102	96	96

Source: 2014 and 2015 surveys; significance level: ***p < 1%; **p < 5%; *p < 10%; ordered logistic regression

(98% local hires) to its entry to the market in the 1980s.[60] As noted earlier, U.S. investment duration and state ownership are correlated due to China's FDI policies. To control for possible confounding effects, I add the number of years of doing business in the U.S. to the tests. Third, the degree to which a Chinese investor owns the U.S. business or asset may have some effect on the allocation of decision-making power between the Chinese headquarters and local managers. Everything else being equal, those Chinese investors with whole ownership may have the headquarters exercise more decision-making authority.

The results strongly indicate that state ownership in a Chinese investor is associated with less management localization (see Table 4.11). In other words, Chinese investors with at least 10% government ownership are more likely to retain their control over major personnel decisions in U.S. affiliates. The variable remains significant in all of the model specifications. Also, the results remain largely unchanged when I modify the way to combine the two-year data (see Table 4.12).

As elaborated earlier, layered personnel management plays a crucial role in how the Chinese government maintains its control over SOEs. In the structure, the central government directly manages only the top-level executives of the largest SOEs, which in turn decide on the careers of mid-level managers. The literature has not empirically examined how control might extend abroad to SOEs' foreign businesses, in particular how personnel decisions are allocated between the Chinese headquarters and local management. If the foreign affiliates share the main characteristics of their parent

60 Interview with an executive of the U.S. affiliate of a large Chinese company in construction and real estate (June 23, 2017).

TABLE 4.12 *State ownership and management localization (personnel decisions re high-level U.S. managers)*

	1	2	3	4	5	6
State ownership (50%)	−1.077***		−1.134***		−1.204***	
	(0.312)		(0.394)		(0.412)	
State ownership (10%)		−1.072***		−0.9196**		−0.954**
		(0.3094)		(0.384)		(0.399)
Investment duration	−0.0078	−0.0115	−0.0121	−0.0183	−0.0123	−0.0195
	(0.0156)	(0.0153)	(0.019)	(0.0187)	(0.0197)	(0.019)
Log U.S. asset			0.0624	0.0674	0.0764	0.086
			(0.1601)	(0.1604)	(0.177)	(0.176)
U.S. business ownership					0.4528	0.412
					(0.528)	(0.529)
number of observations	163	163	104	104	98	98

Source: 2014 and 2015 surveys; significance level: ***p < 1%; **p < 5%; *p < 10%; ordered logistic regression

companies, personnel control would manifest in the Chinese firms' U.S. operations. To be more concrete, managers at the headquarters want to retain control over U.S. investments whereas lower-level U.S. employees are incentivized to limit their risk exposure by surrendering decision-making authority. The regression results support this argument.

Moreover, the 2016 survey inquired about how decisions regarding major U.S. legal and compliance issues are made, which directly addresses the theme of this book. The respondents were asked to make a selection from: (1) entirely decided by Chinese headquarters; (2) decided by Chinese headquarters after consulting with U.S. management; (3) decided by U.S. managers after consulting with Chinese headquarters; (4) entirely decided by U.S. management. I use the respondents' selections as the dependent variable to search for possible association between the varying decision allocation and state ownership in Chinese investors. I include investment duration and investment size as control variables.

As shown in the regression results, state ownership in a Chinese investor is significantly associated with centralized decision-making about major U.S. compliance and legal issues (see Table 4.14). The general finding dovetails well with findings from the preceding tests. U.S. investment size is also significant, so the larger the U.S. investment, the more likely it is that decisions about major U.S. legal and compliance matters are made by U.S. managers.

To summarize, compared to private Chinese investors, those with significant state ownership hold a tighter grip on their U.S. businesses. In other words, they retain more authority to decide major personnel, legal, and compliance matters concerning U.S. operations, which should have complex effects on how Chinese firms react

TABLE 4.13 *Summary statistics*

Variable	Observations	Mean	Std. dev.	Min.	Max.
State ownership (50%)	130	0.3307692	0.4723102	0	1
State ownership (10%)	130	0.4307692	0.4970995	0	1
Net U.S. asset	123	2.02439	1.183655	1	4
Investment duration	129	8.465116	9.321553	0*	36

Source: 2016 survey; * investment of less than a year by the time of the survey

TABLE 4.14 *State ownership and decision on major U.S. compliance and legal matters*

	1	2	3	4
State ownership (50%)	−1.348***		−1.364***	
	(0.426)		(0.43)	
State ownership (10%)		−1.268***		−1.425***
		(0.398)		(0.409)
Investment duration	0.0201	0.0193	0.00996	0.009
	(0.0204)	(0.0204)	(0.0214)	(0.021)
Net U.S. asset			0.3125**	0.387**
			(0.157)	(0.1586)
Number of observations	115	115	112	112

Source: 2016 survey; significance level: ***p < 1%; **p < 5%; *p < 10%; ordered logistic regression

to U.S. legal and regulatory institutions. On the one hand, decision-makers' lack of knowledge about the U.S. institutional context should impede effective responses to U.S. institutions when such responses necessitate decisions on nonroutine matters. Aware of the information asymmetry, some Chinese investors have tried to overcome it by frequent on-site inspection of U.S. operations or luring U.S. talent back to the Chinese headquarters.[61] Such efforts may help mitigate the problem but will not eliminate it, given the large institutional gaps between China and the United Sates. On the other hand, the centralization of decision-making power and the risk-aversion of SOE employees due to the misalignment of risks and rewards may actually lead to inefficient overinvestment in compliance with U.S. laws and regulations. "One may lose the year-end bonus if found responsible for poor

[61] For instance, the CEO and founder of a large Chinese manufacturer of 3C-related products visited the United States several times a year to check on operations. And the company hired a senior manager from IBM to work in its headquarters in Beijing. Interview with an executive of this company (Jan 18, 2017); also, Fuyao's CEO and founder travels to the United States once a month to inspect his invested factories. Ylan Q. Mui, "A Chinese Billionaire Is Staking His Legacy – and Thousands of American Jobs – on This Factory in Ohio," *Washington Post* (Oct. 26, 2016), at www.washingtonpost.com/news/wonk/wp/2016/10/26/a-chinese-billionaire-is-staking-his-legacy-and-thousands-of-american-jobs-on-this-factory-in-ohio/?utm_term=.9b6bed47bd52, last accessed on June 25, 2017.

business judgments or mistakes that caused some losses, or even be demoted if the losses are significant. But only serious violations of law or party discipline can get one fired at a large SOE," explained a manager at the U.S. affiliate of a central-level SOE about the abundant caution they took towards compliance.[62] Meanwhile, the reward for optimal risk-taking is tightly capped: "you get a pat on the shoulder and a 'good job!' And that's pretty much it."[63] Hence, in coping with complex and stringent U.S. laws and regulations, local managers of Chinese state-owned investors "tread on thin ice (*ru lü bo bing*)."[64] In other words, all else being equal, Chinese investors with significant state ownership should appear quite adaptive when routine legal and compliance matters are concerned.

B *Reliance on Local Professionals*

"When in trouble, find a lawyer; when in big trouble, find an expensive lawyer," commented the CEO of Wanxiang America (the U.S. affiliate of a large Chinese manufacturer) on how to succeed in the United States.[65] Given the intricacy of U.S. laws and regulations, reliance on local professionals is crucial for compliance. As illustrated in Chapter 3, the vast majority of Chinese firms have engaged U.S. lawyers in their business. Some do so frequently. At the same time, the majority of the survey respondents either had hired or planned to hire full-time compliance staff. Hence, most of the Chinese firms in the United States appear to rely extensively on U.S. professionals. Yet the data also demonstrate significant variations across different firms. Why do some rely more on U.S. professionals than others? This subsection attempts to answer the question and explores in particular whether state ownership in Chinese investors is associated with the variations.

Again, the existing SOE theories provide some plausible hypotheses. First, because of their general risk-aversion, SOE employees tend to seek professional counsel as a means of mitigating personal risk. If something goes wrong, the professional service providers will take the blame. For instance, the chief counsel for the U.S. affiliate of a major Chinese bank claimed to use only the most prestigious law firms in New York because, having followed the advice of the best banking lawyers in town, he would not be held responsible for any mistakes down the road.[66] Hence, SOEs may be more

[62] Interview with a manager of a large Chinese state-owned company in manufacturing and transportation (Jan. 18, 2017).
[63] Interview with a manager of the U.S. affiliate of a Chinese state-owned asset-management company (June 20, 2017).
[64] Interview with an executive of the U.S. affiliate of a large Chinese company in construction and real estate (June 23, 2017).
[65] Public statement made at the Whitepaper Launching event organized by the CGCC on Jan. 19, 2016.
[66] Interview with the chief counsel of the U.S. affiliate of a large Chinese state-owned company in finance and investment (Aug. 3, 2013).

TABLE 4.15 *Summary statistics*

Variable	Observations	Mean	Std. dev.	Min.	Max.
Full-time in-house counsel (licensed U.S. lawyer)	212	0.2971698	0.4580936	0	1
Full-time compliance staff	209	0.4593301	0.4995397	0	1
Use of U.S. lawyer	99	0.6565657	0.4772715	0	1
Log U.S. asset	64	7.261937	1.372454	4.255272	10.93952
Net U.S. asset	123	2.02439	1.183655	1	4

Note: CGCC 2014 or/and 2016 survey

inclined to rely on U.S. professionals. Second, SOE managers may be less sensitive to profit imperatives,[67] and therefore more tolerant of high legal and compliance costs.

Yet some scholars may contend that SOEs operate in the same way as large companies driven by commercial interests. After all, executives of large non-state-owned corporations have the same incentive to circumvent risk by consulting professional opinions. It almost goes without saying that general counsel at a large U.S. company would hire outside lawyers who "make them look good."[68] Moreover, large corporations, regardless of their ownership type, are generally less sensitive to legal and compliance costs. Reliance on professionals may also be a necessity for SOEs as well as private Chinese firms. According to the manager of a state-owned bank, they had to appoint a seasoned American lawyer as compliance director instead of expatriating someone from the headquarters simply because "compliance is too technical (*tai zhuanye*)."[69] This subsection tests the competing hypotheses about the association between state ownership in Chinese investors and the use of local professionals by their U.S. affiliates.

I explore the topic from two angles: (1) reliance by Chinese-invested firms on in-house compliance and legal professionals, and (2) reliance on outside legal counsel. I begin with several tests of possible associations between state ownership in Chinese investors and the use of in-house professional compliance and legal staff. The 2014 and the 2016 surveys inquired about whether the responding firm had full-time in-house compliance staff. From the data, I constructed a dependent dummy variable that equals 1 if the responding firm had full-time compliance staff, 0 otherwise.

The independent variable of interest is state ownership in the Chinese investors. I use the same dummies as in the previous tests. Also, I add investment size and duration as controls. Chinese companies with large U.S. investments presumably confront more complex legal issues and also tend to have more capacity to handle them professionally. In addition, Chinese investors that entered the U.S. market

67 Bai and Xu, "Incentives for CEOs with Multitasks," 517.

68 "The General Counsel's Perspective on Emerging Markets: What Keeps Them Up at Night – Doing Business in and with Emerging Markets 2015," Friday, July 10, 2015, Practising Law Institute.

69 Interview with a former manager of a large Chinese state-owned company in banking (Jan. 24, 2017).

TABLE 4.16 *State ownership and full-time compliance staff*

	1	2	3	4	5	6
State ownership (50%)	−0.1385 (0.323)		−0.561 (0.627)		−0.356 (0.499)	
State ownership (10%)		0.103 (0.308)		−0.834 (0.6203)		−0.0183 (0.4705)
Investment duration	0.0112 (0.0169)	0.0061 (0.0165)	0.0101 (0.035)	0.011 (0.0348)	−0.008 (0.026)	−0.0153 (0.026)
Net U.S. asset (2016 survey)					0.785*** (0.194)	0.7775*** (0.194)
Log U.S. asset (2014 survey)			0.7415*** (0.254)	0.774*** (0.2597)		
Number of observations	197	197	62	62	109	109

Source: 2014 and 2016 surveys; significance level: ***p < 1%; **p < 5%; *p < 10%; logistic regression

recently may not have had sufficient time to build or acquire in-house compliance capacity.

According to the preliminary test results, state ownership is not significantly associated with the hiring of full-time in-house compliance officers. In other words, the regression output indicates that state-owned Chinese investors are no more or less likely to build internal compliance capacity than private Chinese investors. Nor does investment duration have any significant effect on the likelihood. Given the limited sample size, however, the nonsignificant coefficients offer no more than suggestive evidence. As expected, internal compliance capacity is significantly and positively connected to the size of U.S. investment. Bigger U.S. businesses have more need and capacity to handle compliance issues internally.

I also test the possible association between state ownership in Chinese investors and the employment of full-time in-house counsel who are licensed to practice U.S. law. As shown in Table 4.17, except for model specification (4), state ownership variables are not significantly associated with in-house legal capacity. Put differently, everything else held constant, Chinese investors with significant state ownership are no more or less likely than privately owned Chinese investors to hire U.S. lawyers as in-house counsel. Meanwhile, similar to the finding above, U.S. investment size is a highly significant predictor. Companies with large U.S. investments tend to have both the need for in-house capacity to handle U.S. legal matters and the resources to pay for it.

Given the complexity of the U.S. institutional environment, even those Chinese companies with internal U.S. legal and compliance capacity have to rely on outside counsel. I ran a number of tests to explore why reliance on U.S. lawyers varies, with

TABLE 4.17 *State ownership and full-time in-house counsel with license to practice U.S. law*

	1	2	3	4	5	6
State ownership (50%)	–0.222		–1.517		–0.272	
	(0.353)		(0.811)		(0.5803)	
State ownership (10%)		0.282		–1.532**		0.553
		(0.333)		(0.77)		(0.555)
Investment duration	0.0133	0.0029	–0.029	–0.0399	–0.006	–0.021
	(0.018)	(0.017)	(0.044)	(0.043)	(0.0303)	(0.0302)
Net U.S. asset (2016 survey)					1.265***	1.235***
					(0.247)	(0.246)
Log U.S. asset (2014 survey)			1.078***	1.118***		
			(0.33)	(0.3399)		
Number of observations	199	199	62	62	110	110

Source: 2014 and 2016 surveys; significance level: ***p < 1%; **p < 5%; *p < 10%; logistic regression

a focus on the effect of state ownership in Chinese investors. The 2014 survey included a question about how often the responding firms used U.S. lawyers (never, occasionally, and often). From the response data I created a dummy dependent variable that equals 1 if the survey respondent often engaged U.S. lawyers, 0 otherwise. Regarding the independent variable of interest, I use the same two dummy variables for state ownership as used in the previous tests. I also add several control variables. Chinese companies with large U.S. investments tend to generate more complex legal issues, but they are also more capable of affording the cost of external legal services. Hence, I include U.S. investment size as a control. In addition, I include in the tests the availability of full-time in-house counsel, which approximates the amount of legal matter confronting Chinese investors. Last, I add investment duration to the tests as Chinese investors that entered the U.S. market early may have grown accustomed to high legal costs and rely more frequently on U.S. legal services.

The regression results suggest no significant association between state ownership in a Chinese investor and the frequency of using external U.S. legal services. Given the wide gaps between Chinese and U.S. laws, Chinese companies, regardless of their ownership structure, have to rely extensively on local legal professionals. However, because the sample size is small, the results are suggestive evidence and the conclusions remain merely tentative. Investment size is significant across all the model specifications. The result is intuitive as Chinese investors with substantial U. S. investments have more resources to consume costly U.S. legal services. Meanwhile, in-house legal capacity is also significant and positively associated with the use of external U.S. lawyers. The result serves as more direct evidence

TABLE 4.18 *State ownership and frequent use of U.S. lawyers*

	1	2	3	4	5	6
State ownership (50%)	−0.493		−0.623		−0.514	
	(0.628)		(0.663)		(0.702)	
State ownership (10%)		−0.45		−0.599		−0.526
		(0.616)		(0.649)		(0.679)
Investment duration	−0.055	−0.058	−0.054	−0.058	−0.044	−0.047
	(0.038)	(0.037)	(0.04)	(0.0397)	(0.0409)	(0.0402)
Log U.S. asset	0.826***	0.833***	0.697**	0.708**	0.6484**	0.662**
	(0.281)	(0.283)	(0.301)	(0.303)	(0.308)	(0.31)
Full-time in-house counsel			1.197*	1.208*	1.176*	1.193*
			(0.635)	(0.636)	(0.6496)	(0.652)
Number of observations	63	63	62	62	59	59

Source: 2014 survey; significance level: ***p < 1%; **p < 5%; *p < 10%; logistic regression

that Chinese companies facing frequent and complex legal matters tend to engage outside counsel frequently.[70]

In summary, this section empirically examined the possible effects of state ownership on Chinese investors' ability to adapt to U.S. institutions from two angles: the extent of localized decision-making and the use of local professionals. The results show mixed effects of state ownership. Regarding management localization, the tests return robust evidence that ties state ownership to more centralized decision-making. In other words, everything else being equal, the Chinese headquarters of state-owned investors tend to retain more authority to decide major personnel matters pertaining to the operations of their U.S. investments. This finding also holds for decisions concerning major U.S. legal and compliance matters. On the other hand, in terms of reliance on local professionals, the tests find no significant effects of state ownership, which leads to the tentative conclusion that state-owned Chinese firms are just as likely to engage local professionals as are their privately owned counterparts in the United States.

To recapitulate, the empirical tests of this chapter have returned preliminary evidence that Chinese firms owned by the government differ from privately owned firms in several aspects crucial to their adaptation to U.S. institutions. First, regarding institutional distances between China and the United States, Chinese investors with significant state ownership encounter wider legal and regulatory gaps. Formal-law distances held constant, state-owned Chinese investors have to cross larger enforcement gaps when doing business in the United States. Second, Chinese firms with significant state ownership are more likely than privately owned firms to

70 The sample size is small for logit regressions that are based on maximum likelihood. Nonetheless, the results, robust and highly significant, can be seen as strong suggestive evidence.

have considered Chinese government policies when investing in the United States and are less likely to reinvest U.S. profits. Third, state ownership is associated with less decision-making power allocated to U.S. managers. At the same time, the tests produce no significant evidence that state ownership has any impact on the Chinese managers' generally positive opinions of U.S. institutions. Nor does it affect the use of local professionals by Chinese firms in the United States. Among all the findings of significance, those confirming management centralization for state-owned Chinese investors are highly robust and consistent; the rest, sensitive to model specifications, should be taken as suggestive evidence.

As noted repeatedly throughout this chapter, the regression results are not without limitations. First, the sample sizes are relatively small. Though Chinese investment in the United States has experienced fast growth recently, the entire pool of sizable Chinese-invested businesses in the United States remains modest. Thus, readers should refrain from drawing definitive conclusions from the non-significant coefficients. Second, one may be concerned with biases. In general, foreign firms that perform poorly in a host country would have withdrawn their investments, resulting in a potential survival bias. But in this study, the bias is not a major issue because prominent Chinese companies only recently began to invest in the United States and very few have retreated back to China. More importantly, the focus of the study is on how Chinese companies currently operational in the United States react to U.S. legal institutions, so survival bias is a marginal concern. Additionally, the sample is not a representative one of all Chinese-invested businesses in the United States. For purposes of this book, however, the population of interest is the group of Chinese firms with investments that may have a potential impact on U.S. legal institutions, not small businesses such as take-out restaurants or laundromats invested by Chinese families. As noted in Chapter 3, the survey respondents constitute a relatively neutral and representative sample of prominent Chinese companies in the United States. In summary, despite the limitations, the empirical findings of this chapter offer readers an unprecedented and valuable window into how state ownership in Chinese investors is associated with varying reactions to U.S. institutions.

IV CONCLUSION AND INTRODUCTION TO CHAPTERS 5 TO 7

In the preceding chapter, I formulated a heuristic device that guides the analysis of foreign investors' reactions to host-country legal and regulatory institutions through three inquiries: (1) the legal and regulatory distances between the investor's home country and host country, which consist of the distances in relevant formal laws and the distances in law enforcement; (2) the investors' desire to adapt to host-country institutions, which comprises investment motives and the managers' perceptions of host-country institutions; and (3) the investors' ability to adapt to host-country institutions, which includes the allocation of decision-making power and the use of local knowledge. Following the analytical framework, Chapter 3 found wide gaps between Chinese and U.S. legal and regulatory institutions, a general inclination of Chinese managers to adapt, and a generally adequate yet highly variable capacity of Chinese investors to make the necessary adjustments.

But all Chinese companies in the United States are not the same. Chapter 4 empirically investigated cross-firm variations and made a number of interesting findings. First, due to the peculiar law enforcement environment at home, state-owned Chinese investors confront larger legal and regulatory distances than do private Chinese investors in the United States. Second, regarding the desire to adapt to U.S. institutions, the empirical tests suggest that Chinese investors with significant state ownership are more likely to consider short-term policy factors than are private Chinese investors. However, managers of state-invested businesses in the United States hold the same positive views of U.S. institutions as those working for private Chinese investments. Third, regarding the ability to adapt to U.S. institutions, the test results indicate that state-owned investors retain more decision-making authority than privately owned Chinese investors. The allocation impedes compliance that requires well-informed and prompt high-level decisions, but at the same time it may incentivize inefficient overinvestment in routine and technical compliance matters. Moreover, no significant evidence suggests that state ownership makes any difference in the companies' reliance on local professionals. In spite of certain limitations, the overall results are highly suggestive of a measurable connection between significant state ownership in Chinese investors and how they react to U.S. legal and regulatory institutions.

The remainder of this book will further evaluate and substantiate these findings. Applying the analytical framework, I will empirically explore how Chinese firms in the United States cope with the U.S. tax system, U.S. employment law (in particular laws against employment discrimination), and the U.S. regime on national security review of foreign investments (also known as the CFIUS review regime). I choose to focus on these areas for three reasons. First, every Chinese firm, regardless of its size, sector, location, and ownership type, has to file tax returns and employ a workforce, and, as will be discussed, consider the CFIUS risk; whereas issues about Chinese firms that have received broad media coverage such as pollution and poor product quality do not bear on those that operate in the U.S. service sector. Second, these three areas of law are of great policy and theoretical importance; most of the ongoing debates about the impacts of Chinese ODI revolve around the fiscal, labor, and national security impacts of Chinese investments. Those debates, having relied primarily on anecdotal case studies and limited governmental data, are in need of more systematic empirical research. Third, the U.S. institutions in these three areas vary in terms of their distances from the corresponding Chinese institutions and of the Chinese firms' desire and ability to comply.

As illustrated in Figure 4.1, Chinese companies investing in the United States face considerable institutional distances in all three areas. But relatively speaking, the

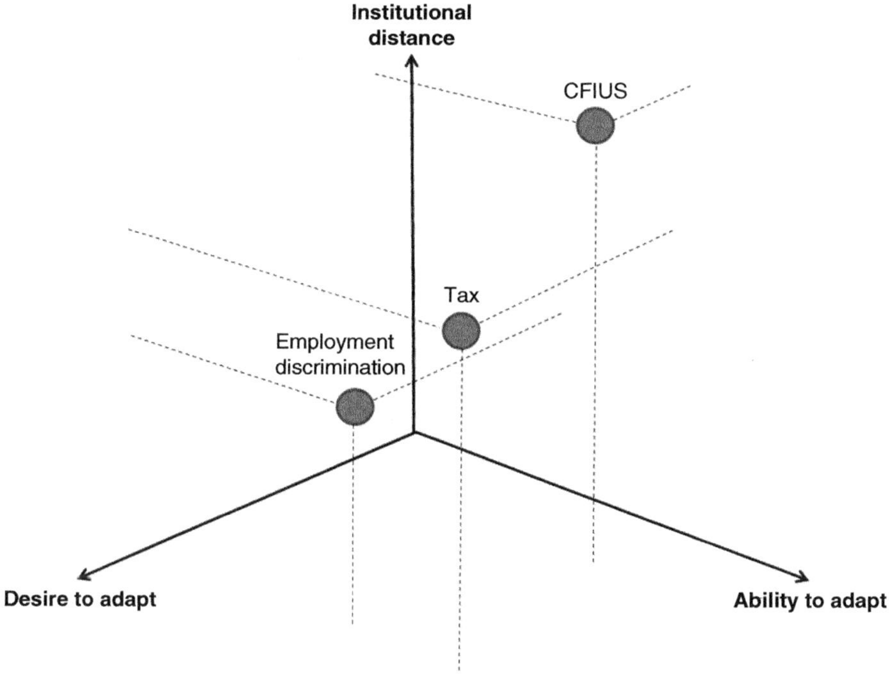

FIGURE 4.1 Mapping the three areas under the analytical framework

gaps in employment discrimination laws are narrower than those in the two countries' tax laws, and both are much narrower than the distance in the laws governing national security review of foreign investments. Thanks to decades of transnational learning and institutional transplant, formal Chinese tax laws and employment discrimination laws have incorporated many of the basic principles and concepts of corresponding U.S. laws. Therefore, Chinese managers in the United States should not feel totally at a loss when coping with those laws. For instance, gender discrimination is legally prohibited in both China and the United States, so even though the law has not been rigorously enforced in China, Chinese managers in the United States should know that a solely gender-based dismissal of a female employee is illegal.

In contrast, CFIUS review is an entirely new institution for Chinese investors, as they did not have to consider national security risk before making any investment back in China. Yet in the United States, CFIUS potentially implicates all Chinese acquisitions of U.S. assets. Also, CFIUS enjoys broad discretion and its review is highly secretive. As a result, most Chinese managers either lack any knowledge of the institution or are critical of it, which shapes their reactions to the CFIUS regime. Moreover, in contrast to U.S. tax and employment laws, the law governing the CFIUS process has been directly impacted by Chinese investment and subsequently undergone substantial modification.

A road map for the rest of this book follows. Chapter 5 empirically examines how Chinese companies investing in the United States respond to the complex U.S. tax system; Chapter 6 explores the reactions of Chinese companies to U.S. laws prohibiting employment discrimination; next, Chapter 7 investigates how Chinese investors interact with the U.S. regime for national security review of foreign investments. Following the general analytical frame previously formulated in Chapter 3, each of Chapters 5 to 7 will begin with a comparative institutional analysis that identifies the legal and regulatory gaps between the two countries in the specific area under study. It will then explore the desire and ability of Chinese companies to adapt by examining how Chinese managers view U.S. institutions and the extent to which local professionals are employed to handle matters in that legal area. Last, each of the three chapters will empirically analyze whether and how state ownership in the Chinese investors associates with their reactions to the U.S. institutions.

5

Chinese Companies in the U.S. Tax System

[China] should abolish VAT and only tax income, just like the U.S.[1]

Cao Dewang, chairman of Fuyao Glass, a Chinese company with substantial investments in the United States

I have long advocated a VAT as the linchpin of reforming [the U.S.] tax system[2]

Michael J. Graetz, professor of tax law at Columbia Law School

An interview in June 2017 with a senior executive of a large state-owned Chinese company began unexpectedly with the executive's solicitation of legal advice. Over the past decade or two, her company had set up a number of entities in the United States with different business objectives. One of them has functioned solely as liaison for the Chinese headquarters. The company initially intended to create and operate it as a foreign office. Then a U.S. lawyer suggested incorporation. Incorporate it did. Since then, however, the entity has never paid any U.S. tax because "it has not had any income."[3] All of its expenses are covered by funds allocated from the Chinese headquarters. On occasion, the headquarters would express some concern that an incorporated business in the United States pays no U.S. tax for an extended period. What prompted the executive's question during the interview was a lunch conversation the day before with managers from several other Chinese companies that had set up liaison offices in the United States. It turned out that they had all done it differently. "Some operate the U.S. offices as

1 Zhang Quanwei, "Cao Dewang: Gongkai Jiang Shuifu Zhiwei Tixing Weijigan" (Cao Dewang: Talk about Tax Burden to Alert Threat), *Xinjingbao* B04–05 (Dec. 21, 2016), at http://cnews.chinadaily.com.cn/2016-12/21/content_27729881.htm, last accessed on Jan. 19, 2017.

2 Michael J. Graetz, "VAT as the Key to Real Tax Reform," in Tax Analyst, *The VAT Reader: What a Federal Consumption Tax Would Mean for America* (2011), 112.

3 Interview with an executive of the U.S. affiliate of a large Chinese company in the energy and natural-resources sector (June 9, 2017).

offices, others treat them as branches."[4] Knowledge about the apparent disparity must have caused confusion and added some justification to the headquarters' concern. "What's the proper form? . . . We are a big state-owned company; we don't want to break any law just to save on taxes."[5]

The conversation echoes what this book has found so far. That is, Chinese investors typically confront wide institutional gaps when doing business in the United States; they rely on local professionals, and are generally inclined to adapt to the host country's legal environment. But does this state-owned conglomerate represent other Chinese companies in the United States? More specifically, do Chinese companies in the United States approach tax compliance with abundant caution, or engage in opportunistic compliance and aggressive tax planning, or, worse yet, evade U.S. taxes whenever they can? And does state ownership of the company have something to do with the reluctance to "break any law to save on taxes"? This chapter answers these questions by empirically investigating how Chinese companies react to the complex and law-based U.S. tax system.

Taxation has been at the heart of the literature on foreign direct investment (FDI); of the many studies on the broad topic, those concerning the taxation of multinational enterprises (MNEs) have probably garnered the most attention from practitioners, scholars, and policymakers. The existing research covers a broad range of tax issues such as the fiscal effect of corporations' tax avoidance on state-sponsored welfare,[6] the corporate response to tax inducement,[7] and the level of international co-operation in tax policymaking and implementation.[8] Despite the expansive thematic coverage, the literature has so far focused on MNEs headquartered in developed countries and offered few clues about soaring outbound FDI (ODI) from developing countries.[9] As noted earlier, the Chinese ODI marks a seismic shift in the global economic order and exhibits two distinct features: (1) most of the Chinese investors have been thriving in poor regulatory

4 Ibid. 5 Ibid.

6 See, e.g., Reuven S. Avi-Yonah, "Globalization, Tax Competition, and the Fiscal Crisis of the Welfare State," 113 *Harvard Law Review* 1573 (2000), 1579.

7 See generally Sebastian Krautheim and Tim Schmidt-Eisenlohr, "Heterogeneous Firms, 'profit shifting' FDI and International Tax Competition," 95 *Journal of Public Economics* [illegible] (2011); Thiess Buettner and Martin Ruf, "Tax Incentives and the Location of FDI: Evidence from a Panel of German Multinationals," 14 *International Tax and Public Finance* 151 (2007); Mihir A. Desai, C. Fritz Foley, and James R. Hines Jr., "Foreign Direct Investment in a World of Multiple Taxes," 88 *Journal of Public Economics* 2727 (2004); Nathan M. Jensen, "Fiscal Policy and the Firm: Do Low Corporate Tax Rates Attract Multinational Corporations?", 45 *Comparative Political Studies* 1004 (2011).

8 See generally Kimberly A. Clausing, "Multinational Firm Tax Avoidance and Tax Policy," 62 *National Tax Journal* 703 (2009); Michael Plowgian, "BEPS: The Shifting International Tax Landscape and What Companies Should Be Doing Now," 65 *Tax Executive* 255 (2013).

9 According to the most recent report on global FDI, "nine of the 20 largest investor countries were from developing or transition economies." UNCTAD, *World Investment Report 2015* (2016), at http://unctad.org/en/PublicationsLibrary/wir2015_en.pdf.

environments,[10] and (2) the "visible hand" of the state exerts a powerful influence,[11] either directly through laws and policies or indirectly through the control over state-owned enterprises (SOE).[12] The two distinct features pose novel and important law and policy questions that the existing literature has failed to address.

This chapter provides some preliminary answers from a tax-compliance perspective. China-based MNEs, having thrived in the Chinese regulatory environment, face daunting compliance challenges in the United States. Of all the challenges, their need to comply with the U.S. tax law clearly stands out as among the most demanding. Thus, a study of how they react to the complex law-based U.S. tax system elucidates their adaptations to other legal and regulatory institutions. Moreover, this chapter explores the effect of government ownership on the Chinese companies' reactions to the U.S. tax system. The findings will shed light on important, albeit underexplored, questions about the taxation of SOEs in a globalized economy. In addition, on a practical level, U.S. tax professionals, and federal and state tax agencies, would benefit from more knowledge about Chinese investors' U.S. tax practices. Furthermore, this chapter will contribute to an informed debate about the costs and benefits, especially long-term fiscal benefits, of burgeoning FDI from China.

The chapter proceeds as follows. In section I, I briefly review the literature on FDI and taxation. In section II, by way of a comparative introduction to the Chinese tax system, I highlight the wide legal and regulatory gaps in this area and the challenges for Chinese investors operating under the U.S. tax law. Section III provides an empirical overview of the desire and the ability of Chinese investors to comply with the U.S. tax system. Next, section IV explores actual compliance by examining Chinese companies' U.S. tax planning and their frictions with the federal tax agency. Section V statistically analyzes the effects of state ownership. A brief conclusion follows.

I FOREIGN DIRECT INVESTMENT AND TAXATION

The existing literature on FDI and taxation revolves around three major themes. First and foremost, the scholarship concentrates on the connections between tax

10 Samuel Adomako and Albert Danso, "Regulatory Environment, Environmental Dynamism, Political Ties, and Performance: Study of Entrepreneurial Firms in a Developing Economy," 21 *Journal of Small Business and Enterprise Development* 212 (2014), 214.

11 See generally Anne S. Tsui, Claudia Bird Schoonhoven, Marshall W. Meyer, Chung-Ming Lau, and George T. Milkovich, "Organization and Management in the Midst of Societal Transformation: The People's Republic of China," 15 *Organization Science* 133 (2004); Benjamin L. Liebman and Curtis J. Milhaupt, "The Institutional Implications of China's Economic Development," in Liebman and Milhaupt, *Regulating the Visible Hand?*.

12 For instance, investment by Chinese state-owned enterprises accounted for approximately 80% of Chinese cumulative investment stock. Ping Deng, "Tongguo Yanjiu Zhongguo Duiwai Touzi Fazhan Lilun: Xianshi yu Jianyi" (Chinese Outward Direct Investment Research: Theoretical Integration and Recommendations), 9 *Management and Organization Review* 513 (2013), 519.

rates and the flow of investment. Some find that changing tax rates significantly impact the amount of FDI.[13] More specifically, corporate tax liability factors into business decisions such as allocation of revenue and expense, direction of capital flow, and location of investment.[14] Most governments, aware of the correlation between tax rates and FDI, engage in a competitive reduction of corporate tax.[15] This "race to the bottom" spurs a major debate on policy reactions and their consequences.[16] Though some sound the alarm of fiscal crisis in welfare countries,[17] others praise the "tax havens" for contributing to efficiency in global capital allocation or being even "welfare-increasing for high-tax countries."[18]

However, when developing countries are brought into the picture, the strong and linear correlation between low tax rates and high FDI weakens. For instance, only middle-income developing countries are found to benefit from bilateral tax treaties,[19] and for the tax inducements to work, a primary condition is good governance.[20] Similarly, when governments of transitional states make tax concessions, they fail to attract FDI.[21] A plethora of research explores such signs of causal

13 See generally Deborah L. Swenson, "The Impact of U.S. Tax Reform on Foreign Direct Investment in the United States," 54 *Journal of Public Economics* 243 (1994); Michael L. Moore, Bert M. Steece, and Charles W. Swenson, "An Analysis of the Impact of State Income Tax Rates and Bases on Foreign Investment," 62 *Accounting Review* 671 (1987); Michael P. Devereux and Harold Freeman, "The Impact of Tax on Foreign Direct Investment: Empirical Evidence and the Implications for Tax Integration Schemes," 2 *International Tax and Public Finance* 85 (1995); Christian Bellak and Markus Leibrecht, "Do Low Corporate Income Tax Rates Attract FDI? Evidence from Central and East European Countries," 41 *Applied Economics* 2691 (2009).

14 See generally Agnès Bénassy-Quéré, Lionel Fontagné, and Amina Lahrèche-Révil, "How Does FDI React to Corporate Taxation?", 12 *International Tax and Public Finance* 583 (2005); John Mutti and Harry Grubert, "Empirical Asymmetries in Foreign Direct Investment and Taxation," 62 *Journal of International Economics* 337 (2004); Steven P. Cassou, "The Link between Tax Rates and Foreign Direct Investment," 29 *Applied Economics* 1295 (1997); Buettner and Ruf, "Tax Incentives and the Location of FDI," 151.

15 See generally Michael P. Devereux, Ben Lockwood, and Michela Redoano, "Do Countries Compete over Corporate Tax Rates?", 92 *Journal of Public Economics* 1210 (2008); Céline Azémar and Andrew Delios, "Tax Competition and FDI: The Special Case of Developing Countries," 22 *Journal of the Japanese and International Economies* 85 (2008).

16 See generally Victor M. Gastanaga, Jeffrey B. Nugent, and Bistra Pashamova, "Host Country Reforms and FDI Inflows: How Much Difference Do They Make?", 26 *World Development* 1299 (1998); David G. Hartman, "Tax Policy and Foreign Direct Investment in the United States," 37 *National Tax Journal* 475 (1984); James R. Hines Jr., "Lessons from Behavioral Responses to International Taxation," 52 *National Tax Journal* 305 (1999).

17 Reuven S. Avi-Yonah, "Globalization, Tax Competition, and the Fiscal Crisis of the Welfare State," 113 *Harvard Law Review* 1573 (2000), 1573.

18 Qing Hong and Michael Smart, "In Praise of Tax Havens: International Tax Planning and Foreign Direct Investment," 54 *European Economic Review* 82 (2010), 84.

19 Eric Neumayer, "Do Double Taxation Treaties Increase Foreign Direct Investment to Developing Countries?", 43 *Journal of Development Studies* 1501 (2007), 1518–19.

20 Dhammika Dharmapala and James R. Hines Jr., "Which Countries Become Tax Havens?", 93 *Journal of Public Economics* 1058 (2009), 1065–6.

21 Jürgen Beyer, "'Please Invest in Our Country': How Successful Were the Tax Incentives for Foreign Investment in Transition Countries?", 35 *Communist and Post-Communist Studies* 191 (2002), 208.

nonlinearity along with the institutional and structural factors that affect tax incentives designed to attract FDI.[22] Moreover, to supplement the findings from the cross-country econometric research, in-depth studies have been undertaken to explore the relationship between tax incentives and FDI in individual developing countries.[23]

Despite the growing attention to developing countries, the existing literature fails to address the two major questions pertinent to the new wave of emerging-market FDI flowing into developed countries. One, having focused narrowly on the relationship between "tax rate" and "investment," very few scholars have systematically examined how investors from developing countries such as China react to complex and law-based tax systems in their host developed countries.[24] Two, the current research lacks any empirical study concerning tax compliance by SOEs investing and operating in developed countries. This chapter narrows the gaps by empirically examining how Chinese companies in the United States interact with the U.S. tax system. It also investigates the possible associations between state ownership of Chinese investors and their tax compliance in the United States.

II THE INSTITUTIONAL DISTANCE IN TAX BETWEEN CHINA AND THE UNITED STATES

Applying the analytical framework formulated in Chapter 3, I first present an institutional comparison of the tax systems in China and the United States. As will be shown, wide institutional gaps exist between the two countries in both formal tax laws and their enforcement. Being an integral part of China's dramatic transformation in the past few decades, Chinese laws in the tax area underwent fundamental changes. Before the dawn of the economic reform, the state owned almost all business organizations in China, rendering a comprehensive tax system redundant. In the decade before 1994, Chinese tax policies and revenue collection methods went through a turbulent period. The government initially implemented the *li gai shui* (profit-to-tax) reform, replacing revenue extraction from state-owned

22 See, e.g., Quan Li, "Democracy, Autocracy, and Tax Incentives to Foreign Direct Investors: A Cross-national Analysis," 68 *Journal of Politics* 62 (2006), 69–71; Nathan M. Jensen, "Fiscal Policy and the Firm: Do Low Corporate Tax Rates Attract Multinational Corporations?", 45 *Comparative Political Studies* 1004 (2011), 1019–20.

23 See, e.g., Samuel Tung and Stella Cho, "The Impact of Tax Incentives on Foreign Direct Investment in China," 9 *Journal of International Accounting, Auditing and Tax* 105 (2000); Samuel Tung and Stella Cho, "Determinants of Regional Investment Decisions in China: An Econometric Model of Tax Incentive Policy," 17 *Review of Quantitative Finance and Accounting* 167 (2001).

24 Recent empirical research on norms and compliance uncovered evidence that foreign institutions such as corrupt social norms exert significant influence on the foreign persons' compliance behavior in the United States. Raymond Fisman and Edward Miguel, "Corruption, Norms, and Legal Enforcement: Evidence from Diplomatic Parking Tickets," 115 *Journal of Political Economy* 1020 (2007), 1022. Another empirical study uncovers a connection between tax noncompliance and U.S. companies controlled by foreign investors based in corrupt societies. Jason DeBacker, Bradley T. Heim, and Anh Tran, "Importing Corruption Culture from Overseas: Evidence from Corporate Tax Evasion in the United States," 117 *Journal of Financial Economics* 122 (2015), 123–4.

enterprises with enterprise tax in order to incentivize management efficiency.[25] To stimulate local economic growth, the central government relied on a fiscal contract scheme according to which provincial governments collected taxes and remitted a negotiated amount to the center. Provincial officials in turn would negotiate with local governments about the allocation of subprovincial revenues. The system greatly benefited the lower governments and led to a sharp decline in the ratio of government revenue to GDP, a contraction of central revenue relative to provincial revenue, and high revenue volatility, which threatened the center's governance capacity.[26]

Following the policy guideline of "unifying tax laws, equalizing tax burdens, simplifying the tax system, and rationalizing the allocation of tax authority,"[27] the central government in 1994 implemented a systematic fiscal reform that laid the groundwork for most subsequent development. The reform institutionalized the allocation of revenues between the central and local governments, greatly expanded the value added tax (VAT), and allocated the lion's share of VAT to the central government.[28] The post-reform taxes fit in three general categories: national taxes, taxes shared by central and local governments, and local taxes.[29] National taxes include customs duty, consumption tax, income tax of central enterprises, income tax of banks, etc. Taxes shared between central and local governments include VAT, resource tax, and securities transaction tax. Seventy-five percent of VAT, the major revenue source after the reform, is allocated to the central government. Most other taxes belong exclusively to local governments. Since the 1994 reform, the government has been fine-tuning the tax system, and recently it converted business tax to the more efficient VAT.[30]

After the 1994 reform and the subsequent amendments that "reflected an incremental process of policy and legal transplants in the name of modernization,"[31] the Chinese government has set up a comprehensive tax regime befitting a market economy. Nevertheless, the tax systems of China and the United States differ in many aspects. In terms of the formal tax institutions, one key difference between China and the United States is VAT. Absent in the United States, VAT accounts for

25 Alfred Tat-Kei Ho and Meili Niu, "Rising with the Tide without Flipping the Boat? Analyzing the Successes and Challenges of Fiscal Capacity Building in China," 33 *Public Administration and Development* 29 (2013).

26 Wang Shaoguang and An'gang Hu, *The Chinese Economy in Crisis: State Capacity and Tax Reform* (2001), 13–17.

27 Deng Liping, *Shuishou zhidu lilun yu shiwu* (Theory and Practice of a Tax System) (2007), 91.

28 Jane K. Winn and Angela Zhang, "China's Golden Tax Project: A Technological Strategy for Reducing VAT Fraud," 4 *Peking University Journal of Law School* 1 (2013), 1.

29 Stephen B. Herschler, "The 1994 Tax Reforms: The Center Strikes Back," 6 *China Economic Review* 239 (1995).

30 Wei Cui, "China's Business-Tax-to-VAT Reform: An Interim Assessment," 5 *British Tax Review* 617 (2014).

31 Jinyan Li, "Tax Transplants and the Critical Role of Processes: A Case Study of China," 3 *Journal of Chinese Tax and Policy* 85 (2013).

more revenue than any other tax in China's government coffers. Moreover, the formal tax laws in China constitute a unified institution, whereas the U.S. tax system mirrors the federalist political structure. In addition, Chinese tax laws on paper are much less complex than U.S. tax laws.

Differences between the two countries are also apparent in formal tax administration. While the U.S. government relies heavily on voluntary compliance for income reporting and tax collection,[32] China depends on a labor-intensive administrative system. Chinese tax bureaus at all levels employ about 755,000 full-time agents, roughly half of whom work for local and regional governments.[33] While the tax administration in the United States reflects its federalist political regime, where state and local tax agencies function largely independently from the IRS, China features a hierarchical dual structure for tax administration. The State Administration of Taxation (SAT) in Beijing leads offices of the State Tax Bureau (STB) at the provincial, municipal and district, and county levels, in order of decreasing rank.[34] Each provincial government also controls a regional tax administration agency, the local tax bureau (LTB), which is subject to the dual leadership of the SAT and the provincial government.[35]

The Chinese tax agencies formally derive their administrative authority from the PRC Law on the Administration of Tax Collection[36] and other substantive laws, such as the PRC Law on Individual Income Tax and the PRC Law on Enterprise Income Tax.[37] Moreover, the SAT and the Ministry of Finance (the Chinese equivalent of the U.S. Treasury Department) possess extensive legislative power.[38] Lawful or not, lower tax agencies also issue rules that Chinese taxpayers generally obey.[39]

Except for matters relating to VAT, formal tax administration and compliance procedures in China and the United States share some common features. Taxpayers in both countries register with relevant tax bureaus, periodically report certain information required by the law, and pay taxes or receive refunds on a regular basis.[40] All these procedures are governed by law; and formal institutions exist to protect taxpayers' legal rights. Similar to the U.S. administrative appeal mechanism, Chinese taxpayers have the legal right to challenge tax agency actions via a petition

[32] J. T. Manhire, "There Is No Spoon: Reconsidering the Tax Compliance Puzzle," 17 *Florida Tax Review* 1 (2014), 2.

[33] *State Administration of Taxation*, official website of the STB (2012), at www.chinatax.gov.cn/n6669073/n6669133/6886063.html.

[34] *Shuiwu Zuzhi Jigou* (Organizational Structure of Tax Administration), official website of the STB, at www.chinatax.gov.cn/n8136506/n8136608/n8138877/n11897218/11901206.html.

[35] Ibid.

[36] PRC Law on the Administration of Tax Collection, arts. 1 and 2, chap. 1, at www.gov.cn/banshi/2005-08/31/content_146791.htm.

[37] Shuishou Zhidu de Falu Jici ("The Ranking of Laws Concerning Tax Collection"), at www.chinatax.gov.cn/n8136506/n8136608/n8138877/n11897113/11900938.html.

[38] Li, "Dare You Sue the Tax Collector?", 64. [39] Ibid.

[40] Various provisions of the PRC Law on the Administration of Tax Collection.

for reconsideration by a designated body in the tax bureau.[41] In contrast to the appeal procedure with the IRS, however, Chinese taxpayers usually have to pay the assessed tax before filing a petition.[42] Once the Chinese taxpayers have exhausted the administrative recourse, they may turn to the courts.[43] Unlike in the United States, Chinese tax agencies typically bear the burden of proof to demonstrate that the disputed administrative acts are lawful.[44] After a trial and a court decision, any unsatisfied parties may then appeal to a higher court.[45]

This brief comparative description demonstrates substantial distances in formal tax laws and tax administration between China and the United States, though in a few respects, such as tax compliance procedures and the availability of judicial review, the two countries share some common features. Moreover, in terms of revenue composition, the Chinese unified tax system depends heavily on VAT, whereas the U.S. federalist tax regime draws most of its revenue from income. Additionally, Chinese tax law on paper is much simpler than U.S. tax law.

In comparison to the large gaps in formal tax laws and administration, the enforcement and compliance gaps between China and the United States are even wider. Though in theory Chinese tax agencies may administer revenue collection strictly according to the law, and Chinese taxpayers, if they so intend, may act in ways akin to their U.S. counterparts in terms of compliance, the Chinese taxpayer's power status relative to the tax agency often dictates the terms of compliance and the actual administration of taxes.[46] Some Chinese taxpayers, such as senior managers of SOEs, hold official status in the state apparatus and therefore enjoy enormous policymaking power as well as power to negotiate favorable tax treatments.[47] The elevated power status of the managers shapes the SOEs' tax compliance and

41 Petitions against bureaus of the STB are handled by the bureau of the next higher level. Petitions against an office of the LTB may be filed with either the corresponding local government or the bureau of a higher rank, unless otherwise stipulated by regional rules. Petitions against the STB in Beijing may be filed with the bureau itself. Petitions should in general be filed, orally or in writing, within sixty days after knowledge of the concrete administrative action. See Shuiwu Xingzheng Fuyi Guize (Rules re Tax Administrative Reconsideration), Guojia Shuiwu Zongju Ling No.21 (STB Rule No. 21) (April 1, 2010), at www.chinatax.gov.cn/n8136506/n8136593/n8137537/n8138502/9563669.html.

42 PRC Law on the Administration of Tax Collection, art. 88.

43 Ibid.

44 PRC Administrative Litigation Law, art. 32. In the case of the United States, the burden of proof may under certain limited conditions shift from the taxpayers to the IRS. See more details in IRC § 7491.

45 PRC Administrative Litigation Law, art. 80.

46 The variation in regulatory compliance has been studied in more detail in non-tax areas such as labor and employment. See, e.g., Sean Cooney, Sarah Biddulph, and Ying Zhu, *Law and Fair Work in China* (2013).

47 Wei Cui, "Taxation of State-Owned Enterprises: A Review of Empirical Evidence from China," in Liebman and Milhaupt, *Regulating the Visible Hand?*, 109; Zhiyong An, "Taxation and Foreign Direct Investment (FDI): Empirical Evidence from a Quasi-experiment in China," 19 *International Tax and Public Finance* 660 (2012), 662. Some, however, argue that SOEs pay more taxes in China. See Oliver Zhen Li, Hang Liu, and Chenkai Ni, "Controlling Shareholders' Incentive and Corporate Tax Avoidance: A Natural Experiment in China" (Feb. 26, 2014), at *SSRN*, http://ssrn.com/abstract=2401619.

precludes tax controversies. If tax disputes ever occur, the powerful taxpayers and relevant tax agencies resolve them as equals via channels within the state apparatus; few would ever adjudicate,[48] not for a general fear of state authorities but for a shared understanding of the lack of judicial efficacy.[49] Of course, due to the high cost of political bargaining, accountants for the SOEs deal with routine tax matters in accordance with rules and conventional practices. Overall, as in other legal areas, the cost of noncompliance with tax law is relatively low for large SOEs in China.

In comparison, small and medium-sized private Chinese companies that do not have much power rely heavily on personal connections with tax agents for tax compliance.[50] Deviation from formal tax law is so widespread that "every company will be found in violation of the tax law if the government seriously investigates."[51] When tax disputes arise, these taxpayers refrain from formal resolution (e.g., administrative appeals or administrative litigation) and strive to settle.[52] Lawsuits against tax agencies only occur in endgame situations.[53]

Because of the high stakes, large private Chinese companies and MNEs put more reliance on formal law. As discussed earlier, the enormous cost of building protective personal connections on a national scale and their lack of formal political status preclude large private firms from the special treatment enjoyed by Chinese SOEs. Though these large private companies may possess some de facto power over government policies, the lack of a common identity vitiates their ability to act collectively.[54] Without substantial political power, large private firms and MNEs in China usually invest more to mitigate the risk of noncompliance.

The three stylized models of tax compliance in China are not mutually exclusive, as most sizable corporate taxpayers in China take multiple measures to mitigate their compliance risk. For instance, despite their formal political status, SOEs nonetheless spend lavishly on entertaining government officials to maintain co-operative personal relationships.[55] And private Chinese companies, while investing heavily in cultivating good connections with government officials, eagerly seek official

48 Li, "Dare You Sue the Tax Collector?", 58.

49 For a detailed discussion about the fear of state authorities and the deterrence effect it generates in tax compliance in China, see Benjamin Van Rooij, "Weak Enforcement, Strong Deterrence: Dialogues with Chinese Lawyers about Tax Evasion and Compliance," 41 *Law and Social Inquiry* 288 (2016).

50 See, e.g., Katherine R. Xin and Jone L. Pearce, "Guanxi: Connections as Substitutes for Formal Institutional Support," 39 *Academy of Management Journal* 1641 (1996).

51 Qian Wang and Xuena Li, "Jie Qiye Er Yu" (Destroying the Tax Basis by Overtaxing Companies), *Xinshiji* (New Century Magazine) (Aug. 27, 2012), at http://magazine.caixin.com/2012-08-24/100428102.html.

52 Li, "Dare You Sue the Tax Collector?", 68–9. 53 Ibid.

54 Kellee S. Tsai, "Capitalists without a Class: Political Diversity among Private Enterprises in China," 38 *Comparative Political Studies* 1130 (2005), 1150.

55 See, e.g., Hongbin Cai, Hanming Fang, and Lixin Colin Xu, "Eat, Drink, Firms, Government: An Investigation of Corruption from the Entertainment and Travel Costs of Chinese Firms," 54 *Journal of Law and Economics* 55 (2011). The study finds no significant variation in travel and entertainment costs incurred by Chinese firms of different ownership structures.

membership in the ruling party or other formal political organizations.[56] Yet despite the overlap, the three stylized models capture the core features of tax compliance in China.[57]

Another main distinction between China and the United States regarding tax administration and compliance concerns the role of the judiciary. In China, tax agencies are almost always the ultimate decision-maker in cases of ambiguity and controversy;[58] and Chinese taxpayers rarely litigate against tax agencies.[59] In the United States, by contrast, taxpayers commonly sue the IRS over tax matters.[60] The U.S. Tax Court, independent of the IRS, plays an essential part in resolving disputes and interpreting the law.[61] U.S. federal courts also adjudicate tax disputes as a neutral third party.[62] In addition, state and local courts adjudicate numerous tax cases each year. Given the largely impartial role of the judiciary, the power distribution between taxpayers and the tax agency matters less in compliance and enforcement, which is in strong contrast to the situation in China. In light of the significant institutional distances between the two countries in the area of tax, how do Chinese companies in the United States react to the complex and law-based U.S. tax system? Moreover, does Chinese government ownership in an investor make any difference? Drawing on the survey data, the following section empirically explores these two topics.

III THE DESIRE AND THE ABILITY TO ADAPT TO THE U.S. TAX SYSTEM

How do Chinese firms in the United States respond to the vast institutional gaps in tax? To be more specific, do they adopt a conservative approach to tax compliance and interact with U.S. tax agencies with great caution? Do they engage in opportunistic compliance and aggressively avoid U.S. tax? Or do they choose to ignore the differences and export their home-state practices? Following the analytical framework presented in Chapter 3, this section answers the questions by empirically examining foreign investors' desire and ability to adapt to U.S. institutions.

A *Perceptions of the U.S. Tax System*

First, I explore the desire of Chinese investors to adapt to the U.S. tax system. In doing so, I focus on two variables, investment motives and perceptions of U.S.

56 Hongbin Li, Lingsheng Meng, Qian Wang, and Li-An Zhou, "Political Connections, Financing and Firm Performance: Evidence from Chinese Private Firms," 87 *Journal of Development Economics* 283 (2008), 296.

57 To a certain extent, the stylized models also describe tax enforcement and compliance in the United States, e.g., the substantial tax benefits due to lobbying by large U.S. corporations. Brian Kelleher Richter, Krislert Samphantharak, and Jeffrey F. Timmons, "Lobbying and Taxes," 53 *American Journal of Political Science* 893 (2009), 906. So the difference is a matter of degree.

58 Li, "Dare You Sue the Tax Collector?", 68–9.

59 Ibid.

60 Ibid., at 57.

61 For an elaborate history of the court and its importance, see David Laro, "Evolution of the Tax Court as an Independent Tribunal," 1995 *University of Illinois Law Review* 17 (1995).

62 K. Martin Worthy, "The Tax Litigation Structure," 5 *Georgia Law Review* 248 (1970), 348–50.

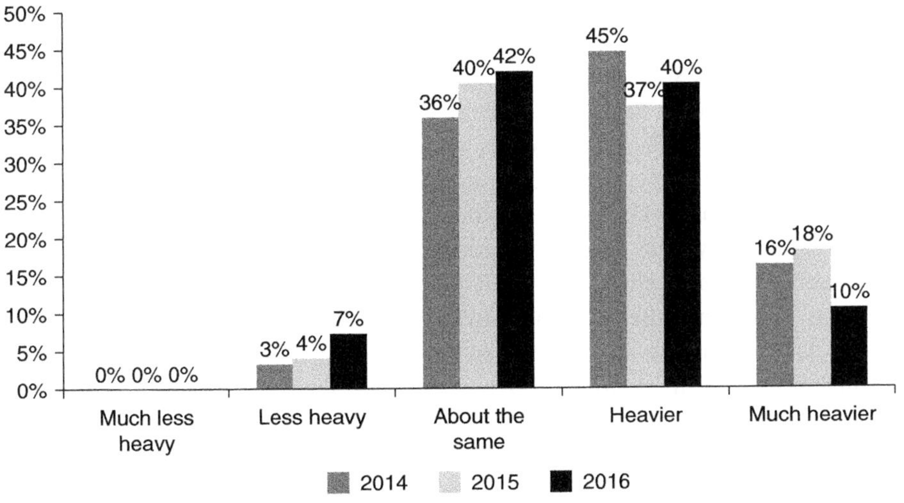

FIGURE 5.1 Perception of the U.S. tax burden in comparison to Chinese tax
Source: 2014–16 surveys

institutions. The former, which does not vary across subject matter areas, has been thoroughly investigated in Chapters 3 and 4. To briefly recapitulate, the vast majority of Chinese investment in the United States has been motivated by long-term commercial interests. To avoid repetition, this subsection concentrates on the Chinese MNE managers' view of the U.S. tax system. I begin with their opinion on the U.S. tax burden.

As noted earlier, the effect of the tax burden on FDI has inspired a vast literature. Many scholars contend that a high tax rate hinders FDI, citing certain empirical findings of a negative correlation between the two.[63] Others argue the opposite, pointing to evidence either of a positive effect of high tax on FDI[64] or of the failure of tax incentives to attract investment.[65] Still others find that tax incentives affect FDI in variable ways.[66]

As shown in Figure 5.1, the majority of the survey respondents consider U.S. tax to be more onerous than Chinese tax. The finding is somewhat surprising given the

63 See, e.g., Kan H. Young, "The Effects of Taxes and Rates of Return on Foreign Direct Investment in the United States," 41 *National Tax Journal* 109 (1988); Harry Grubert and John Mutti, "Taxes, Tariffs and Transfer Pricing in Multinational Corporate Decision Making," 73 *Review of Economics and Statistics* 285 (1991); Hartman, "Tax Policy and Foreign Direct Investment in the United States," 475.

64 Deborah L. Swenson, "The Impact of U.S. Tax Reform on Foreign Direct Investment in the United States," 54 *Journal of Public Economics* 243 (1994), 261–2.

65 See, e.g., David Lim, "Fiscal Incentives and Direct Foreign Investment in Less Developed Countries," 19 *Journal of Development Studies* 207 (1983); Michael L. Moore, Bert M. Steece, and Charles W. Swenson, "An Analysis of the Impact of State Income Tax Rates and Bases on Foreign Investment," 62 *Accounting Review* 671 (1987).

66 Alexander Klemm and Stefan Van Parys, "Empirical Evidence on the Effects of Tax Incentives," 19 *International Tax and Public Finance* 393 (2012), 395.

ongoing debate in China about heavy Chinese tax levied on businesses. The debate was triggered by a Chinese entrepreneur who cited heavy Chinese tax as a major reason for him to shift manufacturing to the United States.[67] In support of the comment, a Chinese tax scholar highlighted a finding of his survey on Chinese businessmen that 87% of respondents considered their tax burdens to be heavy.[68] Other Chinese tax experts and government officials have disagreed and contended that Chinese business taxes were not much higher than those of the United States.

The complexity of tax laws and tax administration thwarts accurate comparison of business tax burdens between the two countries. For instance, Chinese law generally subjects large companies to a flat statutory rate of 25% on their taxable income,[69] much lower than the statutory federal income tax rate of 35% for large U.S. companies.[70] Yet apart from the typical income tax, both governments usually require companies to pay and withhold certain payroll taxes. Under the formal Chinese law, companies should pay for five types of employment-related insurance, totaling 42.3% of the employees' base salaries.[71] In the United States, employers pay for Social Security at a rate of 6.2% of the wage, up to $118,500, and they pay for Medicare at a rate of 1.45%.[72] In addition, some Chinese companies cannot fully shift the VAT to customers or taxpayers down the value chain, which increases their effective tax. On the other hand, corporations in the United States normally have to pay state income tax at varying rates.[73]

Of course, even in the United States few companies pay tax at exactly the statutory rates, and the actual tax burden can vary significantly.[74] By one measure, the effective corporate tax rate in China is much lower than that in the United States.[75] In line with this assessment, the survey results indicate that, from the perspective of Chinese managers, the overall U.S. tax burden is more onerous than the tax burden in China. The finding casts doubts on the claim that excessive tax drove Chinese businesses to the United States.[76]

67 Zhang Quanwei, "Cao Dewang: Gongkai Jiang Shuifu Zhiwei Tixing Weijigan."

68 Hu Chunyan, "Minqi Shuifu 'Tonggan' Mingxian Zhengjie Hezai?" (Private Enterprises Suffer Heavy Tax: What Is the Cause?), *Zhongguo Qingnian Bao* (Dec. 20, 2016), at http://zqb.cyol.com/html/2016-12/20/nw.D110000zgqnb_20161220_5-01.htm.

69 PRC Law on Enterprise Income Tax, sec. 4, chap. 1.

70 Prior to the major tax reform passed in December 2017. IRC § 11(b)(1).

71 PRC Labor Law, sec. 73, chap. 9.

72 *Contribution and Benefit Base*, Official Social Security website, at www.ssa.gov/oact/cola/cbb.html.

73 Six states do not impose income tax on corporations, though three of them impose gross receipts taxes on business. Jared Walczak, "State Corporate Income Tax Rates and Brackets for 2015 (Tax Foundation)," at http://taxfoundation.org/article/state-corporate-income-tax-rates-and-brackets-2015.

74 "Effective Tax Rates Can Differ Significantly from the Statutory Rate," report by the U.S. Government Accountability Office (May 2013), at www.gao.gov/assets/660/654957.pdf.

75 The rate was 21.5% in China, compared to 27.7% in the United States. See "PricewaterhouseCoopers Global Effective Tax Rates" (2006–9), at http://businessroundtable.org/sites/default/files/Effective_Tax_Rate_Study.pdf., 3.

76 Kevin Liu, "Meet the Chinese Billionaire Who's Moving Manufacturing to the U.S. to Cut Costs," *Fortune* (Dec. 22, 2016), at http://fortune.com/2016/12/22/us-china-manufacturing-costs-investment.

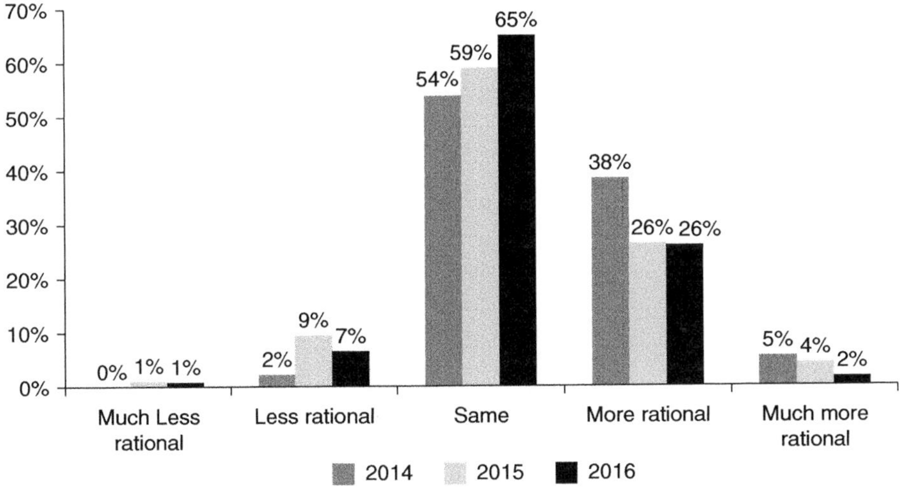

FIGURE 5.2 U.S. tax law in comparison with Chinese tax law
Source: 2014–16 surveys

The tax rate is but one part of the tax system. How do Chinese managers view the complex U.S. tax law? Prior studies have found that, besides corporate tax rates, ambiguous legal language, complex compliance procedures, and frequent and inconsistent changes in tax law all deter FDI.[77] Despite the valuable insights, the prior literature has neglected the fact that these different dimensions of a tax system are often inextricably linked. For instance, relatively stable law may offset ambiguous legal language in terms of the effects on FDI. To account for such interlinks, I adopt a broad and holistic notion of U.S. tax law. Moreover, though the same tax law can be simultaneously complex and simple to different foreign investors, the existing literature neglects the relative fluency with which foreign companies can take account of structural factors. Presumably, companies from the U.K. are more likely than their Chinese counterparts to find U.S. tax law easy to comprehend.

To assess this perception, I inserted in the CGCC survey a question about the respondents' comparative views of U.S. tax law, i.e., whether it is more or less sensible (*he li* in Chinese) than Chinese tax law. As illustrated in Figure 5.2, the survey respondents hold an overall positive perception of U.S. tax law, although about half remain neutral. This finding starkly contradicts the conventional wisdom that has been rather critical about the complex U.S. tax law.[78]

77 See, e.g., Kelly Edmiston, Shannon Mudd, and Neven Valev, "Tax Structures and FDI: The Deterrent Effects of Complexity and Uncertainty," 24 *Fiscal Studies* 341 (2005); Martin Lawless, "Do Complicated Tax Systems Prevent Foreign Direct Investment?", 80 *Economica* 1 (2013).

78 See, e.g., Michael J. Graetz, 100 *Million Unnecessary Returns: A Simple, Fair, and Competitive Tax Plan for the United States* (2010); Michael J. Graetz, "Tax Reform Unraveling," 21 *Journal of Economic Perspectives* 69 (2007); Gary Clyde Hufbauer, *Reforming the US Corporate Tax* (2005); Jane G. Gravelle, "Practical Tax Reform for a More Efficient Income Tax," 30 *Virginia Tax Review* 389 (2010).

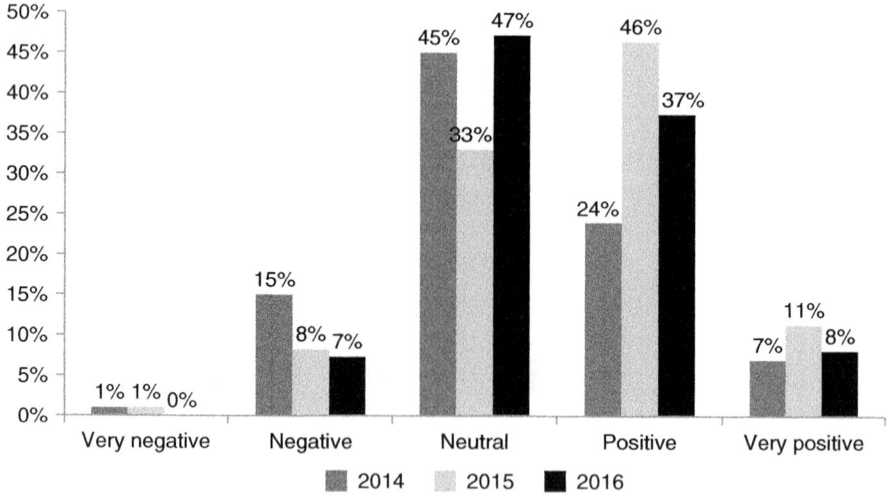

FIGURE 5.3 General view of the U.S. tax system
Source: 2014–16 surveys

Moreover, the survey respondents were asked about their general impression of the U.S. tax system. As shown in Figure 5.3, the views are more positive than those on U.S. tax law. In 2015 and 2016, the respondents on average considered the U.S. tax system to be superior to the one they were accustomed to back home. This suggests that Chinese MNE managers – who are familiar with a Chinese tax administration permeated with official edicts, connections, ambiguous law, and weak courts – prefer the complex, yet law-based, U.S. tax system.

B Reliance on U.S. Tax Professionals

Faced with the large institutional gaps, do Chinese companies have the ability to adapt to the U.S. tax system? In answering the question, I focus on two factors: the allocation of decision-making power and reliance on U.S. tax professionals. Again, the former, which does not vary across different areas of law, was analyzed in Chapters 3 and 4. To briefly recapitulate, the survey data indicate that the Chinese headquarters typically decide major U.S. legal and compliance issues after consulting local managers. To avoid repetition, this subsection concentrates on Chinese companies' reliance on U.S. tax professionals.

Anyone who has filed or attempted to file a tax return in the United States should recognize the importance of tax practitioners for compliance.[79] But few have studied

79 Steven Klepper, Mark Mazur, and Daniel Nagin, "Expert Intermediaries and Legal Compliance: The Case of Tax Preparers," 34 *Journal of Law and Economics* 205 (1991), 228, finding that the use of tax professionals is associated with increasing noncompliance in situations of legal ambiguities; James

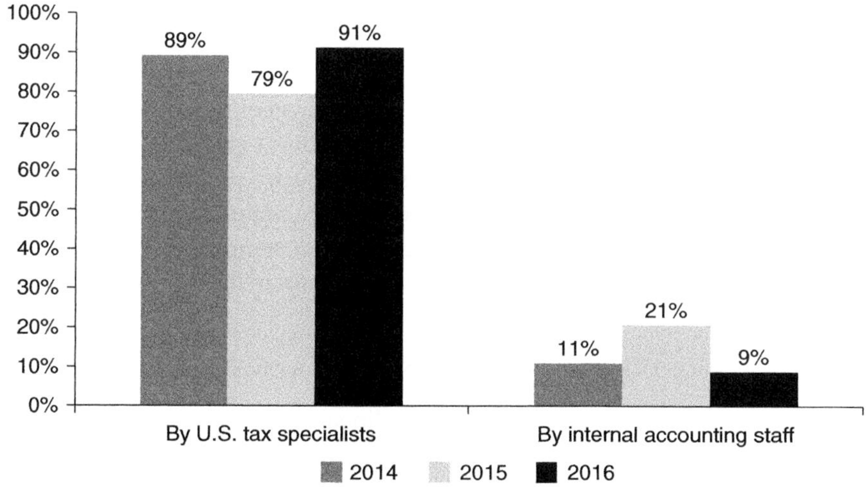

FIGURE 5.4 Dealing with U.S. tax matters
Source: 2014–16 CGCC survey

the use of tax practitioners by MNEs from emerging markets such as China. U.S. tax compliance, highly complex even in the eyes of domestic taxpayers,[80] inevitably constitutes a serious "liability of foreignness" for Chinese companies.[81] Thus, local tax professionals should play a pivotal role in guiding Chinese investors through the maze of U.S. tax rules.

The surveys inquired about respondents' handling of U.S. tax matters, i.e., whether they deal with the matters internally or outsource them to U.S. specialists. According to the survey results, the vast majority of respondents have chosen to delegate the work (see Figure 5.4). I ran separate correlation tests and found a significant link between investment size and the use of internal accounting staff to handle U.S. tax matters, which suggests that staff have the requisite knowledge and skills. In other words, they are likely to be U.S. tax experts as well. Although reliance on U.S. professionals does not, *ipso facto*, indicate high compliance,[82] it certainly

Andreoni, Brian Erard, and Jonathan Feinstein, "Tax Compliance," 36 *Journal of Economic Literature* 818 (1998), 847. Some find that the use of an attorney or CPA to prepare returns increases tax noncompliance. See, e.g., Brian Erard, "Taxation with Representation," 52 *Journal of Public Economics* 163 (1993), 196–7; Yet contradictory empirical evidence also exists. See, e.g., Peggy A. Hite and Gary A. McGill, "An Examination of Taxpayer Preference for Aggressive Tax Advice," 45 *National Tax Journal* 389, 391 (1992).

80 About half of all U.S. taxpayers employ tax practitioners to prepare their tax returns. See Andreoni, Erard, and Feinstein, "Tax Compliance," 846.

81 B. Elango, "Minimizing Effects of 'liability of Foreignness': Response Strategies of Foreign Firms in the United States," 44 *Journal of World Business* 51 (2009).

82 Previous research has suggested that relying on tax practitioners may facilitate compliance in cases of clear tax rules and noncompliance when there is ambiguity. See, e.g., Klepper, Mazur, and Nagin, "Expert Intermediaries and Legal Compliance."

suggests that Chinese companies will adapt to host-country institutions and act like their local counterparts.

To summarize, this section empirically investigated the desire and ability of Chinese investors to adapt to the complex U.S. tax system. It found that Chinese MNE managers consider U.S. tax to be more onerous, but that they nonetheless hold positive views of U.S. tax institutions. Moreover, Chinese companies rely extensively on local professionals to manage U.S. tax matters. Hence, they should adapt to the U.S. tax system quite well and act like local companies, despite the wide institutional gaps between China and the United States in this subject matter area.

IV CHINESE COMPANIES IN THE U.S. TAX SYSTEM

The preceding sections described the institutional gaps between China and the United States in the area of taxation, and evidenced the desire and ability of Chinese companies to adapt to the host-country tax system. Thus, Chinese companies likely adopt isomorphic behavior in dealing with U.S. tax matters. But domestic U.S. companies vary dramatically in their tax compliance: some invest heavily in tax avoidance strategies; others refrain from any risky planning. Which do Chinese companies resemble? In other words, how do they actually react to the U.S. tax system? This section answers the question by examining the following two topics: (1) the degree to which Chinese companies engage in tax planning to avoid U.S. tax, and (2) tax audits and disputes with the IRS.

A Tax Avoidance

Tax planning plays a central role in corporate tax compliance in the United States. It offers a window onto how Chinese companies adapt to the U.S. tax system. As noted earlier, a vast literature has examined the relationship between global capital flows, in particular investment of MNEs, and tax inducements. Most large MNEs cannot afford to stay apart from the U.S. market, so they adopt various tax planning strategies to minimize their U.S. tax.[83] Have Chinese companies followed suit? To be more concrete, we ask whether, and to what extent, Chinese companies in the United States have engaged in tax planning to avoid U.S. tax?

The 2015 and 2016 surveys collected information about the respondent's U.S. tax planning.[84] According to the data, 41% and 53% of the 2015 and 2016 survey respondents

83 For the description and analysis of a few well-known international tax planning strategies, see, e.g., Edward D. Kleinbard, "Through a Latte, Darkly: Starbucks's Stateless Income Planning," 139 *Tax Notes* 1515 (2013); Paul M. Schmidt, John Bates, and Jeffrey Paravano, "Why Tax Inversions Continue to Be an Effective Global Tax Planning Strategy," 32 *Journal of Taxation of Investments* 3 (2015); Joseph P. Brothers, "From the Double Irish to the Bermuda Triangle," 24 *Tax Analysts* 687 (2014).

84 In order to mitigate bias as tax avoidance may be viewed as lacking legitimacy, the respondents were asked whether they had engaged in "legitimate" or "reasonable" tax avoidance.

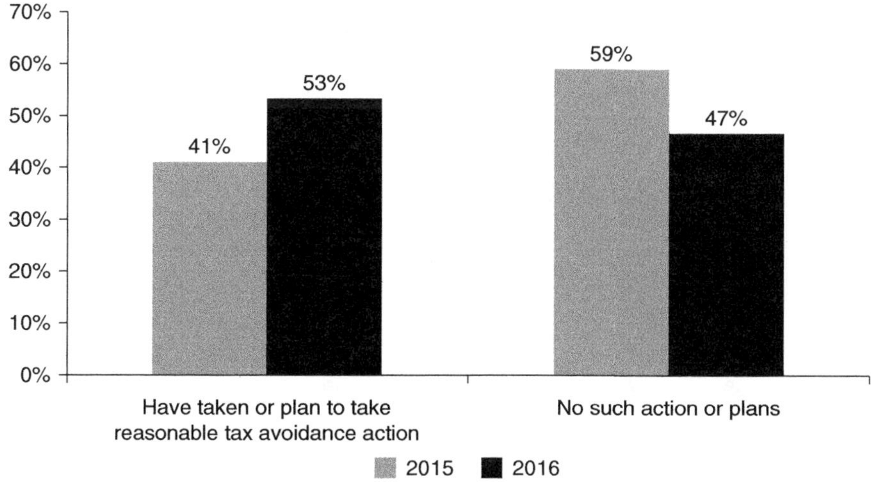

FIGURE 5.5 Tax avoidance by Chinese companies in the United States
Source: 2015 survey (95 responses for this particular survey question); 2016 survey (120 responses for this question)

respectively took, or planned to take, action to avoid U.S. tax. In comparison, a survey study shows that the average public firm in the United States has "a 94.4% probability of investing in a tax shelter."[85] Given the large institutional distances between China and the United States in the area of taxation, especially on the enforcement dimension, one would expect Chinese investors to take extra caution in tackling U.S. tax issues. Moreover, due to the institutional gaps, many Chinese managers have insufficient information about complex U.S. tax planning. According to the 2016 survey data, 58% of those Chinese companies that have neither engaged in tax planning nor prepared to do so in the United States list lack of knowledge as a main reason.

One may suspect that Chinese companies in the United States, which on average report a slight loss, have no urgent need to shelter income through planning strategies. In other words, the companies' apparently cautious compliance approach simply reflects their lack of taxable income. As noted by a New York tax lawyer who has advised Chinese investors, "soon after their business began to make a profit, they would come to solicit planning advice."[86] However, according to the empirical analysis of the following section, Chinese firms' profit level is not significantly associated with their tax avoidance measures. Hence, the survey data, taken together, strongly suggest that Chinese companies in the United States tend to be more conservative in complying with U.S. tax law than are domestic U.S. firms. For those Chinese companies that have

85 John R. Graham, Michelle Hanlon, Terry J. Shevlin, and Nemit Shroff, "Incentives for Tax Planning and Avoidance: Evidence from the Field," 89 *Accounting Review* 991 (2014), 997.

86 Interview with a Chinese lawyer who practiced U.S. tax law for about a decade at a major U.S. law firm (March 31, 2015).

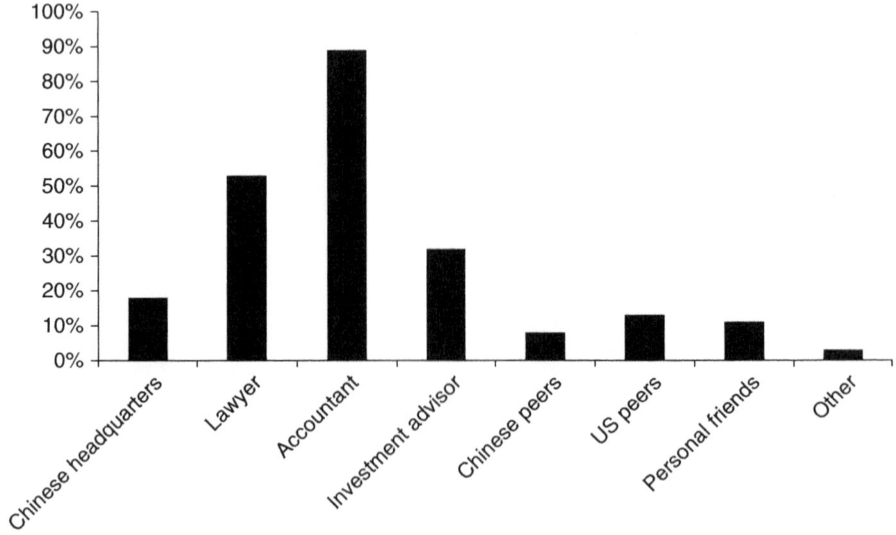

FIGURE 5.6 Sources of information for U.S. tax avoidance
Source: 2015 survey (thirty-eight responded to this particular multiple-choice survey question)

engaged in tax planning, where did they obtain the relevant information? According to the 2015 survey data, 89% acquired the information from accountants, followed by 53% that got it from lawyers (see Figure 5.6). Only a few were advised by their peers or their Chinese headquarters. The data serve as yet another piece of evidence for the essential role of local professionals.

B Tax Audits and Disputes with the IRS

I have shown thus far that Chinese companies in the United States typically face large institutional gaps in the area of tax, yet they are generally inclined to adapt, and capable of adapting, to the complex U.S. tax system. The data also suggest that Chinese companies generally take a more conservative approach in tax compliance than their local counterparts. As a result, Chinese firms should not be tangled in a large number of frictions with the U.S. tax administration. Is this a valid hypothesis? Answers are not yet available.

Administrative enforcement measures, such as tax audits, constitute the fulcrum of tax compliance.[87] Rational taxpayers allegedly comply with tax law if and only if the

[87] See, e.g., Barbara Kastlunger, Erich Kirchler, Luigi Mittone, and Julia Pitters, "Sequences of Audits, Tax Compliance, and Taxpaying Strategies," 30 *Journal of Economic Psychology* 405 (2009); Arthur Snow and Ronald S. Warren, "Ambiguity about Audit Probability, Tax Compliance, and Taxpayer Welfare," 43 *Economic Inquiry* 865 (2005); James Alm, Roy Bahl and Matthew N. Murray, "Audit Selection and Income Tax Underreporting in the Tax Compliance Game," 42 *Journal of*

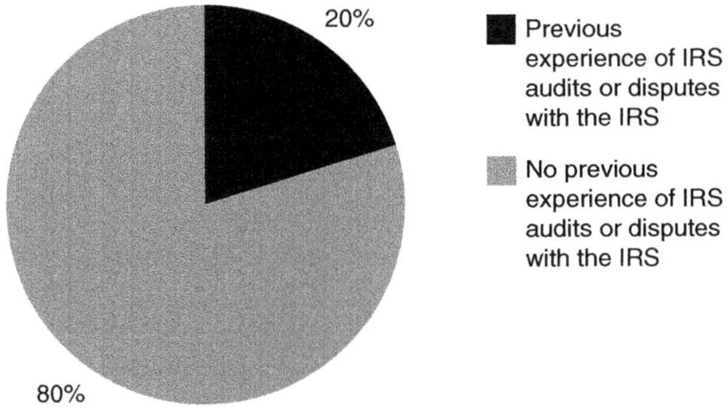

FIGURE 5.7 IRS audits, or disputes with the IRS
Source: 2014 survey (eighty-nine responses for this particular survey question)

costs associated with audit and penalty exceed the benefits of tax evasion.[88] And a sizable body of empirical work has demonstrated the effects of audits and penalties on shaping compliance behavior.[89] Yet again, foreign-controlled firms in the United States have largely been neglected. A closely related issue is tax controversy, which typically follows an audit and a deficiency assessment. As noted earlier, while U.S. taxpayers adjudicate tax disputes from time to time, taxpayers in China rarely sue tax agencies.[90] Does that change when Chinese companies move to operate in the United States?

The 2014 survey collected information about the respondent's prior experience of tax audits or disputes with the IRS. As shown in Figure 5.7, a significant minority of eighteen (20%) did have such prior experiences and seventy-one (80%) Chinese investors did not. The ratio is low considering that the median respondent has operated in the United States for several years and the survey sample includes most of the prominent Chinese investors.[91] The IRS chooses its audit targets using a variety of methods, including random selection and a discriminant information function formula that calculates the probability of positive tax adjustments (i.e., the

Development Economics 1 (1993); H. Cremer, M. Marchand, and P. Pestieau, "Evading, Auditing and Taxing: The Equity–Compliance Tradeoff," 43 *Journal of Public Economics* 67 (1990).

88 For a general introduction of the framework, see Michael G. Allingham and Agnar Sandmo, "Income Tax Evasion: A Theoretical Analysis," 1 *Journal of Public Economics* 323 (1972).

89 See, e.g., Kastlunger et al., "Sequences of Audits," 405; Cremer, Marchand, and Pestieau, "Evading, Auditing and Taxing," 67.

90 Li, "Dare You Sue the Tax Collector?", 58.

91 For comparison, I use as a benchmark a predicted average IRS audit rate for the respondent sample calculated from averaging the rates associated with various asset amounts of C corporations provided in the *IRS Data Book*, at www.irs.gov/pub/irs-soi/12databk.pdf. Assuming the audit is temporally independent and across different Chinese-invested firms, the asset value of the survey respondents did not change, and dividing the respondents into two categories (one assigned the audit rate of 2% for companies with assets of less than ten million, the other 10% for firms with larger assets), the expected probability of having experienced an IRS audit would be 32.7%. That is much higher than the 20.2% from the survey report.

probability of tax evasion multiplied by the amount of tax recovered).[92] Thus, the relatively low rate of friction with the IRS may be attributable to conservative tax compliance by Chinese companies in the United States. As just noted, many Chinese firms have insufficient knowledge about the U.S. system to engage in tax planning. Though they trust local professionals with routine tax and accounting matters, most of the Chinese managers lack adequate capacity to assess the risk associated with planning strategies. For instance, according to the chief finance officer of a Chinese company in the United States, "strictly speaking, there is no lawful tax avoidance planning in the United States. Most of the 'so-called' tax planning strategies carry legal risks ... [so my company] has not taken any such tax avoidance methods."[93] In addition, because expected returns from audits factor into the IRS's calculation, the relatively low audit rate for Chinese companies may be attributed to their insignificant taxable income.[94] However, as the next section will detail, corporate revenue or profit does not adequately explain the lack of friction with the U.S. tax system.

To summarize, drawing on the original survey data, this section presented an empirical overview of how Chinese companies react to the intricate law-based U.S. tax system. Aided by local professionals, roughly half of the Chinese companies have engaged in tax planning to minimize their U.S. tax; the ratio is relatively low compared to sizable U.S. companies. Moreover, the Chinese companies have not experienced a large number of tax audits or disputes with the IRS. Both suggest that prominent Chinese companies, confronting significant institutional gaps in the area of tax, respond to the U.S. tax system in ways similar to, or more cautiously, than U.S. firms.

V THE EFFECT OF CHINESE GOVERNMENT OWNERSHIP

While Chinese companies appear to cope well with the U.S. tax system, one cannot help but notice significant firm-level variations (see Table 5.1). When it comes to tax compliance, all Chinese companies in the United States are not the same. Multiple factors may explain such variations. For instance, available resources may play a role. Prior research has also explored the effects of institutional factors, such as corrupt social norms, on foreigners' tax compliance in the United States.[95] But the defining feature of FDI from China, the prominence of state owned investors, has so far received scant attention. Does the "visible hand of the state" exert any measurable influence on how Chinese companies react to the U.S. tax system?

92 DeBacker, "Importing Corruption Culture from Overseas," 125.

93 Interview with chief finance officer of the U.S. affiliate of a large Chinese company in construction (Feb. 8, 2017).

94 It is common for U.S. companies with substantial taxable income to be audited every year. Lillian Mills, Merle M. Erickson, and Edward L. Maydew, "Investments in Tax Planning," 20 *Journal of the American Taxation Association* 1 (1998), 5.

95 DeBacker, Heim, and Tran, "Importing Corruption Culture from Overseas."

TABLE 5.1 *Summary statistics*

Variable	Observation	Mean	Std. dev.	Min	Max
State ownership (10%)	235	0.485106	0.500845	0	1
State ownership (50%)	235	0.395745	0.490054	0	1
Investment duration	224	11.6875	10.01661	0	40
U.S. revenue	181	2.160221	1.225547	1	4
U.S. profit	173	0.369942	0.48419	0	1
U.S. tax law	218	3.220183	0.663155	1	5
Level of satisfaction with the IRS	217	3.331797	0.726836	1	5
U.S. tax system	220	3.518182	0.79072	1	5

Source: 2015 and 2016 surveys

This section provides some preliminary answers. Recall that earlier chapters have shown that, in general, state-owned Chinese investors tend to be more policy-driven and less committed to long-term investment in the United States, and retain more decision-making authority, than privately owned investors, including making decisions on major U.S. legal and compliance matters. Moreover, in the domestic setting, state ownership has an effect on the dynamics of firm–tax agency interaction. Does the effect get transported to the United States? Or are tax matters too technical and routine to invoke the power of the visible hand? To explore these questions, this section first examines Chinese managers' perceptions. It then empirically tests possible associations between state ownership in Chinese companies and Chinese companies' U.S. tax avoidance, as well as their experiences of tax audits and disputes with the IRS.

A *Opinions of U.S. Tax Institutions*

As shown in Chapter 4, Chinese investors with significant state ownership in general do not differ from private investors in holding overall positive views of various U.S. social, legal, and business institutions. Now, what about U.S. tax institutions? Are SOE managers more or less likely than their peers at private Chinese firms to view U.S. tax laws and agencies positively? To answer the question, I ran a series of statistical tests. As described above, the survey respondents were asked to compare U.S. tax law and the entire U.S. tax system with those in China. Moreover, a question inquired about respondents' level of satisfaction with the IRS. The questions all took the form of a scale from 1 to 5, with 5 being the most favorable. I use the data as the dependent variables.

The independent variable of interest, state ownership in Chinese investors, comprises the same two dummies as used in the preceding chapter. I also include a number of controls to the tests. First, duration of investment in the United States is added to account for possible effects of normative internalization. In other words,

Chinese companies that have operated in the United States for an extended period, which tend to be state-owned due to the restrictions of the earlier FDI policies, may hold different views about U.S. tax institutions than do newcomers. Second, I added the size of Chinese companies' U.S. businesses (as measured by the Chinese companies' U.S. revenue) to the tests. It is plausible that Chinese companies with large U.S. investments encounter more complex U.S. tax issues and, as a result, hold less favorable views of the institution; meanwhile, investment size is associated with state ownership in Chinese investors.[96] Third, I included U.S. profits in the tests. U.S. corporate tax, generally imposed on net income, correlates with the amount of a corporate taxpayer's profit. Therefore, it is possible that those reporting U.S. profits suffer the tax pain and feel less positive toward the institutions. Last, I added a year dummy to account for possible changes in the reported perceptions due to different compositions of Chinese companies in the two years.

As shown in Table 5.2, in none of the tests is the state-ownership dummy significant, which indicates that Chinese investors with significant state ownership do not differ from those privately owned in expressing largely positive views of U.S. tax law, the tax system, and the work of the IRS. In other words, Chinese MNE managers, regardless of their employers' ownership characters, think positively of the U.S. tax system.

In one model specification, U.S. investment size as measured by the company's revenue is weakly significant and negatively associated with the Chinese managers' perception of the IRS. In other words, the Chinese investors with larger U.S. businesses may think less of the work of the U.S. tax agency. It is possible that larger Chinese companies have more complex tax issues and find their more frequent dealings with the IRS less satisfactory. The result, however, is not robust. None of the other variables are significant. Thus, the variation in the generally positive opinions about the U.S. tax system appears to be idiosyncratic. In this case the universal reliance on U.S. tax professionals may be attributable to the lack of systematic variation in how the managers view the U.S. tax system. The professionals have shielded them from the complexity and the flaws of the institutions. As noted by a Chinese manager, he never had any direct contact with tax agents in the United States. "Here it's all taken care of by the accountants and tax lawyers. Whereas in China, managers are supposed to wine and dine with tax officials from time to time."[97] Keep in mind that the sample size limits what one can infer for the findings of nonsignificance.

B Tax Planning to Avoid U.S. Tax

Are SOEs more or less likely to avoid U.S. tax than private Chinese companies? As previously discussed, the renaissance of SOEs in the global economy has triggered

96 The simple correlation calculated using the 2015 and 2016 data is more than 0.33.

97 Interview with the CEO of the U.S. affiliate of a large Chinese real estate and investment company (June 14, 2017).

TABLE 5.2 *State ownership of Chinese investors and perceptions of U.S. tax institutions*

	U.S. tax law		U.S. tax system		Work of the IRS	
	1	2	3	4	5	6
State ownership 10%	−0.0167444 (0.3653863)		−0.1516864 (0.3465966)		.0524241 (0.3595112)	
State ownership 50%		0.1579258 (0.3726196)		0.2160591 (0.3511129)		0.3067754 (0.3698773)
Duration of investment	0.0054337 (0.0168449)	0.0036707 (0.0170499)	0.0159274 (0.0165188)	0.0123976 (0.0165873)	−0.0050977 (0.0168714)	−0.00823 (0.0170209)
U.S. revenue	−0.0415288 (0.1556502)	−0.0535127 (0.1520217)	−0.0329319 (0.1475493)	−0.0644635 (0.1434884)	−0.2459016 (0.156086)	−0.2580131* (0.1529648)
U.S. profits	0.6154115 (0.4383752)	0.5664489 (0.441497)	−0.1449544 (0.4230493)	−0.2642214 (0.4281702)	0.336046 (0.4272527)	0.2711697 (0.429412)
Survey year	0.3087264 (0.4279571)	0.3073023 (0.4272203)	−0.0117548 (0.4134343)	−0.0478259 (0.4118037)	−0.2134426 (0.4261365)	−0.2045884 (0.4253323)
Number of observations	159	159	157	157	157	157

Note: data source: 2015 and 2016 CGCC surveys; significance level: ***$p < 1\%$; **$p < 5\%$; *$p < 10\%$; ordered logistic regressions.

some renewed interest in their tax behavior.[98] Under the conventional view, SOEs should be insensitive to corporate tax because the government shareholder is also the tax collector.[99] However, the agency problem inherent in all large corporations, state-owned or not, suggests that the answer is less than clear.[100] On the one hand, the managers of SOEs may engage in empire building by maximizing after-tax earnings and profits. On the other, they may refrain from aggressive tax planning for lack of compensatory incentives. Recent empirical research on the tax behavior of SOEs has yet to produce conclusive evidence and no study has explored the tax planning of Chinese SOEs outside China.[101] This subsection begins to narrow the gap.

First of all, it is important to note that the unity argument for SOEs' lack of tax sensitivity does not apply. Apparently, the government owner of the investors (i.e., the Chinese government) and the taxing authority (i.e., governments in the United States) are not identical, at least not for the investors' U.S.-sourced income. But that does not necessarily mean that Chinese state-owned investors are as sensitive to U.S. tax as their private counterparts. While inherent agency problems may justify the taxation of SOEs domestically, the same problem also weakens managers' incentives to engage in tax avoidance behavior. In other words, the tax compliance of SOEs is more complex and sensitive to context. What is the U.S. context? The chapter has thus far demonstrated that Chinese investors, regardless of their ownership form, perceive U.S. tax institutions positively and uniformly rely on tax specialists. Meanwhile, the investors with significant state ownership distinguish themselves by retaining more decision-making authority and paying more attention to Chinese government policies. Are these ownership effects sufficient to alter the companies' tax planning behavior in the United States?

To answer the question, I ran a series of tests using U.S. tax planning as the dependent variable. From relevant 2015 and 2016 survey data I constructed a dummy variable that equals 1 if the respondent has taken, or plans to take, any action to avoid U.S. tax, and 0 if the respondent has not taken, and does not plan to take, any tax avoidance action.

98 Cui, "Taxation of State-Owned Enterprises."

99 Harry Huizinga and Soren Bo Nielsen, "Privatization, Public Investment, and Capital Income Taxation," 82 *Journal of Public Economics* 399 (2001).

100 Cui, "Taxation of State-Owned Enterprises."

101 See, e.g., Hanwen Chen, Song Tang, Donghui Wu, and Daoguang Yang, "The Political Dynamics of Corporate Tax Avoidance: the Chinese Experience," working paper, at https://papers.ssrn.com/sol3/papers.cfm?abstract_id=2640111; Clemens Fuest and Li Liu, "Does Ownership Affect the Impact of Taxes on Firm Behavior? Evidence from China," working paper, at http://papers.ssrn.com/sol3/papers.cfm?abstract_id=2603177; Lixing Li and Guangrong Ma, "Government Size and Tax Evasion: Evidence from China," 20 *Pacific Economic Review* 346 (2015); Tanya Y.H. Tang, "Privatization, Tunneling, and Tax Avoidance in Chinese SOEs," 24 *Asian Review of Accounting* 274 (2016); Oliver Zhen Li, Hang Liu, and Chenkai Ni, "Controlling Shareholders' Incentive and Corporate Tax Avoidance: A Natural Experiment in China," 44 *Journal of Business Finance and Accounting* 697 (2017).

The independent variable of interest is state ownership in the Chinese investor. I use the same two state-ownership dummies to alternatively test their hypothetical effects. I also include several control variables to the regression tests. First, the duration of a respondent's business operation may be associated with tax planning and state ownership. Chinese companies that have done business in the United States for an extended period, which are disproportionately state-owned,[102] may have accumulated more knowledge necessary for tax avoidance. According to an experienced U.S. tax lawyer, some of his Chinese clients seek tax-related information from all sources possible and are able to acquire over time a rudimentary understanding of major U.S. tax rules pertinent to their businesses.[103] Second, tax practitioners may play a crucial part in Chinese companies' tax compliance.[104] As shown earlier, Chinese companies rely uniformly on U.S. tax experts, and the vast majority outsourced their tax work instead of handling it internally. Doing so may have notable implications on their tax avoidance behavior.[105] Additionally, including the variable is of interest by itself because no prior study has thus far explored the use of tax practitioners by developing-country MNEs. From the survey data I created a dummy variable that equals 1 if the survey respondent delegates its tax work to external specialists, otherwise the dummy is set to 0. Third, as noted, corporate tax is normally levied on net income,[106] and state ownership may correlate with both profit level and tax avoidance behavior. So the statistical tests control for the profit level of a Chinese-invested business. Fourth, the size of a Chinese investor's U.S. business may also relate both to its ownership structure and to tax avoidance. The Chinese government may invest disproportionately in companies having larger operations in the United States, while higher revenues may raise both U.S. tax and the incentive for tax planning.[107] Last, I add a survey-year dummy to account for changes that might occur over the two years.

The results, as shown in Table 5.4, are mixed. In models 1 and 3, the state-ownership dummy is significant at the 10% level and the coefficient is positive. That is to say, Chinese investors with significant state ownership are more likely than the rest to have taken or planned to take action to avoid U.S. tax. The results, however, are not robust. In the other six specifications, the state-ownership dummy is not significant, indicating that Chinese investors with state ownership act like private Chinese investors in terms of avoiding U.S. tax.

102 Buckley et al., "Historic and Emergent Trends," 723.

103 Interview with a Chinese tax lawyer who has practiced U.S. tax law for more than a decade at a large U.S. law firm (March 31, 2015).

104 Klepper, Mazur, and Nagin, "Expert Intermediaries and Legal Compliance."

105 Erard, "Taxation with Representation"; Hite and McGill, "An Examination of Taxpayer Preference for Aggressive Tax Advice."

106 IRC §§ 162, 163, 165.

107 As a result of the SOE reforms in the 1990s, the state retained ownership mainly in large enterprises. See Zheng and Chen, "China's State-Owned Enterprise Reform and Its Discontents."

TABLE 5.3 *Summary statistics*

Variable	Mean	Std. dev.	Min.	Max.	Observations
State ownership (10%)	0.485106	0.500845	0	1	235
State ownership (50%)	0.395745	0.490054	0	1	235
Investment duration	11.6875	10.01661	0	40	224
U.S. revenue	2.160221	1.225547	1	4	181
U.S. profit	0.369942	0.48419	0	1	173
Tax planning	0.47907	0.500728	0	1	215
U.S. tax professional	0.8565022	0.3513684	0	1	223

Source: 2015 and 2016 annual surveys

The findings contribute to the emerging debate about SOEs and taxation. On the conventional view, SOEs should be indifferent to tax because the state shareholder is also the receiver of tax revenue.[108] And some empirical research has bolstered the claim by showing Chinese SOEs to be less tax aggressive than non-SOEs in the domestic setting. Recent scholarship, however, points out that SOEs can be sensitive to tax due to the multilayered agency problem in corporate governance.[109] The findings of this section lend some support to this latter argument.

Among the control variables, the use of external accountants is negatively and significantly associated with tax avoidance in the United States in models 5 and 6. I discussed earlier that those Chinese companies that relied on internal accounting staff to manage U.S. tax matters are larger ones probably equipped with the requisite in-house tax knowledge and capacity. Thus, they are more likely to engage in tax planning to reduce U.S. taxes. U.S. investment size is significant and positively associated with the companies' tax planning efforts, according to the results from model 8. As expected, other things held equal, Chinese companies with larger U.S. businesses tend to have both the capacity and the need to engage in tax planning. Last, the companies in 2016 are more likely to avoid U.S. tax than those in 2015. However, none of these results are robust. Further research is necessary to draw definitive conclusions.

C *Tax Audits and Disputes with the IRS*

Power status plays a pivotal role in shaping the interactions between corporate taxpayers and tax agencies in China. While routine tax matters may be handled in accordance with formal rules and conventional practices, different compliance models apply in cases involving legal uncertainty or substantially diverging interests. The SOEs, given their political status, treat Chinese tax agencies as peers in the government structure and resolve thorny tax issues or disputes through negotiation;

108 Huizinga and Nielsen, "Privatization, Public Investment, and Capital Income Taxation."
109 Cui, "Taxation of State-Owned Enterprises."

TABLE 5.4 *U.S. tax avoidance*

	1	2	3	4	5	6	7	8
State owning more than 10% of Chinese investor	0.53636*		0.5459396*		0.4351979		0.2867378	
	(0.2970049)		(0.3018057)		(0.3639124)		(0.3778607)	
State owning more than 50% of Chinese investor		0.3541819		0.4452557		0.4600699		0.3558072
		(0.3081277)		(0.3122889)		(0.3792251)		(0.388492)
Years of investment in U.S.	−0.0135858	−0.0124687	−0.0116318	−0.0115268	−0.0168151	−0.0178459	−0.0224693	−0.0241339
	(0.0144547)	(0.0147294)	(0.0153676)	(0.0156077)	(0.018017)	(0.0182739)	(0.0185817)	(0.0189153)
Tax matters dealt with by outside accountants			.0408154	.0352397	−0.9901422*	−1.041076*	−0.8706494	−0.9018838
			(0.236793)	(0.2359112)	(0.5618796)	(0.5620255)	(0.5710053)	(0.5721871)
U.S. profit					0.5434674	0.5399483	0.2920099	0.2661255
					(0.4321086)	(0.4321329)	(0.4622435)	(0.4646803)
U.S. revenue							0.2730373	0.2795644*
							(0.1674436)	(0.1650283)
Survey year					1.315869*	1.390711*	1.110995	1.149865
					(0.7390518)	(0.7361988)	(0.756087)	(0.7553225)
Number of observations	199	199	195	195	155	155	155	155

Note: significance level: ***p < 1%; **p < 5%; *p < 10%; data source: 2015 and 2016 surveys; logistic regressions.

not in the shadow of the law, but according to their political status and the interests at stake.[110] Because of the relatively larger institutional distance, state-invested Chinese companies in the United States may confront more challenges than their large private peers in adapting to a law-based regulatory environment.

In addition, centralized decision-making in Chinese investors with significant state ownership, plus the organizational rigidity and the multilayered agency problem, may hinder their ability to take major business actions. Prior research has demonstrated that Chinese SOEs are less efficient at making investment decisions.[111] The same logic should apply to the companies' decisions regarding major tax compliance issues, manifesting in a higher probability that Chinese SOEs will experience tax audits and disputes with the IRS than will their privately invested counterparts. I ran a series of regression tests to assess this hypothesis. The dependent variable to be used is reported experience of tax audits and disputes with the IRS. From the 2014 CGCC survey I constructed a dummy variable that takes the value of 1 if the survey respondent reported prior audits or disputes with the IRS, otherwise the dummy variable takes the value of 0.

For the independent variable of interest – Chinese government ownership – I use alternately the same two dummy variables as in prior tests. I also include a number of control variables. First, the duration of a company's operation in the United States. Presumably, everything else being equal, Chinese companies that have operated in the United States for an extended period, which tend to be state-owned, are more likely to have experienced tax audits or controversies. Second, I include U.S. profit level in the tests. As noted earlier, U.S. corporate tax is generally levied on net income,[112] and the probability of tax audits positively correlates with corporate taxable income, so I control for the profit level of a Chinese business in the United States. A 2014 survey question inquired about the respondents' profit or loss.[113] The question was structured on a scale of 1 to 5, with 1 being "incurred heavy losses" and 5 being "highly profitable." The control variable draws data directly from this question.

As discussed, Chinese companies in the United States rely heavily on local professionals to handle their tax matters. Existing research on this topic has detected measurable effects of professional tax service on compliance behavior. So the variable is included as a control. Moreover, the size of a Chinese investor's U.S. business may also relate to both its ownership structure and the dependent variables of interest. As noted above, the Chinese government may invest in companies with larger operations in the United States that inevitably have more U.S. tax and compliance issues.[114] Survey questions about the companies' U.S.

110 Ibid.

111 See, e.g., Shimin Chen, Zheng Sun, Song Tang, and Donghui Wu, "Government Intervention and Investment Efficiency: Evidence from China," 17 *Journal of Corporate Finance* 259 (2011).

112 IRC §§ 162, 163, 165.

113 The question was only asked in the 2014 survey.

114 As a result of the SOE reforms in the 1990s, the state retained ownership mainly in large enterprises. See, e.g., Zheng and Chen, "China's State-Owned Enterprise Reform and Its Discontents."

TABLE 5.5 *Summary statistics*

Variable	Observations	Mean	Std. dev.	Min.	Max.
State owning more than 10% of Chinese investor	95	0.568	0.498	0	1
State owning more than 50% of Chinese investor	95	0.484	0.502	0	1
Tax matters handled by external accountants	92	0.891	0.313	0	1
Previous experience of audit or dispute with IRS	89	0.202	0.404	0	1
Years of investing in U.S.	98	10.60204	9.438613	1	35
Profit level	85	2.882353	1.00489	1	5
Asset (log)	64	3.386937	1.388602	0.2552725	6.939519
Revenue (log)	61	2.994716	1.670203	−3	5.439175

Source: 2014 survey

revenues and U.S. assets provide the data for the control variables. Adding these covariates, however, reduces the sample size, as some respondents were reluctant to disclose the information (see Table 5.5). I used the logarithmic values of reported revenue and asset amounts alternately in the regression tests.

The test results presented in Table 5.6 below suggest that majority government ownership is associated with a heightened probability of being audited or becoming involved in a dispute with the IRS.[115] When broadened to include significant minority ownership, the variable loses much of its significance. Moreover, outsourcing the work to U.S. accountants does not appear to alter the odds, nor does the size of the investment or its profitability seem to matter.[116]

The regression result preliminarily confirms the hypothesis that Chinese government-owned firms experience more tax audits and disputes with the IRS. As noted above, in China's domestic context elevated political status allows the SOEs to follow a mixed political–legal model in tax compliance. While routine tax matters are dealt with by accountants, the SOEs normally resolve controversies through negotiation with the agencies as equals. And the Chinese government generally makes or amends tax rules to accommodate the special interests or needs of the SOEs.[117] Having exited the power-based regulatory ecosystem, state-owned Chinese

115 Given the limited sample size and the binary dependent variable, I first apply the exact logistic regression method to assess the relationship between state ownership in Chinese investors and the company's probability of experiencing an IRS audit or a dispute with the agency.

116 IRS audit rates typically correlate well with the amount of total assets of corporations and pass-through entities; see, e.g., *Internal Revenue Service Data Book* (2012), at www.irs.gov/pub/irs-soi/12databk.pdf. The counterintuitive finding may be explained by the fact that most of the Chinese-invested companies in the sample are still at an early stage of loss-generating operations.

117 Cui, "Taxation of State-Owned Enterprises."

TABLE 5.6 *IRS audits, or disputes with the IRS*

	1	2	3	4	5	6	7	8
State owning more than 10% of Chinese investor		2.93		2.74		3.11		4.23*
State owning more than 50% of Chinese investor	3.66*		3.43*		3.98*		5.63**	
Years of investment in U.S.	1.03	1.04	1.03	1.04	1.05	1.05	1.03	1.03
Profit level	1.68	1.64	1.65	1.61	1.23	1.22	1.12	1.11
Tax matters dealt with by U.S. professionals			1.37	1.31	1.10	0.98	1.37	1.22
Revenue 2013 (log)							1.48	1.51
Asset (log)					1.46	1.46		
Number of observations	73	73	72	72	56	56	56	56

Note: significance level: ***$p<1\%$; **$p<5\%$; *$p<10\%$; data source: CGCC 2014 annual survey; models 1 to 4 use exact logistic regressions; the rest of the models (5–8) use regular logistic regressions due to lack of software computation power; the table reports odds ratios.

companies no longer possess the bargaining leverage vis-à-vis law enforcement agencies. Instead, their old ways of dealing with tax rules and government agencies amplify the risk of audit and tax controversy in the United States. More importantly, Chinese state-owned investors retain the authority to make decisions regarding major U.S. legal and compliance issues. Centralized decision-making not only impedes the handling of audits and disputes with the IRS, but also amplifies the home-state effects in the process. Hence, the test results suggest a significant positive association between majority state ownership in Chinese investors and the likelihood of experiencing audits and disputes with the U.S. tax agency.

Alternatively, the link between Chinese government ownership and tax audit experience may result from the IRS systematically targeting Chinese state-owned companies in the United States. The IRS is certainly not immune from politicized exercise of its authority.[118] This study, however, does not contain sufficient evidence to evaluate this hypothesis directly. But given the earlier finding that Chinese companies with or without significant state ownership are equally satisfied with the work of the IRS (see Table 2), the claim of discriminatory enforcement targeting state-owned Chinese companies in the United States requires further empirical analysis.[119]

[118] Zachary A. Goldfarb and Karen Tumulty, "IRS Admits Targeting Conservatives for Tax Scrutiny in 2012 Election," *Washington Post* (May 10, 2013), at www.washingtonpost.com/business/economy/irs-admits-targeting-conservatives-for-tax-scrutiny-in-2012-election/2013/05/10/3b6a0ada-b987-11e2-92f3-f291801936b8_story.html?utm_term=.8f4f9c974ceb, last accessed on Dec. 24, 2016.

[119] The 2015 and 2016 CGCC survey contained a question about selective enforcement of rules in the United States. According to the data, quite a few survey respondents believe that U.S. tax agencies unfairly target foreign companies for audits.

To summarize, the Chinese companies report a relatively low rate of IRS audit or tax controversy. However, all the companies are not the same. Chinese government ownership correlates significantly with heightened probability of agency scrutiny or conflict, which indicates that Chinese state-owned firms in the United States may face higher hurdles than Chinese companies of other types in tackling major legal and compliance issues in the area of tax.

To recapitulate, this section empirically explored the state's visible hand in Chinese companies' tax behavior in the United States. According to the test results, state ownership is not associated with variations in Chinese MNE managers' perceptions of U.S. tax institutions. Moreover, Chinese investors universally rely on local professionals to handle U.S. tax matters. Both facilitate adaptation to the complex U.S. tax system. Moreover, Chinese companies with significant state ownership do not differ from private companies in terms of avoiding U.S. tax, which I attribute to broad reliance on local professionals and the fact that tax planning is a routine and technical matter decided locally. For major U.S. tax compliance matters, by contrast, state ownership matters. The preliminary tests find that Chinese companies with majority state ownership are more likely than firms of other ownership types to experience tax audits and disputes with the IRS. While the finding might reflect politicized exercise of discretion by the IRS, it is better explained by the large institutional gaps confronting state-owned companies investing in the United States and their centralized decision-making that hinders adaptation as well as prompt conflict resolution.

VI CONCLUSION

Chinese companies exhibit two rather unique features: they prosper in an environment with weak legal institutions and they function well with an overarching state. When these firms invest in the United States, important new issues about their impact on the host country inevitably emerge. For instance, will the companies, having thrived in a poor legal and regulatory environment, export legal and regulatory noncompliance? This chapter offered some preliminary answers by empirically investigating Chinese firms in the U.S. tax system.

Earlier, Chapter 3 presented an analytical framework for studying how foreign investors react to host-country legal and regulatory institutions, and empirically explored Chinese companies' adaptation to U.S. institutions in general. It identified large but varying institutional gaps between the two countries, and found Chinese companies to be both inclined and able to cross the gaps and act like local firms. Applying the analytical framework, this chapter made similar findings in the area of U.S. tax. Despite a widely shared perception of onerous U.S. tax, Chinese investors generally hold a positive view of both U.S. tax law and the overall tax system. As expected, Chinese firms rely heavily on local professionals to manage U.S. tax matters. Moreover, they act like prudent U.S. companies in terms of tax planning, and encounter relatively infrequent tax disputes and audits. In short, Chinese companies in the United States have largely adapted to the complex law-based U.S. tax system.

That being said, cross-company variations are evident. Previously, Chapter 4 examined how state ownership of Chinese investors may relate to such variations. Through a series of statistical tests, it found preliminary evidence that state-owned Chinese companies are relatively more attentive to home-government policies and less committed to their U.S. businesses. Moreover, Chinese investors with significant state ownership retain more authority to decide major U.S. legal and compliance issues. Meanwhile, state ownership of Chinese investors does not alter the managers' overall positive opinions about various U.S. institutions. Nor does it affect how Chinese companies rely on U.S. professionals.

This chapter continued the journey and explored how state ownership may be associated with variations in Chinese investors' tax compliance in the United States. Consistent with the findings from the previous chapter, Chinese managers view U.S. tax institutions favorably, regardless of their employers' ownership type. Also, state ownership of Chinese investors has no robust link to tax avoidance in the United States, which contradicts some prior research about SOEs' tax compliance behavior in the domestic setting. However, Chinese investors with majority state ownership are more likely to experience audits and disputes with the IRS.

The findings of this chapter contribute to the scholarship about FDI and taxation. If companies from China can adapt to and comply with the intricate and law-based U.S. tax system, MNEs from other developing countries should be able to do the same in the United States as well as in other developed countries with less complex tax systems. The chapter also adds to the emerging debate about SOEs and tax avoidance. The finding that outside the home state Chinese SOEs act similarly to private companies in terms of tax planning. Moreover, the empirical evidence of this chapter aids the debate about the fiscal effects of soaring Chinese FDI. Competing fiercely for Chinese investment, local and state governments in the United States have offered generous incentives such as tax credits worth millions of dollars, assuming implicitly that they will not only invest for the long term but also pay taxes at rates comparable to, if not higher than, those for similarly situated U.S. firms.[120] The empirical evidence offers some substance to that assumption.

120 Mui, "A Chinese Billionaire Is Staking His Legacy." For a general survey of governments' competition for corporate investment with incentive packages, see Louise Story, "As Companies Seek Tax Deals, Governments Pay High Price," *New York Times* (Dec. 1, 2012), at www.nytimes.com/2012/12/02/us/how-local-taxpayers-bankroll-corporations.html.

The preliminary and broad-stroke survey of Chinese firms' tax practices inevitably leaves a myriad of nuances unexplored.[121] Also, as is typical in most empirical scholarship, the tests uncover as many questions and puzzles as they answer. Take, for example, the heightened probability of tax audits and disputes for Chinese state-owned firms. While I attribute it partially to SOEs' hampered adaptation, the exact internal cause awaits future inquiry.

[121] Many factors have been shown to bear on tax evasion behavior. See, e.g., Graham et al., "Incentives for Tax Planning and Avoidance."

6

Chinese Companies and U.S. Employment Law

They constantly remind us that that's how they do things in China ... We'll make statements that we're in America, and we have codes that we have to go by.[1]

Cynthia Harper, a worker at a Chinese-invested factory in Ohio

In most people's minds, the American rust belt has been a victim of globalization. For decades, U.S. manufacturers in the region have been relocating to developing countries, especially China, to reduce costs and maintain profits. Most of the workers who lost their factory jobs moved away from the industrial cities and often had to trade down, working for much less than their previous wages. The resulting anger and frustration have shaped U.S. political discourse, and China-bashing has become a stationary feature of presidential campaigns. During the most recent one, both candidates made full use of the rhetoric. "They're stealing our jobs, they're stealing our companies, they're taking our money," Trump told his cheering supporters in Ohio. "We have drugs, we have debt, we have empty factories."[2]

The recent surge of Chinese investments in the United States, however, has added an unexpected twist to the familiar story. In 2016, Moraine, Ohio, a typical industrial city on the rust belt, celebrated the opening of a $600-million factory manufacturing automotive glass. The factory is a renovated assembly plant that was previously built by General Motors (GM) to produce SUVs but was shut down in 2008. That very day about a thousand American workers lost their jobs.[3] The exodus of businesses and residents accelerated, and there emerged the scene typical of most cities in the rust belt: "buildings closed down. Parking lots growing up with weeds. For sale signs."[4] In 2014, a Chinese company, Fuyao Glass, took over the abandoned GM facility,

[1] Mui, "A Chinese Billionaire Is Staking His Legacy." [2] Ibid. [3] Ibid.

[4] Lewis Wallace, "A Chinese Company Brings Hope to Former GM Workers in Ohio," *NPR* (Jan 28, 2014), at www.npr.org/2014/01/28/267777577/a-chinese-company-brings-hope-to-former-gm-workers-in-ohio.

spent millions of dollars on renovation, and employed more than 2,000 workers to produce windshield glass for sale to U.S. customers.[5] Citing proximity to customers, low costs, and, notably, "government regulations easier to operate under,"[6] Fuyao intends to further expand its investment in the United States. While most of the employees were hired locally, about 10%, including some of the most senior managers, were sent from China.[7] The owner of Fuyao Glass, Cao Dewang, flies to Moraine from China once a month to inspect the U.S. operations.

"If you want to invest in the U.S., you must first love it," commented Mr. Cao in front of a large audience in New York City right before the Ohio plant opened.[8] And love he has shown, by, among other things, "donating to the local university and entertaining clients at the Pine Club, a famous local steakhouse – even though he doesn't eat beef."[9] Yet despite the expressed affection for and dedication to the host country, the Chinese investor soon encountered "an acrimonious union campaign" at its plant and a lawsuit by a former manager.[10] According to Mr. Cao, the manager "didn't do [his job] but squandered my money,"[11] whereas the American manager alleged that discrimination was part of the reason he was let go.[12] Are the employment-related problems of Mr. Cao at his plant in Ohio representative of most Chinese investors in the United States? Are they due to gaps in regulatory institutions? Do they herald rising frictions between Chinese employers and their American employees as Chinese investments in the United States continue to grow?

This chapter answers these questions by empirically exploring how Chinese companies react to U.S. employment laws, with a focus on the laws prohibiting employment discrimination. Chinese outbound investors' employment practices in host countries have grabbed enormous public and academic attention worldwide, and negative press abounds. Also, U.S. employment laws apply broadly to Chinese companies doing business in this country. As noted earlier, U.S. laws in many other controversial areas such as environmental protection or product safety typically do not bear on Chinese companies operating primarily in the service sector, yet most of the Chinese companies in the United States employ a sizable work force and therefore should comply with U.S. rules proscribing employment discrimination.

5 Mui, "A Chinese Billionaire Is Staking His Legacy."

6 Matt Rivers, "Chinese Firm Creates Jobs in Rust Belt County that Voted for Trump," *CNN* (April 10, 2017), at http://money.cnn.com/2017/04/09/news/economy/china-us-jobs-ohio-glass-factory.

7 Mui, "A Chinese Billionaire Is Staking His Legacy."

8 Statement made by Cao Dewang (Cho Tak Wong), chairman and founder of Fuyao Glass, at New Neighbors: Chinese Investment in the U.S. by Congressional District, organized by National Committee on U.S.–China Relations (May 20, 2015).

9 Mui, "A Chinese Billionaire Is Staking His Legacy."

10 Noam Scheiber and Keith Bradsher, "Culture Clash at a Chinese-Owned Plant in Ohio," *New York Times* (June 10, 2017), at www.nytimes.com/2017/06/10/business/economy/ohio-factory-jobs-china.html.

11 Ibid. 12 Ibid.

By the most recent account, Chinese investors employ as many as 90,000 U.S. workers.[13] Though multinational enterprises (MNEs) based in several industrialized countries, such as the UK and Japan, hire far more U.S. employees,[14] Chinese firms stand out for the pace at which their hiring is growing in the United States. According to a consulting agency that has been tracking China's outbound foreign direct investment (ODI), Chinese companies are likely to employ 200,000 to 400,000 Americans by 2020.[15] That prospect will certainly add a new angle to the ongoing debates about U.S.–China economic relations, which have so far centered on the impacts of foreign direct investment (FDI) moving solely from the United States to China.[16]

Although the popular press has begun to cover the new phenomenon, as evidenced by numerous reports about Fuyao Glass and its problems at the Ohio factory, systematic research to guide the debates is lacking. Caught unprepared by the sharp reversal of the net investment flow between the world's two largest economies, scholars have not explored its impacts on the U.S. labor market. Therefore, one has to consult the existing literature on Chinese MNEs operating in less developed countries. A cursory review of that literature, however, reveals polarizing views. Some express deep suspicion about expanding Chinese companies for, among other things, their alleged abuses of labor rights in the host countries.[17] Others contend that the Chinese investors are generally on par with those from elsewhere in terms of employee management.[18] The juxtaposing views, plus the huge structural differences between the United States and the resource-rich developing countries that have absorbed the bulk of Chinese ODI in the past, offer few clues to the question of this chapter – how do Chinese investors respond to sophisticated U.S. institutions safeguarding employment rights, especially employment equality?

This chapter, beginning the process of answering the question, proceeds in five sections. Section I presents a comparative introduction to the Chinese laws

13 Rhodium Group, "New Neighbors (2016 Update): Chinese Investment in the United States by Congressional District 2," available at http://rhg.com/wp-content/uploads/2016/04/RHG_New-Neighbors_2016-Update_Full-Report.pdf.

14 For example, Japanese MNCs employ more than 700,000 U.S. workers. "Select USA – Foreign Direct Investment (FDI): Japan (2014)," at http://selectusa.commerce.gov/country-fact-sheets/2015–09-10%20Japan%20Fact%20Sheet.pdf.

15 Hanemann and Lysenko, "The Employment Impacts of Chinese Investment in the United States."

16 See, e.g., Mary A. Marchant and Sanjeev Kumar, "An Overview of U.S. Foreign Direct Investment and Outsourcing," 27 *Review of Agricultural Economics* 379 (2005); Richard Freeman, "Are Your Wages Set in Beijing?", 9 *Journal of Economic Perspectives* 15 (1995); David H. Autor, David Dorn, and Cordon H. Hanson, "The China Syndrome: Local Labor Market Effects of Import Competition in the United States," 103 *American Economic Review* 2121 (2013); Ann Harrison and Margaret McMillan, "Offshoring Jobs? Multinationals and U.S. Manufacturing Employment," 93 *Review of Economics and Statistics* 857 (2011).

17 Smith and Zheng, "The Management of Labour in Chinese MNCs," 379.

18 Yan Hairong and Barry Sautman, "'The Beginning of a World Empire'? Contesting the Discourse of Chinese Copper Mining in Zambia," 39 *Modern China* 131 (2013), 136.

governing employment discrimination. Thanks to remarkable legislative progress in the past two decades, the formal Chinese laws proscribing employment discrimination share the key principles embodied in corresponding U.S. laws. However, wide and varying gaps in compliance with and enforcement of the law persist. Next, section II critically reviews the existing research about Chinese MNEs' employment practices abroad and highlights its inadequacy to tackle the questions raised herein. Section III then empirically surveys how Chinese companies in the United States react to various U.S. labor and employment institutions. Section IV statistically analyzes the possible effects of state ownership in several major aspects pertaining to the firms' antidiscrimination efforts. Lastly, section V enumerates the limitations of the findings and concludes the chapter.

I CHINESE LAWS AGAINST EMPLOYMENT DISCRIMINATION

When reporting the problems Fuyao Glass encountered at its Ohio factory, the *New York Times* journalists observed that Chinese investments in the United States "can suffer when investors are unfamiliar with the American regulatory and political environment, as is true for many executives in China, where labor standards tend to be less strictly enforced."[19] That is an intuitive application of the analytical framework presented in Chapter 3 for understanding foreign investors' compliance with host-country laws: the reactions of foreign investors hinge on the institutional distances between the investors' home and host states, and their desire and ability to adapt to host-country institutions. Proceeding under the analytical framework, this section first examines the institutional gaps between China and the United States in the area of workplace equality. And I begin by sketching Chinese laws and comparing them to the corresponding U.S. laws.

After seizing power in 1949, the Chinese Communist Party (CCP) implemented a series of policies allegedly in conformity with the ideological teachings of communism, including the "eradication of gender and ethnic oppression." Article 96 of the 1954 Constitution provided Chinese women with the same political, economic, cultural, social, and familial rights as men.[20] For instance, the government encouraged women, who had "experienced a bitter history of prolonged oppression, degradation, and abasement,"[21] to join the workforce on equal terms to men.[22] The subsequent nationalization of private businesses, ideological indoctrination, and the expansion of the government's reach alleviated gender inequality.[23]

19 Scheiber and Bradsher, "Culture Clash at a Chinese-Owned Plant in Ohio."

20 Article 96, PRC Constitution of 1954, at www.npc.gov.cn/wxzl/wxzl/2000–12/26/content_4264.htm.

21 "The Situation of Chinese Women," Information Office of the State Council of the People's Republic of China, at http://news.xinhuanet.com/zhengfu/2002–11/18/content_633184.htm.

22 Xiaoling Shu, "Education and Gender Egalitarianism: The Case of China," 77 *Sociology of Education* 311 (2004), 316.

23 Bennis Wai-yip So, "The Policy-Making and Political Economy of the Abolition of Private Ownership in the Early 1950s: Findings from New Material," 171 *China Quarterly* 682 (2002), 682.

In addition, state-sponsored services such as public childcare eased the burden of household duties traditionally imposed on women.[24] As a result of all these changes, the participation of women in China's labor force increased dramatically.[25] According to a 2011 national survey, 71.1% of working-age women in China were employed,[26] compared to 64% in Japan and 63% in the United States.[27]

Similarly, the government adopted a wide array of preferential measures to boost employment for members of ethnic minority groups. For example, large state-owned enterprises in the autonomous regions were at one time required to meet a certain quota for hiring minority workers.[28] The "affirmative actions" mandated by the state in this period had lasting effects. Though "the gap in occupational attainment between Han Chinese and ethnic minorities increased" in the 1980s,[29] when the market reform began, the employment rates for the latter remained higher than those for the former until the 1990s.[30] Even in the current market environment, only certain ethnic groups appear to suffer employment discrimination.[31] In short, Chinese government policies favoring ethnic minority groups have arguably achieved some success in rectifying ethnicity-based discrimination.[32]

In engineering social changes, however, a strong state invariably wields a double-edged sword. Although some policies of the Chinese government ameliorated employment inequality, a number of others adopted in this formative period had enduring discriminatory effects.[33] Take, for example, the household registration system (also known as the *hukou*), which affixes each Chinese citizen to a locality categorized as either urban or rural.[34] For decades the Chinese government

24 Yan Tian, "Chongsi Zhongguo Fanjiuyieqishifa de Dangdai Xingqi" (Rethinking the Rise of Chinese Employment Discrimination Law), 3 *Zhongwai Faxue (Peking University Law Journal)* 560 (2012), 568.

25 More than 70% of working-age Chinese women were employed by the end of the first five-year plan (1954–8). Yu Yaping, "Woguo Funu Jiuye de Xianzhuang yu Duice Yanjiu" (Analysis of the Current Situation of Women Employment and Policy Response), at http://shcdf.eastday.com/epublish/gb/paper381/1/class038100003/hwz902477.htm.

26 All-China Women's Federation and National Bureau of Statistics in China, "Report on Major Results of the Third Wave Survey on the Social Status of Women in China" (Oct. 21, 2011), at http://landwise.resourceequity.org/record/228.

27 Danielle Paquette, "How American Women Fell behind Japanese Women in the Workplace," *Washington Post* (Oct. 7, 2015), at www.washingtonpost.com/news/wonk/wp/2015/10/07/how-american-women-fell-behind-japanese-women-in-the-workplace.

28 Barry Sautman, "Preferential Policies for Ethnic Minorities in China: The Case of Xinjiang," 4 *Nationalism and Ethnic Politics* 86 ([illegible]).

29 Ibid.

30 Margaret Maurer-Fazio, James Hughes, and Dandan Zhang, "An Ocean Formed from One Hundred Rivers: The Effects of Ethnicity, Gender, Marriage, and Location on Labor Force Participation in Urban China," 13 *Feminist Economics* 159 (2007), 177.

31 Ibid.

32 Timothy Webster, "Ambivalence and Activism: Employment Discrimination in China," 44 *Vanderbilt Journal of Transnational Law* 643 (2011), 649.

33 Ibid.

34 Kam Wing Chan and Li Zhang, "The Hukou System and Rural–Urban Migration in China: Processes and Changes," 160 *China Quarterly* 818 (1999).

redistributed the surplus generated by the rural populace to urban households,[35] and to maintain the dual system, it restricted rural residents from traveling and working outside the registered localities.[36] Coincidental with the economic liberalization, the rigid *hukou*-based restrictions started to loosen. Millions of rural residents sought low-skilled jobs in the cities, fueling the double-digit growth of the Chinese economy. While the market reform alleviated some of the unfair treatments under the *hukou* system, it has survived repeated calls for total abolition.[37] And discrimination against workers of rural registration remains common in Chinese cities.[38]

Certain state policies also led to entrenched gender inequality in Chinese workplaces. For instance, the 1951 Labor Insurance Rules set the retirement age for women at fifty (or fifty-five for cadres), five to ten years earlier than that for men.[39] In 1978 the State Council promulgated the Provisional Rules re Worker Retirement and Leave, which reinforced the disparity.[40] In the then-existing "cradle-to-grave" welfare system, such an arrangement symbolized paternalistic "favors" for female workers.[41] But when the market replaced the state as the primary mechanism for resource allocation, the mandated retirement ages inevitably conflict with the material interests of private employers, exacerbating gender discrimination in the workplace.[42] Besides gender-based discriminatory policies, the Chinese government had until recently treated carriers of infectious diseases unfairly.[43] For instance, carriers of the hepatitis B virus (HBV), which infected about 90 million Chinese, used to be excluded from most civil service jobs.[44]

The state's policy of discrimination against groups of certain traits did not stem from profit motives. The pre-reform employment system, having embodied "a fusion of Soviet regulation with Buddhist values for harmony and obedience,"[45] featured "centrally regulated job allocation, high job security, egalitarian pay system and

35 Tiejun Cheng and Mark Seldon, "The Origins and Social Consequences of China's Hukou System," 139 *China Quarterly* 644 (1994), 650–1.

36 Ibid.

37 Leng Lee, "Decomposing Wage Differentials between Migrant Workers and Urban Workers in Urban China's Labor Markets," 23 *China Economic Review* 461 (2012); Kam Wing Chan and Will Buckingham, "Is China Abolishing the Hukou System?", 195 *China Quarterly* 582 (2008).

38 Yang Song, "What Should Economists Know about the Current Chinese Hukou System?", 29 *China Economic Review* 200 (2014).

39 Lin Jia, "Tuixiu Nianling de Fali Fenxi ji Zhidu Anpai" (Analysis of Retirement Age and Institutional Arrangements), 359 *Zhongguo Faxue* (China Legal Science) 5 (2015), 6.

40 Article 1, Guowuyuan Guanyu Gongren Tuixiu Tuizhi de Zanxing Banfa (State Council Provisional Rules re the Retirement and Leave for Workers) (May 24, 1978), at www.npc.gov.cn/wxzl/wxzl/2000–12/07/content_9552.htm.

41 Ibid.

42 Lin Jia, "Analysis of Retirement Age and Institutional Arrangements," 8; Christine M. Bulger, "Fighting Gender Discrimination in the Chinese Workplace," 20 *Boston College Third World Law Journal* 345 (2000), 353–4.

43 Webster, "Ambivalence and Activism," 646. 44 Ibid.

45 Shaohui Chen and Marie Wilson, "Standardization and Localization of Human Resource Management in Sino-Foreign Joint Ventures," 20 *Asia Pacific Journal of Management* 397 (2003), 398.

cradle-to-grave social welfare systems."[46] Thus, most of the systemic workplace inequalities simply reflected conflicting state policy goals. But when the state gave up on parts of socialist ideology and withdrew from micromanaging the economy, rampant employment discrimination ensued.[47] Having shed its ownership control over most employers, the Chinese government had to rely on law to regulate the workplace. Hence, labor and employment law legislation in China evolved concurrently with market reform.[48]

The Chinese Labor Law, which took effect in 1995 and set forth the basic legal rights for workers, marked the dawning of decades-long active labor and employment legislation. It codified the right of Chinese workers to nondiscrimination. Article 12 of the statute prohibits discrimination based on ethnicity, race, gender, or religion. The legislation, however, failed to effect significant behavioral changes,[49] and widespread employment discrimination persisted.[50] In response to mounting social discontent, the Chinese legislature passed additional employment-related laws.[51] The Chinese Labor Contract Law (2007), for instance, closed some of the loopholes in the existing laws and reallocated the legal rights and obligations between employers and employees to favor the latter.[52]

Following immediately was the enactment of the Chinese Employment Promotion Law in 2008,[53] which signaled the Chinese legislature's determination to promote employment equality. For instance, the language of Articles 28 and 29 advocates the hiring of minority candidates and those with disabilities,[54] and Article 30 of the statute bars discrimination against carriers of infectious diseases such as HIV or HBV. In addition, to address discrimination caused by the household registration system, Article 31 stipulates equal treatment for both urban and migrant workers.[55] Furthermore, Chinese government agencies have promulgated a wide array of administrative rules aimed at safeguarding the employment rights of

46 Ibid., 398.

47 Maurer-Fazio, Hughes, and Zhang, "An Ocean Formed from One Hundred Rivers," 160; Alvin Y. So, "The Changing Pattern of Classes and Class Conflict in China," 33 *Journal of Contemporary Asia* 363 (2003), 366–7.

48 Yan Tian, "Rethinking the Rise of Chinese Employment Discrimination Law," 565.

49 In that respect, the PRC Labor Law is probably not unique, as labor law legislation in other countries is often the result of symbolic politics. See, e.g., Alan Hyde, "Theory of Labor Legislation, A," 38 *Buffalo Law Review* 383 (1990).

50 Sean Cooney, "Making Chinese Labor Law Work: The Prospects for Regulatory Innovation in the People's Republic of China," 30 *Fordham International Law Journal* 1050 (2007), 1060.

51 Virginia E. Happer Ho, "From Contracts to Compliance? An Early Look at Implementation under China's New Labor Legislation," 23 *Columbia Journal of Asian Law* 35 (2009), 39.

52 Hilary K. Josephs, "Measuring Progress under China's Labor Law: Goals, Processes, Outcomes," 30 *Comparative Labour Law and Policy Journal* 373 (2008), 386.

53 Zonghua Renmin Gongheguo Jiuye Cujin Fa (P.R.C. Law on Employment Promotion) (promulgated Aug. 30, 2007 by Standing Comm. Nat'l People's Cong., effective Jan 1, 2008), www.gov.cn/flfg/2007–08/31/content_732597.htm.

54 Ibid. 55 Ibid.

"disadvantaged Chinese, including women, ethnic minorities, the disabled, and carriers of infectious diseases."[56]

In short, after two decades of cumulative lawmaking, the Chinese employment laws in the books converged on international standards set by countries featuring comprehensive legal safeguards of workers' rights.[57] According to an OECD report, China ranks among the top of all major economies in terms of employment protection legislation.[58] Since it largely adopted the continental European model, the legal protection of workers' rights even exceeds that of the United States in selected areas. Moreover, regarding employment discrimination, a variety of Chinese laws have incorporated the basic principles of equality embodied in Title VII of the Civil Rights Act.[59] But the devil is in the lack of details. The existing statutory language fails to clearly define and specify the key legal and factual elements necessary for effective compliance and enforcement.[60] To a certain degree, the Chinese laws in their current form resemble the vaguely defined and weakly enforced U.S. employment equality rules before and immediately after the enactment of Title VII.[61]

Thus, vast compliance and enforcement gaps remain in this area between China and the United States. While the United States has by no means eradicated unlawful employment-related discrimination, the issue plagues Chinese workplaces.[62] Consider gender discrimination as an example. A recent survey claims that 50% of female workers in China frequently encounter gender-based workplace discrimination, 47% experience occasional discrimination, and merely 3% reported having no such experience.[63] Another survey by the National Confederation of Women also

56 Webster, "Ambivalence and Activism," 645.

57 China has ratified a series of international conventions against discrimination, for instance the Discrimination (Employment and Occupation) Convention, 1958 (No. 111), ratified on Jan. 12, 2006, at www.ilo.org/dyn/normlex/en/f?p=1000:11200:0::NO:11200:P11200_COUNTRY_ID:103404; and the Convention on the Elimination of All Forms of Discrimination against Women, ratified on Nov. 4, 1980, https://treaties.un.org/pages/viewdetails.aspx?src=treaty&mtdsg_no=iv-8&chapter=4&lang=en.

58 See OECD, "OECD indicators on Employment Protection Legislation 2013," data available at www.oecd.org/els/emp/EPL-data2013.xlsx.

59 However, the coverage of Chinese law is not as broad as that of U.S. law. For instance, unlike in the United States, age discrimination is not one of the enumerated prohibitions under the Chinese Employment Promotion Law (CEPL), though one may argue that the general legal principles of nondiscrimination embodied in the CEPL extend to age discrimination, and there have been anecdotal cases where the government held age discrimination to be a violation of the law. See, e.g., You Chunliang, "Shenzhen Zhengquan Jiaoyisuo Zhaopin Nianling Qishi bei Rending Weifa" (Shengzhen Stock Exchange Hiring Concerns Illegal Age Discrimination), *Fazhiwang* (April 12, 2012), at www.legaldaily.com.cn/index/content/2012–04/12/content_3491318.htm.

60 Webster, "Ambivalence and Activism," 702.

61 Kim Soohan, Alexandra Kalev, and Frank Dobbin, "Progressive Corporations at Work: The Case of Diversity Programs," 36 *NYU Review of Law and Social Change* 171 (2012), 178.

62 Webster, "Ambivalence and Activism," 660–2.

63 Wang Yejie, "Diaocha Xianshi: 50% Nuxing Gongzuozhong Jingchang Shoudao Xingbie Qishi" (Report Shows 50% of Women Frequently Experience Workplace Discrimination), *Zhongguo*

shows rampant gender-based discrimination. Nearly half of all employers in China consider the gender and marital status of job candidates and more than half of women candidates are asked questions relating to childbearing and marriage.[64] By comparison, only 18% of women in the United States report having experienced gender-based discrimination at work;[65] according to other recent research, merely 4.4% of employees in the United States perceived sex-based discrimination within the prior year.[66] Very few systematic comparative studies have been conducted in this area between China and the United States, with one exception that offers preliminary evidence showing that working women in China are more likely than those in the United States to report that gender influences decisions related to their hiring, pay, performance appraisal, and career progress.[67]

Besides vague and ambiguous legal terms in the Chinese law prohibiting employment discrimination, one may ascribe the law's comparatively poor enforcement to inadequate judicial intervention in China. Although the substantive laws entitle the victims to sue,[68] litigation has proved a futile tool for combating discrimination in China.[69] Chinese plaintiffs must cross higher evidentiary barriers to win discrimination cases than their U.S. counterparts. In the United States, plaintiffs may prove "intentional" discrimination entirely from circumstantial evidence,[70] and they may prevail when circumstantial evidence suggests that the defendant employers' motives for the personnel actions at issue were mixed.[71] Moreover, plaintiffs in the United States may use "disparate impact" evidence to make a prima facie case of discrimination and shift the burden of proof to the defendant. In such cases the

Qingnian Bao (China Youth Daily) (March 28, 2016), at http://zqb.cyol.com/html/2016–03/28/nw.D110000zgqnb_20160328_5–04.htm.

64 Lin Zizhen, "Sun Xiaomei Daibiao: Fan Jiuye Qishi Zhuanmen Lifa Ying Naru Guihua" (Sun Xiaomei Representative: Special Anti-employment Discrimination Statute Should Be Included in Legislation Plan), *Caixinwang* (March 7, 2017), at http://topics.caixin.com/2017–03-07/101063007.html.

65 "On Pay Gap, Millennial Women Near Parity: For Now Despite Gains, Many See Roadblocks Ahead," Pew Research Center (Dec. 11, 2013), at http://assets.pewresearch.org/wp-content/uploads/sites/3/2013/12/gender-and-work_final.pdf.

66 The percentage is calculated based on the entire survey sample, including both men and women. However, the breakdown of the numbers suggests that women were nearly 12.5 times more likely than men to perceive sex-based discrimination. Derek R. Avery, Patrick F. McKay, and David C. Wilson, "What Are the odds? How Demographic Similarity Affects the Prevalence of Perceived Employment Discrimination," 93.2 *Journal of Applied Psychology* 235 (2008).

67 Margaret A. Shaffer et al., "Gender Discrimination and Job-Related Outcomes: A Cross-cultural Comparison of Working Women in the United States and China," 57.3 *Journal of Vocational Behavior* 395 (2000).

68 Article 62 of the PRC Employment Promotion Law entitles workers to sue for employment discrimination.

69 In comparison, Chinese courts play an important role in resolving other types of labor dispute. See, e.g., Cynthia Estlund, "Will Workers Have a Voice in China's 'Socialist Market Economy'? The Curious Revival of the Workers Congress System," 36 *Comparative Labor Law and Policy Journal* 69 (2014), 93.

70 *Reeves* v. *Sanderson Plumbing Prods. Inc.*, 530 US 133 (2000).

71 *Desert Palace* v. *Costa*, 539 US 90 (2003).

plaintiffs only need to show that the employer uses personnel practices with a disparate impact across protected groups.[72] The employer's motive is irrelevant. In sharp contrast, plaintiffs in China generally bear the burden of providing *direct* evidence of discrimination in order to obtain judicial relief.[73] Such evidence being hard to obtain in most circumstances, victims of work-related discrimination fight an uphill battle in Chinese courts.[74]

Inadequate incentives also contribute to poor enforcement of employment discrimination laws. Under pressure from business-friendly local governments,[75] Chinese courts usually award winning plaintiffs no more than a few thousand yuan (a few hundred U.S. dollars), and punitive damages are almost unheard of.[76] Inadequate awards and penalties undercut the incentives not only for the victims to sue for work-related discrimination but also for employers to comply with the law.

Though the law is a frail weapon for the disadvantaged in China's workplaces, some observe significant variations among Chinese employers in their compliance. By and large, Chinese state-owned enterprises (SOEs) have a better record of complying with employment-related laws.[77] As previously noted, SOEs' political status enables them to influence legislation that may implicate their core interests, so subsequent compliance does not significantly alter the status quo for the most powerful SOEs.[78] Moreover, SOE managers do not fully internalize the cost of legal compliance due to the inherent multilayered agency problem, nor are they subject to the same profit imperatives as managers of private companies.[79] Furthermore, commanding vast state resources and enormous market power, the largest SOEs are more capable than firms of other types of sustaining high-standard work conditions.[80] More importantly, SOEs are inclined to pacify employees, who collectively form an important constituency and a solid power base of the political regime. In sum, SOEs, while not entirely immune to workplace discrimination,[81] are more likely to treat current employees equally than are Chinese firms of other

72 42 USC Sec. 2000e-2(k)(1).

73 Yan Tian, "Fan Jiuye Qishifa de Yiban Lilun: Zhongmei Liangguo de Jiangou yu Fansi" (The General Principle of Law against Employment Discrimination – Comparing China and the United States), 36 *Huanqiu Falu Pinglun (Global Law Review)* 59 (2014), 70.

74 Ibid.

75 Mary E. Gallagher, "China's Workers Movement and the End of the Rapid-Growth Era," 143 *Daedalus* 81 (2014), 83.

76 Yan Tian, "The General Principle of Law against Employment Discrimination," 72.

77 Boy Lüthje, Siqi Luo, and Hao Zhang, *Beyond the Iron Rice Bowl: Regimes of Production and Industrial Relations in China* (2013).

78 Ji Li, "Does Law Matter in China? An Empirical Study of a Limiting Case," 46 *George Washington International Law Review* 119 (2014), 159.

79 Garry D. Bruton, Mike W. Peng, David Ahlstrom, Ciprian Sten, and Kehan Xu, "State-Owned Enterprises around the World as Hybrid Organizations," 29 *Academy of Management Perspectives* 92 (2015), 93.

80 Lüthje, Luo, and Zhang, *Beyond the Iron Rice Bowl.*

81 Xiaowei Zang, "Affirmative Action, Economic Reforms, and Han–Uyghur Variation in Job Attainment in the State Sector in Urumchi," 202 *China Quarterly* 344 (2010).

ownership characters.[82] That being said, SOEs have been found to engage in serious discrimination when screening job candidates.[83]

Besides the SOEs, large MNEs in China are typically in compliance with Chinese law, as they "tend to copy traditional Western company styles."[84] Sizable private Chinese companies, without the political clout of the SOEs, also invest in legal compliance to lower the risk of high-stakes governmental interference. However, as their compensation is better aligned with corporate profits, the managers of private Chinese firms tend to be more opportunistic than SOE managers in making compliance decisions. Take, for example, the controversial reaction of Huawei, one of the largest and most competitive private companies in China,[85] to the Chinese Labor Contract Law. In December 2007, shortly before the statute went into effect, about 7,000 Huawei employees were offered "voluntary" resignation followed by employment contracts for one to three years.[86] The Labor Contract Law provides that "workers who have served in a company for ten consecutive years" should be treated as having entered into an "open-ended labor contract" without a definite termination date, which entitles the employees to extraordinary rights.[87] The maneuver by Huawei illustrates both the attention of large private Chinese companies to legal compliance and, at the same time, their willingness to take full advantage of legal loopholes.[88]

In contrast, the vast majority of small and medium-sized private Chinese companies account for most of the employment law violations in China.[89] Prior research has found them to engage in "large scale exploitation of migrant workers, including long work hours, violation of legal standards and low wages and usually no presence

82 Margaret Maurer-Fazio, "Ethnic Discrimination in China's Internet Job Board Labor Market," 1 *IZA Journal of Migration* 1 (2012).

83 Zhou Xiangyi and Song Xuetao, "Zhaopin Shichang shang de Xingbie Qishi: Laizi Zhongguo 19130 fen Jianli de Zhengju" (Gender Discrimination in the Employment Market: Evidence of 19,130 CVs), 8 *Zhongguo Gongye Jingji* 145 (2016). Many Chinese courts even consider the antidiscrimination provisions inapplicable to hiring practices. Aaron Halegua, "Who Will Represent China's Workers? Lawyers, Legal Aid, and the Enforcement of Labor Rights," report for the Ford Foundation (2016).

84 Lüthje, Luo, and Zhang, *Beyond the Iron Rice Bowl*.

85 The company ranked 129 on Fortune Global 500 in 2015, at http://beta.fortune.com/global500.

86 Chen Hong, "Thousands of Huawei Staff 'Quit'," *China Daily* (Nov. 3, 2007), at www.chinadaily.com.cn/china/2007–11/03/content_6228172.htm.

87 Article 14, PRC Labor Contract Law (effective Jan. 1, 2008).

88 Guangdong Provincial High Court later decided that such maneuvers would be void. Lin Jie, "Guangdong Laodong Zhengyi'an Jingpen, Huawei Wanren Cizhi bei Rending Wuxiao" (Guangdong Province Saw Labor Disputes Surge, Huawei Massive Resignation Void), *Zhongguo Qingnian Bao* (China Youth Daily) (July 21, 2008), at http://news.xinhuanet.com/legal/2008–07/21/content_8707282.htm.

89 Note that the varying degree of compliance with employment law across employers of different size and ownership is not unique to China. In the United States, for instance, large employers in the private sector and governmental instrumentalities tend to follow the law of workplace equality more closely than small and medium-sized private employers. See, e.g., Cynthia L. Estlund, "The Workplace in a Racially Diverse Society: Preliminary Thoughts on the Role of Labor and Employment Law," 1 *University of Pennsylvania Journal of Labor and Employment Law* 49 (1998), 59.

of unions."[90] Chinese workers are well aware of the variation in employment practices. According to a 2010 survey of college graduates in China, 41% of respondents preferred to work for SOEs, 26% multinationals, 17% government, and 7% private firms.[91]

To summarize, Chinese employment laws have made notable progress; in less than two decades, the state passed a whole set of new statutes to replace the cradle-to-grave system befitting a Soviet-style planned economy. While bearing various institutional vestiges,[92] the market-based legal regime embodied "unbridled enthusiasm for 'following international practices and norms.'"[93] However, despite the remarkable legislative progress, serious compliance and enforcement issues persisted. Because of the formal laws' lack of applicability and ineffective judicial intervention, discrimination in its multiple forms remains widespread in Chinese workplaces. That being said, compliance varies across employers of different sizes and ownership types.[94] For instance, Chinese SOEs are less likely than others to engage in ethnic discrimination and both state- and foreign-owned firms are significantly more likely to treat candidates equally than are domestic firms.[95] As Chinese companies of diverse sizes and ownership structures invest in the United States, how do they react to the U.S. institutions governing employment practices, especially those prohibiting employment discrimination? Are they going to be entangled in the same problems as are currently facing Fuyao Glass in its Ohio plant?

Before proceeding, it is worth reminding readers that U.S. workplaces, especially those of small firms,[96] are by no means free from discrimination, though blatant forms of discrimination may have been replaced by discrimination in more subtle forms.[97] And a vast body of literature has highlighted the flaws in the current U.S. legal system to battle discrimination. For instance, even in the United States, "discrimination litigants face difficult odds" in courts, as "less than 5% of all discrimination plaintiffs will ever achieve any form of litigated relief."[98] They fare

90 Lüthje, Luo, and Zhang, *Beyond the Iron Rice Bowl.*

91 Yan and Sautman, "The Beginning of a World Empire?", 134.

92 Taylor C. Boas, "Conceptualizing Continuity and Change the Composite-Standard Model of Path Dependence," 19 *Journal of Theoretical Politics* 33 (2007).

93 Yu Zhou, Xiao-Yu Liu, and Ying Hong, "When Western HRM Constructs Meet Chinese Contexts: Validating the Pluralistic Structures of Human Resource Management System in China," in Malcolm Warner, ed., *Whither Chinese HRM? Paradigms, Models and Theories* (2013), 24.

94 Smith and Zheng, "The Management of Labour in Chinese MNCs," 370.

95 Margaret Maurer-Fazio, "Ethnic Discrimination in China's Internet Job Board."

96 Richard J. Pierce Jr., "Small Is Not Beautiful: The Case against Special Regulatory Treatment of Small Firms," 50 *Administrative Law Review* 537 (1998).

97 See, e.g., Kathryn M. Neckerman and Joleen Kirschenman, "Hiring Strategies, Racial Bias, and Inner-City Workers," 38 *Social Problems* 433 (1991), 433–4; David Neumark, Roy J. Bank, and Kyle D. Van Nort, "Sex Discrimination in Restaurant Hiring: An Audit Study," *Quarterly Journal of Economics* 915 (1996), 917–19.

98 Katie R. Eyer, "That's Not Discrimination: American Beliefs and the Limits of Anti-discrimination Law," 96 *Minnesota Law Review* 1275 (2012), 1276.

better only than prisoners.[99] The institutional difference between China and the United States, though substantial, is a matter of degree.

II EMPLOYMENT PRACTICES OF CHINESE COMPANIES IN FOREIGN COUNTRIES

China has long been a magnet for FDI, and a vast literature has accumulated that explores the employment practices of MNEs doing business in the world's largest developing country.[100] Yet in stark contrast, much remains unknown about the employment practices of Chinese companies in foreign countries, mainly because Chinese ODI, despite its rapid growth, is a rather recent phenomenon. Media reports have preceded systemic research on how they comply with foreign employment laws. Overall, the coverage has been rather negative. For instance, one analogized Chinese investment to a "Trojan Horse" destroying "established norms and policies, from human rights to labour laws."[101] Another has accused Chinese companies

> of breaking rules on working hours and health and safety; using coercive forms of labour control, including withholding wages to inhibit mobility and taking deposits to control migrant workers, whether irregular or regular; trafficking forced labour; ignoring or suppressing trade unions; paying wages below subsistence levels, and even employing prison labour on construction and civil engineering projects.[102]

Most NGOs hold similarly critical views about Chinese companies' overseas labor practices. According to Human Rights Watch, for instance, Chinese investors' worker management in Zambia evidences "cruelty and disregard for human life."[103]

By comparison, recent research has drawn a more nuanced picture. From in-depth case studies, Yan and Sautman find no proof that Chinese companies in Zambia, compared to their peers from other countries, were unusually cruel in treating the local workers.[104] Some scholars detect pro-labor effects of state

[99] Wendy Parker, "Lessons in Losing: Race Discrimination in Employment," 81 *Notre Dame Law Review* 889 (2006), 891.

[100] Evi Hartmann, Edda Feisel, and Holger Schober, "Talent Management of Western MNCs in China: Balancing Global Integration and Local Responsiveness," 45 *Journal of World Business* 169 (2010); Cherrie Jiuhua Zhu, Brian K. Cooper, Di Fan, and Helen De Cieri, "HR Practices from the Perspective of Managers and Employees in Multinational Enterprises in China: Alignment Issues and Implications," 48 *Journal of World Business* 241 (2013); Jiafei Jin, Chih-Chieh Chen, Patricia Fosh, and Yang Chen, "Understanding Chinese Non-managerial Employees' Response to Western HRM: Changes in Turnover Intention," 52 *Asia Pacific Journal of Human Resources* 316 (2014); Christian Schmidt, Sebastian Mansson, and Harald Dolles, "Managing Talents for Global Leadership Positions in MNCs: Responding to the Challenges in China," 12 *Asian Business and Management* 477 (2013); Adam Smale, Ingmar Björkman, and Jennie Sumelius, "Examining the Differential Use of Global Integration Mechanisms across HRM Practices: Evidence from China," 48 *Journal of World Business* 232 (2013).

[101] Smith and Zheng, "The Management of Labour in Chinese MNCs," 379. [102] Ibid.

[103] Yan and Sautman, "The Beginning of a World Empire?", 136. [104] Ibid.

ownership in Chinese investors,[105] and attribute deteriorating employment practices to the withdrawal of state financial support and the subsequent profit imperatives for the managers.[106] Comparing two Chinese-invested businesses in Zambia and Tanzania, Lee reveals tensions between the Chinese managers and the local employees. Chinese investment coincided with the casualization of employment relations, and local employees complained about, among other things, long work hours, unfair treatment, and low pay.[107] Yet Lee also finds varying dynamics of employer–employee relationships in the two cases and cautions against overgeneralization.[108] Similarly, Pal's research about Chinese companies in Cambodia cautions against oversimplification of their employment practices. While large state-owned Chinese investors won praise from the local workers for their paternalistic management style, the employment practices of small and private Chinese firms spurred much resentment.[109]

Additionally, research about Chinese companies in developing countries finds heavy reliance on expatriated employees. China dispatched nearly 5 million workers abroad from 1978 to 2009,[110] and by the end of 2015 as many as a million Chinese workers were working in 190 foreign countries.[111] The expatriates "follow Chinese firm tenets," live in "company-based industrial dormitories," and are "tightly controlled and more likely to focus on work during the contract period and submit to compulsory overtime."[112] The ethnic enclaves formed by Chinese expatriates "reinforce home-country habits"[113] and aggravate problems such as "language barriers, lack of awareness of host society practices, or hostility in host societies towards new migrants."[114]

The employment practices of Chinese MNEs may also vary according to the host country's level of economic development. One study reports that Chinese MNEs pay high wages and provide good working conditions in developed countries and the opposite in developing countries.[115] Another study finds Chinese investors indistinguishable from those of other countries in dealing with unions and workers in

105 Peter Kragelund, "Part of the Disease or Part of the Cure: Chinese Investments in the Zambian Mining and Construction Sectors," 21 *European Journal of Development Research* 644 (2009), 649.

106 Haglund, "In It for the Long Term?", 645–6.

107 Ching Kwan Lee, "Raw Encounters: Chinese Managers, African Workers and the Politics of Casualization in Africa's Chinese Enclaves," 199 *China Quarterly* 627 (2009), 647.

108 Ibid.

109 Nyíri Pál, "Chinese Investors, Labour Discipline and Developmental Cosmopolitanism," 44 *Development and Change* 1387 (2013), 1397.

110 Shambaugh, *China Goes Global*, 179.

111 "News Conference for COFCOM Platform about 'Going Global' Service, i.e. Investment Host Countries (Regions) Guide 2015," MOFCOM (Dec. 9, 2015), at www.mofcom.gov.cn/article/ae/slfw/201512/20151201206646.shtml.

112 Smith and Zheng, "The Management of Labour in Chinese MNCs," 379.

113 Ibid., 375–6.

114 Ibid.

115 Jie Shen, "Approaches to International Industrial Relations in Chinese Multinational Corporations," 18 *Management Revue* 410 (2007).

European countries.[116] Moreover, Zhang and Edwards uncover evidence of not only the adoption of employment practices in developed countries, but also reverse diffusion of the practices back home.[117] However, some contend that, even in developed countries, Chinese firms fall short of full compliance. Wu and Sheehan compare Chinese-owned and Italian-owned businesses in Italy and find the former to have worse work conditions, lower hourly pay, and inadequate benefits.[118]

The variance in the employment practices of Chinese MNEs has convinced some that "there is not a single dominant labor process model, except perhaps a management focus on tight cost consciousness, competition, and authoritarian control."[119] In other words, Chinese outbound investors may retain a few home-state traits, but rational cost–benefit calculations also guide them to adjust corporate behavior in accordance with host-country institutions. Recent studies have found that some Chinese SOEs, despite their preference for expatriates, yielded to pressure from host-country institutions and employed local workers.[120] Hence, "Chinese multinational companiess are well capable of embracing locality norms and working with the agencies of local institutions,"[121] especially in host countries with robust institutions such as the United States.[122]

To summarize, the surge of Chinese ODI has generated much negative coverage of Chinese companies' employment practices. The emerging literature on the topic, however, presents a more nuanced picture. While some further highlight the management–employee tensions in Chinese-invested businesses, others question the claim that Chinese employers treat local workers any worse than MNEs based in other countries. Moreover, scholars demonstrate that the employment practices of Chinese MNEs defy oversimplified generalization. How Chinese employers interact with local employees and institutions depends on a variety of factors such as ownership characteristics and host-country contexts.

Though the burgeoning literature offers valuable insights about the employment practices of Chinese companies in developing countries, the debate remains largely unsettled. It also leaves us in the dark as to how Chinese companies will react to the sophisticated employment regulatory system in the United States, especially the complex institutions prohibiting employment discrimination. The following section provides some questions.

116 Burgoon and Raess, "Chinese Investment and European Labor," 179 (2014).

117 Miao Zhang and Christine Edwards, "Diffusing 'Best Practice' in Chinese Multinationals: The Motivation, Facilitation and Limitations," 18 *International Journal of Human Resource Management* 2147 (2007).

118 Bin Wu and Jackie Sheehan, "Globalization and Vulnerability of Chinese Migrant Workers in Italy: Empirical Evidence on Working Conditions and Their Consequences," 20 *Journal of Contemporary China* 135 (2011), 151–2.

119 Smith and Zheng, "The Management of Labour in Chinese MNCs," 374.

120 Ibid., at 376.

121 Ibid., at 380.

122 Ji Li, "I Came, I Saw, I . . . Adapted," 143.

III CHINESE COMPANIES' EMPLOYMENT PRACTICES IN THE UNITED STATES

Section I briefly chronicled the development of Chinese employment-related law in the past decades. The legislators adopted European standards for the protection of employment rights, and the formal laws share the basic concepts and principles of U.S. laws prohibiting employment discrimination. But below the surface, significant differences still exist between the two countries in this area of law. The laws in China remain vague and expressive, and Chinese courts have provided weak enforcement. As a result, employment discrimination, while still existing even in the United States, remains rampant in Chinese workplaces. Having highlighted the institutional distances, I now turn my attention to the desire and ability of Chinese investors to adapt to U.S. employment law. Again, I examined in Chapter 3 two of the factors (i.e., investment motive and the allocation of decision-making power) that do not vary across different areas of law. The following subsections focus on the other two variables – perceptions of U.S. employment rules and reliance on local professionals.

A *Views on the U.S. Employment Market and Rules*

Labor and employment issues keep Chinese managers in the United States awake at night. According to the CGCC surveys, "high labor cost" tops the list of challenges and risks of doing business in the United States (see Figure 6.1). This is hardly surprising, given the relatively precocious nature of Chinese ODI. Compared to Japan and South Korea, "the internationalization of Chinese firms is occurring at a much earlier stage of economic development."[123] Therefore, the labor shortage experienced by the former two countries during the peak years of their development is not the primary driver of Chinese firms' ODI in developed countries.[124] Though labor cost is growing rapidly in China, it is still way below the cost in the United States. As Chairman Cao of Fuyao Glass recently noted, "all the major costs for doing business are higher in China than in the United States, except for labor."[125]

Besides high labor costs, the survey respondents also expressed concerns with the shortage of management talent. Managing Chinese investments in the United States requires a unique set of skills and knowledge. Ideal candidates should be able to traverse the huge divide in culture, language, and management style. Such talent is certainly in short supply.[126] As observed by a China expert, "the Achilles' heel of Chinese multinationals is human resources – particularly management."[127]

123 Smith and Zheng, "The Management of Labour in Chinese MNCs," 375. 124 Ibid., 368.

125 Shen Zewei, "Cao Dewang Pao Le? 'Boli Dawang' Cheng Zaimei Kaichang Lirun Gaoyu Zhongguo" (Cao Dewang Fled China? "Glass King" Argues Profits from Manufacturing in the US Higher than in China), *Lianhe Zaobao* (Dec. 19, 2016), at www.zaobao.com.sg/realtime/china/story20161219-703939, last accessed on Dec. 25, 2016.

126 Jie Shen, "Approaches to International Industrial Relations."

127 Shambaugh, *China Goes Global*, 186.

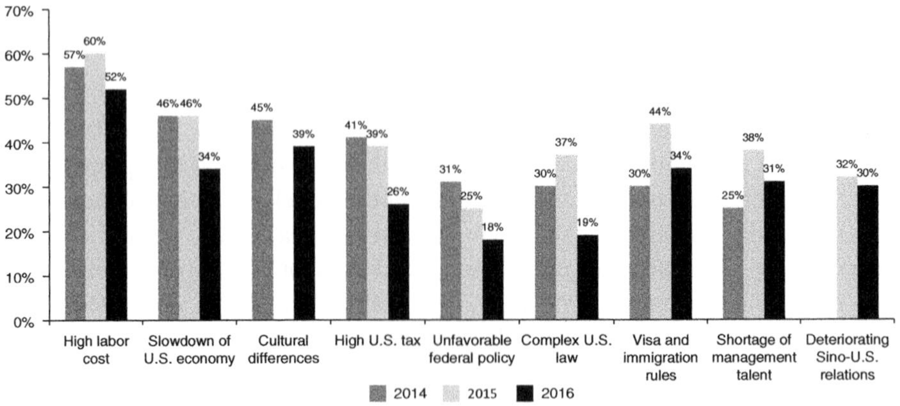

FIGURE 6.1 Major challenges and risks of doing business in the United States
Source: 2014–16 surveys (in the 2016 survey, "cultural differences" refers specifically to the difference in management culture between China and the United States)

Labor unions in the United States rank low on the list of the concerns. According to the 2015 survey, only 12% of respondents consider union issues to be a challenge of doing business in the United States. Though almost all large Chinese firms host well-organized "grassroots" affiliates of the All-China Federation of Trade Unions (ACFTU) and therefore have some experience dealing with labor organizations, unions in the United States are much more adversarial. The ACFTU chapters, while serving certain management functions and representing the workers' interests,[128] ultimately hold dear the government's core interests in facilitating business investment and maintaining stability.[129] Prior experiences of working with the ACFTU do not aid Chinese managers' interactions with the more confrontational unions in the United States. The lack of concern shown in the survey data, therefore, is attributable to the low rate of unionization in the United States and the fact that Chinese companies have not invested heavily in sectors with high union representation.[130]

The 2016 survey contained a question inquiring specifically about Chinese managers' perception of the effects of U.S. labor and employment rules. As illustrated in Figure 6.2, only about 10% of the respondents hold negative views. In contrast, more than 46% considered U.S. laws to have positive effects. The rest find the rules to have little effect on their businesses.

To summarize, this subsection has shown that employment matters top the list of concerns for Chinese MNE managers in the United States. Their opinions about

[128] Simon Clarke, Chang-Hee Lee, and Qi Li, "Collective Consultation and Industrial Relations in China," 42 *British Journal of Industrial Relations* 235 (2004), 242.

[129] Feng Chen, "Between the State and Labour: The Conflict of Chinese Trade Unions' Double Identity in Market Reform," 176 *China Quarterly* 1006 (2003), 1011.

[130] Aaron Halegua, "United States," in Minawa Ebisui, Sean Cooney, and Colin Fenwick, eds., *Resolving Individual Labor Disputes: A Comparative Overview* (2016), 313.

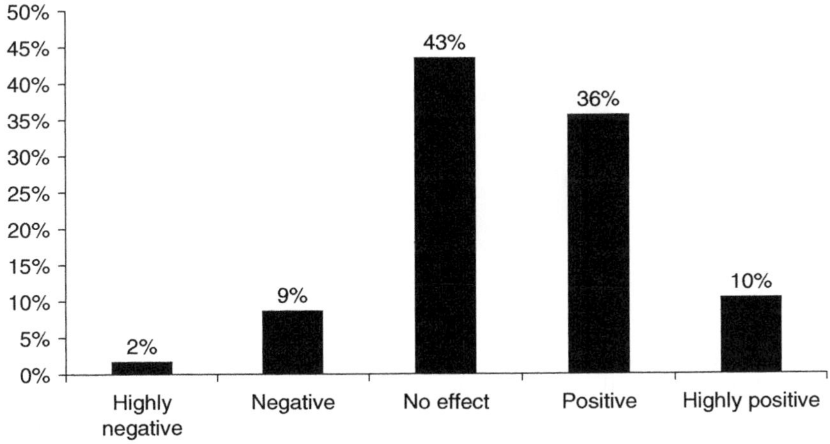

FIGURE 6.2 View on the effect of U.S. labor and employment rules
Source: 2016 survey

U.S. employment rules, though positive in general, vary significantly across the firms. Given the overall positive view and their long-term investment commitment, illustrated earlier, Chinese firms in the United States should exhibit a general, albeit variant, inclination to make the necessary adjustments to U.S. law regulating the workplace.

B Reliance on Local Professionals

Compliance with host-country legal and regulatory institutions governing U.S. workplaces also hinges on foreign investors' ability to comply. Chapter 3 demonstrated that Chinese investors localize decision-making to a great extent but retain the power to decide major personnel and compliance matters. To avoid repetition, this subsection focuses on the second factor crucial to the ability to adapt, i.e., reliance by Chinese investors on local professionals to handle human resource matters in the United States.

The survey results present a nuanced picture. First, the vast majority of the surveyed companies have either set up separate departments for human resource management (HRM) or employed full-time HRM staff, indicating the importance of the issue to Chinese investors. According to the 2015 survey, only about 17% of survey respondents reported having no full-time HRM position. Second, for those that had full-time HRM staff, 34% reported having expatriated the staff from the Chinese headquarters. In other words, while the majority of full-time human resource managers in the Chinese companies were local recruits, a significant minority relied on the headquarters' expertise.

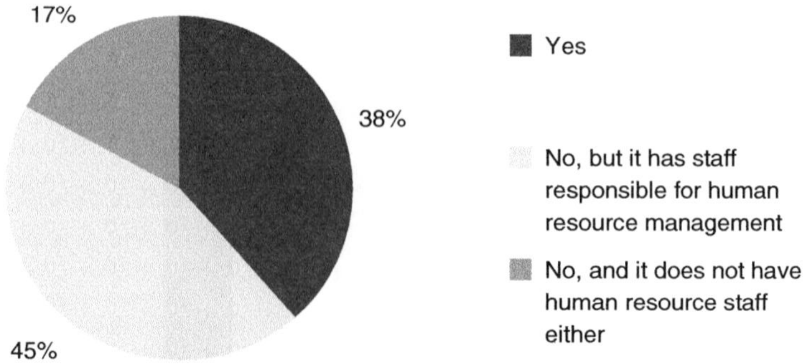

FIGURE 6.3 Human resource staff (survey question: whether your firm has a human resource department in the United States)
Source: 2015 survey (ninety-nine respondents for this question)

In addition to HRM staff, legal and compliance personnel should add to the capacity of Chinese companies to cope with U.S. employment law. For instance, the in-house counsel of a major Chinese developer with substantial U.S. businesses repeatedly advised the Chinese managers not to ask female job candidates about their marital status or plans for having children.[131] However, as discussed earlier, only a minority of Chinese firms have developed in-house legal and compliance capacity. Moreover, some Chinese firms may outsource certain human resource matters to local professional firms, such as designing employee manuals and reviewing employment contracts.[132] Some may rely on local service providers for recruiting and training.[133] In summary, regarding Chinese companies' capacity to comply with U.S. employment rules, the data portray a nuanced picture. While the majority relied on local recruits to handle human resources, a significant minority of survey respondents either have no full-time HRM staff or have expatriated the staff from China. Those relying on U.S. legal and compliance professionals may further mitigate the risk of violating employment discrimination law. Thus, Chinese investors should possess generally adequate but varying capacity to conform to U.S. employment institutions.

C *Adaptation to U.S. Employment Institutions*

To briefly recapitulate, though the formal Chinese and U.S. laws proscribing employment discrimination share the same basic principles, their enforcement

131 Interview with in-house counsel for the U.S. affiliate of a large Chinese company in real estate and investment (May 14, 2017).

132 Interview with the manager of a branch of a Chinese bank in the United States (June 26, 2017); interview with an executive of the U.S. affiliate of a Chinese company in construction and transportation (June 23, 2017).

133 Interview with the manager of a small Chinese pharmaceutical company (June 21, 2015).

and compliance notably differ in the two countries. Facing large institutional gaps, are the Chinese companies in the United States willing and able to make necessary adjustments? The empirical evidence presented up to this point has foreshadowed general but variant adaptation.

The survey data bear this out. In designing human resource systems for their U.S. operations, most of the Chinese companies have used U.S. local companies as a benchmark model; however, a significant minority of companies have also taken into account the practices of their Chinese headquarters. Also, some Chinese MNEs have used other Chinese firms in the United States as reference in designing their human resource systems (see Figure 6.4).

Figure 6.5 further illustrates both the general adaptation and the variance among Chinese companies on a variety of employment-related matters. For instance, in the handling of labor relations, 24% of responding companies duplicate the practices of their local U.S. competitors. Meanwhile, about 10% have adopted strategies that are generally or entirely different from what the managers consider to be those of U.S. peers. Similar distributions are evident in recruiting, training, compensation, and performance evaluation.

The varying adaptation of Chinese companies also manifests in the area of workplace equality. As illustrated by Figure 6.6, while the majority of Chinese firms in the United States have adopted formal policies to prevent employment discrimination (e.g., internal rules or training programs), a significant minority have either provided mere oral warning or taken no preventive measures at all. It would be unimaginable for U.S. companies, especially those large enough to engage in FDI,

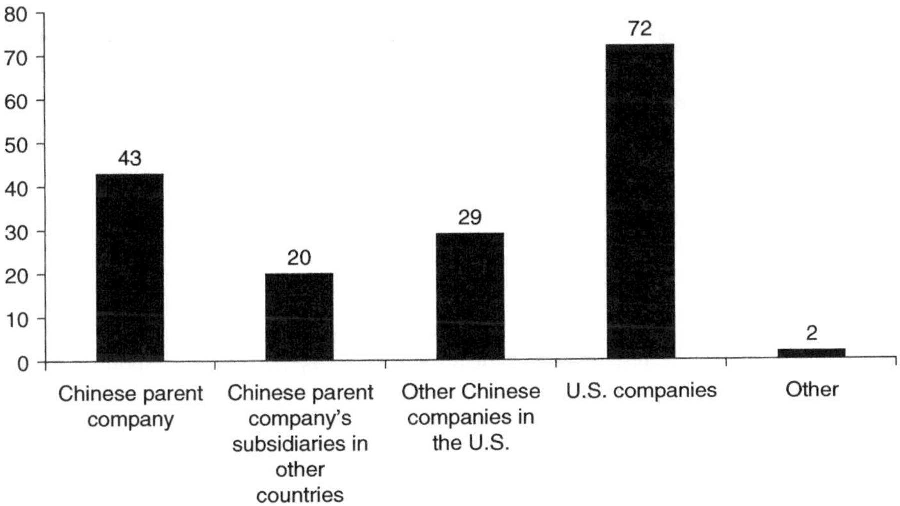

FIGURE 6.4 Benchmark model used in designing the human resource system
Source: 2015 survey (multiple-choice question)

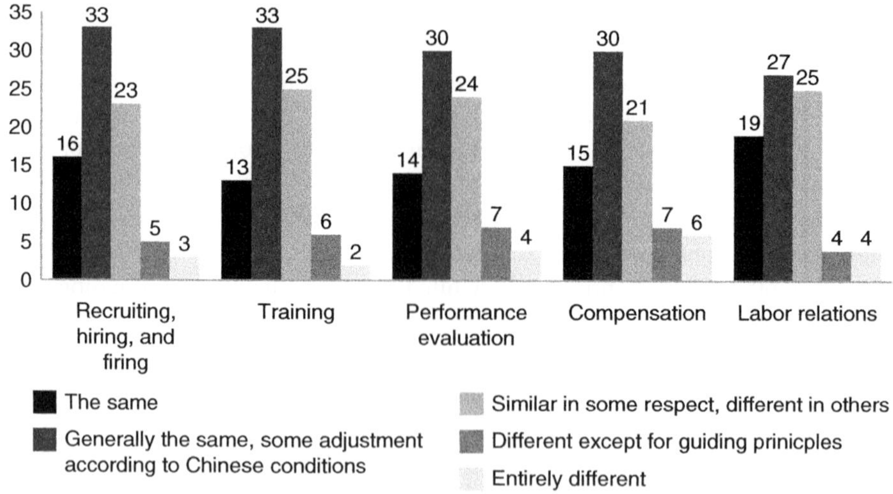

FIGURE 6.5 HRM compared to local U.S. companies
Source: 2015 survey

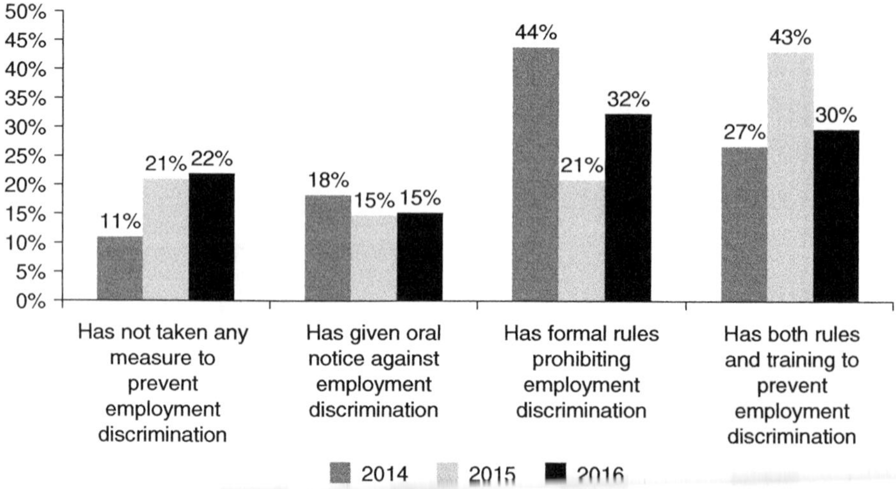

FIGURE 6.6 Measures taken to prevent employment discrimination
Note: 2014 survey (82 responses for the question); 2015 survey (81 responses to the question); 2016 survey (114 responses to the question).

to omit clear and specific instructions about nondiscrimination in their employee manuals.[134]

Given the wide gaps between China and the United States in the regulatory environment for employment equality and the varying ability of Chinese companies to adapt, Chinese managers should be prone to violating U.S. rules against discrimination that would lead to discrimination complaints and lawsuits. Yet according to the survey data, the vast majority of the responding firms have not received any complaints from their U.S. employees about discrimination. Among those that have handled such complaints, most settled with the employees. Only about 4–5% had litigated discrimination complaints in the United States.[135] These figures are low compared to those reported by U.S. firms. For instance, in 2014, U.S. companies had at least an 11.7% chance of having an employment charge filed against them at the U.S. Equal Employment Opportunity Commission (EEOC) or the equivalent state fairness agency.[136] Because only a portion of the discrimination complaints result in formal charges, the probability of a U.S. firm receiving at least one such complaint in any one year easily doubles. Moreover, the cumulative probability of multiple years is presumably still higher. What might explain the finding that appears to contradict the conventional wisdom portrayed by the popular press?

Prior to offering some tentative explanations, I want to stress that the data, reported by Chinese MNE managers, may fall below the actual frequency of discrimination complaints. Also, the focus here is on the relatively low probability that Chinese firms in the United States will receive discrimination complaints, not on the actual occurrence of workplace discrimination. For a myriad of organizational and social reasons, victims of discrimination may be reluctant to lodge a complaint with their employers.[137] That said, the workplace homogeneity in the Chinese companies and their relatively small workforces may limit discrimination complaints. It is common for Chinese firms in the United States to prefer that their locally hired employees, especially those that need to report to the headquarters, speak the Chinese language, because the managers at the headquarters, born in the 1960s and 1970s, barely speak any English.[138] Effective communication requires U.S. employees with key responsibilities to be conversational in Chinese. Also, as shown by the survey data, Chinese firms consider cultural differences a main

[134] For example, as early as 1976 nearly 70% of surveyed industry leaders in the United States offered equal-opportunity training for managers. Kim, Kalev, and Dobbin, "Progressive Corporations at Work."

[135] The percentages are calculated from the 2014 survey data.

[136] "Employee Charge Trends across the United States: The 2015 Hiscox Guide to Employee Lawsuits 4," at www.hiscox.com/shared-documents/The-2015-Hiscox-Guide-to-Employee-Lawsuits-Employee-charge-trends-across-the-United-States.pdf.

[137] Laura Beth Nielson and Robert L. Nelson, "Rights Realized: An Empirical Analysis of Employment Discrimination Litigation as a Claiming System," 2005 *Wisconsin Law Review* 663 (2005), 668.

[138] Interview with the head of the U.S. investment department of a large private Chinese company with business in multiple sectors (March 11, 2016).

challenge for investing in the United States. Therefore, despite the fact that many of the companies recruit most of their staff locally, the local hires tend to be Chinese educated in the United States, Chinese-American or East Asian.

The size of the staff may also have an effect on the likelihood of discrimination complaints. Because Chinese investors only recently ventured into the U.S. market, most of them have a small workforce. According to the most recent CGCC survey data, 72% of Chinese companies have no more than fifty employees in the United States (42% have no more than ten, and 30% have between eleven and fifty).[139] As noted, small businesses are exempt from some of U.S. employment discrimination rules.[140] Moreover, without the organizational complexity and inefficiency of large corporations, small firms may resolve discrimination grievances more effectively, preventing them from escalation.[141] Of course, structural factors may also play a role. Research has shown that complainants about employment discrimination by minority employers expect poor odds to prevail in U.S. courts.[142] If most managers at Chinese companies in the United State are Chinese or ethnic Chinese, discrimination complaints may not receive their due attention.

As Chinese companies further expand their U.S. businesses, however, their U.S. workforces will most likely diversify. Motivated by long-term commercial interests, especially the objective of developing the U.S. market, Chinese investors are incentivized to adjust their employee composition to reflect business needs, even at the cost of linguistic or cultural uniformity. For example, a Chinese company in transportation recently recruited a non-Chinese employee for the purpose of cultivating institutional customers in the United States.[143] "He signed two deals in the first month! We asked him to share his secrets. He gave a presentation which boiled down to one sentence, 'don't talk business with clients, talk stories, sports, jokes.' We [the Chinese employees] are not good at this. I just hired another one like him."[144] Even pure cost concerns may lead to workforce diversity for Chinese companies in the United States. According to the literature on the economic theory of labor market discrimination, foreign firms as outsiders may benefit from actively

139 China General Chamber of Commerce—USA, "2017 Annual Business Survey Report on Chinese Enterprises in the US," at www.cgccusa.org/wp-content/uploads/2017/06/Survey-Report-2017-ENG.pdf, 10.

140 Most of the U.S. laws prohibiting discrimination, e.g., Title VII of the Civil Rights Act of 1964, the Equal Pay Act, Titles I and V of the Americans with Disabilities Act, etc., apply to all private employers that employ fifteen or more individuals; the Age Discrimination in Employment Act applies to private employers that employ twenty or more employees. Nonetheless, small firms may be subject to state and municipal rules against discrimination.

141 As noted earlier, small firms may be more likely than large employers to engage in discrimination. The focus of discussion here is possible relations between firm size and discrimination complaints.

142 Mary L. Inman and Robert S. Baron, "Influence of Prototypes on Perceptions of Prejudice," 70 *Journal of Personality and Social Psychology* 727 (1996), 732.

143 Interview with the CEO of the U.S. affiliate of a large Chinese state-owned company in transportation (June 14, 2017).

144 Interview with the CEO of the U.S. affiliate of a large Chinese state-owned company in transportation (June 14, 2017).

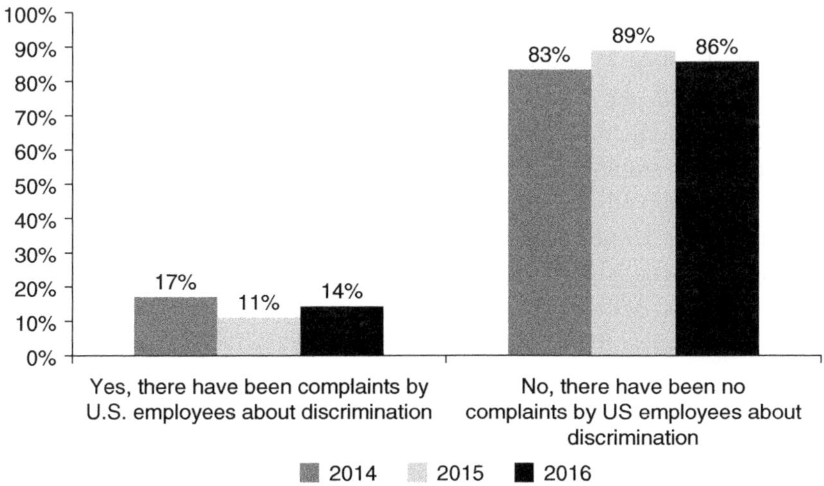

FIGURE 6.7 Complaints about discrimination by U.S. employees
Source: 2014–16 surveys

exploiting bigotry in their host countries by hiring the excluded group.[145] Echoing that argument, a Chinese manager reported that he would often hire non-Asian minority employees simply because, in his view, they tend to be "undervalued" in the U.S. labor market, "so we can find high-quality candidates and retain them at relatively low cost."[146]

To summarize, Chinese firms investing in the United States face large institutional gaps in the area of employment discrimination. According to the overall empirical evidence, Chinese MNE managers on average hold a generally positive, yet varying, view of U.S. employment-related law. Meanwhile, their capacity to adapt varies significantly. While the majority relied on locally recruited staff to handle human resource matters according to U.S. models, a significant minority of firms have applied home-state practices. Accordingly, the firms' antidiscrimination measures vary. That said, Chinese companies are less likely than local firms to receive discrimination complaints, which may be ascribed to their relatively small workforce and to workplace homogeneity. However, as the Chinese firms diversify their workforces in the United States, employment discrimination is set to pose a major challenge.

145 Jordan I. Siegel, Lynn Pyun, and B. Y. Cheon, "Multinational Firms, Labor Market Discrimination, and the Capture of Competitive Advantage by Exploiting the Social Divide," Harvard Business School: Strategy Unit Working Paper (2010), 2.

146 Interview with the CEO of the U.S. affiliate of a large Chinese company in manufacturing and construction (March 27, 2016).

IV STATE OWNERSHIP AND ADAPTATION TO U.S. EMPLOYMENT LAW

Section III sketched Chinese companies' employment practices in the United States, which evidence varying adaptation to host-country institutions. A number of questions naturally follow: why do some Chinese managers hold more positive views about U.S. employment law and make more efforts to prevent employment discrimination than others do? And why do only some firms receive discrimination complaints in the United States? This section sets out to explore cross-firm variations, and the focus is again trained on the effects, if any, of state ownership in Chinese investors. According to the preliminary test results, issues of employment discrimination appear to transcend the ownership character of Chinese companies.

A *Opinions of U.S. Employment Laws*

Figure 6.2 clearly illustrates significant inter-firm variation in how the surveyed managers think of U.S. employment law. This subsection empirically investigates the variation. The dependent variable is coded directly from the scale question (5 representing the most positive view, and 1 the most negative view). The independent variable of interest is state ownership in the Chinese investors. As discussed earlier, prior studies have generated conflicting conclusions. Some contend that Chinese SOEs typically comply well with Chinese employment laws, which are highly protective of workers' interests. Yet others show that SOE managers also engage in some types of employment discrimination, especially at the hiring stage. The tests run in Chapter 4 suggest that the perceptions of U.S. institutions are detached from the Chinese investors' ownership type. Rather, they vary in a highly idiosyncratic manner. The following statistical tests further assess the link in the area of employment law. In doing so, I use the same two alternative dummies as used in the prior tests (50% state ownership and 10% state ownership).

Additionally, a number of control variables are added to the tests. First, investment duration is included to account for the possible effect of internalization. Second, the size of the Chinese investors' U.S. business appears in some of the tests. As noted, small businesses in China tend to violate employment law more frequently. It is possible that managers of small and medium-sized businesses, when investing in the United States, hold different views of U.S. labor and employment law due to mind-set inertia. Meanwhile, there are certain exemptions in U.S. law for small businesses, which may affect managers' perception as well. I use the number of U.S. employees as a measure of business size. Last, taking a cue from the test results in Chapter 4, I include U.S. profit level to account for the possible effect of business performance on managers' perceptions of host-country institutions.

As shown in Table 6.2, state ownership is significantly associated with the dependent variable in model 2. Managers of Chinese companies with significant state

TABLE 6.1 *Summary statistics*

Variable	Observations	Mean	Std. dev.	Min.	Max.
View of U.S. law	115	3.443478	0.860348	1	5
State ownership (50%)	130	0.330769	0.47231	0	1
State ownership (10%)	130	0.430769	0.4971	0	1
Investment duration	129	8.465116	9.321553	0	36
U.S. profit level	119	2.798319	0.898019	1	5
U.S. employees	127	263.9449	1157.523	1	10000

Source: 2016 survey

TABLE 6.2 *State ownership and opinions of U.S. labor and employment law*

	1	2	3	4	5	6
State ownership (50%)	0.573		0.249		0.208	
	(0.402)		(0.417)		(0.418)	
State ownership (10%)		1.018***		0.593		0.5897
		(0.39)		(0.411)		(0.409)
Investment duration	–0.02	–0.028	–0.032	–0.0365*	–0.032	–0.037*
	(0.02)	(0.02)	(0.021)	(0.02)	(0.021)	(0.021)
U.S. profit level			0.865***	0.794***	0.784***	0.7086***
			(0.25)	(0.256)	(0.259)	(0.265)
U.S. employees					0.00017	0.00018
					(0.00016)	(0.00016)
Number of observations	109	109	104	104	104	104

Note: data source: 2016 survey; ***$p < 0.01$; **$p < 0.05$; *$p < 0.1$; ordered logistic regressions

ownership are more likely to express a positive view about U.S. labor and employment law. However, when profit level is added to the tests, state ownership is no longer significant. In all the other model specifications, U.S. profit is positively linked to the perception of U.S. employment law. One may infer from the finding that the business performance of Chinese companies has a feedback influence on how managers view U.S. institutions.[147] Investment duration is negatively and significantly associated with the perception in two model specifications (4 and 6), suggesting that the newcomers tend to hold more positive views of U.S. employment law. Yet the results are not robust. Moreover, investment size is not significant. The combined findings match those from Chapter 4, which explored variations in

147 One may contend that the causal relationship is indirect and goes in the opposite direction, i.e., positive perception leads to more compliance, which then results in higher business profits. Even though I agree with the long-term effects of perception on compliance, the second part of the logical chain is too tenuous to have short-term measurable effect.

Chinese managers' opinions about various general U.S. institutions and found them to be highly idiosyncratic. Keep in mind, however, that the sample size for this set of tests is relatively small, so the preliminary results should be taken as merely suggestive evidence.

B *Anti-discrimination Measures*

While the majority of the surveyed firms have written rules or provided training to prevent discrimination, a significant minority of Chinese firms have either done nothing or merely given oral warnings. This subsection explores this variation, with a focus on the possible association with state ownership in the Chinese investors. To measure the varying efforts to prevent employment discrimination, I created an ordinal dependent variable from the survey data that coded the four levels of effort. The dependent variable equals 1 if the Chinese company in the United States has not taken any measure to prevent employment discrimination; 2 if the company has orally advised employees against discrimination; 3 if the company has put in place formal rules prohibiting discrimination; and 4 if the company has both implemented formal rules and provided training against employment discrimination.[148]

Multiple factors may bear on efforts to prevent employment discrimination in the United States. Some of the factors are of theoretical and practical interest; others are trivial but should be controlled for due to their potentially confounding effects. First, the independent variable of interest is state ownership in the Chinese investors. As previously noted, some research indicates that SOEs in China are more compliant with Chinese employment law, and that SOE managers tend to be highly risk-averse. Both raise the odds that SOE managers in the United States adopt preventive measures on workplace equality. Conversely, some preliminary research finds Chinese SOEs to engage in more discrimination than do their private counterparts at the hiring stage.[149] In addition, private firms, which tend to engage in opportunistic compliance in China, should avoid the risk when operating in a more stringent enforcement context in the United States. Moreover, in dealing with routine and technical U.S. matters, SOEs may not differ from private Chinese companies. Following this line of argument, Chinese investors of different ownership types may react similarly to U.S. employment law. To evaluate the competing hypotheses, I include the same two ownership dummies (50% state ownership and 10% state ownership) alternately in the statistical tests.

In addition, the size of a Chinese company's U.S. investment may have some effect, as it determines the availability of necessary resources for adaptation and compliance. I use the Chinese companies' U.S. revenue as a measure of investment size. I also include investment duration as a control for internalization and temporal

148 Because the question in the 2015 survey was formulated as a multiple-choice one, the coding is based on the highest level of preventive measure selected by the respondents.

149 Zhou Xiangyi and Song Xuetao, "Gender Discrimination in the Employment Market," 145–60.

changes in the institutional distance between the two countries. Additionally, it is possible that Chinese companies having experienced some labor and employment issues in the United States have reacted by taking more preventive measures.[150] A Chinese manager noted that his firm had not paid much attention to the issue until a dismissed female employee filed a discrimination claim.[151]

Presumably, Chinese investors teaming up with U.S. firms are more likely to delegate HRM to local partners, which should have an impact on antidiscrimination measures. Although the survey data indicate that most Chinese investors invest in the United States through wholly owned subsidiaries instead of joint ventures or minority equity ownership, I nonetheless add the variable as a control given its importance. Moreover, I add the size of a Chinese company's U.S. workforce. As noted above, the number of employees in the United States may correlate with efforts to counter discrimination as the current U.S. employment discrimination laws generally exempt businesses with fewer than fifteen workers.[152] Also, issues of discrimination are more likely to occur in Chinese companies with a large workforce in the United States, which justifies more preventive measures. Lastly, I control for the survey year to account for possible omitted variables that might significantly affect the data over the two years.

As shown in Table 6.4, state ownership does not appear to be significantly associated with companies' antidiscrimination measures. Everything else being equal, the Chinese investors with substantial state ownership do not differ from the rest regarding the measures taken to prevent employment discrimination. Such measures are routine compliance actions that do not require decisions by the Chinese headquarters; and, as discussed earlier, Chinese investors with state ownership are indistinguishable from their private peers when dealing with routine matters in their U.S. business. In addition, private Chinese companies may adapt rationally to the more rigorously enforced U.S. antidiscrimination rules by engaging in less opportunistic compliance. As a result, they act like those with significant state ownership in the U.S. regulatory environment.

Investment size has the most significant effect on the measures taken by the Chinese companies to prevent employment discrimination; the larger the U.S. assets invested by a Chinese company, the more efforts it will make to address workplace discrimination. The finding is intuitive. Chinese companies with substantial U.S. assets naturally have more resources for compliance. They also face narrow institutional gaps in the area. In addition, large investment usually incurs substantial initial cost that can only be recouped over the long run. Such long-term commitments incentivize the investors to conform to the host-country institutions.

150 The opposite may also be true. Anti-discrimination measures such as training may raise the awareness of employees, who may subsequently file such complaints.

151 Interview with the CEO of the U.S. affiliate of a large Chinese company in the manufacturing and construction sector (March 27, 2016).

152 See *supra* n. 140 for a brief discussion of the small-business exemption.

TABLE 6.3 *Summary statistics*

Variable	Observation	Mean	Std. dev.	Min.	Max.
Anti-discrimination measure	195	2.769231	1.150113	1	4
State ownership (50%)	232	0.396552	0.490239	0	1
State ownership (10%)	232	0.487069	0.500914	0	1
Investment duration	225	11.66222	10.01925	0	40
U.S. revenue	181	2.160221	1.225547	1	4
U.S. business ownership	232	0.823276	0.38226	0	1
Discrimination complaints	199	0.130653	0.337871	0	1
U.S. employees	177	202.6215	986.3675	1	10000

Source: 2015 and 2016 surveys

TABLE 6.4 *State ownership and measures to prevent employment discrimination*

Variables	1	2	3	4	5	6
State ownership (50%)	0.1299		0.1234		–0.0426	
	(0.2931)		(0.341)		(0.382)	
State ownership (10%)		0.1591		–0.1999		–0.309
		(0.284)		(0.337)		(0.378)
Investment duration	0.0065	0.0064	–0.0099	–0.0063	–0.0075	–0.0046
	(0.0147)	(0.0144)	(0.017)	(0.0169)	(0.0185)	(0.0183)
Discrimination complaints			0.9729**	0.9612**	1.108**	1.107**
			(0.4546)	(0.4576)	(0.4972)	(0.499)
U.S. revenue level			0.5101***	0.5503***	0.453***	0.4947***
			(0.1378)	(0.1412)	(0.1564)	(0.1615)
U.S. business ownership					0.6368	0.657
					(0.4609)	(0.46)
Number of total employees in the U.S.					0.00056	0.00056
					(0.00043)	(0.00042)
Survey year	–0.157	–0.16	–0.087	–0.086	–0.243	–0.225
	(0.291)	(0.29)	(0.352)	(0.352)	(0.414)	(0.414)
Number of observations	183	183	149	149	127	127

Note: 2015 and 2016 surveys. ***p < 0.01; **p < 0.05; *p < 0.1; ordered logistic regressions

Additionally, prior receipts of discrimination complaints are significantly associated with antidiscrimination measures taken by Chinese investors. As discussed earlier, a complaint may function as a wake-up call to Chinese managers. Of course, one may contend that preventive measures raise awareness of discrimination, which then triggers more complaints. While interviews with Chinese managers support the former scenario, prior research has found no effects of discrimination lawsuits on the adoption of diversity programs.[153] Thus, further research is needed to examine the causality. None of the other control variables is significant, though definitive conclusions cannot be drawn from the nonsignificant coefficients given the limited sample size.[154]

C Discrimination Complaints

As noted at the beginning of this chapter, soon after it opened the Ohio plant, Fuyao Glass faced a lawsuit by a former American manager alleging that discrimination played a role in his dismissal.[155] According to the survey data, Fuyao's experience does not represent that of the majority of Chinese companies in the United States. Why the variation across different Chinese firms? This subsection explores this question. According to the empirical tests of the preceding subsection, Chinese investors of state and private ownership alike make similar efforts to prevent employment discrimination in the U.S. context when other variables are held constant. Thus, the working hypothesis for the following tests is that state ownership in Chinese investors is not significantly associated with the probability of receiving discrimination complaints. For the dependent variable, I use a dummy that equals 1 if the survey respondents reported having received employment discrimination complaints from their U.S. employees, 0 otherwise.

The independent variable of interest (i.e., state ownership in Chinese investors) is represented by the same two alternative dummy variables as used in the prior tests. I add investment duration as a control because the longer a Chinese company has operated in the United States, the more likely it is that it has received complaints about discrimination. I also include the number of employees in the United States as a control. Everything else being equal, a large U.S. workforce raises the probability that some employees would complain about discrimination. Moreover, I add to the tests antidiscrimination measures taken by the companies, as diversity training may raise awareness and trigger more discrimination complaints.[156] Lastly,

153 Frank Dobbin, Soohan Kim, and Alexandra Kalev, "You Can't Always Get What You Need: Organizational Determinants of Diversity Programs," 76.3 *American Sociological Review* 386 (2011), 406.

154 In a separate set of tests using only the 2015 survey data (because the question about HRM staff was included only in that year's survey), I tested the effects of human resources staff on the preventive measures. According to the results, the Chinese companies with full-time HRM capacity are more likely to take measures against employment discrimination. Though the sample size is small, the coefficient is significant and robust across several specifications. The finding is consistent with prior studies. Kim, Kalev, and Dobbin, "Progressive Corporations at Work."

155 Scheiber and Bradsher, "Culture Clash at a Chinese-Owned Plant in Ohio."

156 See, e.g., Elizabeth Hirsh and Julie A. Kmec, "Human Resource Structures: Reducing Discrimination or Raising Rights Awareness?", 48.3 *Industrial Relations: A Journal of Economy and Society* 512 (2009).

TABLE 6.5 *Summary statistics*

Variable	Observation	Mean	Std. dev.	Min.	Max.
Discrimination complaints	199	0.130653	0.337871	0	1
State ownership (50%)	232	0.396552	0.490239	0	1
State ownership (10%)	232	0.487069	0.500914	0	1
Investment duration	225	11.66222	10.01925	0	40
U.S. employees	177	202.6215	986.3675	1	10000
Anti-discrimination measure	195	2.769231	1.150113	1	4

Source: 2015 and 2016 surveys

TABLE 6.6 *State ownership and discrimination complaints*

Variables	1	2	3	4	5	6
State ownership (50%)	−0.193		−0.336		−0.527	
	(0.476)		(0.521)		(0.559)	
State ownership (10%)		−0.184		−0.235		−0.313
		(0.453)		(0.4899)		(0.524)
Investment duration	0.0038	0.0032	0.0008	−0.0012	0.0049	0.0011
	(0.0242)	(0.0238)	(0.0252)	(0.0248)	(0.0272)	(0.0267)
Number of employees in the U.S.			0.00058**	0.00057**	0.00039*	0.00038
			(0.00028)	(0.00027)	(0.00024)	(0.00023)
Preventive measures					0.7989***	0.793***
					(0.297)	(0.2967)
Survey year	0.3207	0.319	−0.426	−0.416	−0.0717	−0.067
	(0.482)	(0.483)	(0.532)	(0.531)	(0.5628)	(0.5598)
Number of observations	185	185	151	151	143	143

Note: data from 2015 and 2016 surveys. ***$p < 0.01$; **$p < 0.05$; *$p < 0.1$; logistic regressions

I include a survey year dummy to control for systematic changes in the data over the two survey years.

As shown in Table 6.6, state ownership is not significantly associated with the dependent variable. In other words, Chinese investors with significant state ownership do not differ from those privately owned in the likelihood of receiving discrimination complaints from their U.S. employees. The finding naturally follows prior test results that ownership characteristics in Chinese investors play at most a marginal role on their efforts to prevent employment discrimination in the United States. As noted earlier, the lack of significant ownership effect may stem from the technicality and routineness of employment matters. Discrimination complaints, unlike tax controversies or audits, may not amount to major legal or compliance issues that require high-level management attention.[157] Hence, the significant difference in how Chinese investors with different ownership characters allocate decision-making authority does not manifest in employment discrimination matters.

As expected, the size of the local workforce is significant. Everything else being equal, Chinese companies with more U.S. employees are more likely to have received discrimination complaints from them. The coefficient is not significant in model 6 after "preventive measures" is added, which is likely due to a very high correlation between the two variables. As shown in the prior tests, taking measures against discrimination is significantly and positively associated with the probability of getting discrimination complaints. Causality in both directions may be at work. On the one hand, preventive measures raise the awareness of the employees about discrimination and possible remedies, including the voicing of complaints; such measures enable employees to name and blame.[158] On the other hand, the complaints may have alerted the managers to the legal risks and the necessity of preventive measures, though the measures may not achieve the intended effects of actually reducing workplace discrimination.[159]

In summary, this section ran a set of statistical tests to explore the variations in Chinese investors' opinions about and reactions to U.S. laws against employment discrimination, with a focus on the possible effects of state ownership in the investors. First, the overall test results relating to the managers' perceptions suggest no more than marginal effects of state ownership in Chinese investors. In other words, Chinese investors with or without significant state ownership hold the same views about U.S. employment law. Second, the statistical tests do not detect a link between state ownership in Chinese investors and the measures taken to prevent employment discrimination; in comparison, the size of U.S. investment does matter. Third, the test results suggest that Chinese investors with larger U.S. workforces tend to receive more discrimination complaints, but not any association between the complaints and the investors' ownership type. As previously discussed, state ownership manifests its effects when the investors deal with major compliance matters; regarding routine practices in everyday operations, state-owned businesses and their

157 Some companies have purchased business insurance that covers employment-related lawsuits. That will further routinize the matter and prevent it from catching the attention of the Chinese headquarters.

158 William L. F. Felstiner, Richard L. Abel, and Austin Sarat, "The Emergence and Transformation of Disputes: Naming, Blaming, Claiming . . .," 15 *Law and Society Review* 631 (1980).

159 Juan Sanchez and Medkik Nohora, "The Effects of Diversity Awareness Training on Differential Treatment," 29 *Group and Organization Management* 517 (2004); Carol Kulik and Loriann Roberson, "Common Goals and Golden Opportunities: Evaluations of Diversity Education in Academic and Organizational Settings," 7 Academy of Management Learning and Education 309 (2008); Alexandra Kalev, Frank Dobbin, and Erin Kelly, "Best Practices or Best Guesses? Assessing the Efficacy of Corporate Affirmative Action and Diversity Policies," 71 *American Sociological Review* 589 (2006), finding that training had the least effect on moderating managerial bias.

private peers act comparably. Hence, they differ neither in the measures taken to prevent discrimination in the United States nor in the probability of receiving discrimination complaints.

V CONCLUSION

Many intense debates about the soaring Chinese ODI revolve around labor and employment issues, which also rank high on the list of risks and challenges for Chinese companies investing in the United States. Despite their importance, few have systematically researched how Chinese companies tackled the issues in the U.S. context. For instance, do Chinese companies generally comply with U.S. laws safeguarding workers' interests? Or do they neglect or even violate local workers' legal rights, as some recent media reports have portrayed?[160] To preliminarily answer the questions, this chapter first examined the institutional gaps between China and the United States in the area of employment discrimination. After nearly two decades of progressive legislation, China's comprehensive employment laws converged with the international standard set by OECD countries. As a result, the formal laws share the basic principles embodied in U.S. employment discrimination rules. Yet in practice, the laws are poorly enforced and complied with, resulting in wide institutional gaps between the two countries in this subject matter area.

Crossing the gaps necessitates adequate desire and ability of the Chinese investors to adapt. According to the empirical evidence, the Chinese MNE managers on average hold positive views of the complex U.S. law governing the workplace, even though they complain about exorbitant labor costs in the United States. Yet inter-firm variation is evident in this regard. Meanwhile, the majority of the Chinese companies relied on local staff for human resources management, but a significant minority still have expatriates handling such matters. Hence, the Chinese firms vary in their employment practices. While the majority have adopted the HRM model of their U.S. peers, a significant minority have followed the headquarters or other Chinese companies in the United States. Similarly, regarding measures taken to prevent employment discrimination, the majority acted like typical U.S. companies, adopting written policies and offering training programs, yet a large fraction of Chinese companies have taken perfunctory or no preventive action. Despite the varying efforts, the vast majority of the Chinese firms have not received any discrimination complaints from local employees, which is partially attributable to the homogeneity of their workforces in the United States. The fast growth of Chinese firms in the U.S. market will inevitably expand and diversify their local staff, and the significant minority of the firms that have not taken

160 See, e.g., Scheiber and Bradsher, "Culture Clash at a Chinese-Owned Plant in Ohio"; Carolyn Cui and Esther Fung, "A Chinese Conglomerate Finds Managing Businesses Is Tougher than a Spending Spree," *Wall Street Journal* (July 5, 2017), at www.wsj.com/articles/chinas-swashbuckling-hna-discovers-the-struggles-of-american-dealmaking-1499247001.

U.S. antidiscrimination law seriously will soon find themselves entangled in discrimination complaints and lawsuits.

This chapter also assessed possible links between state ownership in Chinese companies and their adaptation to host-country employment law. Between size and state ownership, the two variables that affect an employer's compliance with employment law in China, size appears to play a more important role in the United States. Companies with large U.S. investments implement more preventive measures; and those employing a large U.S. workforce receive more discrimination complaints. The insignificance of Chinese companies' ownership type is attributable to the routineness of employment discrimination matters in the United States.

The findings of this chapter add to the burgeoning literature about Chinese MNEs and their employment practices. Instead of expatriating Chinese workers, as many have done when investing in developing countries, Chinese firms in the United States have to a great extent localized their workforces, despite high labor cost and the shortage of management talent (see Figure 6.1). Regulations restricting the use of foreign workers certainly play a role, but market power drives Chinese investors' workforce localization. Since the vast majority of Chinese investors seek to develop the U.S. market, they have to hire local employees who, according to an expatriated Chinese manager, "can crack a joke with the client."[161]

[161] Interview with the CEO of the U.S. affiliate of a large Chinese state-owned company in the transportation sector (June 14, 2017).

7

Chinese Companies and the U.S. National Security Review

Foreign ownership – especially from Chinese companies designated as "state champions" that often benefit from illegal subsidies designed to gain strategic access to markets like the United States – may pose a strategic rather than overt national security threat[1]

Congressman Pittenger's request to GAO

Can bacon be a national security issue? Yes, according to some American politicians, if a Chinese investor is involved. In 2013, Shuanghui, China's largest meat processor, attempted to acquire Smithfield Foods for the staggering amount of US$4.72 billion. Out of "an abundance of caution," the Chinese company notified the Committee on Foreign Investment in the United States (CFIUS) about the proposed acquisition.[2] While the agency review was under way, a bipartisan group of U.S. legislators held a hearing and urged a heightened CFIUS review that would take into account "the full range of national security interests."[3] The Chinese investor eventually "brought home the bacon,"[4] but the political drama highlighted the suspicion and national security concerns regarding Chinese foreign direct investment in the United States. Also, it prompted questions about the conceptual boundary of national security. If pork can potentially be a U.S. national security issue when Chinese companies invest in it, what cannot? The political fire drawn to the Shuanghui–Smithfield deal showcased the exposure of seemingly nonthreatening Chinese investments in the United States to possible regulatory scrutiny on a national security basis.[5]

1 Congressman Robert Pittenger's request to review CFIUS, at https://pittenger.house.gov/sites/pittenger.house.gov/files/Letter%20to%20GAO%20re%20CFIUS%20Report%209.15.16.pdf (Sept. 15, 2016), last accessed on Jan. 3, 2017.

2 Doug Palmer, "More U.S. Senators Concerned by Shuanghui–Smithfield Deal," *Reuters* (June 21, 2013), at http://articles.chicagotribune.com/2013-06-21/business/sns-rt-us-usa-china-smithfield bre95k16u-20130621_1_u-s-treasury-u-s-beef-u-s-meat, last accessed on May 24, 2017.

3 Ibid. 4 Ibid. 5 As will be explained, greenfield investment is exempt from CFIUS review.

The concern of the security risk associated with foreign direct investment preceded the current wave of Chinese investment in the United States. As will be elaborated in a moment, the institutional foundation of CFIUS review initially took form under political pressure following the surge of FDI from Japan and several oil-exporting countries in the 1970s and 1980s, when 70% of Americans believed that foreign ownership of U.S. firms was bad for the country.[6] For decades, however, the agency engaged in a loose review of foreign investment as most of it originated from U.S. allies. The arrival of Chinese investors broke the equilibrium and gave lawmakers the incentive to ratchet up CFIUS review. Unlike U.S. laws on tax and employment discrimination, the current rules governing CFIUS review differentiate foreign investors according to their ownership types. Those controlled by a foreign government are singled out for heightened scrutiny. Moreover, in contrast to how tax law and employment law are enforced in the United States, CFIUS review is opaque and, until recently, was generally assumed to fall outside judicial review. The vagueness of national security also contributes to the agency's nearly unlimited discretion. "Like beauty, [national security] is very much in the eyes of the beholder,"[7] as demonstrated by the debate revolving around the Shuanghui–Smithfield deal.

How do Chinese companies react to such an institution, which was intended to scrutinize foreign acquisitions of U.S. assets by investors from non-ally countries such as China, especially those investors subject to foreign government influence? Readers should not find it surprising that the reactions differ greatly from those in the areas of tax and workplace equality. First of all, given the huge institutional distance, many Chinese investors are unaware of CFIUS review; those with knowledge about the process consider it non-transparent and politicized. Meanwhile, a significant minority did not consult U.S. specialists about CFIUS review. Consequently, more than half of Chinese investors did not consider CFIUS at all when investing in the United States, and about half of those that did consider CFIUS review applicable to their deals decided not to notify the agency. Such reactions inevitably spawn conflict with the powerful agency, as exemplified by *Ralls* v. *CFIUS*, the first and only lawsuit by a foreign investor against CFIUS in its entire history. The lawsuit had a lasting impact on the U.S. institution by bringing parts of the agency's actions under constitutional review.

The tensions manifest more clearly when Chinese companies with government ownership attempt to invest in U.S. businesses. They are more likely to hold negative views about the CFIUS process. In addition, because the agency is mandated to

6 Edward M. Graham and David Marchick, "U.S. National Security and Foreign Direct Investment" (2006), executive summary, xv, available at https://piie.com/publications/chapters_preview/3918/esiie3918.pdf.

7 Brandt J. C. Pasco, "United States National Security Reviews of Foreign Direct Investment: From Classified Programmes to Critical Infrastructure, This Is What the Committee on Foreign Investment in the United States Cares About," 29 *ICSID Review* 350 (2014), 355.

scrutinize foreign investment that would result in foreign government control, state-owned Chinese companies are more likely to consider CFIUS than their private peers. However, state ownership does not have a significant effect on the actual filing of notice with CFIUS, when other variables such as sector and investment size are held constant.

To guide readers through this chapter, a brief road map is as follows. Section I below conducts an institutional analysis. It demonstrates the unique features of the formal rules of the CFIUS regime, how the rules evolved as a result of Chinese FDI, and, in a highly stylized way, the calculations of foreign investors about the filing of a notice with CFIUS. Next, section II presents an empirical overview of how Chinese companies react to the CFIUS review regime. In contrast to the findings from the two prior chapters, Chinese managers either lacked any knowledge about CFIUS review or expressed a generally negative view of the process. Correspondingly, the majority did not consider it when investing in the United States. Section III conducts statistical tests on the potential links between state ownership in Chinese investors and their reactions to CFIUS institutions. According to the results, state ownership has an effect on managers' opinion of the CFIUS process and on their filing consideration, but not on their actual filings. Section IV discusses the contributions of the empirical findings and concludes the chapter.

I THE CFIUS REGIME: THE RULES AND THEIR ENFORCEMENT

Unlike U.S. tax institutions and the institutions governing workplace equality, the CFIUS regime is entirely new to Chinese companies. Though the Chinese government has created an equivalent system, it applies, just like the CFIUS regime, exclusively to foreign investment.[8] Moreover, in contrast to the generally nondiscriminatory U.S. tax and employment laws, the formal rules governing CFIUS review differentiate state-owned enterprises (SOEs) from private investors. Regarding enforcement, the CFIUS regime also differs from U.S. tax law and U.S. employment law in its highly discretionary and opaque nature. Therefore, in this subject matter area Chinese investors face an enormous institutional gap.

To fully appreciate the gap, readers should first understand how the U.S. institution works. Moreover, unlike in the areas of tax and employment equality where Chinese companies have largely been rule followers, the U.S. law governing CFIUS review has born clear impacts of Chinese investment. It is, therefore, necessary and important to describe in more detail the CFIUS institutions so that readers will be able to comprehend the disruption and its causes.

Legal restraints on foreign investment in the United States due to national security concerns can be traced back to World War I. Enacted in 1917, the Trading with the

[8] Article 31, PRC Antimonopoly Law.

Enemy Act (TWEA) gave the president broad powers to act, in times of war or national emergency, against foreign-controlled businesses in the United States.[9] Following the war, Congress passed additional sector-specific restrictions on foreign investment in radio broadcasting, telecommunications, shipping, oil, and air transport.[10] These formal laws were deemed sufficient for safeguarding U.S. assets from foreign investors with sinister intent, until the 1970s, when OPEC members poured substantial capital into the U.S. market. The subsequent political pressure led to the establishment of CFIUS.

Created in 1975 by an executive order, CFIUS was initially responsible merely for monitoring the impact of foreign investment in the United States and co-ordinating federal policies.[11] The agency's institutional evolution since then has been a "crisis-driven development."[12] In the 1980s, the surge of investment from Japan and the fear of a rapidly growing economic competitor surpassing the United States led to the 1988 Exon-Florio Amendment to Section 721 of the Defense Production Act (DPA) of 1950. The amendment formally authorizes the president to block foreign investment that threatens to impair U.S. national security.[13]

Japan's subsequent economic slowdown eased the collective panic, and CFIUS, chaired by the Secretary of the Treasury,[14] had a rather hands-off attitude towards scrutinizing foreign investment. In the past decade, however, political pressure for heightened scrutiny of foreign investment mounted again due to the rise of China, widely seen as potentially posing a formidable economic and geopolitical challenge, and the war on terrorism. Eventually, a few high-profile acquisition attempts by foreign investors (including one by CNOOC, a Chinese state-owned energy conglomerate) triggered the passage of the Foreign Investment and National Security Act (FINSA) of 2007, which amended and codified the CFIUS review process and significantly enhanced congressional oversight.[15]

Under Section 721 of the DPA, as amended by FINSA, the president has the authority to block any "covered transaction," broadly defined as "any merger, acquisition, or takeover ... by or with any foreign person which could result in foreign control of any person engaged in interstate commerce in the United States"[16] that threatens to impair U.S. national security, provided no other existing laws could

[9] Graham and Marchick, "U.S. National Security and Foreign Direct Investment," 5. [10] Ibid., xvi.

[11] Dustin Tingley, Christopher Xu, Adam Chilton, and Helen V. Milner, "The Political Economy of Inward FDI: Opposition to Chinese Mergers and Acquisitions," 8 *Chinese Journal of International Politics* 27 (2015), 10.

[12] David Zaring, "CFIUS as a Congressional Notification Service," 83 *Southern California Law Review* 90 (2009), 90.

[13] Marc Greidinger, "The Exon-Florio Amendment: A Solution in Search of a Problem," 6 *American University International Law Review* 111 (1991), 112–14.

[14] Composition of CFIUS, official webpage of the U.S. Department of the Treasury, at www.treasury.gov/resource-center/international/foreign-investment/Pages/cfius-members.aspx.

[15] Margaret Merrill, "Overcoming CFIUS Jitters: A Practical Guide for Understanding the Committee on Foreign Investment in the United States," 30 *Quinnipiac Law Review* 1 (2011), 6.

[16] 50 U.S.C. app. § 2170(a)(3) (2006).

mitigate the threat. For foreign investors, the uncertainties due to the potential exercise of this broad authority may be lessened and managed by a voluntary filing of a notice with CFIUS for review and approval prior to the transaction. Following the receipt of a completed notice, CFIUS has thirty days to review and approve the investment or otherwise initiate a forty-five-day investigation.[17] By the end of the forty-five-day period, unresolved issues will be submitted to the president, who must either approve or block the transaction within fifteen days.[18] Because the filing of a notice (by a foreign investor or any other party to a covered transaction) with CFIUS is mostly voluntary,[19] only 5% of all foreign investments in the United States go through the process.[20] Absent a voluntary filing, however, the committee has the authority to initiate a review unilaterally of a covered transaction by requiring the foreign investor to file a notice.[21]

Acting as the president's agent, CFIUS's jurisdiction is limited to "covered transactions." CFIUS's mandate is to "conduct an investigation of the effects of a covered transaction on the national security of the United States, and take any necessary actions in connection with the transaction to protect the national security of the United States."[22] To allow maximum executive discretion, Congress did not precisely define the scope of "national security."[23] The current law nonetheless provides a non-exhaustive list of considerations, including investment that impacts "domestic production needed for ... national defense," "United States critical technologies," "long-term requirements for ... critical resources," and "critical infrastructure."[24] In addition, as briefly noted earlier, FINSA mandates CFIUS investigation in situations where the covered transaction results in foreign government control or foreign control of U.S. critical infrastructure.[25] Because of this legal requirement, sizable Chinese companies, a significant fraction of which are state-owned, are particularly sensitive to CFIUS investigation.[26] Finally, CFIUS is not

17 31 C.F.R. §§ 800.502–5 (2011); 50 U.S.C. app.§ 2170(b)(2)(C) (2006). Note that in practice it may take much longer for foreign investors to go through the process as CFIUS gets to determine the application's completeness. The clock starts to run only after the filing is deemed complete. Jingli Jiang and Gen Li, "CFIUS: For National Security Investigation or for Political Scrutiny," 9 *Texas Journal of Oil, Gas, and Energy Law* 67 (2013), 97.

18 31 C.F.R. § 800.506(b)(l)–(3) (2011); 50 U.S.C. app.§ 2170(d)(2) (2006).

19 31 C.F.R. § 800.401(a) (2011).

20 Richard A. Chesley and Daniel M. Simon, "Initiating Substantial Uncertainty into an Already Uncertain Process: The Intersection of National Security and Bankruptcy," *Global Insight* (March 25, 2013), at www.dlapiper.com/en/us/insights/publications/2013/03/initiating-substantial-uncertainty-into-an-alrea__/.

21 Section 721(b)(1)(D) of 50 U.S.C. App. 2170, Defense Production Act of 1950, as amended by FINSA.

22 Section 721 (50 U.S.C. App. § 2170(d)(2) (2006)), Defense Production Act of 1950, as amended by FINSA.

23 Jose W. Fernandez, "Lessons from the Trenches," 33 *International Financial Law Review* 44 (2014), 44.

24 50 U.S.C. App. § 2170(f) (2006).

25 Section 721(b)(2)(B) (50 U.S.C. App. 2170), Defense Production Act of 1950, as amended by FINSA.

26 50 U.S.C. app. § 2170(b)(1)(B) (2006).

time-barred from opening a review of a covered transaction,[27] and the law shields the findings and actions of the president from judicial review.[28]

From 2008 to 2014, 782 notices were filed,[29] mostly by companies from countries that are considered U.S. allies. The U.K. topped the ranking of source countries until 2012, when it was overtaken by China (see Figure 7.1). Since 2012, Chinese investors have accounted for the most notices filed each year. Shrouded in secrecy, the CFIUS review process is a "legal black hole."[30] Congress intended the agency to operate at a high level of secrecy. "Almost nothing is known about the internal functioning of the Committee. CFIUS does not disclose its deliberations, nor does it explain its decisions."[31] Moreover, "the Committee's legal mandate is replete with discretion."[32] Researchers have had to deduce from observable cases and data the factors affecting the decision-making in CFIUS, and they have come to conflicting opinions. Some view CFIUS as conducting apolitical review using standards narrowly tailored to U.S. national security risk. Others find that foreign investment in the United States faces constant political opposition that is reflected in CFIUS actions.[33]

And the agency itself has spawned a debate about its efficacy and legitimacy. Though some applaud it as an institutional innovation able to pool diverse administrative knowledge, block political pressure, and reach rational and consistent decisions,[34] others are not so sanguine about the efficacy of the agency and its independence from political influence.[35] In their view, the breadth of CFIUS's

[27] Andreas Heinemann, "Government Control of Cross-border M & A: Legitimate Regulation or Protectionism?", 15 *Journal of International Economic Law* 843 (2012), 844.

[28] 50 U.S.C. app. § 2170(e) (2006).

[29] 538 notices from 2008 to 2012, "Covered Transactions, Withdrawals, and Presidential Decisions 2008–2012," www.treasury.gov/resource-center/international/foreign-investment/Documents/CFIUS%2520Stats%25202008-2012.pdf, last accessed on Oct. 22, 2014; there were ninety-seven notices filed in 2013 and 147 notices filed in 2014. "Annual Report to Congress," CY 2014, CFIUS, at www.treasury.gov/resource-center/international/foreign-investment/Documents/Annual%20Report%20to%20Congress%20for%20CY2014.pdf.

[30] See, e.g., Christopher M. Tipler, "Defining 'National Security': Resolving Ambiguity in the CFIUS Regulations," 35 *University of Pennsylvania Journal of International Law* 1223 (2014), 1243; Joshua C. Zive, "Unreasonable Delays: CFIUS Reviews of Energy Transactions," 3 *Harvard Business Law Review Online* 169 (2013), 169.

[31] Zaring, "CFIUS as a Congressional Notification Service," 83. [32] Ibid., 84.

[33] Tingley et al., "The Political Economy of Inward FDI," 27.

[34] Jon D. Michaels, "The (Willingly) Fettered Executive: Presidential Spinoffs in National Security Domains and Beyond," 97 *Virginia Law Review* 878 (2011), 878. For a more thorough discussion of the pros and cons of agency structure designed to pool resources, see Daphna Renan, "Pooling Powers," 115 *Columbia Law Review* 211 (2015).

[35] Friedrich Wu and Andreas Bakke Frøystadvåg, "China Investment Corporation's Forays into Europe and the United States: Explaining the Different Receptions," 25 *Journal of Contemporary China* 91 (2016), 91; Joshua Zive, "Unreasonable Delays: CFIUS Reviews of Energy Transactions," 3 *Harvard Business Law Review* 169 (2013); Matthew C. Sullivan, "CFIUS and Congress Reconsidered: Fire Alarms, Police Patrols, and a New Oversight Regime," 17 *Willamette Journal of International Law and Dispute Resolution* 200–1 (2009).

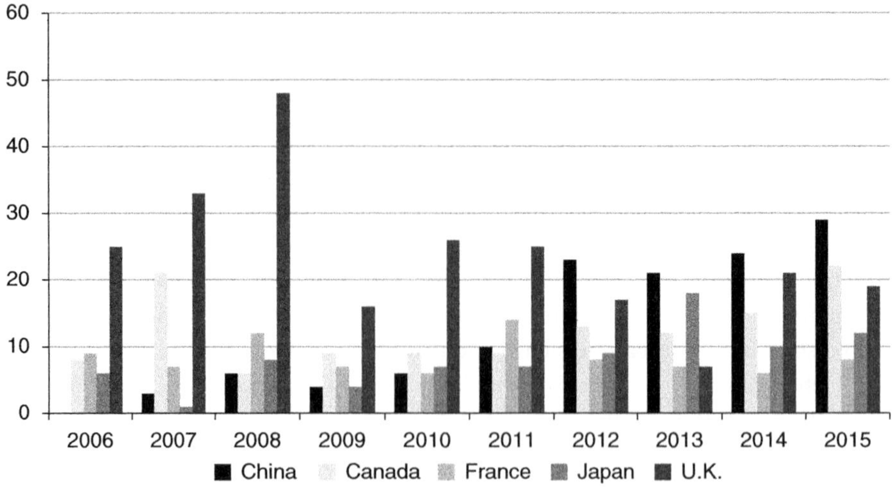

FIGURE 7.1 CFIUS-reported covered transactions by investor's home country (2006–15)
Source: Annual Reports to Congress (2008–17) by Committee on Foreign Investment in the United States, available at www.treasury.gov/resource-center/international/foreign-investment/Pages/cfius-reports.aspx

membership and the diversity of institutional interests represented by the member agencies are a principle source of the uncertainty that foreign investors have to face in coping with the system.[36] Vague terms and broad discretion also expose the agency to political influence. One scholar goes as far as labelling CFIUS "essentially a congressional notification service."[37] Because of congressional encroachment in the area, traditionally and constitutionally reserved for the executive branch, committee staff would sometimes "advise foreign acquirers to consult with Congress before embarking on mergers."[38]

Despite the secrecy and uncertainty associated with CFIUS review, until recently no foreign investor had ever challenged a CFIUS action in a U.S. court, likely due to the relatively loose enforcement prior to the enactment of FINSA,[39] the vague statutory language and broad discretion of the agency, the underlying national security nature of the process, and the statutory provision clearly constraining judicial review.[40] But after CFIUS stepped up its scrutiny of foreign investments after FINSA (see Figure 7.2), and investment originating from China continued to grow exponentially, the disproportionate impact on Chinese investment is evident. While CFIUS turned more proactive, it reviewed a high percentage of Chinese investments,[41] and quite a

36 Pasco, "United States National Security Reviews of Foreign Direct Investment," 350, 355.
37 Zaring, "CFIUS as a Congressional Notification Service," 83. 38 Ibid., 99. 39 Ibid.
40 50 U.S.C. app. § 2170(e) (2006).
41 Wu and Frøystadvåg, "China Investment Corporation's Forays into Europe and the United States," 99.

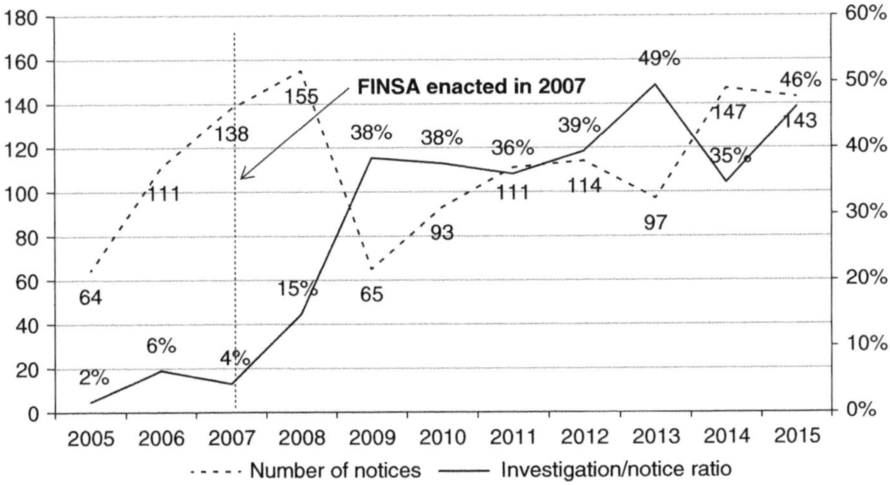

FIGURE 7.2 CFIUS notices filed and investigation–notice ratio (2005–15)
Source: Annual Reports to Congress (2008–17) by Committee on Foreign Investment in the United States, available at www.treasury.gov/resource-center/international/foreign-investment/Pages/cfius-reports.aspx

few large investments failed due to the review.[42] Section II will elaborate in detail the perceptions and reactions of Chinese investors during this transitional phase. For now, the key points to know are that serious friction occurred from time to time between Chinese companies and CFIUS, which generally ended in the former ceasing the investment and bearing all the losses. Eventually, a Chinese investor threw down the gauntlet and sued CFIUS and the president for actions taken against its acquisition in the United States.

In March 2012, Ralls Corporation, a company incorporated in Delaware but owned by two Chinese nationals who were senior managers at Sany (a large Chinese private company manufacturing heavy machinery[43]), purchased four U.S. companies with the intent to develop windfarms on the land they owned in north-central Oregon.[44] The targeted sites are located in and around the "region of a restricted airspace and bombing zone maintained by the U.S. Navy."[45] Likely due to the large institutional distance, Ralls did not pay adequate attention to potential CFIUS risk and failed to file a notice prior to the transaction. Prompted by the U.S.

[42] Thilo Hanemann and Daniel Rosen, "Don't Misread Old Tealeaves: Chinese Investment and CFIUS" (Feb. 24, 2016), at http://rhg.com/notes/dont-misread-old-tealeaves-chinese-investment-and-cfius.

[43] The founder and chairman of Sany Group, Liang Wengen, is a member of the Communist Party of China and a deputy of the 17th and 18th National Congresses of the CPC. "Entrepreneurs' Presence Grows at CPC Congress," *Xinhua* (Nov. 12, 2012), at http://usa.chinadaily.com.cn/business/2012-11/12/content_15919618.htm.

[44] *Ralls Corp.* v. *Comm. on Foreign Inv. in U.S.*, 758 F.3d 296, 319 (D.C. Cir. 2014).

[45] Ibid., at 304.

Navy, Ralls subsequently made the filing, and CFIUS determined that the transaction threatened to impair U.S. national security and issued interim mitigation orders restricting Ralls's access to the windfarm sites pending the president's final decision.[46] Now fully aware of the graveness of the matter, Ralls negotiated a sale of the assets at a discounted rate to a U.S. company, assuming that would address the national security concern. The sale fell through due to the interim orders. Ralls also engaged former U.S. government officials to lobby the agency, to no avail. President Obama subsequently concurred that the transaction posed a national security threat and issued a presidential order, pursuant to which Ralls had to divest from the U.S. companies within ninety days;[47] disassemble its equipment, which must be done by U.S.-born American citizens; and acquire CFIUS approval for its sale of the assets to a third party.[48] Due to the onerous conditions, Ralls stood to lose all its U.S. investment, worth at least US$20 million.[49] In addition, Sany's managers were concerned that the official determination that its acquisition threatened U.S. national security would jeopardize the company's other and future investment in the United States.[50]

In sharp contrast to how U.S. government bodies typically operate in the area of tax and workplace equality, throughout the CFIUS process Ralls received no explanation and was given no opportunity to rebut any evidence against it.[51] In response to the actions of CFIUS and later the president, Ralls filed a lawsuit claiming, inter alia, the violation of its due-process right under the Fifth Amendment.[52] The district court initially dismissed most of Ralls's claims as moot or for lack of subject matter jurisdiction,[53] and later tossed out the due-process claim as well for failure to state a claim.[54] Upon Ralls's appeal, the D.C. Circuit surprisingly reversed the lower court's decisions.[55]

The D.C. Circuit rejected the argument that Ralls's due-process claim was a nonjusticiable political question as the claim did not "encroach on the prerogative of the political branches," "did not require the exercise of non-judicial discretion," and was "susceptible to judicially manageable standards."[56] The D.C. Circuit decided that Ralls had been denied due process as it was neither informed of the nature of the national security concern with the acquisitions or the evidence on which the determination was based, nor allowed an opportunity to rebut.[57] The D.C. Circuit remanded the case to the district court with instructions that Ralls be

46 Ibid., at 302. 47 Ibid., at 306.

48 *Ralls Corp.* v. *Comm. on Foreign Inv. in the U.S.*, 926 F. Supp. 2d 71, 80 (D.C. Dist. 2013).

49 Jasmine Wang, "Sany Affiliate May Lose $20 Million on US Wind-Farm Ban," *Bloomberg* (Oct. 3, 2012), at www.bloomberg.com/news/articles/2012-10-04/sany-affiliate-may-lose-20-million-on-u-s-wind-farm-ban.

50 Tang Ya, Chen Jing, and Chen Daixi, "Sanyi Zhonggong: Women Ruhe Gaoying Obama" (Sanyi Zhonggong: How We Won against Obama), *Shangye Pinglun* (Aug. 5, 2016), at www.ebusinessreview.cn/articledetail-286709.html.

51 Ibid. 52 *Ralls Corp.* v. *Comm. on Foreign Inv. in U.S.*, 758 F.3d 296, 315 (D.C. Cir. 2014).

53 Ibid., at 306. 54 Ibid., at 307. 55 Ibid., at 309. 56 Ibid., at 307–13. 57 Ibid., at 325.

provided access to the unclassified evidence on which the decision was based and an opportunity to respond thereto.[58] It also instructed the lower court to fully adjudicate several other legal issues raised by the investor. After CFIUS handed over 3,000 pages of documents to Ralls, the two parties negotiated an undisclosed settlement, under which Ralls was allowed to sell its interests to desired purchasers.[59] The settlement, however, left unresolved several important legal issues concerning the CFIUS process, such as the boundary of the agency's statutory authority.[60]

Viewed from a jurisprudential perspective, *Ralls* is no doubt a watershed case. As discussed earlier, Exon-Florio authorizes the president to block a covered transaction that threatens to impair U.S. national security. This power is not time-barred. So, essentially, all foreign investment in U.S. businesses is exposed to the risk of a presidential veto.[61] To manage and mitigate the risk, however, foreign investors may get an approval from CFIUS, which bars the agency's future review and investigation. In other words, foreign investors may seek CFIUS review prior to a covered transaction, which, if approved, will be protected from the president's future exercise of the veto power.[62] So, at its core, CFIUS approval offers a safe-harbor protection to a covered transaction.[63] Accordingly, the trial judge in the *Ralls* case considered the investor's decision not to file a CFIUS notice as a willing assumption of the risk of a presidential veto.[64] In other words, foreign investors who opt not to obtain the safe harbor of CFIUS approval merely acquire "contingent" property rights in U.S. assets.[65]

The D.C. Circuit disagreed and proffered the constitutional due-process protection over foreign investors' U.S. assets acquired through a covered transaction. The court ordered CFIUS to provide the foreign investor with unclassified evidence and an opportunity to rebut.[66] The constitutional protection extended to foreign investors should have altered the expected payoffs of the decision not to file a notice with CFIUS before investment. After *Ralls*, if a foreign investor fails to make a filing with CFIUS prior to a covered transaction, and CFIUS subsequently initiates an investigation and decides to sanction the foreign investor, the agency will have to follow

58 Ibid.

59 Paul Welitzkin, "Lawsuit Settlement Seen as Unlikely to Affect CFIUS," *China Daily* (Nov. 11, 2015), at http://usa.chinadaily.com.cn/epaper/2015-11/06/content_22387282.htm.

60 Briefly, the claims to be fully adjudicated on remand include: (1) CFIUS exceeded its statutory authority in dealing with Ralls's property interests, (2) CFIUS violated the Administrative Procedures Act in exercising its authority, and (3) CFIUS and President Obama acted in an *ultra vires* manner. *Ralls Corp.* v. *Comm. on Foreign Inv. in U.S.*, 758 F.3d 296 (D.C. Cir. 2014).

61 Though the D.C. Circuit decision proffered due-process protection on foreign investors' property interests in U.S. business, it does not at all diminish the president's power to find national security risk in the covered transaction and order divestiture.

62 50 USC app. S 2170(b)(1)(D).

63 Pasco, "United States National Security Reviews of Foreign Direct Investment," 350, 354.

64 *Ralls Corp.* v. *Comm. on Foreign Inv. in the United States*, 987 F. Supp. 2d 18, 27 (D.C. Dist. 2013).

65 Ibid.

66 *Ralls Corp.* v. *Comm. on Foreign Inv. in the United States*, 758 F.3d 296, 325 (D.C. Cir. 2014).

more onerous procedural requirements. In theory, that should increase the expected payoffs for the investor from skipping the filing. More importantly, the *Ralls* decision altered foreign investors' expectation about judicial scrutiny of CFIUS actions, i.e., a higher probability of active judicial review. Of course, it is costly to litigate in the United States against a federal agency, so the foreign investor will take that approach only if substantial interest is at stake.

In other words, the *Ralls* case further separated the foreign investor's expected payoffs from the two diverging initial decisions, i.e., to file or not to file prior to embarking on a covered transaction. If the foreign investor chooses to file prior to a covered transaction, it has not yet acquired property interests in any U.S. assets. So the judicial review, which is more conceivable after *Ralls*, does not concern protected interests for constitutional due-process purposes.[67] The courts will be highly deferential towards the agency, so the foreign investor reasonably expects negative payoffs from litigating an unfavorable CFIUS decision. In other words, the D.C. Circuit decision does not alter the pre-*Ralls* world if the foreign investor chooses to file a notice with CFIUS prior to a covered transaction. As some practitioners observed, "since the D.C. Circuit's opinion, CFIUS has shown no inclination to offer foreign investors rights to rebut evidence in standard CFIUS cases, nor even in cases in which the relations between CFIUS and the parties become acrimonious."[68]

In contrast, if the foreign investor invests without first filing a notice with CFIUS, it acquires property interests in the U.S. assets. Such property ownership, under *Ralls*, entitles the foreign investor to constitutional due-process protection. Thus, CFIUS's administrative actions will be subject to more intrusive judicial scrutiny. Everything else being equal, *Ralls* transformed the payoffs for foreign investors in such a way that they have more incentives to skip CFIUS filing before investing in U.S. assets.

Of course, everything else may not be equal. Evidently, if CFIUS intends to maintain the same payoffs from filing a notice, all it has to do is change the probability of detection or the probability of investigation. In order to do so, however, CFIUS has to boost its administrative capacity. The agency will need to collect more information about foreign acquisitions of U.S. assets that may potentially pose a national security threat, and more resources to investigate the transactions. Moreover, the agency can achieve the same objective by significantly altering the probability of approving a covered transaction if the foreign investor failed to make a pre-transaction filing.

Alternatively, the agency may adjust the payoffs for filing the notice in order to achieve the same outcome as in the pre-*Ralls* regime. It can do so by raising the expected return from filing the notice, e.g., making it easier to obtain approval for the foreign investor that files a notice with CFIUS. Though the D.C. Circuit decision does not substantively implicate agency actions following the "filing prior

67 *Ralls Corp. v. Comm. on Foreign Inv. in the United States*, 987 F. Supp. 2d 18, 27–9 (D.C. Dist. 2013).

68 Stewart Baker and Stephen Heifetz, "Ralls May Give Foreign Investors More Leverage with CFIUS," *Law360* (Dec.11, 2014), at www.law360.com/articles/603312/ralls-may-give-foreign-investors-more-leverage-with-cfius.

to investment" branch of the decision tree, and CFIUS has not yet shown any sign of altering its procedures, the agency would nonetheless feel some pressure in the future to reform its procedures in order to narrow the payoff gap between the "to-file" decision and the "not-to-file" decision.

In short, *Ralls* could potentially trigger a series of chain effects on the calculation of foreign investors engaging in covered transactions. A new equilibrium of the interactions between CFIUS and foreign investors will emerge in due course. Its final form, however, will also be affected by several contextual factors. As noted, the probability of CFIUS attention and investigation is a variable not only of agency administrative capacity, but also of media coverage and the relations between the U.S. government and the home country of the foreign investors.[69] Investors from a country that is a close ally of the U.S. (e.g., Korea or Japan) will inevitably be treated differently from those of non-allies (e.g., China or Russia) for the analysis of a national security threat.[70]

To summarize, the CFIUS regime evolved over time in response to recurring political concerns with the negative impacts of foreign investment in the United States. Prior to FINSA, most foreign investment in the United States originated from U.S. allies, so CFIUS did not actively investigate or block covered transactions. Absent active interference from the agency, foreign investors tolerated the uncertainty and arbitrariness of the process and never sued. FINSA altered the equilibrium by requiring heightened agency scrutiny of certain covered transactions. The legislative change coincided with surging investment from China. Tensions have since been growing between, on the one hand, a more active CFIUS exercising broad power and discretion in a non-transparent way and, on the other, Chinese investors lured by the U.S. market and the government's open policy to acquire substantial U.S. assets in diverse sectors. The tensions culminated in *Ralls* v. *CFIUS*. The case allows the public to peek into the "legal black hole" of the CFIUS review process and underscores the importance of understanding how Chinese investors view and cope with the institution, as elaborated in the following section.

II CHINESE INVESTMENT UNDER THE CFIUS REGIME

As noted in Chapter 2, the United States has become the largest national recipient of China's ODI, yet the economic interdependence can barely disguise the political distrust between the two governments. Chinese investment into the United States, therefore, poses an acute problem for CFIUS. Since 2012 Chinese investors have filed the most CFIUS notices each year, surpassing both the UK and Japan. And the only four transactions officially blocked by the president in the entire history of the

69 Jiang and Li, "CFIUS: For National Security Investigation or for Political Scrutiny," 67, 95–6.
70 Ibid., 96.

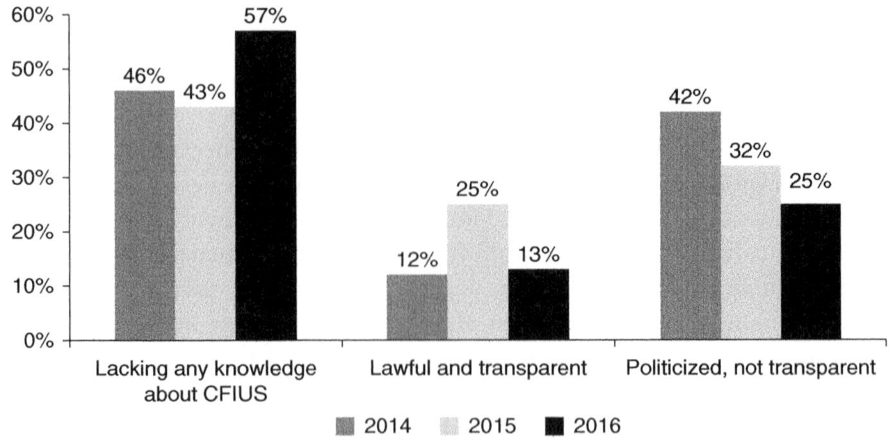

FIGURE 7.3 Views of the CFIUS process
Source: 2014–16 surveys

CFIUS regime were all by Chinese investors.[71] In short, analyzing how Chinese companies view and react to the CFIUS regime is crucial to understanding not only their interactions, but also the context of the *Ralls* case and its impact on the U.S. institution for national security review of foreign investment.

Section I detailed the enormous institutional distance Chinese investors confront in this subject matter area. Traversing such a wide gap, according to the analytical framework set forth in Chapter 3, necessitates strong desire and compliance capacity on the side of Chinese MNE managers. This section empirically examines the two elements and focuses on how managers view the system and their use of U.S. specialists in CFIUS compliance. Thereafter, I will empirically survey how Chinese companies actually reacted to the CFIUS process.

A *Opinions about CFIUS*

By their nature, rules such as those regulating CFIUS review apply only to foreign-sourced investment. Chinese investors, having no experience of complying with such laws in the home state, face an enormous institutional gap. Therefore, it is not a great surprise that about half of the survey respondents reported having no knowledge about CFIUS (Figure 7.3). The gap is a shield that blocks information about CFIUS review from Chinese investors. The finding certainly affects how they react to the institution. How can Chinese investors take any rational action in the shadow of the presidential veto if they lack basic information about CFIUS review? As articulated by the district

[71] The fourth and most recent veto was by President Trump on Sept. 13, 2017. Ana Swanson, "Trump Blocks China-Backed Bid to Buy U.S. Chip Maker," *New York Times* (Sept. 13, 2017), at www.nytimes.com/2017/09/13/business/trump-lattice-semiconductor-china.html?_r=0.

judge in the *Ralls* case, the long-standing assumption about foreign investors' behavior has been that they are fully informed of the CFIUS review mechanism, so their decisions not to notify the agency prior to a covered transaction should be interpreted as a rational assumption of the risk. Hence, no legal protection is available once the risk materializes, e.g., when the agency orders a detrimental divestiture without due process. The empirical finding that about half of Chinese investors lacked any knowledge of the CFIUS system clearly falsifies the assumption. Foreign investors' rational reactions to U.S. legal and regulatory rules are bounded by their knowledge. In this subject matter area, the wide institutional divide blocks the knowledge.

Even those Chinese investors informed about CFIUS review expressed negative views. As previously discussed, relative to U.S. tax law and U.S. employment discrimination law, CFIUS rules are intentionally vague, broad, and ambiguous. In addition, the rules mandate CFIUS to thoroughly scrutinize investment from non-allies and those subject to strong foreign-government influence. According to the survey data, among those that have some knowledge about CFIUS, the majority considered the regime politicized and non-transparent, which contrasts sharply with how the same managers opined about U.S. institutions governing tax and employment equality.

The distribution of opinions shifted over time. As noted earlier, minor shifts are insignificant given the changing composition of the survey samples. But here something significant is probably at work, as the percentage of investors considering CFIUS to be lawful and transparent in 2015 was more than twice those of the other two years. Two factors might have contributed to the dramatic change. First, as will be illustrated, more Chinese investors consulted U.S. lawyers who are mostly former government agents working for CFIUS and who were able to provide some guidance to investors about the review process.[72] Second, *Ralls* may have some positive influence as the investor plaintiff eventually prevailed in the D.C. Circuit. As commented by the CEO of Sany, the Chinese-affiliated company of Ralls, on the unexpected ruling, "the case is a win–win as it helps foreign investors to understand the United States."[73] It may be hard for U.S. scholars to conceive that an otherwise obscure D.C. Circuit decision could have any major impact outside the CFIUS Bar. But *Ralls* is different in that the judgment made headlines in all Chinese newspapers and online news channels within days of its publication.[74] The outcome might have

[72] Diane Bartz and Greg Roumeliotis, "The Washington Insiders Who Work to Get Chinese Deals Approved," *Reuters* (Feb. 25, 2016), at www.reuters.com/article/us-usa-china-deals-advisors-insight-idUSKCN0VX2PX.

[73] Peng Fei, "Sanyi Zhonggong 'Zunyan Susong' Jiewei Zhongqi Fumei Shougou Nanti" (Sanyi's Dignity Suit Solves the Problem for Chinese Buyers of U.S. Assets), *Fa Ren* (Dec. 6, 2016), at http://finance.sina.com.cn/roll/2016-12-06/doc-ifxyiayr9306297.shtml.

[74] See, e.g., Wu Chengliang, "Sanyi Zhonggong Zai Meiguo Daying Guansi" (Sanyi Heavy Machinery Won Suit in US), *People's Daily* (July 17, 2014), at http://world.people.com.cn/n/2014/0717/c1002-25290956.html; Liu Jiao, "Sanyi Zhonggong Guanlian Qiye zai Meiguo Gaoying Aobama" (Affiliate of Sanyi Heavy Machinery Won Suit against Obama in US), *Xinhua Net* (July 16, 2014), at www.sn.xinhuanet.com/2014-07/16/c_1111647316.htm; SINA, one of the most popular online news portals,

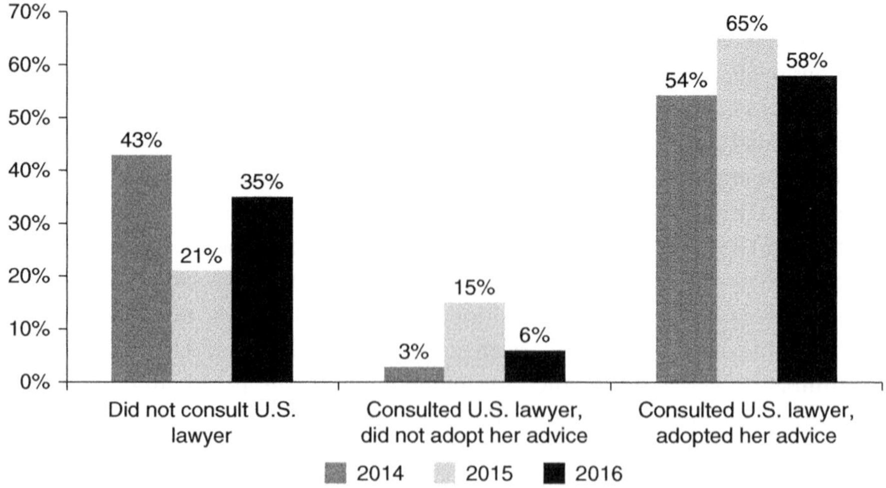

FIGURE 7.4 Whether U.S. lawyers were engaged in CFIUS review
Source: 2014–16 surveys

convinced many Chinese investors that the CFIUS regime is, after all, governed by law. However, the ruling failed to spur actual change in how CFIUS conducted its business, so the positive view waned after 2015. Of course, some other variables that changed over the years might have contributed to the improved perception. I will conduct more rigorous analysis later to assess the possible effects of *Ralls*.

B Reliance on U.S. Professionals

The CFIUS process is complex and opaque; many foreign investors therefore "rely on a relatively small group of experienced lawyers who deal regularly with CFIUS."[75] Do Chinese investors also depend on U.S. lawyers to navigate the system? Prior chapters suggested that, in general, Chinese investors would rely extensively on local professionals to cope with U.S. legal and regulatory institutions. For instance, in dealing with U.S. tax matters, about 90% of Chinese companies outsourced it to outside tax specialists. In the area of national security review, however, the results are mixed. Though the majority of respondents with knowledge of CFIUS consulted U.S. lawyers on the matter, a significant minority did not (Figure 7.4).[76] However, the vast majority of those that did consult specialists ended up adopting the professional advice.

operated a special column for the lawsuit titled "Sanyi Group Won Lawsuit against Obama," at http://finance.sina.com.cn/focus/sanyiabm.

75 Michaels, "The (Willingly) Fettered Executive," 881.

76 Because the sample comprises sizable Chinese MNEs and state-owned firms are overrepresented, the percentage for 2014 for legal consultation in a random sample of all Chinese MNEs in the United States should be lower than 57%.

The big picture portrayed by the survey data remains roughly the same over the three years, and minor changes are expected due to different sample compositions. That said, a notable shift in 2015 merits some discussion. Compared to the previous year, a higher percentage of the Chinese investors (80%) solicited legal advice regarding CFIUS. Conversely, the percentage of investors not consulting a U.S. lawyer about CFIUS dropped by more than half from 43% to 21%. Meanwhile, interactions with U.S. lawyers led to different outcomes in 2015. While the percentage of investors who consulted U.S. lawyers and followed their legal advice increased from 54% in 2014 to 65% in 2015, the percentage of investors who dismissed lawyers' advice surged from 3% in 2014 to 15% in 2015. What explains the drastic change? I speculate that the D.C. Circuit decision in *Ralls* plays an important role. As noted, the case made headline news in China,[77] which educated Chinese investors about the value of law in the CFIUS process. Subsequently, more consulted U.S. lawyers on the matter.[78]

On the other hand, *Ralls* probably vitiated the credibility of CFIUS "experts." The appellate decision took most of them by surprise.[79] The outcome probably taught Chinese investors to take their lawyers' advice with a grain of salt, hence the much higher percentage of respondents who refused to follow the legal advice of their lawyers. Moreover, it is possible that, having learned about CFIUS from reading news reports of the *Ralls* case, some investors that would have been better off skipping the filing felt it necessary to get a professional opinion. Lawyers, being risk-averse and incentivized by potential legal fees, likely advised in favor of filing a notice in most situations. Their clients, however, ran different calculations and some might have decided not to adopt the lawyers' advice.[80] Similar to the managers' view about CFIUS, the impact of *Ralls*, if any, appears to have faded in 2016. The distribution of the 2016 data resumes the pattern of 2014.

To summarize, despite the media portrait of CFIUS as a major barrier to Chinese FDI in the United States, the study finds that the majority of Chinese MNE managers lacked any knowledge of the review. I attribute the finding to the large

77 See, e.g., Wu Chengliang, "Sanyi Heavy Machinery Won Suit in US"; Liu Jiao, "Affiliate of Sanyi Heavy Machinery Won Suit against Obama in US"; SINA online news portal "Sanyi Group Won Lawsuit against Obama."

78 Ralls was decided on July 15, 2014. Most of the 2014 survey questionnaires (59/101) were collected before the D.C. Circuit decided *Ralls* v. *CFIUS* on July 15, 2014.

79 CFIUS experts all opined that the trial court got the law right. See, e.g., Daniel B. Pickard, Nova J. Daly, and Usha Neelakantan, "The Ralls Case: Why CFIUS and the Court Got It Right," 8 *Global Trade and Customs Journal* 192 (2013); Jeremy Zucker and Hrishikesh Hari, "Gone with the Wind II: The Ralls Decision and Lessons for Foreign Investors," 9 *Global Trade and Customs Journal* 44 (2014). Prior to the initial district court ruling, CFIUS experts estimated the probability of Ralls's prevailing in court to be less than 1%. "Sanyi Su Aobama An Lushi Xia TingKang: Hexin Suqio Huo Shouli" (Lawyer Xia TingKang for Ralls v. Obama: Core Claim Accepted), *Xinlangcaijing* (March 2, 2013), at http://finance.sina.com.cn/hy/20130302/100514697913.shtml.

80 Of course, caution should be exercised not to overinterpret the change in percentages from 3% to 15%, as the corresponding change in absolute numbers is relatively insignificant.

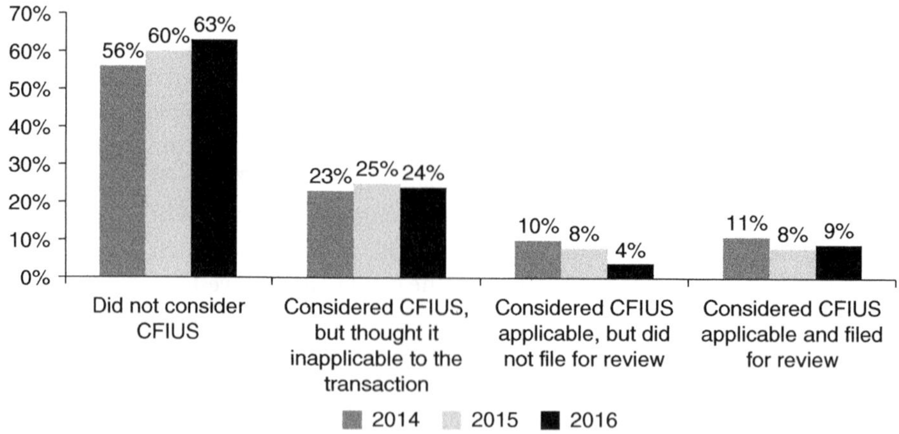

FIGURE 7.5 Consideration and filing with CFIUS when investing in the United States
Source: 2014–16 surveys

institutional distance in this area. Chinese investors never had to deal with national security review at home, so they had to cross huge gaps in this area when investing in the United States. Moreover, unlike the enforcement of U.S. tax law and employment law, CFIUS review is discriminatory and highly discretionary. Naturally, the vast majority of those with some knowledge about CFIUS considered the review process politicized and non-transparent. In addition, reliance on professionals varies significantly across different firms. Though the majority of Chinese companies having some knowledge about CFIUS consulted U.S. lawyers and followed their professional advice, a significant minority either ignored the lawyers' opinions or failed to get one in the first place.

C *Consideration and Filing with CFIUS*

Given the findings regarding the desire and ability of Chinese investors to cope with CFIUS review, how did they actually respond? As shown in Figure 7.5, the majority did not consider filing a CFIUS notice when they invested in the United States. The finding is not surprising considering that nearly half of survey respondents admitted lacking any knowledge about CFIUS review. Moreover, under the current law, greenfield investments fall outside CFIUS's jurisdiction, so those respondents who entered the U.S. market by building businesses from scratch did not have to contemplate the legal issue and risk.[81]

[81] The definition of greenfield investment for purposes of CFIUS review is not entirely free of ambiguity. Would Ralls have been exempted from CFIUS review had the company purchased the sites directly from individual U.S. owners who bought the sites from the four U.S. companies? The answer is not entirely clear.

Among those that had considered U.S. national security review when making their investments, the majority concluded that it was inapplicable to their transactions. As noted, CFIUS review applies only to covered transactions. Greenfield investment is exempt. Moreover, some Chinese investors may have concluded that acquisitions of U.S. business posing minimal threat to U.S. national security would not incur any significant CFIUS risk.

Among those that had considered CFIUS review to be applicable to their transactions, only about half filed a notice with the agency. As previously discussed, foreign investors that do not voluntarily file the notice violate no law. By not filing the notice, informed investors simply assume the risk of a subsequent CFIUS investigation and, in case of a finding of national security threat, sanctions such as an ordered divestiture. Fully informed rational foreign investors would have no incentive to make a CFIUS filing when the expected return from doing so is lower than that from skipping the filing. Suppose a medium-sized Chinese company with 20% voting interest owned by a provincial government intends to invest in a U.S. firm manufacturing low-end auto parts, and the investor expects a quick return on the investment. Though under the current law, CFIUS should initiate an investigation if notified, the risk of a finding of national security threat is so low that the Chinese investor is probably better off skipping it before making the investment, especially given their negative view about the CFIUS process.

To summarize, this section presented an empirical overview of how Chinese companies viewed and responded to the CFIUS process. According to the survey data, about half of the Chinese investors lacked any knowledge of CFIUS when investing in the United States. Among the rest, the majority considered CFIUS review politicized and non-transparent. Those with knowledge about the regime generally relied on U.S. lawyers for guidance. The evidence, taken together, suggests that Chinese investors do not all contemplate the legal issues and risks associated with CFIUS review and it is highly likely that they will respond to CFIUS in ways deviating from the regime's legislative intent. Indeed, according to the survey data, the majority of the companies failed to consider CFIUS filing prior to their investment and half of those who thought the rules applicable to their cases decided not to file the notice.

The data also reveal some interesting developments over time. A higher percentage of Chinese investors in the 2015 survey reported a positive view of CFIUS and consulted U.S. lawyers over CFIUS matters. The *Ralls* decision probably plays a role in shifting the distribution. The D.C. Circuit ruling demonstrated that the agency and the president were bound by law, leaving Chinese investors a positive impression of the lawfulness of the CFIUS process. It also educated investors about the importance of U.S. law, so more solicited legal advice. The effects of *Ralls*, however, faded quickly as CFIUS showed no sign of altering its behavior in the review process; hence the resemblance of the 2014 and 2016 distributions.

III STATE OWNERSHIP AND CHINESE COMPANIES' REACTIONS TO CFIUS

The control of U.S. assets by foreign governments, especially those considered non-allies, has always drawn much suspicion. Readers may recall the bacon deal. What some U.S. legislators found particularly unappetizing in Shuanghui's acquisition of Smithfield Foods was the possible involvement of the Chinese government.[82] As noted earlier, under the current law, acquisitions that will result in foreign government control over U.S. assets trigger automatic investigation once CFIUS is notified. Though the law is on the face of it neutral in that the heightened scrutiny applies to acquisitions controlled by any foreign government, its impact falls disproportionately on Chinese investors given their close and intricate relationships with a government that is often considered a geopolitical challenge to the United States. Chinese SOEs, which play a prominent role in the Chinese business expansion into the United States, are easy suspects. As discussed earlier, the attempt by CNOOC, a Chinese state-owned conglomerate in the energy sector, to acquire UNOCAL and the political aftermath contributed to the enactment of FINSA. But even Chinese investors without significant state ownership may find themselves in the spotlight of CFIUS investigation. As noted, the formal law governing CFIUS review does not mark any equity-holding threshold for finding foreign government control. Instead, the agency is allowed to consider all facts and circumstances. Hence, Huawei, an employee-owned company that has resisted Chinese government ownership, had several of its acquisitions in the United States blocked by CFIUS.[83]

Given the special features of the institution, the intricate yet often uneasy U.S.–China relations, and the prominence of SOEs in China's FDI in the United States, one would expect state ownership in Chinese investors to have measurable effects on how they view and react to the CFIUS process. Using data from the annual surveys, this section statistically analyzes the possible effects. First, do managers of Chinese companies with significant state ownership see the CFIUS regime differently? In the two preceding chapters, the Chinese managers, regardless of their employers' ownership type, expressed generally positive views about U.S. tax law and U.S. employment law. But the law governing CFIUS review is different in that it differentiates state-controlled foreign investors from the rest. In addition, CFIUS enjoys wide discretion and its review process has been likened to a legal black hole. So, intuitively, managers of state-owned investors would be less likely to view the CFIUS process as lawful and transparent. The statistical tests below confirm the hypothesis. Second, under what conditions are Chinese investors more likely to

[82] Parija Kavilanz, "Is Pork a National Security Asset?", *CNN* (May 31, 2013), at http://money.cnn.com/2013/05/31/news/companies/smithfield-foods, last accessed on May 23, 2017.

[83] See more detailed discussion about Huawei's investment experiences in the United States in Chapter 2.

consider the CFIUS risk when making their U.S. investments? Particularly, are Chinese companies with significant state ownership more likely to consider CFIUS review when investing in the United States? As will be detailed, the regression analysis suggests that state ownership in a Chinese investor is positively associated with the filing of a CFIUS notice. Moreover, Chinese companies with substantial U.S. investments, operations in sensitive sectors, or prior experience of mergers and acquisitions in the United States are more likely to have considered CFIUS notification. Third, when do Chinese investors actually file a notice with CFIUS? Does state ownership make a difference in this regard? The regression tests suggest that the effect of Chinese government ownership is insignificant. When it comes to the costly filing, business sector, investment size, prior M & A experience, and knowledge of CFIUS review appear to play more important roles in the decision.

A *Perception of the CFIUS process*

In contrast to the generally positive views of U.S. tax law and employment law, Chinese managers either lacked knowledge about the CFIUS process or described it as non-transparent and politicized. Given the opaqueness of the review and the broad discretion enjoyed by the agency, it is hard to blame the Chinese managers for the overall negative view. Those working for state-owned companies should be more critical since U.S. law subjects their employers to heightened scrutiny. If the hypothesis holds, it will be in strong contrast to the findings from prior chapters that detached Chinese investors' ownership type from varying opinions about U.S. institutions.

I created a dummy dependent variable that equals 1 if the respondent not only knew about the CFIUS review process but also viewed it as transparent and in accordance with law, 0 otherwise. I added a set of independent and control variables. The independent variable of interest is Chinese government ownership in the investors. I use the same two dummies (50% state ownership and 10% state ownership) alternately, as in prior chapters. Current U.S. law specifies that, when notified of a covered transaction that may result in foreign government control of U.S. assets, CFIUS should automatically initiate an investigation. However, Congress did not equate foreign government control to majority or whole government ownership in a U.S. business. CFIUS is authorized to examine all facts and circumstances of a covered transaction in order to make the determination. One would reasonably expect the vague and ambiguous language to cause more concern for Chinese investors with significant government ownership intending to enter the U.S. market via mergers and acquisitions.

In addition, the sector of a Chinese company should matter. First of all, sectoral distribution may correlate with Chinese investors' ownership structures because under current Chinese law and policies government-owned enterprises tend to occupy strategically important sectors in China.[84] Second, some sectors tie closely to national security. For instance, covered transactions targeting U.S. critical infrastructure have been singled out to automatically trigger a CFIUS investigation upon notice.[85] Similarly, foreign investment in telecommunications has frequently been investigated.[86] Though Congress refuses to provide a clear definition of national security, it offers a list of considerations for CFIUS analysis, which closely relate to a foreign acquirer's sector. I created a dummy that equals 1 if the foreign investor operates in a "sensitive sector," 0 otherwise. The tricky issue in coding for this variable is how to define "sensitive sector" when the formal definition remains ambiguous. Based on the enumerated factors in the regulations and prior research, I define the term broadly to include crucial infrastructure, information, transportation, heavy machinery with dual-use potential, public utilities, and the defense industry.

Moreover, how much a foreign investor invests in the United States should matter, as it affects the expected payoffs from a CFIUS investigation and sanction. The amount should also correlate with the investor's ability to bear the cost of CFIUS filing and subsequent litigation, if necessary. The 2014 and 2015 surveys inquired about the dollar amounts of the responding companies' revenues in the United States. Due to the low response rate for this question, the 2016 survey replaced it with a scale question. For the regression tests, I converted the 2014 and 2015 data to a scale of 1 to 4 to match the 2016 measurement.

Furthermore, the current law exempts greenfield investment from CFIUS review. Foreign investors that build business operations from scratch do not pose, in the eyes of lawmakers, any national security threat that cannot be addressed by other U.S. laws.[87] To account for the variation in the mode of investment, I added a dummy variable that equals 1 if the Chinese investor has previously engaged in a merger or acquisition in the United States, 0 otherwise. The statistical tests also include as a control the duration of a company's operation in the United States because it is relevant to the calculation of expected payoffs relating to the CFIUS filing.

Additionally, ownership in a U.S. business may have an effect. A prior study shows that Chinese SOEs may strategically invest through joint ventures to reduce political risk.[88] The factor may also have an indirect effect as CFIUS considered having U.S. citizens managing the U.S. assets to be a key mitigating factor for national security risk.[89] In response, savvy Chinese investors have promised to retain U.S. senior management even after full acquisition in order to reassure

84 Lüthje, Luo, and Zhang, *Beyond the Iron Rice Bowl.*

85 31 CFR s 800.503(b)(2).

86 For instance, the Chinese telecommunications company Huawei has been investigated several times by CFIUS and its acquisitions of U.S. businesses have been prohibited. Li, "I Came, I Saw, I … Adapted," 143.

87 31 CFR s 800.301(c), example 3.

88 Lin Cui and Fuming Jiang, "FDI Entry Mode Choice of Chinese Firms: A Strategic Behavior Perspective," 44 *Journal of World Business* 434 (2009).

89 Zaring, "CFIUS as a Congressional Notification Service," 81.

TABLE 7.1 *Summary statistics*

Variable	Mean	Std. dev.	Min.	Max.	Observations
State ownership (50%)	0.423313	0.494844	0	1	326
State ownership (10%)	0.51227	0.500618	0	1	326
Investment duration	11.36646	9.76049	0	40	322
CFIUS as lawful and transparent	0.159259	0.366597	0	1	270
U.S. revenue	2.3125	1.28324	1	4	240
U.S. business ownership	0.83758	0.369425	0	1	314
Sensitive sector	0.242604	0.429293	0	1	338
Prior M & A	0.338926	0.474141	0	1	298
Consulted CFIUS lawyer	0.187675	0.391001	0	1	357
Knowledge of CFIUS	0.477778	0.500434	0	1	270
Considered CFIUS	0.4	0.49076	0	1	285
Filed CFIUS notice	0.094737	0.293366	0	1	285

Source: 2014–16 surveys

concerned U.S. officials.[90] This factor should also affect consideration by Chinese investors as they are entitled to only part of the expected future profits of the invested U.S. business. According to the survey data, however, the variable does not vary much; most Chinese investors invest through wholly owned subsidiaries, instead of joint ventures or minority equity ownership.

Professional opinion may also influence the view of Chinese managers. Earlier chapters have documented the extensive reliance by Chinese companies on local professionals. With little knowledge about the entirely alien CFIUS review, Chinese managers should form their opinions based on what they learn from U.S. specialists.

Last, the effect of *Ralls* will be tested. The surveys straddled the D.C. Circuit decision in *Ralls*. In the summer of 2014, most of the survey questionnaires had been completed and collected before the D.C. Circuit decided *Ralls* on July 15, 2014. So for most respondents, the 2014 survey recorded their knowledge, if any, about the trial court decision, which dismissed all of Ralls's claims, and the generally shared expectation that the D.C. Circuit would uphold the lower court's decision. When the 2015 survey was conducted, *Ralls* had prevailed in the lawsuit against CFIUS and the president, and the case had been remanded to the district court for a full trial on several open issues. And the 2016 survey was able to capture the aftermath, if any, of *Ralls* and the subsequent lack of change in how CFIUS reviews covered transactions. I add two survey-year dummies to catch the effect of the *Ralls* decision over the three years from 2014 to 2016, with the baseline being 2015.

90 Marilyn Geewax, "Can a Huge Hog Deal Pose a National Security Risk?", *NPR* (May 31, 2013), at www.npr.org/2013/05/31/187351539/can-a-huge-hog-deal-pose-a-national-security-risk, last accessed on May 24, 2017.

As shown in Table 7.2, state ownership in Chinese investors is significant across all the model specifications. The coefficients are negative, indicating that the Chinese companies with significant government ownership were less likely than the rest of Chinese investors to consider the CFIUS review process as transparent and in accordance with the law. The finding contrasts strongly with the test results in the prior chapters that Chinese investors' state ownership is unrelated to managers' views about U.S. institutions, either general institutions (e.g., the U.S. legal system) or specific ones in the areas of taxation and employment. The finding here, however, is not surprising. Foreign government control triggers CFIUS investigation automatically, irrespective of the underlying threat to U.S. national security. Such a categorical agency response inevitably results in the perception of arbitrariness and lack of transparency. As noted, much of the opaqueness of the review is designed to "protect military and proprietary information," and is an inherent nature of national security review. "It's hard to think of a national security review process anywhere in the world that is done in the sunlight."[91] Further complicating the matter are fluctuating U.S.–China relations. While the world's two titans are moving ever closer in trade and investment, their political objectives diverge in multiple respects.[92] Many in the United States consider the Chinese government a rising contender for global leadership and potentially disrupting the existing international order.[93] Meanwhile, many in China cannot help but interpret U.S. foreign policies as aimed at maintaining its leadership by containing and stalling China's legitimate rise in the world.[94] Against this backdrop, key stakeholders in the U.S. government inevitably treat Chinese SOEs differently from foreign companies based in its ally countries, such as Japan and Canada.[95] Yet the differentiation cannot be openly stated as it would negatively implicate diplomatic relations with China and contradict other long-held U.S. policies. The maintenance of a "superficial friendship" by the governments greatly adds to the uncertainties of the CFIUS process for Chinese state-owned investors.[96]

In addition, lawyers matter, and the coefficients are positive. So, everything else being equal, Chinese investors that have consulted U.S. lawyers about CFIUS review are more likely to consider the process transparent and law-bound. Experts

91 Ibid.

92 See, e.g., Xuetong Yan, "The Instability of China–US Relations," 3 *Chinese Journal of International Politics* 263 (2010); John J. Mearsheimer, "The Gathering Storm: China's Challenge to US Power in Asia," 3 *Chinese Journal of International Politics* 381 (2010).

93 David Fagan, "The US Regulatory and Institutional Framework for FDI," in Karl P. Sauvant, ed., *Investing in the United States: Is the U.S. Ready for FDI from China* (2009), 3.

94 Ibid.

95 Ibid. The suspicion of investments from Chinese SOEs may materialize in the CFIUS process as concerns with espionage risk. Paul Connell and Tian Huang, "An Empirical Analysis of CFIUS: Examining Foreign Investment Regulation in the United States," 39 *Yale Journal of International Law* 131 (2014), 135.

96 Yan, "The Instability of China–US Relations," 263.

TABLE 7.2 *Viewing the CFIUS process as lawful and transparent*

	1	2	3	4	5	6
State ownership (50%)	−1.072016**		−1.273227**		−1.433018**	
	(0.4607762)		(0.530504)		(0.5539218)	
State ownership (10%)		−0.7334935*		−1.066661**		−1.062675**
		(0.4159689)		(0.5061185)		(0.5130232)
Sensitive sector	0.3605241	0.2253366	0.4475739	0.4158517	0.0126707	−0.0227896
	(0.4702478)	(0.4652864)	(0.5031306)	(0.5086917)	(0.5978042)	(0.5920907)
Investment duration	0.0161766	0.0102084	0.0141553	0.0067999	−0.0016132	−0.0084507
	(0.0188277)	(0.018276)	(0.0227126)	(0.0218704)	(0.0252362)	(0.0243443)
U.S. business ownership			−0.4566048	−0.4375028	−0.3817419	−0.3793351
			(0.5126338)	(0.5121974)	(0.5392631)	(0.5367861)
Prior M & A			0.5792008	0.6225623	0.6222451	0.6570148
			(0.4181951)	(0.4191617)	(0.4413032)	(0.4417278)
U.S. revenue			0.2382222	0.2582098	0.211546	0.2263525
			(0.1713293)	(0.1735079)	(0.1893152)	(0.1906502)
Legal advice re CFIUS					1.122911**	0.9854249*
					(0.5677732)	(0.5475199)
Survey year 2014					−1.746231**	−1.689706**
					(0.6883401)	(0.6781978)
Survey year 2016					−1.085277**	−0.9900033**
					(0.5023315)	(0.496705)
Number of observations	249	249	184	184	184	184

Note: ***$p < 0.01$; **$p < 0.05$; *$p < 0.1$; 2014–16 surveys; logistic regressions

in the CFIUS bar-trade their know-how and insiders' information. Aided by their expertise, investors consider the process more predictable and transparent.

Moreover, the coefficients of the survey-year dummies are significant and negative. Everything else being equal, a Chinese investor's perception of CFIUS in 2015 is much more likely to be positive than in 2014 and 2016. As noted, the surprising *Ralls* decision by the D.C. Circuit in favor of the Chinese investor probably improved perception of the system. However, CFIUS did not change its actions subsequent to the ruling, so the improvement was temporary.

Sectoral sensitivity is not significantly associated with the probability of a positive perception of the CFIUS system, after controlling for the other variables. Though related, perception of CFIUS is a step away from the payoff calculations. Nor are duration of investment and U.S. business ownership significantly associated with the probability of viewing the CFIUS system as transparent and in accordance with the law. Given the limited sample size, however, I would refrain from drawing definitive inference from the nonsignificant coefficients.[97]

B Considering CFIUS Review When Investing in the United States

In theory, the current law governing CFIUS review subjects almost all foreign acquisitions of U.S. assets to the contingency of a presidential veto on a national security ground that is not time-barred and is barely reviewable by the court even after *Ralls*. Therefore, Chinese investors should at least consider the issue even if they eventually conclude that the investments do not impair U.S. national security. Yet the survey results suggest otherwise: the majority of Chinese companies failed to take CFIUS into account when investing in the United States (see Figure 7.5).

Lack of knowledge about the CFIUS regime due to the enormous institutional gap certainly explains why a significant fraction of investors failed to consider it. What else? For instance, does foreign government ownership matter, as it triggers an automatic investigation by CFIUS? This subsection explores how various factors, especially state ownership, may be associated with the likelihood that Chinese investors take CFIUS review into account when investing in the United States. The dependent variable is a dummy that equals 1 if the survey respondent reported having considered CFIUS review, 0 otherwise.

Again, the independent variable of interest is state ownership in the Chinese investors. The same two dummies (50% state ownership and 10% state ownership) will be tested alternately. I also include a number of other variables in the tests. Awareness of CFIUS certainly matters. Sectoral sensitivity may also play a role

97 Because the coding of the dummy dependent variable groups those without knowledge of CFIUS with those expressing a negative view, the tests may return false significance. Hence, I recode the dummy dependent variable by grouping those without knowledge with those holding positive views and run a set of similar tests. The results are consistent, i.e., Chinese investors with state ownership hold negative views of the CFIUS system.

because the current law treats differently those sectors that tie closely to national security. For instance, notification of a covered transaction targeting U.S. critical infrastructure automatically triggers a CFIUS investigation.[98] I also include U.S. investment size as a control to account for the effects of the expected legal risks from skipping CFIUS. Investors with insignificant U.S. investments stand to lose little even if CFIUS orders a divestment after identifying a national security threat. In addition, I add prior M & A experience, as the current law excludes greenfield investment from CFIUS jurisdiction.[99] I also include investment duration and the two survey-year dummies to assess possible effects over time and those of the *Ralls* case. Last, I include ownership in a U.S. business as a control. As previously discussed, the presence of local partners may mitigate U.S. national security concerns.

Table 7.3 reports the test results of different model specifications where the dependent variable is whether the Chinese investors considered CFIUS review when investing in the United States. As expected, the coefficients for state ownership in the Chinese investors are positive and significant across all the models. So, everything else being equal, an investor with significant Chinese government ownership is more likely than the rest to have considered CFIUS review when investing in the United States.

Knowledge about CFIUS is positive and significant. Intuitively, those ignorant of the system are less likely to have considered it. The sector in which the Chinese investor operates is also significant. Chinese companies doing business in sensitive sectors are more likely than investors in nonsensitive sectors to have contemplated CFIUS review when investing in the United States. Moreover, the Chinese investor's investment size is also highly significant. Those with larger investment tend to be more likely to consider CFIUS review. In addition, the coefficient for prior M & A experience is positive and highly significant.

These empirical findings, taken together, resonate well with what one predicts rational foreign investors would do in response to the formal CFIUS rules as long as they possess the requisite information. The DPA, as amended by FINSA, specifically provides that CFIUS investigate covered transactions resulting in foreign government control of U.S. assets, and that investment in sensitive sectors such as critical infrastructure receive the heightened scrutiny of the agency. Thus, these two variables directly affect the probability of a CFIUS investigation and sanction. On the other hand, the size of investment determines the payoffs calculated by investors. Foreign investors should carefully consider CFIUS review before they make substantial investments with long-term returns, as CFIUS investigation may result in a divestiture order. In the words of a specialist, "for any significant deal, it's prudent to go forward with a CFIUS review."[100]

[98] 31 CFR s 800.503(b)(2). [99] 31 CFR s 800.301(c), example 3.

[100] Geewax, "Can a Huge Hog Deal Pose a National Security Risk?".

TABLE 7.3 *Considering CFIUS when investing in the United States*

	1	2	3	4	5	6
State ownership (50%)	1.090436***		0.7129091*		0.8900088*	
	(0.3055199)		(0.3902114)		(0.4559053)	
State ownership (10%)		1.051983***		0.7512741*		0.8432221*
		(0.2998476)		(0.3906401)		(0.4591979)
Sensitive sector	1.136613***	1.140372***	1.494378***	1.444011***	1.384393***	1.308429**
	(0.3365705)	(0.3354841)	(0.4157208)	(0.4213107)	(0.4991828)	(0.5053729)
Investment duration	0024719	0.0070143	−0.0037769	−0.0014188	−0.0238329	−0.0191441
	(0.0150568)	(0.0147156)	(0.0194725)	(0.0191262)	(0.0251462)	(0.0244638)
U.S. Business ownership			−0.7890301	−0.8109722	−0.5570175	−0.562969
			(0.4832026)	(0.4842714)	(0.5884603)	(0.587384)
Prior M & A			1.084664***	1.030636***	1.13576***	1.067142**
			(0.36496)	(0.3650287)	(0.4355275)	(0.4336729)
U.S. revenue			0.5559714***	0.5458125***	0.7195319***	0.7036065***
			(0.1487447)	(0.1492951)	(0.1890115)	(0.1885897)
Awareness of CFIUS					2.458151***	2.435291***
					(0.4556204)	(0.4543495)
Survey year 2014					0.5355394	0.5434553
					(0.6499541)	(0.648701)
Survey year 2016					0.7906765	0.7617333
					(0.5299651)	(0.5273266)
Number of observations	266	266	191	191	181	181

Note: ***p < 0.01; **p < 0.05; *p < 0.1; 2014–16 surveys; logistic regression tests

Other variables are not significant in all the model specifications. Duration of investment, for instance, does not appear to affect the consideration of CFIUS review. Presumably, Chinese companies that have operated in the United States for a long time should constitute less of a national security threat, otherwise they would have already caught the attention of CFIUS and been ordered to divest. The finding that the variable is insignificant when other variables are included in the regression suggests that duration itself may not be the crucial factor. A private Chinese company in a nonsensitive sector (e.g., textiles), regardless of how long it has operated in the United States, would have less incentive to consider CFIUS review when acquiring U.S. businesses in its sector. The fact that CFIUS rarely orders divestiture might also diminish the incentive for private Chinese companies in nonsensitive sectors to consider CFIUS before making investment.

Additionally, U.S. business ownership is insignificant. Prior studies have shown that CFIUS considered the threat to U.S. national security to be less acute if American citizens participate in or control certain management activities. Yet according to the regression result, whether the Chinese investor wholly owns its U.S. business or has a local partner does not appear to affect whether it considers CFIUS review, when other variables are held constant.

Finally, the *Ralls* decision by the D.C. Circuit does not appear to have any significant impact on whether Chinese investors would consider CFIUS review. It is possible that when other variables, such as state ownership and investment size, are controlled, Chinese investors do not expect the *Ralls* decision to substantially alter the payoffs regarding the CFIUS process. After all, CFIUS still enjoys wide discretion despite the due-process requirement imposed by the D.C. Circuit.[101]

I also ran separate tests using the survey data of each year. Though some coefficients are no longer significant due to the much smaller sample size, the results are not substantially different from those of the pooled sample. In sum, the results from the regression analysis confirmed some predictions and dispelled others about Chinese investors' consideration of CFIUS when investing in the United States. Investors with state ownership and in sensitive sectors are more likely to consider CFIUS review when they have some knowledge about the system; and those who invest substantial amounts are more inclined to do so as well. Other potential variables are not significant in all of the model specifications.

C Filing with CFIUS

As discussed earlier, the current law allows foreign investors to seek a safe harbor for their U.S. investments by filing a notice with CFIUS and obtaining an approval. Who among the Chinese investors in the United States will actually make the costly filing? The filing is costly not only because the fees paid to the professionals are

[101] Li, "I Came, I Saw, I . . . Adapted," 143.

substantial; also, satisfying the request for information can delay the proposed transaction. Though the law limits the time for a determination regarding the national security implications of a declared transaction, the clock does not start until CFIUS deems the notice to be complete. Moreover, CFIUS may impose onerous conditions on the acquisition, or push the investor to amend the notice and refile. This subsection statistically analyzes the variation in filing behavior. For this set of tests, the dependent variable is a dummy that equals 1 if the Chinese respondent filed a notice with CFIUS. Because the calculation for the filing is essentially the same as that for the consideration, I use the same set of independent and control variables.

Table 7.4 shows the results from six model specifications. Chinese investors' sectoral background continues to be a significant predictor of filing with CFIUS. Everything else held constant, investors in sensitive sectors are more likely to file CFIUS notices than those outside those sectors. Likewise, Chinese investors with larger investment assets in the United States are more likely to have filed a CFIUS notice about their investments. Chinese companies with substantial U.S. investments will benefit more from obtaining a safe-harbor protection in the form of a CFIUS approval. Intuitively, both knowledge about CFIUS and prior M & A experience in the United States are significant and positively associated with the likelihood of filing a notice.

Chinese government ownership in the investors, however, is no longer significant, for two possible reasons. First, though foreign government ownership may increase the probability of a CFIUS investigation, the factor per se will not result in sanctions. So, after controlling for sectoral sensitivity and asset size, Chinese government ownership becomes insignificant. Recall the earlier example of a textile manufacturer owned by a Chinese government entity. The management planning to acquire a U.S. peer company reasonably expects the risk of a CFIUS finding of national security threat to be minimal. Thus, the Chinese investor should feel comfortable skipping the filing, despite its government ownership. Another possible explanation is that some state-owned investors consider the probability of CFIUS rejection or sanction too high and that they give up certain acquisitions. In line with this explanation, the survey data indicates that all of the responding firms that have ever abandoned a merger or acquisition of a U.S. business due to CFIUS concerns are at least majority-owned by the Chinese government.[102]

Having a local partner is not associated with any major change in the propensity of the Chinese investor to file a notice with CFIUS, though how a joint venture is formed is typically a factor that CFIUS considers to make determination of a covered transaction.[103] Additionally, survey-year dummies are not significant, indicating that

102 Among those validly answering the survey question, about 10% reported having given up certain proposed U.S. investments due to concern with CFIUS review.

103 31 CFR s 800.301(d).

TABLE 7.4 *Filing with CFIUS when investing in the United States*

	1	2	3	4	5	6
State ownership (50%)	0.3512889		0.873249		0.8622532	
	(0.5160741)		(0.7741942)		(0.7689734)	
State ownership (10%)		0.6652911		1.153569		1.163465
		(0.5306602)		(0.775552)		(0.774035)
Sensitive sector	1.582732***	1.469951***	1.428403**	1.419818**	1.399524*	1.368307*
	(0.4939569)	(0.4853699)	(0.7237944)	(0.7047164)	(0.7210308)	(0.7053684)
Investment duration	−0.0351829	−0.0370293	−0.0876363**	−0.0867805**	−0.0844239**	−0.0832042**
	(0.0237163)	(0.0235)	(0.0356018)	(0.0343059)	(0.0359796)	(0.0347555)
U.S. Business ownership			−1.038858	−1.129942	−1.111279	−1.208721
			(0.7493421)	(0.7576859)	(0.7712598)	(0.7821531)
Prior M & A			2.778529***	2.786546***	2.864419***	2.877936***
			(0.7516377)	(0.7547824)	(0.7769182)	(0.7785844)
U.S. revenue			0.5079364**	0.4934905*	0.4535361*	0.4368271*
			(0.2541477)	(0.2536059)	(0.2633366)	(0.2644924)
Awareness of CFIUS			3.661794***	3.772581***	3.729833***	3.8448***
			(1.132029)	(1.152538)	(1.141524)	(1.172949)
Survey year 2014					0.6286791	0.5991785
					(0.9536847)	(0.9615702)
Survey year 2016					−0.1506975	−0.2175999
					(0.7956111)	(0.8003402)
Number of observations	266	266	181	181	181	181

Note: ***$p < 0.01$; **$p < 0.05$; *$p < 0.1$; 2014–16 surveys; logistic regression tests

Ralls did not change the filing behavior of Chinese investors. As discussed earlier, though the D.C. Circuit decision has the potential to alter the payoffs in such a way that, everything else being equal, foreign investors are more incentivized not to file a notice with CFIUS prior to embarking on a covered transaction, many other factors may affect the expected payoff. Because CFIUS has not notably altered its behavior since *Ralls*, neither should the Chinese investors.[104] In sum, when it comes to filing notices with CFIUS, investment size, sectoral sensitivity, knowledge of the process, and prior M & A experience play significant roles. State ownership is not significant. But it is premature to draw definitive conclusions from the finding, as it could mean either that government ownership per se is unimportant for filing decisions or that state-owned companies have self-selected out of risky investments that necessitate CFIUS filings.

To summarize, the empirical tests identified, in two aspects, the significant roles of state ownership in Chinese investors. First, Chinese investors with state ownership are less likely to view the CFIUS process as lawful and transparent. The finding, in stark contrast to those from the tests in the preceding two chapters on tax and employment equality, is not entirely surprising given the CFIUS rules concerning the distinction of investment that may result in foreign government control of U.S. assets, the vagueness of the rules, and the secrecy-shrouded review mechanism. Second, for the same reasons, Chinese investors with state ownership are more likely to have considered the CFIUS risk when investing in the United States. In addition, Chinese companies' U.S. investment size, their sector of business, and their awareness of the system are significant in all the tests for considering the CFIUS risk and the actual filing with the agency.

IV CONCLUSION

Nothing is certain in life but death and taxes. The famous quote of Benjamin Franklin is universally applicable, so when Chinese companies invest in the United States they understand compliance with U.S. tax law to be an integral part of their business. Similarly, thanks to legal transplants the Chinese laws prohibiting employment discrimination share many of the core principles embodied in U.S. law on workplace equality. So when Chinese managers deal with U.S. workers, the concept of nondiscrimination does not sound foreign. But if asked about consideration of CFIUS review, an average Chinese manager in the United States will likely respond with a confused look, followed by "What sea fears?" At home, Chinese managers never had to deal with national security review prior to an investment, so they face an enormous formal institutional gap in this subject matter area. In addition, the CFIUS rules are ambiguous and their enforcement spotty and highly discretionary. Therefore, nearly half of the survey respondents confessed to having

104 It is also possible that not many Chinese companies have contemplated new acquisitions since *Ralls*.

no knowledge about the regulatory system. Those informed about it generally considered the CFIUS process politicized and non-transparent. As a result, most Chinese investors either failed to take it into account when investing in the United States or adopted a relatively opportunistic approach to the regulatory risk, which, coupled with the agency's highly discretionary and opaque exercise of its power, led to the disruption of *Ralls*. Here, the word "disruption" carries no derogatory connotation. In the area of national security review of foreign investments, the major disruption took the form of a federal circuit court decision that appears justified on Constitutional and fairness grounds. Quite ironically, it took a lawsuit by a Chinese-invested company to bring CFIUS under judicial review. The landmark decision of *Ralls* had a positive, albeit temporary, impact on Chinese investors' perception of the system, and it failed to alter their reactions to the institution.

Again, Chinese companies exhibit varying attitudes and reactions towards the U.S. institution. According to preliminary statistical analysis, the variations in how Chinese managers viewed the CFIUS mechanism turn on the investors' ownership type and on consultation with U.S. specialists; whereas the variation in the companies' reactions is associated with their government ownership, sectoral sensitivity, and prior M & A experience, and with the size of their U.S. investments. One can infer from the findings that Chinese companies in the United States are generally rational given the institutional context, to the extent that they are aware of the U.S. regulatory risk.

Apart from substantiating the theme of this book, this chapter has presented much-needed information about foreign investors' perception of and reaction to the CFIUS process. As noted, prior research has centered on the legal and political aspects of CFIUS and ignored the receiving end of the review mechanism. Thus, the debate about the regime's efficacy has to date been educated guesses. Though we know about how foreign investors react to the review from integrated annual data publicized by CFIUS and from anecdotal reports, a systematic study of the topic has been lacking. The "silent majority," those that invest without filing a CFIUS notice, do not appear in any archival data. This study presents such information.

Moreover, the surprising decision by the D.C. Circuit in *Ralls* has attracted much attention from scholars as well as practitioners. Some argue that the case marks a major development in the regime of national security review of foreign investment.[105] Others downplay the significance of the decision in terms of its practical impact.[106] This study weighs in on this debate. The findings suggest that the decision

105 See, e.g., Anne W. Salladin and Amelia J. Schmidt, "CFIUS Post-Ralls: Ramifications for Sovereign Wealth Funds," 2015 *International Review of Law* 1 (2015), 3.

106 Charles A. Blanchard et al., "Will Ralls Decision Really Bring CFIUS Transparency?", *Law360* (Aug. 12, 2014), at www.law360.com/articles/566033/will-ralls-decision-really-bring-cfius-transparency.

only temporarily improved views of Chinese investors about the CFIUS process, and it has not affected investors' actual behavior.

Furthermore, the findings highlight the potential for future conflict in the area. *Ralls*, despite its theoretical implications, has failed to alter CFIUS behavior in regular cases, curtail its broad discretion, or narrow the enormous institutional gap in this subject matter area. If anything, the reach of the CFIUS regime has only expanded. On December 2, 2016, President Obama issued an executive order prohibiting a Chinese-owned German company from acquiring control of a publicly traded German manufacturer, Aixtron.[107] That was only the third time in CFIUS history that a U.S. president exercised the veto power, and all the three were cast against Chinese acquisitions. As before, the order cited national security concerns but provided no details. Presumably, Aixtron's U.S. subsidiary in California and the company's products used in the semiconductor industry caught the attention of CFIUS. This time, however, the attempted takeover had not been consummated and the Chinese buyer simply abandoned the deal. Without fully vested property interest in the United States, the Chinese investor did not have a constitutional due-process claim established by the *Ralls* case. As Chinese investment in the United States is set to grow in the long run, the CFIUS regime will continue to evolve under a confluence of legal, political, and business factors. Soon after Trump won the presidential election various stakeholders proposed drastic expansion of CFIUS review authority to counter the perceived risks of Chinese FDI and to coerce the Chinese government to further open its market to U.S. companies.[108] Given the findings of this chapter, the dynamic interactions between Chinese investors and CFIUS will undoubtedly provide fertile soil for abrupt institutional changes.

107 Mozur, "Obama Moves to Block Chinese Acquisition of a German Chip Maker."

108 For an example of such proposals, see testimony of Robert D. Atkinson before the U.S.–China Economic and Security Review Commission, Hearing on Chinese Investment in the United States: Impacts and Issues for Policymakers (Jan. 26, 2017), at www2.itif.org/2017-us-china-testimony.pdf, last accessed on May 29, 2017.

8

Implications and Questions for the Future

Chinese FDI in the United States has been growing exponentially in the past few years. Even though fears over capital flight have caused the Chinese government to tighten foreign-currency control and put the brakes on "irrational" outbound FDI,[1] Chinese investment in the United States will most likely continue on a long-term upward trajectory. Given the size of the Chinese economy, China will before long surpass Japan, Canada, and the UK to be the largest source of FDI in the United States. How will Chinese companies investing in the United States interact with the complex legal and regulatory institutions of the host country? Will they exercise extra caution in complying with U.S. law as if "treading on thin ice," or superficially comply but aggressively exploit any legal loopholes, or, worse yet, trample on U.S. laws and regulations, as some Chinese investors have allegedly been doing in other host states?

In addressing these new and important questions, this book presents an eclectic analytical framework that guides research about foreign investors' compliance with host countries' laws and regulations. The framework encompasses interdisciplinary inquiries about the need, desire, and ability of foreign investors to adapt and conform to a host country's legal institutions. To be more specific, the need to adapt turns on relevant institutional distances between the investors' home and host states, the analysis of which entails comparative law and comparative institutional research; the desire to adapt hinges on the investors' motives and perceptions of host states' institutions; and the foreign investors' ability to adapt is a function of the allocation of decision-making power and reliance on local professionals.

The heuristic device should be broadly applicable. One may use it to organize research about Chinese investors' compliance with Japanese employment law or

[1] Chinese ODI during the first half of 2017 decreased by 46% compared to the same period of 2016. Ellen Sheng, "Chinese Outbound Investment Drops 46% in First Half of 2017 as Government Tightens Controls," *Forbes* (July 14, 2017), at www.forbes.com/sites/ellensheng/2017/07/14/deal-breakers-chinese-outbound-investment-dropped-46-in-first-half-of-2017/#62c401aa55a3.

with German law on national security review of foreign investment, as well as about Indian investors' compliance with U.S. tax law. Despite its conceptual parsimony and broad applicability, however, the analytical frame will benefit from further refinement. As previously noted, the three components – the need, desire, and ability of foreign investors to conform to host-country legal institutions – are neither independent nor mutually exclusive; and the firm-level factors on which I choose to focus certainly do not exhaust all that matters for foreign investors' desire and ability to adapt. For instance, whether a foreign investor's stock is publicly traded may have some effect on its compliance behavior worldwide. Presumably, the disclosure requirement and additional oversight imposed on listed companies incentivize compliance. Even the factors already examined in this book should be subject to more fine-grained analysis. For example, future research should unpack the reliance by foreign investors on local professionals and examine closely the extent to which managers adopt professional advice. As Chapter 7 illustrates, Chinese investors do not always dance to the lawyers' tune. "Sometimes the executives, especially those who previously worked at big firms like [firm's name omitted], have their own ideas and would stick to them," lamented a U.S. lawyer serving primarily Chinese corporate clients.[2] In short, the framework articulated in this book serves as a prelude to future interdisciplinary research about the compliance of foreign investors with host-country laws and regulations.

Preliminary as it may be, the analysis guided by the current framework has generated a variety of important empirical findings about Chinese firms' compliance in the United States. Transnational learning and institutional transplant have narrowed the gaps of major market-facilitating institutions between China and the United States. And Chinese investors in general have shown both the desire and the ability to adapt and comply with most U.S. laws. Hence, surging FDI from China will not cause systematic friction with most existing U.S. legal and regulatory institutions, let alone wreak havoc on them. However, instead of settling the debate, some of the empirical findings may also substantiate the pessimistic view of Chinese FDI in the United States. Major divides remain between the two countries in terms of how laws are enforced and complied with, even in areas where the laws on the books have been converging. In addition, despite the overall inclination and efforts to conform, Chinese companies in the United States vary considerably; some are critical of host country institutions, invest for short-term policy considerations, and distrust local managers and professionals. So the pessimists may reasonably predict increasing conflict to follow soaring Chinese investment in the United States.

To make the matter more interesting, the variations are partially tied to the ownership structure of Chinese investors. Chinese FDI, originating from a large, diverse, and rapidly transforming economy, inevitably exhibits a great deal of variation and contradiction, for which one may find many explanatory variables. Within

2 Interview with an associate at the New York office of a China-based global law firm (July 18, 2017).

the scope of this book is the one that has stimulated most of the debate about Chinese FDI – whether and how China's intricate state–business relations are associated with Chinese investors' varying reactions to U.S. legal and regulatory institutions. The book finds that Chinese investors with significant state ownership do exhibit certain distinctive features, especially with regard to the allocation of management decision-making power. They also behave differently in subject matter areas where foreign government ownership is a salient legal factor.

The many findings of this book suggest new directions for research about outward FDI from China. First, Chinese FDI in developed countries such as the United States shares few common features with Chinese FDI in the developing world. For instance, private Chinese companies in the United States are committed to long-term investment, even more so than SOEs. Also, very few Chinese investors seek to acquire U.S. natural resources. Moreover, Chinese business elites embrace free-market capitalism and its enabling institutions, so they invest in the United States to "learn advanced management skills and technologies."[3] In the words of a Chinese executive, "we are humble students when doing business in the United States."[4] Furthermore, Chinese investors generally adopt a localization strategy and the U.S. labor and service market is largely sufficient to meet the demand.

The notable differences, however, bring to the fore the overall rationality and adaptiveness of Chinese outbound investors. When investing in a resource-rich country with poor governance and an undeveloped labor market, Chinese companies expatriate workers and export domestic management and compliance practices. By comparison, when investing in a country with robust state institutions and a mature service and labor market, Chinese firms adapt by localizing recruitment and management. Future research should explore the possibility of applying a modified version of the analytical framework presented herein to examining the compliance of Chinese investors in host-country institutional settings of both types.

Second, Chinese FDI in the United States is inextricably intertwined with domestic state–business relations, U.S. politics, and China–U.S. relations. All three are undergoing dramatic changes. In China, the ruling party has recently tightened its grasp over the SOEs, marking a sharp turn from the prior policies aimed at curtailing political intervention in SOEs' business and management decisions.[5] Will enhanced party control further impede the adaptation of state-owned Chinese investors to U.S. institutions? Concurrently, tectonic political changes are unfolding on the other side of the Pacific Ocean. Trump's presidency has introduced a great deal of uncertainty to U.S. investment policies as well as to

3 See the discussion of Chinese companies' investment motives in Chapter 3.

4 Interview with the CEO of a large Chinese investment firm in the real estate sector (June 20, 2017).

5 Zhou Xin, "Communist Party the Top Boss of China's State Firms, Xi Jinping Asserts in Rare Meeting," *South China Morning Post* (Oct. 12, 2016), available at www.scmp.com/news/china/economy/article/2027407/communist-party-top-boss-chinas-state-firms-xi-jinping-asserts.

U.S.–China relations, over which Chinese investors have expressed grave concern. According to the most recent survey, possible deterioration of U.S.–China relations and unfavorable U.S. government policies towards Chinese companies have overtaken "high labor cost" to top the list of business risks and challenges.[6] Although the vast majority of the Chinese investors, committed to long-term investment in the United States, have not yet altered their U.S. business plans, how they will respond to the largely unexpected political risk is a question of immense importance and interest. For instance, future research could explore the changes in their lobbying activities and their possible connections with the shifts in U.S. government policies towards China and Chinese investments.

Third, how will Chinese FDI engender incremental changes in U.S. law? Although Chinese companies will unlikely cause systemic disruption to existing U.S. legal and regulatory institutions, conflicts at the firm level are unavoidable, especially in areas of large institutional gaps. *Ralls* v. *CFIUS*, the case that has modified U.S. law governing national security review of foreign investments, is an illustrative example of how the friction may alter U.S. law piecemeal. Such impacts will certainly manifest in other areas where certain characteristics of Chinese state capitalism raise legal issues that are new or unclarified under current U.S. law. For instance, AVIC, a large Chinese SOE, recently invoked the sovereign-immunity defense in U.S. courts and forced the judges to clarify the issue in light of China's intricate state–business relationship.[7] The Foreign Sovereign Immunities Act of 1976 granted general immunity from U.S. courts' jurisdiction to foreign states and their "agencies and instrumentalities." Though the statute contains an exception for certain commercial activities,[8] the Sixth Circuit allowed the Chinese SOE defendant to assert sovereign immunity to challenge the basis of a U.S. court's jurisdiction and shift the burden of production to the plaintiff.[9] The decision has a far-reaching practical effect of raising the cost of litigation in the United States against SOEs.

In another case, involving the New York branch of the Bank of China, U.S. courts had to tackle the dilemma that enforcing U.S. discovery rules would force the bank to violate Chinese law.[10] To facilitate a trademark infringement action, Gucci requested that the bank's New York branch disclose relevant account information. The branch refused to fully comply with the subpoena, for doing so would violate China's banking secrecy law. Gucci then sued the bank branch and prevailed in a U.S. district court. The bank appealed and the Second Circuit remanded the case

[6] Merely 8% of the surveyed companies plan to reduce their U.S. investment due to concerns with the policies. See "2017 Annual Business Survey Report on Chinese Enterprises in the U.S.," at www .cgccusa.org/wp-content/uploads/2017/06/Survey-Report-2017-ENG.pdf.

[7] *Global Technology Inc.* v. *Yubei*, 807 F.3d 806 (2015).

[8] 28 U.S.C. § 1606(a)(2).

[9] *Global Technology Inc.* v. *Yubei*, 807 F.3d 806, 810–11 (2015).

[10] *Gucci Am., Inc.* v. *Weixing Li*, 2011 U.S. Dist. LEXIS 97814 (S.D.N.Y. Aug. 23, 2011); *Gucci Am.* v. *Bank of China*, 768 F.3d 122 (2d Cir. Sept. 17, 2014); *Gucci Am., Inc.* v. *Weixing Li*, 135 F. Supp. 3d 87 (S.D.N.Y. Sept. 29, 2015).

and instructed the trial judge to reconsider the bank's argument in light of the U.S. Supreme Court's decision in *Morrison*, which curtailed personal jurisdiction of U.S. courts over MNEs.[11] The district court judge then managed to reach the same substantive conclusion and compelled the bank to comply.[12] The case has raised the risk that many foreign banks with branches in the United States may violate their home-state law restricting the disclosure of banking information in order to comply with U.S. procedural law. Going forward, as more Chinese companies invest in the United States and litigate in U.S. courts, legal issues pertinent to the Chinese model of state capitalism will inevitably confront U.S. judges. Future research should analyze the long-term incremental impacts of such litigation on U.S. law.

The book also contributes to the debate about state capitalism. Overall, its findings should ease the concern in the United States that Chinese companies, either the SOEs or the privately owned national champions, are conquering the business world. At least in the bastion of free-market capitalism, Chinese companies are nowhere close to being formidable competitors; and the majority of them report U.S. profits lower than the global average. Doing business in the United States has been analogized by Chinese managers to "climbing a mountain." Not unlike other foreign investors, the Chinese suffer the "liability of foreignness" for which they have to pay "very expensive tuition."[13] Those that have overcome the learning curve are fully localized and "are no longer Chinese."[14] In addition, host-state governments usually have ample regulatory tools (e.g., CFIUS review) to restrain or deter acquisitions by Chinese SOEs and other Chinese investors under the home state's influence. Also, it is easy to overstate the visible hand's influence on China's decision to invest in a foreign country. In the case of investing in the United States, though China's policy objectives seem to have played some role, especially in the decisions of state-owned investors, commercial considerations have clearly been dominant. Insofar as China's ODI is concerned, state capitalism with Chinese characteristics is more about capitalism than about the state, at least for the time being.[15]

That said, marks of Chinese government ownership in SOE investors remain visible upon close examination. As noted above, compared to their private counterparts, state-owned Chinese investors are more likely to centralize the power to decide major personnel, legal, and compliance matters concerning their U.S. investments. State ownership may also matter in the institutional distances that Chinese companies have to traverse when entering the U.S. market and in their investment incentives. All these ownership-related differences, however, are relative

11 *Gucci Am.* v. *Bank of China*, 768 F.3d 122 (2d Cir. Sept. 17, 2014).

12 *Gucci Am., Inc.* v. *Weixing Li*, 135 F. Supp. 3d 87 (S.D.N.Y. Sept. 29, 2015).

13 Public statement by Zhu Hong, minister for commercial affairs, Embassy of the People's Republic of China, at SelectUSA 2017 (June 20, 2017).

14 Statement by Peter Wu, vice president of China Construction America, during a panel at Roads to USA – Greenfield Investment vs. Cross-border M & A Forum (June 20, 2017).

15 See, e.g., Nicholas R. Lardy, *Markets over Mao: The Rise of Private Business in China* (2014).

and should be viewed in light of Chinese companies' general adaptiveness. In addition, most Chinese investors, regardless of their ownership structure, rely extensively on local professionals and hold positive views of U.S. institutions. Taken together, these empirical findings suggest nuanced effects of state ownership on Chinese investors' U.S. investments. For instance, while state-owned firms may cope less effectively with major legal and compliance issues in the United States, in dealing with routine matters concerning U.S. operations, state ownership may lower the employees' risk tolerance and raise investment in compliance.

However, all Chinese SOEs are not equal. China's state capitalism features a blurry line between the party state and business actors.[16] Although this book has already broadened the scope of analysis to include significant minority state ownership (more than 10%), the focus is still trained on equity ownership. In practice, apart from varying state ownership percentage, SOEs' actions may be shaped by a confluence of other factors such as density of state ownership, rank in the political hierarchy, and corporate leaders' political connections and stature.[17] For instance, prior studies have shown that central-level Chinese SOEs and local SOEs respond to different sets of incentives when investing overseas.[18] Future research should explore whether and how these other variables affect Chinese SOEs' compliance behavior in the United States.

The book also adds to the literature on tax and FDI. Because outward FDI from developing countries is a relatively recent phenomenon, few have systematically explored the topic. The findings herein suggest that, quite intuitively, the incentive to avoid tax has no part in Chinese FDI in the United States. As a matter of fact, many Chinese investors complain about onerous U.S. taxation. Yet, counterintuitively, Chinese managers prefer the burdensome, notoriously complex but law-based U.S. tax system to the one in the home state. Overall, Chinese firms approach U.S. tax compliance with abundant caution. The findings also contribute to the emerging scholarship on tax and SOEs. Based on the preliminary test results, Chinese investors' ownership type is associated with the experience of tax audits and controversy in the United States, but not their U.S. tax planning.[19] To further evaluate the findings, future research should use corporate financial data to explore the factors pertinent to tax disputes and planning.

16 See, e.g., Milhaupt and Zheng, "Beyond Ownership."

17 See, e.g., Ming Hua Li, Lin Cui, and Jiangyong Lu, "Varieties in State Capitalism: Outward FDI Strategies of Central and Local State-Owned Enterprises from Emerging Economy Countries," 45 *Journal of International Business Studies* 980 (2014); Shangkun Liang, Zhen Li, Donghua Chen, and Shimin Chen, "Political Ranks, Incentives and Firm Performance," 3 *China Journal of Accounting Studies* 87 (2015); Li, "State-Owned Enterprises in the Current Regime"; Hongquan Chen, Xiaodong Li, Saixing Zeng, Hanyang Ma, and Han Lin, "Does State Capitalism Matter in Firm Internationalization? Pace, Rhythm, Location Choice, and Product Diversity," 54 *Management Decision* 1320 (2016).

18 See, e.g, Li, Cui, and Lu, "Varieties in State Capitalism," 980.

19 As noted repeatedly, readers should refrain from drawing definitive conclusions from tests based on certain self-reported data such as incidents of tax audits or controversy.

Those interested in Chinese companies' overseas employment practices should find the book useful. Prior studies of the topic, which focused mainly on Chinese FDI in developing countries, have generally cast Chinese employers in a negative light. According to this book, Chinese companies in the United States have to a great degree localized their human resource management. Though significant inter-firm variations exist, the vast majority of Chinese employers in the United States have not found discrimination to be a major issue. Future research should explore more rigorously how much workplace homogeneity explains the lack of discrimination complaints and how the situation will change as Chinese businesses in the United States continue to expand.

This book also furnishes much-needed empirical evidence for the debate about Chinese FDI and its national security implications. Despite the significance of the topic, few have examined it from the perspective of foreign investors. Filling the void, this book has found the majority of Chinese investors to lack knowledge about CFIUS review. Those with such knowledge considered the process politicized and non-transparent, and a high percentage of Chinese investors took an opportunistic approach in dealing with the CFIUS risk. Compared to tax, employment equality, and most other subject matter areas, the CFIUS regime stands to bear more direct impact from Chinese FDI. Future research should continue to investigate the dynamic interactions between the agency and Chinese investors.

Though much remains unknown and awaits further research, the findings of this book nonetheless offer useful guidance for policymaking concerning Chinese FDI in the United States. Policymakers have long debated the pros and cons of Chinese FDI and have not waited for rigorous empirical research before implementing laws and regulations with far-reaching implications. A case in point is the reform of CFIUS in the past two decades. Prior to this book, no one has systematically examined the effects of CFIUS on foreign investment in the United States. Yet the lack of rigorous research did not prevent Congress from enacting FINSA or contemplating further reform of the regime.[20] Similarly, most of the policies intended to magnify the benefits and mitigate the harms allegedly associated with Chinese investment rest on either case studies or basic analysis of aggregated official data. This book ameliorates the shortage of empirical evidence.

In light of the findings, how should policymakers respond? First of all, panic or fear is unnecessary as Chinese companies, having to overcome high hurdles in order to survive the fiercely competitive U.S. market, typically do not outperform local firms. And they generally conform to the host-country institutional environment. At least in the near term, Chinese companies will not cause major disruption to the existing U.S. system, except in isolated areas such as national security review of foreign investment. Even in those areas the regulators and agencies have ample

[20] Kate O'Keeffe, "Lawmakers Push for Tighter Scrutiny of Chinese Investment in U.S.," *Wall Street Journal* (Feb. 21, 2017), at www.wsj.com/articles/lawmakers-push-for-tighter-scrutiny-of-chinese-investment-in-u-s-1487678403.

leeway to preserve their broad power and discretion. If restrictive policies have to be made, they should be tailored, and attention should be devoted to areas where huge institutional gaps exist between the two countries, yet the Chinese firms lack the desire and capacity to adapt. Second, given the extensive reliance by Chinese investors on U.S. professionals, the governments of both countries may consider regulating Chinese FDI through these third-party intermediaries. For instance, intensified prosecution of U.S. tax practitioners promoting aggressive tax planning tools may not rein in U.S. companies since some of the largest ones have strong in-house tax capacity. But it will certainly tame Chinese companies in the United States as they lack internal tax capacity. Third, U.S. policymakers have assumed that foreign investors make fully informed rational reactions to laws and regulations. The findings of this book suggest that the assumption, which is shown to be valid in general, should be weakened in certain areas of significant institutional gaps. The gaps prevent investors from acquiring the basic knowledge to be aware of the legal risk, let alone assess it. For instance, the CFIUS regime operates on the supposition that rational foreign investors fully recognize the risk of a presidential veto and that therefore their decisions to skip notification prior to engaging in a covered transaction reflect a deliberate assumption of the risk. The findings of this book have refuted that premise. Future reforms of CFIUS and other U.S. legal and regulatory institutions that vary significantly from those in China should take account of the boundedness of investors' rationality. Otherwise they will fall short of achieving the legislative intent.

Finally, some advice is in order for Chinese investors who recently invested in the United States or are planning to take the plunge. Though varying across different subject areas, institutional gaps between China and the United States are wide in general. This structural factor is certainly beyond the control of any individual Chinese company. But crossing the gaps can be made easier by assigning to head the U.S. operations Chinese managers who have worked in countries the institutions of which bear more resemblance to those of the United States. Some Chinese companies have already done that, e.g., relocating managers from their UK or Canadian affiliates to lead the U.S. investment. Some Chinese firms, including some of the largest Chinese SOEs, typically expatriate Chinese employees that have passed certain qualifications on language and knowledge about the host countries. More Chinese investors should adopt such measures if they cannot fully delegate management to locally recruited staff.

It is no doubt a delicate matter to allocate the power to decide major legal and compliance matters concerning U.S. operations. In general, Chinese investors, especially those with significant state ownership, tend to export their domestic vertical control models to their U.S. affiliates. Problems with centralized management such as information asymmetry, delays in decision-making, and high transaction costs hamper efficient resolution of major legal and compliance issues in the United States. A senior executive of a Chinese MNE considered "lack of trust in local managers" the primary cause of investment failure in the United States. "Chinese investors should realize that they cannot run a U.S. business like a provincial subsidiary."[21] Yet too much delegation risks agency abuse of power.[22] Also, in the case of Chinese SOEs, the preservation of control over state assets often precludes the delegation of core management authority to local recruits. Therefore, the key challenge for all Chinese investors, especially the state-owned, is to design and implement a management model that properly balances investors' control and local management autonomy.

Chinese investors should pay special attention to their compliance in areas identified with substantial legal and regulatory institutional distance. Also, some Chinese companies operate in sectors heavily regulated by laws and regulations at different levels (e.g., banking and real estate). These companies should rely more on U.S. professionals to navigate the local regulatory system. Sometimes even U.S. professionals fail to fully grasp the legal and compliance concerns particular to Chinese investment, and it is advisable that Chinese companies operating in highly regulated and localized sectors consider developing in-house legal and compliance capacity at an early stage of investment by recruiting experienced U.S. lawyers with knowledge of the relevant industries; and for those that have built up such capacity, it is imperative that managers take seriously the opinions of in-house counsel and compliance officers.[23]

On June 20, 2017, an event co-organized by the China General Chamber of Commerce was held in Washington, D.C. as a part of the SelectUSA program to promote FDI in the United States. Hundreds of Chinese investors, managers, and business owners were packed into a hotel conference room to hear a group of panelists share their thoughts on how to succeed in the U.S. market. "For Chinese companies to thrive in the United States," a Chinese executive commented in English during a panel discussion, "*you need to think American way, speak American way, and do American way. That is the only path.*"[24] That path taken, Chinese investment in the United States does not foreshadow a clash of capitalisms.

21 Statement by Fang Peng, president of GCL International, during a panel at Roads to USA – Greenfield Investment vs. Cross-border M & A Forum (June 20, 2017).

22 Chen et al., "Ownership Structure, Corporate Governance, and Fraud," 431.

23 According to the 2017 CGCC survey, the majority of the Chinese companies that have full-time in-house legal and compliance staff take their professional opinions seriously. That being said, 44% of the survey respondents consider the opinions of the compliance staff to have only some influence or little influence on major management decisions. Similarly, 45% of respondents considered the advice of the legal staff to have some or little effect on major management decisions.

24 Statement by Peter Wu, vice president of China Construction America, during a panel at Roads to USA – Greenfield Investment vs. Cross-border M & A Forum (June 20, 2017).

Index